PAPACY AND LAW IN THE GREGORIAN REVOLUTION

The Canonistic Work of Anselm of Lucca

KATHLEEN G. CUSHING

CLARENDON PRESS · OXFORD
1998

Oxford University Press, Great Clarendon Street, Oxford OX2 6DP

Oxford New York

Athens Auckland Bangkok Bogotá Buenos Aires Calcutta
Cape Town Chennai Dar es Salaam Delhi Florence Hong Kong Istanbul
Karachi Kuala Lumpur Madras Madrid Melbourne Mexico City Mumbai
Nairobi Paris São Paolo Singapore Taipei Tokyo Toronto Warsaw
and associated companies in
Berlin Ibadan

Oxford is a registered trade mark of Oxford University Press

Published in the United States
by Oxford University Press Inc., New York

British Library Cataloguing in Publication Data
Data available

Library of Congress Cataloging in Publication Data
Cushing, Kathleen G.
Papacy and law in the Gregorian revolution: the canonistic work
of Anselm of Lucca / Kathleen G. Cushing. p. cm.—(Oxford historical monographs)
A revision of the author's thesis (D. Phil.)—University of Oxford.
Includes bibliographical references and index.
1. Canon law—History. 2. Anselm II, Saint, Bishop of Lucca,
1036–1086 3. Gregory VII, Pope, ca. 1015–1085. 4. Papacy—
History—To 1309. I Title. II. Series.
262.9'22—dc21 98–13282
ISBN 0–19–820724–7

1 3 5 7 9 10 8 6 4 2

Typeset by Hope Services (Abingdon) Ltd.
Printed in Great Britain
on acid-free paper by
Biddles Ltd., Guildford and King's Lynn

Acknowledgements

THE following work began first as a Master of Philosophy, and, subsequently, as a Doctor of Philosophy thesis at Oxford. A number of organizations supported that research, among whom I would like to recognize: the Faculty of Archaeology, History and Letters of the British School at Rome; the Christina Drake Fund for Italian Studies; the Isaiah Berlin Fund Bursary; St John's College, Oxford; and the Committee of Vice-Chancellors and Principals of the Universities of the United Kingdom for their grant from the ORS Awards Scheme.

In the course of my studies and in bringing such a work to publication, I have been assisted by many people, whose advice, suggestions, comments, and, above all, patience have been invaluable. I am particularly grateful to: Robert Benson, Martin Brett, Kate Cooper, John Cowdrey, Jeff Denton, Henrietta Leyser, Conrad Leyser, Henry Mayr-Harting, R. I. Moore, Alexander Murray, Mark Philpott, Robert Somerville, and Patrick Wormald. I would especially like to thank my parents, family, and friends for their inspiration and understanding.

A special word of thanks is owed to Glyn Redworth, not only for his support and encouragement over the years at the 'Ferry Road Research Centre', but most especially for his painstaking reading of the typescript. His criticisms were of the greatest value.

A slightly different version of Chapter 4 appeared previously as 'Anselm of Lucca and the Doctrine of Coercion: The Legal Impact of the Schism of 1080?' in *The Catholic Historical Review*, 81 (1995), 353–71. I would like to thank the editor, Monsignor Trisco, and the Catholic University of America Press for permission to republish that material here.

Karl Leyser, who from the beginning guided my faltering footsteps through the tangled mire of the Gregorian epoch, sadly did not see this work in its final and present form. To him, I owe not only 'revolution', but so very much more.

K.G.C.

Contents

List of Tables   ix

Abbreviations   x

Introduction   1

**Part I: Papacy and Law on the Eve of the
Gregorian Revolution**   9

Part II: A Canonist in the Age of Reform   41

1. Anselm of Lucca: A Sainted Gregorian Bishop   43

2. Anselm and His Canonical Sources   64
   1. Anselm and The 'Reform' Collections: New Sources and
     New Methods   64
   2. Anselm and the Pseudo-Isidore   72
   3. Anselm and the 74T   78
   4. Some Other Genuine and Patristic Sources   86
   5. Anselm and Deusdedit   95
   Conclusion   102

3. Roman Primacy and the Legal Vindication of Reform   103

4. Anselm and Coercion: A Legal Form of Persuasion   122

Conclusion: A Canonist of Reform   142

Appendices

I: Anselm's Canonical Sources: Some Documentary Evidence   147
   Ia. Anselm's Transmission of Independent Ps.Isidorian Texts   147
   Ib. Anselm's Transmission of Ps.Isidorian Texts from the 74T   157
   Ic. Anselm's Transmission of Gelasian Texts from the 74T   169
   Id. Anselm and the Swabian Appendix   175

II: Abridged Edition of Books XII and XIII of the *Collectio canonum* of Anselm of Lucca from Biblioteca Apostolica Vaticana, MS Vat. lat. 1363

II: Abridged Edition of Books XII and XIII of the *Collectio canonum* of Anselm of Lucca from Biblioteca Apostolica Vaticana, MS Vat. lat. 1363   179

Bibliography   225
Index   241

Tables

I. Breakdown of Anselm's Material Sources   203
II. Dispersion and Disposition of Pseudo-Isidorian Texts in the *Collectio canonum*   210
III. Dispersion and Disposition of 74T Texts in the *Collectio canonum*   213
IV. Anselm's '*Dictatus papae*' Texts   216
V. The Canonical Sources of the *Liber contra Wibertum*   223

Abbreviations

Anselm	*Anselmi episcopi Lucensis collectio canonum una cum collectione minore*, ed. F. Thaner (Innsbruck, 1906, 1915)
BMCL, n.s.	*Bulletin of Medieval Canon Law*, new series
Bull. Ist. Stor. Ital.	*Bullettino dell'istituto storico italiano per il medio evo e archivio Muratoriano*
CSEL	*Corpus scriptorum ecclesiasticorum latinorum*
Coustant	*Epistolae Romanorum pontificum . . . s. Clemente usque ad Innocentium III*, I, ed. P. Coustant (Paris, 1721)
DA	*Deutsches Archiv für Erforschung des Mittelalters*
Dp	*Dictatus papae*
Ep. vag.	*The Epistolae Vagantes of Pope Gregory VII*, ed. H. E. J. Cowdrey (Oxford, 1972)
Gratian	*Concordia discordantium canonum [Decretum magistri Gratiani]*, ed. E. Friedberg (Leipzig, 1879)
Gregory I, *Reg.*	*Gregorii I. papae Registrum epistolarum*, I–II, ed. P. Ewald and L. M. Hartmann (*MGH, Epp.*, 1, 2; Berlin, 1891–9)
JK, JE, JL	*Regesta Pontificum Romanorum*, I, ed. P. Jaffé, 2nd edn. by S. Loewenfeld (JL: an. 882–1198), F. Kaltenbrunner (JK: an. ?–590), P. Ewald (JE: an. 590–882) (Berlin, 1885)
JEH	*Journal of Ecclesiastical History*
Mansi	*Sacrorum conciliorum nova et amplissima collectio*, ed. G. D. Mansi, 53 vols. in 60 pts. (Paris–Arnhem, 1901–27)
MGH	*Monumenta Germaniae Historica*:
BdK	*Briefe der deutschen Kaiserzeit*
Const.	*Constitutiones et Acta publica imperatorum et regum*
Deutsches Mittelalter	*Kritische Studientexte des Reichsinstitut für ältere deutsche Geschichtskunde*
Epp.	*Epistolae*
Ep.sel.	*Epistolae selectae*

LdL	*Libelli de lite imperatorum et pontificum saeculis XI. et XII.conscripti*, 3 vols.
Legum	*Legum, sectio IV*
Schriften	*Schriften* (monograph series)
SS	*Scriptores* (in folio)
SRG	*Scriptores rerum Germanicarum in usum scholarum ex Monumentiae recusi*
MIC	Monumenta Iuris Canonici
PL	*Patrologiae cursus completus, Series latina*, ed. J. P. Migne (Paris, 1841–64)
Ps.Is.	*Decretales Pseudo-Isidorianae et Capitula Angilrammi*, ed. P. Hinschius (Leipzig, 1863)
Rangerius	*Vita Metrica Anselmi Lucensis episcopi auctore Rangerio Lucensi* (*MGH, SS*, 30, pt. II), 1152–1307
Reg.	*Registrum Gregorii VII.*, ed. E. Caspar (*MGH, Ep. sel.*, t.2, I–II; Berlin, 1920–3)
Reindel	*Die Briefe des Petrus Damiani*, ed. K Reindel, 4 vols. (*MGH, BdK* V/1–4; Munich, 1983–93)
RIS, n.s.	Rerum Italicarum Scriptores, new series, (Bologna, 1900–)
Sant'Anselmo vescovo di Lucca	*Sant'Anselmo vescovo di Lucca (1073–86) nel quadro delle trasformazioni sociali e della riforma ecclesiastica*, ed. C. Violante (Istituto storico italiano per il medio evo, studi storici, 13; Rome, 1992)
Sant'Anselmo, Mantova	*Sant'Anselmo, Mantova e la lotta per le investiture*, ed. P. Golinelli (Atti del convegno internazionale di studi, Mantova, 23–25 maggio 1986; Bologna, 1987)
74T	*Diversorum patrum sententie sive Collectio in LXXIV titulos digesta*, ed. J. T. Gilchrist (MIC, Ser. B: Corpus Collectionum, 1; Vatican City, 1973)
SG	*Studi Gregoriani*
Thiel	*Epistolae Romanorum Pontificum genuinae et quae ad eos scriptae sunt a s.Hilaro usque ad Pelagium II.*, ed. A. Thiel (Braunsberg, 1868)
TRHS	*Transactions of the Royal Historical Society*
Vita Anselmi	*Vita Anselmi episcopi Lucensis* (*MGH, SS*, 12), 1–35
ZSSRG, kan. Abt.	*Zeitschrift der Savigny-Stiftung für Rechtsgeschichte, kanonistiche Abteilung*

Introduction

ANSELM of Lucca, like many of his contemporaries, is a shadowy figure in a world dominated by the towering personality of Pope Gregory VII. His importance, however, has been underestimated. Anselm was clearly a pivotal and influential man, and was described as such in the sources of the time. Three characteristics were emphasized in these sources: his knowledge and intellectual abilities, especially of the law; his tireless devotion to the cause of Pope Gregory VII; and his indisputable sanctity.

The anonymous author of the first *Vita Anselmi*—written shortly after Anselm's death in 1086—emphasized all of these aspects, but especially stressed the perfect devotion and obedience of Anselm to Gregory VII. These were clearly factors which, to this author, in some way accounted for the bishop's sanctity.[1] Anselm's second biographer, Bishop Rangerius of Lucca, whose *Vita Anselmi* was heavily dependent upon the earlier life, echoed these attributes while focusing predominantly upon the sanctity and the miracles of his predecessor.[2] The priest Donizo, biographer of Countess Matilda of Tuscany, made much of Anselm's exceptional knowledge, particularly of the laws of God.[3] Bernold of Constance, recording the circumstances of Anselm's death, summed up the bishop's life by focusing upon the miraculous as a justification of the reform principles that Anselm had followed.[4] Gregory VII himself, even

---

[1] *Vita Anselmi episcopi Lucensis (MGH, SS, 12), 1–35, e.g. c. 31, p. 22: 'Ante omnia vero id studii semper habuit, quatenus sanctissimum magistrum suum papam Gregorium imitaretur in omnibus, adeo ut discrepare ab illo prorsus nollet etiam in aliquo.'

[2] *Vita Metrica Anselmi Lucensis episcopi auctore Rangerio Lucensi (MGH, SS, 30, pt. II), 1152–1307. It contains a lengthy catalogue of miracle stories, due in part perhaps to the poetic style of the text.

[3] *Vita Matildis celeberrimae principis Italiae carmine scripta a Donizone presbytero*, ed. L. Simeoni (*RIS*, n.s. 5, pt. II), e.g. II, c. 2, vv. 281–6.

[4] Bernold of Constance, *Chronicon a. 1086 (MGH, SS, 5), 400–67, p. 445: 'Beatus Anselmus, quondam Lucensis episcopus, ipso eodem depositionis suae anno innumerabilibus miraculis cepit coruscare, qui post obitum venerabilis papae Gregorii VII. fideles sancti Petri contra tirannidem Heinrici adhuc in carne vivens multum incitavit, set multo plus post obitum suum miraculis coruscans eosdem contra eundem persistere confortavit.'

contentious issues, and these very much coloured Rangerius' treatment of Anselm's life. While Rangerius was certainly far better informed about the situation in Lucca and the Lucchesia, and often added considerable detail as well as new information, his main preoccupation was with the cataloguing of Anselm's miracles. These were evidence of the righteousness of Anselm's cause, and consequently of his own. Rangerius at the same time clearly saw the composition of the *Vita* as an opportunity to demonstrate his apparent classical training, and education.[12] A good deal of his information regarding Anselm must therefore be taken with a pinch of salt.

Unfortunately, Anselm's own written works also present difficulties. It is clear that he was the author of several works.[13] One of the most significant was the polemical tract, the *Liber contra Wibertum*, written between June 1085 and his death in March 1086.[14] Another extremely interesting work is the more recently discovered *Sermo de caritate*, written sometime between late 1085, and early 1086.[15] Anselm also composed a commentary on the Lamentations of Jeremiah, a number of devotional prayers for Matilda of Tuscany, and apparently undertook an exposition of the Psalms at her request.[16] There are in addition a number of other fragments which have been attributed to Anselm, the bulk of which, however, remain suspect.[17] One of these—a commentary on

[12] See G. Severino, 'La "Vita metrica" di Anselmo di Lucca scritta da Rangerio', 223–71. Cf. P. Golinelli, *'Indiscreta sanctitas'*, 151 ff.

[13] *Vita Anselmi*, c. 26, p. 21: 'Multos libellos propriis manibus conscripsit.'

[14] *Liber contra Wibertum*, ed. E. Bernheim (*MGH, LdL*, 1), 517–28. On the *Liber*, see C. Märtl, 'Zur Überlieferung des *Liber contra Wibertum* Anselms von Lucca', *Deutsches Archiv*, 41 (1985), 192–202. Robert Somerville discovered a text in the British Library, Harley MS 3052, which may be part of Anselm's earlier letter to Wibert (noted in the *Liber*, p. 520), see: 'Anselm of Lucca and Wibert of Ravenna', *Bulletin of Medieval Canon Law*, n.s. 10 (1980), 1–13.

[15] *Sermo Anselmi episcopi de caritate*, ed. E. Pasztor, in 'Motivi dell'ecclesiologia di Anselmo di Lucca in margine a un sermone inedito', *Bull. Ist. Stor. Ital.*, 77 (1965), 45–104, text 96–104. On the dating, see 47–8.

[16] *Vita Anselmi*, c. 26, p. 21: 'In lamentationes Hieremiae dilucidissimam fecit expositionem.' This is no longer extant. 'Cinque textes de prière composés par Anselme de Lucques pour la Comtesse Mathilde', ed. A. Wilmart, *Revue d'ascétique et de mystique*, 19 (1938) 23–72, texts 49–72. Cf. *Vita Anselmi*, c. 80, p. 34, where Matilda's vision was miraculously restored when she placed against her eyes parchment on which Anselm had written some prayers for her. Fragments of Anselm's Commentary on the Psalms are preserved in Paul of Bernried, *Vita Gregorii VII*, c. 112, ed. J. M. Watterich, *Pontificum Romanorum Vitae*, I, (Leipzig, 1862), 541 ff. Cf. *Catalogus Sigeberti Gemblacensis monachi de viris illustribus*, ed. R. Witte, no. 162, p. 100.

[17] *S. Anselmo Collectanea* (*PL* 149, cols. 475–8). There is a religious poem, entitled 'Meditationes de gestis Iesu Christi', in Oxford, MS Bodleian 57 (fo. 155ʳ beginning: 'Iesu mi dulcissime'), erroneously attributed to Anselm.

the Cleansing of the Temple (which was a critical symbol for the reformers)—does appear to be genuine.[18] Three important letters have also survived: one to Bishop Hermann of Metz in 1085, one to William I of England in 1085, and an earlier one *circa* 1078 to Abbot Ponzio of Frassinoro.[19]

It is, however, for his *Collectio canonum* that Anselm of Lucca is principally known. The collection was completed between 1081 and 1086, but probably after 1083. Termed *'apologeticus'* by the *Vita Anselmi*, the collection presents an important, and perhaps unrivalled, example of the ways in which the movement for ecclesiastical reform had given impetus to developments in canon law, and vice versa.[20] The significance of the collection lies not merely in its polemical ambitions, and content, but also in its creative, and even innovative, use of canonical sources, particularly the Pseudo-Isidore. Opening with an unrelenting insistence upon the absolute supremacy and primacy of the Roman pontiff, and concluding with an innovative vindication (at least in legal terms) of the Church's right to coerce her enemies, Anselm's collection seems to present a pointed and conscious justification of the reform movement's primary objectives.[21] As such, it offers an extremely important, and hitherto largely unexplored, testimony of the reformers' attitude towards, and understanding of, the canon law.

The *Collectio canonum* is, however, a problematic text.[22] The collection exists in an incomplete, idiosyncratic, and, frankly, poor edition, which leaves the crucial twelfth and thirteenth books unavailable to many scholars.[23] It is clear that the collection was very much a *texte*

---

[18] Anselm of Lucca, 'In libro secundo Matthaeum', (*PL* 149, cols. 476–7). Also printed in R. H. Rough, *The Reformist Illuminations in the Gospels of Matilda, Countess of Tuscany* (The Hague, 1973), appendix, 52–3.

[19] Anselm to William I, and to Hermann of Metz, in *Briefsammlungen der Zeit Heinrichs IV.*, ed C. Erdmann and N. Fickermann (*MGH, BdK*, 5; Weimar, 1950), no. 1 and 21, pp. 15–17, 50–1; and Anselm to Abbot Ponzio of Frassinoro, in Hugh of Flavigny, *Chronicon* (*MGH, SS*, 8), 444.

[20] *Vita Anselmi*, c. 26, p. 21: 'Apologeticum unum diversis ex sanctorum patrum voluminibus compilavit, quibus domni papae sententiam et universa eius facta atque praecepta canonicis defenderet rationibus et approbaret orthodoxis auctoritatibus.'

[21] Both Stickler and Fuhrmann described Anselm's collection as the most important of the Gregorian reform. A. M. Stickler, 'Il potere coattivo materiale della chiesa nella riforma gregoriana secondo Anselmo di Lucca', *SG* 2 (1947), 235–85, here 241; H. Fuhrmann, *Einfluss und Verbreitung der pseudoisidorischen Fälschungen*, 3 vols. (*MGH, Schriften*, 24/1–3; Stuttgart, 1972–4), II, 510.

[22] On the basic problems of the *Collectio canonum*, see S. Kuttner, 'Some Roman Manuscripts of Canonical Collections', *BMCL*, n.s. 1 (1971), 7–29.

[23] *Anselmi episcopi Lucensis Collectio canonum una cum collectione minore*, ed. F. Thaner, (Innsbruck, 1906, 1915). This edition covers only up to the early chapters of Book XI. Cf.

vivante, with interpolations and changes coming almost immediately. This resulted in a number of different versions or recensions. Though the interrelationships between the texts have recently been clarified by Peter Landau, questions continue.[24] Four principal recensions have been identified, all of which to a greater or lesser degree contain significant interpolations. The so-called 'A' recension has three manuscripts containing the entire collection of thirteen books: Biblioteca Apostolica Vaticana, MS Vat.lat. 1363; Paris, Bibliothèque Nationale, MS Par.lat. 12519; and Cambridge, Corpus Christi College, MS 269. The 'B' recension—noteworthy for its lack of Book XI, the penitential—is represented by four manuscripts, three of which contain the complete collection: MS Vat.lat.1364, MS Vat.lat.6381, and Berlin, Staatsbibliothek Preussicher Kulturbesitz 597. The 'C' recension exists only in a much interpolated sixteenth-century manuscript on linen paper, MS Vat.lat.4983. The 'Bb' recension is represented by MS Barberini lat.535, which contains only the first seven books. There are a number of further variations—largely offshoots of the 'A' recension— and partial collections.[25] No original or *Urform* exists; the bulk of the manuscripts date from the early twelfth-century. A new edition of the entire collection, as scholars agree, seems

Kuttner, 'Some Roman Manuscripts', 13: 'It is no great secret that in the unfinished edition of Anselm, Friedrich Thaner gave us less than one might have expected from his great scholarship.' Thaner used a number of recensions interchangeably, unfortunately without a stemma; he did not know of the Cambridge 'A' recension.

[24] On the various recensions, see P. Fournier, 'Observations sur les diverses récensions de la collection canonique d'Anselme de Lucques', *Annales de l'université de Grenoble*, 13 (1901), 427–58, and more recently, P. Landau, 'Erweiterte Fassungen der Kanonessammlung des Anselm von Lucca aus dem 12. Jahrhundert', (also Italian as 'Intorni alle redazioni più ampie del XII secolo della raccoltà dei canoni di Anselmo da Lucca'), in *Sant'Anselmo, Mantova*, 323–37 (German), 339–48 (Italian), which includes a stemma at p. 338. On the Vatican A and B MSS, see now *A Catalogue of Canon and Roman Law Manuscripts in the Vatican Library*, ed. S. Kuttner with R. Elze, 2 vols. (Studi e testi, 322, 328; Vatican City, 1986–7); G. Motta, 'La redazione A "aucta" della *Collectio Anselmi episcopi Lucensis*', in *Studia in honorem eminentissimi cardinalis A. M. Stickler*, ed. R. I. Card. Castillo Lara (Studia et textus historiae iuris canonici, 7; Rome, 1992), 375–449; J. T. Gilchrist, 'The *Collectio canonum* of Bishop Anselm II of Lucca (d. 1086): Recension B of Berlin, Staatsbibliothek Preussicher Kulturbesitz Cod. 597', in *Cristianità ed Europa: Miscellanea di studi in onore di Luigi Prosdocimi*, ed. C. Alzati (Rome, 1994), 377–403; on C, see P. Landau, 'Die Rezension C. der Sammlung des Anselms von Lucca', *BMCL*, n.s. 16 (1986), 17–54. See now also K. Zechiel-Eckes, 'Eine Mailänder Redaktion der Kirchenrechtssammlung Bischof Anselms II. von Lucca (1073–1086)', *Zeitschrift der Savigny-Stiftung für Rechtsgeschichte, kanonistische Abteilung*, 112 (1995), 130–47. Gilchrist's article raises the question of whether B may have relied on an earlier exemplar or parent of A. Zechiel-Eckes suggests that Milan, Biblioteca Ambrosiana A. 46 represents an early recension of Anselm (Y) to which B and C were indebted.

[25] See the stemma in Landau, 'Intorni alle redazioni', p. 338, and the listing of manuscript sources in this present work's bibliography.

to be impossible, at least until such time as the manuscript tradition can be more firmly fixed.

It must be conceded at once, though, that Anselm's authorship of the *Collectio canonum*, particularly Books VIII–XIII, has been questioned, notably by Gérard Fransen.[26] The attribution to Anselm is based upon an inscription found in but one contemporary manuscript: Biblioteca Apostolica Vaticana, MS Barberini lat.535.[27] This manuscript, however, contains only the first seven books of the thirteen-book collection. This, as Fransen argued, weighs against the entire collection being Anselm's work. (The manuscript does contain a complete *capitulatio librorum* for the entire collection.) Fransen also questioned the arguments that have been used in the past to justify Anselm's authorship, namely that the thematic and textual similarities between the collection and Anselm's other works, especially the *Liber contra Wibertum*, should be set against any doubts. Fransen's contentions, while reasonable, are not wholly convincing, as he himself seemed to appreciate. While pointing to 'une différence dans l'économie interne des livres', he concluded that the tradition of Anselm as the author should remain intact, at least for the present. Needless to say, throughout this present work, not only will Anselm be regarded as the compiler of the collection that bears his name, but the present author has few doubts as to his authorship of the bulk of his works.

In an article for the International Congress on Anselm held in Mantua in 1986, Edith Pasztor included a transcription of Book XIII of the collection from several of the Vatican manuscripts. Unfortunately, this was not a critical edition of Book XIII.[28] The same must be said for my present use of the A group (with the Vatican A as the base text, and with reference to B and C, especially for the unedited Books XII and XIII) to provide a working edition. I do not pretend to be providing a

[26] G. Fransen, 'Anselme de Lucques, canoniste?', in *Sant'Anselmo vescovo di Lucca*, 143–56. Cf. Landau, 'Intorni alle redazioni', 339–48. See also G. Picasso, 'La *Collectio canonum* di Anselmo nella storia delle collezioni canoniche', in *Sant'Anselmo, Mantova*, 313–21, who argues for Anselm's authorship.

[27] Biblioteca Apostolica Vaticana, MS Barberini lat. 535: [fo. 14ᵛ]: 'Incipit authentica et compendiosa collectio regularum et sententiarum sanctorum patrum et auctorabilium concilium facta tempore VII. Gregorii sanctissimi papae a beato Anselmo Lucensi episcopo eius diligenti imitatore et discipulo, cuius iussione et precepto desiderante consummavit hoc opus.' The manuscript dates from the first quarter of the 12th cent.; the catalogue of the Roman pontiffs [fos. 1ʳ–3ᵛ] ends with Honorius II. Although the *capitulatio librorum* [fo. 14ᵛ] contains entries for all thirteen books, this manuscript contains the text of only the first seven books.

[28] E. Pasztor, 'Lotta per le investiture e "ius belli": la posizione di Anselmo di Lucca', *Sant'Anselmo, Mantova*, 375–421, at 405–21. There is no critical apparatus.

comprehensive, critical, edition of these important texts. I do, however, hope that my use of A, with clear delineations of the respective recensions, will at the least have the virtue of consistency.[29]

Martin Brett has recently discussed the problems of such provisional, and therefore, partial texts, questioning whether they facilitate or impede a proper edition. He has performed a tremendous service by reminding us that 'establishing texts is the laborious, often almost mindless, precondition of asking more interesting questions'.[30] It will, no doubt, be argued by some that the attempt of the following work to pose some of those questions, along with the 'edition' of Books XII and XIII, are premature without the clarification of the manuscript tradition. It is, however, to be hoped that by asking some of those more interesting questions, and with the aid of a provisional, partial text, a step in the right direction may have been taken.

---

[29] All subsequent references to Books XII and XIII will be from Biblioteca Apostolica Vaticana, MS Vat. lat. 1363, fos. 208ᵛ–240ʳ (with reference to Cambridge, Corpus Christi College 269 and Paris, Bibliothèque Nationale lat. 12519 (A group) where necessary). Texts will be cited Anselm, book and chapter number, rubric title and identification of material source. Foliation will be noted *only* when quotations from the actual canonical text appear. After the first citation, in the interest of brevity, the identification of material sources will not contain the full details of the edition, for which see the Abbreviations or Bibliography.

[30] M. Brett, 'The Manuscripts of the *Collectio Tripartita*', paper presented at the Tenth International Congress of Medieval Canon Law, at Syracuse University, 12–18 August 1996. The paper will appear in the *Proceedings of the Tenth International Congress of Medieval Canon Law* (MIC, ser. C: Subsidia; Vatican City, forthcoming). I would like to thank Dr Brett for his comments, and discussion with me, on this issue.

PART I

Papacy and Law on the Eve
of the Gregorian Revolution

Papacy and Law on the Eve
of the Gregorian Revolution

THE reformers of the middle and second half of the eleventh century
were perhaps unparalleled in their ability to find fault and to apportion
blame. Rarely, as Karl Leyser noted, were the forces of heaven summoned so directly, and so confidently, as by these men, especially
Gregory VII, as they sought to articulate and entrench their vision for
Christian society.[1] Not only were less than co-operative rulers condemned, derided, and reminded of their nefarious origins, even the
pious kings and rulers of Europe were firmly shown their place in the
new order of things.[2] Ecclesiastics, however, often fared little better. It
was no longer enough simply to hold the privilege of clergy. Churchmen
were now obliged to take an active part: to make it their business to
eradicate the existing conditions in order to allow the new truth of the
reformers to take root.[3]

Driven in part by their need to muster support for reform, but most
especially by their need to individualize and define their position, men

---

[1] K. J. Leyser, 'The Polemics of the Papal Revolution', in *Medieval Germany and Its
Neighbours* (London, 1982), 138–60, here 152.

[2] e.g. *Der sogenannte Traktat 'De ordinando pontifice': Ein Rechtsgutachten im
Zusammenhang mit der Synode von Sutri (1046)*, ed. H. H. Anton (Bonner Historische
Forschungen, 48; Bonn, 1982), lines 183–281, where Henry III is called 'nequissimus', and
is accused of infamy. See also *Die Briefe des Petrus Damiani*, ed. K. Reindel (*MGH, BdK*,
4/1–4; Munich, 1983–93), I, no. 2; II, nos. 43, 64, 89, 99; *Registrum Gregorii VII.*, VIII:
21, p. 552: 'Quis nesciat reges et duces ab iis habuisse principium, qui Deum ignorantes
superbia rapinis perfidia homicidiis postremo universis pene sceleribus mundi principe
diabolo videlicet agitante super pares, scilicet homines dominari caeca cupidine et intoller-
abili presumptione affectaverunt?'; cf. *Reg.*, I: 19, 45, 61, 63; II: 11, 30, 31, 45; III: 10; IV:
28; V: 10, 19; VII: 14a; IX: 17; *The Epistolae Vagantes of Pope Gregory VII*, ed. H. E. J.
Cowdrey (Oxford, 1972), nos. 14, 16, 26, 27, 45; and Anselm of Lucca to William I of
England, in *Briefsammlungen der Zeit Heinrichs IV.*, 17: 'Non sine causa gladium portas.
. . .'

[3] e.g. *Reg.* I: 56, 57, 60; II: 1, 15, 29; III: 2; IV: 23; V: 12; VI: 26; IX: 29, 35; and *Ep.
vag.*, nos. 2, 6–10, 13, 24, 31. See also Reindel, II, nos. 57, 58; III, nos. 99, 107, where
Damian was forced to protest his innocence first to Nicholas II, and then to Alexander II.

as diverse as Leo IX, Peter Damian, Humbert of Silva-Candida, Nicholas II, Alexander II, Hildebrand/Gregory VII, the compiler of the 74T, Anselm of Lucca, and Deusdedit, although perhaps with very different agendas, drew a curtain on the immediate past, and aimed at restoring what they understood as the pristine state of the Church of the Fathers. In reality, however, their attitude to the past was an ambivalent one. Challenging custom, tradition, and long-established practice with their own vision, the reformers on the whole subordinated the weight of antiquity—to which they incessantly appealed—to a general principle of papal discretion. Less concerned with day-to-day working laws than with the establishment of a constitution, they set about a redefinition of the Church as an institution separate from all else. The strengthening of the papacy, and of the law, were simultaneously their principal ambitions, and the instruments by which their wider strategies for reform could be realized.

Since the publication between 1924 and 1937 of Augustin Fliche's three-volume work, *La Réforme grégorienne*, the movement for ecclesiastical reform in the eleventh century has largely been identified with the fiery personality of Pope Gregory VII (1073–85).[4] More recently, this historiography has been challenged by Ryan, Gilchrist, Capitani, and Somerville among many others, who have shown that the reform movement was not a homogeneous unit, that it was infinitely more complex, and that there were often radically different opinions and agendas. In particular, they have shown that Gregory VII's 'reforms' had in large if not most part been initiated by his predecessors.[5] As a consequence, Fliche's '*réforme grégorienne*' is now commonly known as the '*so-called* Gregorian reform'.

While some would argue that this is a question of semantics, there is no doubt that these historiographical revisions have been useful. Indeed, it has become increasingly clear that it is unwise to speak of a reform movement in the eleventh century in perhaps any monolithic sense. There were many transformations, many reforming movements, in the eleventh century. Whether or not these constituted a 'social revolution'

---

[4] A. Fliche, *La Réforme grégorienne*, 3 vols. (Spicilegium sacrum Lovaniense, études et documents, fasc. 6, 9, 13; Paris, 1924–37).

[5] e.g. O. Capitani, 'Esiste un'età gregoriana? Considerazione sulle tendenze di una storiografia medievistica', *Rivista di storia e letteratura religiosa*, 1 (1965), 454–81; J. T. Gilchrist, 'Was There a Gregorian Reform Movement in the Eleventh Century?', *Canadian Catholic Historical Association, Study Sessions*, 37 (1970), 1–10; now repr. in id., *Canon Law in the Age of Reform, Eleventh and Twelfth Centuries* (Variorum, Collected Studies Series, CS406; Ashgate, 1993).

which progressively blurred into the papal sponsored movement for reform that gathered pace from the middle of the century, or whether these forces were purposefully compacted by the reformers in their search for what Tellenbach called 'the right order in the world', remains a matter of much debate.[6]

Most recently of all, much interest has been directed to the notion of 'revolution' in the eleventh century.[7] There has been discussion of the peace movement and the related 'social revolution': the growth of consciousness, and perceptions among the previously almost silent mass of the *laboratores*—what R. I. Moore boldly termed 'the emergence of the crowd on the stage of history'.[8] There has been consideration of the urban, and the economic revolution.[9] There has been discussion of the castellan revolution, what is often known as the '*mutation de l'an mil*', or the feudal transformation.[10] There has been discussion of the 'papal revolution in law'.[11] Last, but not least, there has been discussion of the 'Gregorian revolution'—a term, and concept which has found favour as against the 'clash of *regnum* and *sacerdotium*' and the even more problematic 'Investiture Contest'.[12]

---

[6] G. Tellenbach, *Church, State and Christian Society at the Time of the Investiture Contest*, trans. R. Bennett (Oxford, 1939), 1; cf. G. Tellenbach, *The Church in Western Europe from the Tenth to the Early Twelfth Century*, trans. T. Reuter (Cambridge, 1993).

[7] C. Violante and J. Fried (eds.), *Il secolo XI: una svolta?* (Annali dell'istituto storico italo-germanico, 35; Bologna, 1993).

[8] R. I. Moore, 'Family, Community and Cult on the Eve of the Gregorian Reform', *Transactions of the Royal Historical Society*, 5th ser. 30 (1980), 49–69; and id., 'Postscript: The Peace of God and the Social Revolution', in *The Peace of God: Social Violence and Religious Response in France Around the Year 1000*, eds. T. Head and R. Landes (Ithaca, NY–London, 1992), 308–26.

[9] H. Pirenne, *Medieval Cities: Their Origins and the Revival of Trade*, trans. F. D. Halsey (Princeton, 1925); R. Lopez, *The Commercial Revolution of the Middle Ages* (Englewood Cliffs, NJ, 1971). Cf. L. K. Little, *Religious Poverty and the Profit Economy in the Medieval West* (London, 1978).

[10] e.g. G. Duby, *Three Orders: Feudal Society Imagined*, trans. A. Goldhammer (Chicago, 1980); J. Poly and E. Bournazel, *La Mutation féodale Xe–XIIe siècles*, 2nd edn. (Paris, 1991); G. Bois, *The Transformation of the Year 1000: The Village of Lournand from Antiquity to Feudalism*, trans. J. Birrell (Manchester, 1992); and T. N. Bisson, 'The Feudal Revolution', *Past and Present*, 142 (1994), 6–42.

[11] H. J. Berman, *Law and Revolution: The Formation of the Western Legal Tradition* (Cambridge, Mass., 1983). Berman's work, however, has not been widely accepted by medievalists. R. Schieffer, 'The Papal Revolution in Law', paper presented at the Tenth International Congress of Medieval Canon Law, Syracuse University, August 1996, offers a recent critique. Schieffer's paper will be published in the *Proceedings of the Tenth International Congress of Medieval Canon Law* (MIC, Subsidia—forthcoming).

[12] K. J. Leyser, 'On the Eve of the First European Revolution', in *Communications and Power in Medieval Europe: The Gregorian Revolution and Beyond*, ed. T. Reuter (Rio Grande–London, 1994), 1–20.

But how appropriate is it to rename the great clash between *regnum* and *sacerdotium* the 'Gregorian revolution'? Is there something that can be salvaged of 'Gregorian', given recent historiographical revisions? More to the point perhaps, is it one specific revolution—the clash of Gregory VII and Henry IV—or is it in some way the amalgamation of the transformations, radical and otherwise, that characterize this period? It has long been held that the eleventh century was a pivotal epoch, on account of its social upheaval, its move from a gift to a profit economy, and, most especially perhaps, on account of the enormity of the urban advance. The 'transformation of the year 1000'—the view developed in particular by French historians over the past two generations—in many ways envisages the eleventh century as the time when European civilization, as we know it, was created. It was a time which was characterized by a process of definition and distinction in all sectors and aspects of human existence. Not only were groups and spheres of life being more sharply delineated, both individuals and groups were also distinguishing themselves: the *signorie* from the old *curtes*; the city, both economically and juridically, from the country; the clergy from laymen; the spiritual from the temporal.

Contemporaries reflect this process of distinction. It is clear that on a number of levels there were perceptions not only of disorder, but also of change. Men and women clearly felt themselves to be existing in a time of transformation. There was a new impatience, and a new intolerance, towards everyday, age-old, conditions. The signs of doubt and unease, a new preoccupation with purity and pollution, are evident. Gone was the optimism, or self-assuredness of the Ottonian world.[13]

On the most basic level perhaps, the movement for ecclesiastical reform was an attempt to define the moral position of a newly-ascendant Church in relation to this transformation of European society. Does this count as revolution? Not perhaps in a Marxist sense. One of the great paradoxes of the reform movement was that, in their efforts to articu-

---

[13] e.g. *Rodulfi Glabri Historiarum Libri Quinque*, III. 13, ed. J. France (Oxford, 1989), 117; *Lamperti monachi Hersfeldensis Annales*, a. 1074, ed. O. Holder-Egger (*MGH, SRG*), p. 184, 190. See also G. Constable, 'Past and Present in the Eleventh and Twelfth Centuries: Perceptions of Time and Change', in *L'Europa dei secoli XI e XII fra novità e tradizione sviluppi di una cultura* (Miscellanea del centro di studi medioevali, 12; Milan, 1989), 135–70; T. Struve, 'Le trasformazioni dell'XI secolo alla luce della storiografia del tempo', in *Il secolo XI: una svolta?*, 41–72; K. J. Leyser, 'On the Eve of the First European Revolution', 8 ff.; and id., *The Ascent of Latin Europe: An Inaugural Lecture delivered at the University of Oxford, November, 1984*, and now in *Communications and Power in Medieval Europe: The Carolingian and Ottonian Centuries*, ed. T. Reuter (Rio Grande–London, 1994), 215–37.

late their own position, the clergy both sanctioned, and protested against, the hegemony of the powerful over the poor. Moreover, it was a process that took some time. But the conflict, when it broke in the rupture between Gregory VII and Henry IV in 1076, was perhaps unexpected. Events had gone beyond contemporaries' abilities to understand them. The participants found themselves confronted with questions which had not been part of their experience, and for which they had no easy answers. The flurry of polemical literature, the search for past authorities to vindicate positions, the canonical collections, but most especially, the awkwardness and inconsistencies found in all of these, reveal not only the suddenness of the conflict, but the determination to forge ahead. Although in Marxist terms, one class did not replace another, this was a revolution, and it was 'total'. As Karl Leyser wrote: 'It knew no restoration, from it there was no way back, and any reaction only meant that the hotheads of reform had been unable to gain their ends in full and without compromises.'[14]

On the eve of this Gregorian revolution, however, impending conflict, while perhaps discernible on the horizon, was not as yet inevitable, as it would be when Anselm of Lucca compiled his collection. The reformers were only beginning to identify problems, and were only beginning to devise strategies for their correction.

One of the pre-requisites of this transformation was distance. The reformers found their scapegoat in the papacy of the tenth and early-eleventh centuries, depicting it in the bleakest possible colours. A historical consciousness, albeit a false one was imparted above all by Humbert of Silva-Candida, who, in his *Libri III. adversus simoniacos*, vilified these popes along with their foul partners, the Ottonian and Salian kings, for being directly responsible for the degradation which the reformers were obliged to correct.[15] The Tusculum popes were consistently reviled, and the reputations of Benedict VIII (1012–24) and John XIX (1024–32) were sullied by the sordid deeds of their successor and nephew Benedict IX (1032–44, March–May 1045). Such

---

[14] K. J. Leyser, 'On the Eve of the First European Revolution', 1.

[15] *Humberti cardinalis libri III adversus simoniacos*, III, 15 (*MGH, LdL*, 1), 95–253, here 217. Another explicit condemnation of the 'Germans' is found in a speech delivered by Hildebrand at the Roman council in April 1059. See text in A. Werminghoff, 'Die Beschlusse des Aachener Concils im Jahre 816, App. 4: Bruchstuck aus Verhandlungen der Lateransynode im Jahre 1059', in *Neues Archiv der Gesellschaft für altere deutsche Geschichtskunde*, 27 (1902), 669–75. Cf. *Concordia discordantium canonum*, pars III, D. 5, c. 15, ed. E. Friedberg (Leipzig, 1879), col. 1416, and variant note (h) [editio Romana]: '. . . Romani vero diverso modo agere coeperunt, maxime a tempore, quo Teutonicis concessum est regimen nostrae ecclesiae.'

characterizations, however, vastly underestimated the reformers' eleventh-century predecessors.

Benedict VIII, in particular, was a vigorous pontiff. He kept order in Rome, revived papal authority, and was a leading figure in Italian affairs. Benedict worked in close co-operation with Henry II, confirming privileges for the king's foundation of Bamberg, and crowning him as emperor in 1014.[16] Although Benedict's chief priority seems to have been the conservation of ecclesiastical property, he supported Henry II's aims for reforming the Church, first at Ravenna, and notably at the synod of Pavia in 1022, where stringent prohibitions against clerical concubinage were promulgated.[17] Benedict seems to have had great personal admiration for Abbot Odilo of Cluny, and on the whole favoured reforming abbeys.[18] His successor, John XIX, if a somewhat colourless figure who was not as adept as his brother at finding a climate of co-operation with the new king and emperor, Conrad II, was by no means an entirely ineffectual pontiff.[19] Even more closely associated with Odilo of Cluny, John was particularly solicitous of the cause of monastic immunity, twice confirming Cluny's privileges, and taking action against the encroachment there of Gauzlin, Bishop of Mâcon.[20] Even their nephew Benedict IX, the reports of whose crimes and deviance seemed to grow in wickedness as Hildebrand/Gregory VII increased in stature, was, at least for the first twelve years of his pontificate, an adequate and credible, if not immensely ascetic, pontiff.[21]

[16] For the privileges to Bamberg, see *Papsturkunden 896–1046*, ed. H. Zimmermann, 3 vols. (Veröffentlichungen der Historischen Kommission, 3: Denkschriften, 174, 177, 198; Vienna, 1984–9), II, no. 478, pp. 906–9, and no. 528, pp. 1004–5. For Bamberg's foundation, II, no. 435, pp. 830–3.

[17] See *Heinrici II. Constitutiones*, no. 30 (Ravenna), no. 34 (Pavia) (*MGH, Const. 1*), 61–2; 77–8. Benedict's opening remarks at Pavia attest to his concern with ecclesiastical property: see 71–6. Cf. M. Fornasari, 'Enrico II e Benedetto VIII ed i canoni del presunto concilio di Ravenna del 1014', *Rivista della storia della chiesa in italia*, 18 (1964), 46–55.

[18] *Papsturkunden*, II, e.g. no. 474–5 (immunity for St Bénigne de Dijon); no. 489 (privilege to Montecassino); no. 505 (immunity for Fécamp); no. 530 (papal protection for Cluny).

[19] John was forced by Conrad II to decree not only that Grado was subject to Aquileia (an invalidation of his earlier privilege to Grado, no. 561), but that Aquileia was the metropolitan of all of the churches of Italy: *Papsturkunden*, II, no. 576; and to comply in the translation of Zeitz to Naumberg (no. 581). Cf. *Conradi II. Constitutiones*, no. 38 (*MGH, Const. 1*), 82–4.

[20] *Papsturkunden*, II, no. 558 and 570–4.

[21] See R. L. Poole, 'Benedict IX and Gregory VI', *Proceedings of the British Academy*, 8 (1917), 199–235, esp. 217 ff. Benedict presided over a noteworthy early bull of canonization for Simon of Trier, *Papsturkunden*, II no. 599; placed Montecassino under papal protection (no. 611); and in 1044, after Conrad II's death, restored Grado's patriarchical status (no. 618).

These are but a few examples. Yet they serve to demonstrate that little credence should be given to the later reports concerning the despicable status of Rome and its bishop before reform began in earnest. One does well here to recall the testimony of Richard Southern on the exalted position that both Rome, and the papacy, enjoyed in the tenth and early eleventh centuries.[22] Rome was the ultimate source of spiritual power. In Rome were the tombs of Peter and Paul, the relics of the blessed martyrs: figures who actively worked on behalf of petitioners. They were the links between this world and the next, the concrete manifestations of spiritual power. St Peter, above all, who worked on behalf of and through the pope, drew the Christian world towards Rome in a never-ending pilgrimage. He was, as Southern noted, the universal figure in an otherwise local world.[23]

Many years ago, Monsignor Duchesne described the pope of the tenth and early eleventh centuries as 'the high-priest of the Roman pilgrimage, the dispenser of benedictions, privileges and anathemas'.[24] This characterization is confirmed by a cursory glance through the *Papsturkunden* from 896 to 1046, recently edited by Harald Zimmermann. The papacy which emerges from these documents is a vital one. Not only do the texts reveal an increasing demand for papal privileges (there are nearly as many for the period 996–1046 as for the entire preceding century), but they also point to a growing consciousness on the part of local ecclesiastical figures and institutions, of the need for a central authority. As religious institutions proliferated, as their rights and possessions multiplied, and became increasingly valuable and contested, the need for central confirmation of existing privileges, as well as sanction for new ones, became essential. The foundations of the Sees of Magdeburg and Bamberg, and the translation of Zeitz to Naumberg, for instance, would have been utterly inconceivable without papal validation. Such privileges, along with the growing conferral of *pallia* upon archbishops, and occasionally on favoured bishops, formed an essential bond in a vital Latin Church, over which presided the crucial figure of St Peter's vicar.

These privileges, however, also indicate that the papacy was a compliant entity, providing what Karl Leyser called 'a customer's service'.[25]

---

[22] R. W. Southern, *The Making of the Middle Ages* (London, 1953), 135 ff.

[23] Southern, 138.

[24] L. Duchesne, *The Beginnings of the Temporal Sovereignty of the Popes* (London, 1908), 271; quoted by Southern, 135.

[25] K. J. Leyser, review of Zimmermann (as in note 16), *JEH*, 39 (1988), 247–8.

For the bulk of the privileges show that the papacy was prepared to approve the requests of petitioners, provided that these were, or at least appeared to be, suitably sponsored. The telling phrase 'qui postulasti a nobis'—an explicit acknowledgement by the pope that he was not acting spontaneously, but rather was responding to an external request—is found in the bulk of the papal privileges of these centuries, particularly those in the period 996–1046. These documents show that the papacy of this time was an essentially passive institution acting at the behest of other, indeed, inferior, elements, rather than a deliberate force seizing the initiative to extend its authority over the Latin Church.

The transformation of the papacy from a passive institution to a deliberate force seizing the initiative was the reformers' most basic, if unspoken, goal. The elevation of Bishop Bruno of Toul as Pope Leo IX in 1049 marks the beginning of this change. By reviving the old practices of authorizing papal legates, and especially by presiding at councils, Leo became a template for how the Roman papacy would, and could, become not only the focal point of, but the spearhead for, reform. It was a transformation that was to have a revolutionary impact on the canon law.

Like many of the reformers, Leo IX had a great sense of the Church's historical past, particularly that of the Fathers. Yet within this vision, there was a developed, although perhaps selective, sense of the Church's legal past. Leo IX seems to have been the first of the reformers, along with Peter Damian, to recognize the need for a thorough declaration of the validity of ecclesiastical law, and the reassertion of the papacy's legislative prerogatives. This preoccupation with the correct observance and entrenchment of canon law was apparent from the outset of his pontificate. When he was designated by Henry III as successor to Pope Damasus II, Leo declared that he could not ascend the papal throne unless the clergy and people of Rome unanimously elected him pope.[26] His demands should not be seen as implying a rejection of the imperial role in papal elections, though, nor indeed a denial of the emperor's right in general to designate candidates to vacant sees and abbacies. The problem was not with imperial designations in themselves. Rather it was that they had to be seen to accord with the wishes of the diocese or abbey in question.

Leo's preoccupation with the rigorous observance of the forms of ecclesiastical law was not limited to the issue of free and canonical elec-

---

[26] *Leonis IX. Vita ab ipsius in ecclesia Tullensi archdiacono Wiberto conscripta*, II, c. 2, in *Pontificum Romanorum Vitae*, I, ed. J. M. Watterich (Leipzig, 1862), 149–51.

tions. Taking his pontificate as a whole, it is clear that Leo had a wider, more encompassing, idea of ecclesiastical law. This can be seen at Rome in April 1049, where he held the first of his reforming synods. Leo opened the proceedings with a solemn corroboration of the canons of the first four ecumenical councils.[27] He then ordered that all of the decrees of his predecessors on the Apostolic throne be confirmed, and obeyed as part of the authentic *corpus* of ecclesiastical law.[28] It was almost as if Leo was attempting to consolidate the arsenal of ecclesiastical law in order to reactivate papal legislative prerogatives. Only then did he proceed to the main business at hand: thorough legislative condemnations of simony and other abuses.[29]

It was at the synod in October later that year at Rheims that Leo clearly revealed the extent to which canon law and reform were intertwined.[30] As he had previously done at Rome in April, Leo reaffirmed past papal and ecclesiastical law, stipulating that it was to rank among the canons. But Leo also specifically acknowledged the importance and significance of the reform legislation he had enacted not only at this, but all his synods, by reconfirming it at Rheims.[31] More telling, however, is

---

[27] *Leonis IX. Vita*, II, c. 4, p. 154: 'Quantum autem solertiam in catholica lege conservanda adhibuerit, in primo concilio . . . demonstravit; ubi, statuta quatuor synodorum principalium viva voce corroboravit . . . '

[28] Ibid., p. 154: ' . . . decretaque omnium antecessorum suorum pontificum tenenda confirmavit.'

[29] The canons from Leo IX's Roman synod are no longer extant. Simony was undeniably the main issue: see *Herimanni Augiensis Chronicon a. 1049* (*MGH, SS*, 5), 128; and *Vita Leonis*, II, c. 4, which also noted the deposition of bishops who had obtained their rank through simony. The fullest account is provided by Peter Damian, in the *Liber gratissimus* (Reindel, I, no. 40), 498–500, where he described Leo's initial attempts to depose from office ecclesiastics of every rank who had entered by simony, or who had knowingly allowed themselves to be ordained by simonists. When great protests that all divine service would cease, and that the flocks would be left without pastors if this was enacted, Leo agreed to repromulgate the more moderate decree of Clement II which had imposed a penance of 40 days on those knowingly ordained by simonists. According to Damian in *Contra clericorum intemperantiam* (Reindel, III, no. 112), at pp. 280–1, Leo also attacked the practice of clerical concubinage by decreeing that all wives and concubines of priests in Rome were to be declared unfree, and were to become the property of the Lateran palace.

[30] *Historia dedicationis sancti Remigii apud Remos*, ed. J. Mabillon (Acta Sanctorum O.S.B.; Paris, 1701), 6, I, 711–27. Only the Mabillon edition gives the complete version of the text. See also U.-R. Blumenthal, 'The Beginnings of the Gregorian Reform: Some New Manuscript Evidence', in *Reform and Authority in the Medieval and Reformation Church*, ed. G. F. Lytle (Washington, DC, 1981), 1–13, here 7–8, and O. Capitani, *Immunità vescovili ed ecclesiologia in età 'pregregoriana' e 'gregoriana': l'avvio alla 'restaurazione'* (Spoleto, 1966), 164–7.

[31] Leo IX, 'Compertum charitati vestrae' in *Historia dedicationis*, 726: ' . . . et postea, in omnibus synodis quas habuimus, idipsum confirmare curavimus.'

the notice in Leo's letter from the council that he had seen this measure as being necessary for the *utilitas* of the Christian religion.[32] Papal discretion gave him not only the right to decide what was essential, but also a legal position from which to legislate for what was necessary. Perfection in Christian terms had long been seen as entailing adherence to an established code of behaviour. At Rheims, Leo demonstrated that the pope was the appropriate person to determine what that code should be.

Other evidence supports this.[33] The so-called St Magloire canons, which add new information regarding the pope's legislation at Rheims, include a number of provisions directed towards assuring the stability, peace, and well-being of the 'ordinary' Christian layman. It was already apparent from the *Historia dedicationis* that Leo had issued canons aimed at protecting both clergy and laymen from violence.[34] Leo's actions have been described as emanating from the similar concerns involved in the peace movement gathering strength first in France, and then throughout Europe during this period. In the legislation at Rheims, Leo seems to have been especially concerned with filling the void created by Henry I of France's inactivity and ineffectiveness with regard to the promotion of God's peace.[35] What is made clear, however, by the St Magloire canons is that Leo was not only legislating for the Church, but was also extending his prerogatives into the world of the laity.

Leo IX's preoccupation with the laity at the Rheims council is significant in a number of ways. While reinforcing ideas about the pope's identification with the peace movement, the St Magloire canons also underscore Leo's concern with the establishment of a stable, well-ordered society. What is especially striking is that, once again, the pope turned to the law as the means of establishing desired ends. The legislation at Rheims, moreover, shows Leo taking a more pro-active role. In many ways, he seems to have been looking to incorporate local concerns, and the local world, into the Roman Church, thereby solidifying the lat-

---

[32] Ibid., 726–7: ' . . . plurima ad utilitatem christianae religionis necessaria . . . statuendo confirmavimus: quae omnia capitulis digesta inter canones haberi precipimus . . . '

[33] See U.-R. Blumenthal, 'Ein neuer Text für das Reimser Konzil Leos IX (1049)?', *DA* 32 (1976), 23–48 (the St Magloire canons (V) are edited and compared with those from the *Historia dedicationis* (H) at 29–36). Cf. 'The Beginnings of the Gregorian Reform', 1–13.

[34] *Historia dedicationis*, 724, c. 9 Ne quis cum aliquibus sacri ordines inter agentibus violentiam ullam inferre auderet; and c. 10 Ne quis pauperes homines rapinis vel captionibus vexaret.

[35] See H. Hoffmann, *Gottesfriede und Treuga Dei* (*MGH, Schriften*, 20; Stuttgart, 1964), 185, 218; and Blumenthal, 'Ein neuer Text', 43–6.

ter's position in the Christian west at large. With his prohibition against the invasion of ecclesiastical property and the accumulation of additional rights by laymen; with his provision that disputes among laymen be settled in the presence of the local bishop; and with his absolute ban of the customary blood-feud, Leo IX was endowing elements of the local peace movements with a new, and wider import—in short, with a new universality.[36]

At first glance the measures in themselves are not especially innovative, or revolutionary. Perhaps not surprisingly, Leo was clearly anxious to demonstrate that the consensus of the past underlay his decisions. He frequently requested that the sacred writings, and canons of the Fathers, be read aloud to the assembly before he made a final judgement.[37] Even with the peace legislation, Leo by and large depended upon similar pronouncements from the council at Le Puy in 994.[38] It was not that these local conciliar canons were insufficient, but rather that they lacked the universal or cohesive authority that only the papacy, in the eleventh century, could give.

It is, however, Leo's very self-consciousness over his actions at Rheims that strikes a new chord. His reaffirmation of existing law, and the incorporation of his own reform legislation, indicate a desire both to reinforce and supplement the older precepts, in order to fulfill the new requirements of Christian society. In so doing, Leo united the wider idea of reform with the sacred law, thereby implicitly emphasizing that true reform was feasible only within the institutional, and juridical structure of the Roman Church. His actions not only gave reform a seal of legitimacy, but also exalted the position of the papacy. Convinced of the absolute independence of the ecclesiastical juridical order, Leo

---

[36] Blumenthal, 'Ein neuer Text', canons [V]: c. 14, pp. 32–3: Terras sanctuarii laicus invadere non presumat nec novas consuetudines adcrescat; c. 16, p. 33 Si aliqua querimonia inter homines exhortat fuerit, ante episcopum veniant et capitale si fuerit aut fundum terrae reddant; sin autem ante archiepiscopum, quod si noluerint itidem sicut alii, ab omni christianitate priventur, et episcopi litteras suas papae mittant; c. 22, p. 35 Pax de homicidiis patrum, filiorum, nepotum vel consanguineorum omnino fiat.

[37] e.g. *Hist. dedicat.*, 721: ' . . . lectis sententiis super hac re olim promulgatis ab orthodoxis patribus, declaratum est quod solus Romanae sedis pontifex universalis ecclesia primas est et apostolicus. . . . '; 723: ' . . . quod in canonibus de sacrorum ordinum venditoribus sit decretum, eius iussit tantummodo recitari; lectaque sententia ad praeceptum ex concilio chalcedonensi, capitulo videlicet secundo . . . '; and 723: 'Tunc ex praecepto ipsius Papae, lecta sunt sententiae super huiuscemodi re promulgatae ab orthodoxis Patribus . . . '

[38] See Blumenthal, 'Ein neuer Text', 44, and notes on textual comparison, 29–36. On the council of Le Puy, see Hoffmann, 14, 17–20.

sought to underline the capacity of the papacy to respond to the changing requirements of Christian society.

Alongside his reassertion of the legislative prerogatives of the papacy, Leo's more enduring legacy was perhaps the establishment of a reforming circle amongst his entourage at Rome. Although men such as Humbert, Hildebrand, and Peter Damian in no way held a homogeneous set of principles or agendas, their association with the Apostolic city ensured that reform would continue to be directed from Rome. The symbolism or significance of Rome cannot be underestimated; it gave common cause to these otherwise perhaps disparate men. Rome, and above all, the Roman Church not only helped to define the reformers' objectives, and ambitions, it also provided universality for their ideas and policies.

Peter Damian is particularly instructive in this respect.[39] Not only did his adult life span the entire 'pre-Gregorian phase' of reform, but his ideology, ecclesiology, and position on ecclesiastical law hinged upon a subtle understanding of Rome's place within the universal Church. Damian, however, is a notorious and contradictory character. While an extremist in the language with which he articulated and defended his position, Damian often placed himself on the conservative side, at least in the increasingly sharper ecclesio-political context of the reform movement which prevailed after the synod of Sutri in 1046.[40] Although he believed that Rome should take the lead, and be the principle of renewal, he did not exclude but welcomed the intervention of the emperor in the promotion of reform, likening it to Christ's Cleansing of the Temple.[41] Early in his career, Damian had undertaken action at Henry III's request, and often used the occasion to remind his audience of the

[39] For biography, see J. Leclercq, *St Pierre Damien: Ermite et homme d'église* (Uomini e dottrini, 8; Rome, 1960); and L. K. Little, 'The Personal Development of Peter Damian', in *Order and Innovation in the Middle Ages: Essays in Honor of J. R. Strayer*, ed. W. C. Jordan *et al.* (Princeton, 1976), 317–41, 523–8. J. J. Ryan, *St. Peter Damiani and His Canonical Sources* (Toronto, 1956), remains indispensable.

[40] See Ryan, 154. Damian followed in the model of early 11th-cent. reforming imperial bishops, especially that of Burchard of Worms. Although he sought to turn the whole world into a hermitage, Damian, like his favourite formal source, Burchard's *Decretum libri XX*, also reflected the practical concerns of a conscientious pastor of souls.

[41] Reindel, I, no. 11, p. 139: 'Et necesse est iam, ut eadem sit renovandae principium, quae nascentis humanae salutis extiterat fundamentum.' Cf. Reindel, I, no. 20, where Damian praised Henry III for his deposition of Widiger, Archbishop-elect of Ravenna; and I, no. 40, pp. 501–2, for his praise of Henry III's actions at Sutri. The Cleansing would become an important reform symbol, with the pope, however, figuring in the place of Christ: R. Rough, *The Reformist Illuminations in the Gospels of Matilda, Countess of Tuscany* (The Hague, 1973).

apparent lack of papal or episcopal interest in reform.[42] Later, during the Cadalan schism, Damian was so convinced of the co-operation ordained by God between *regnum* and *sacerdotium* that he wholeheart-edly supported the idea that the problem be settled in a council in the presence of the king—a suggestion not entirely welcomed by Hildebrand and Pope Alexander II.[43]

Damian was also the first to call explicitly for an overhaul of the sacred canons. In the *Liber Gomorrhianus* written around October 1049, and addressed to Leo IX, he expressed grave concern over the quality of the available canonical collections, many of which included what he termed 'pernicious fables'. His anxiety stemmed from the fact these 'fables' were understood by the clergy as being divinely-inspired, and binding ecclesiastical law.[44] Damian focused initially upon apocryphal texts in penitential collections which effectively sanctioned sodomy and other homosexual practices by imposing only minimal periods of pre-scribed penance.[45] This led him on to express anguish over the state of canon law as a whole. Since, as Damian believed, canons received their power and authenticity from the Holy Spirit, it was essential that the *corpus* of canon law live up to that testing standard. It was, therefore, of paramount importance that canon law be free of contradictions and unsound doctrine. In consequence, Damian advocated a thorough reform which would remove all dubious or contradictory canons.[46]

One of the problems that clearly troubled him was that of how the authentic canons were to be distinguished from those in error. Damian here assumed a degree of historical consciousness. He turned first to the

---

[42] e.g. Reindel, I, no. 26, p. 241: 'Quid iuvat, cum quis limati mucronis ferro succin-gitur, si circumfusis hostium cuneis non vibratur?'

[43] See his letter to Anno of Cologne, Reindel III, no. 99, pp. 97–100, where Damian, using Gelasius, stressed the ideal state between the two spheres.

[44] *Liber gomorrhianus* (Reindel, I, no. 31), p. 300: 'Sed quoniam quaedam neniae sacris canonibus reperiuntur admixtae, in quibus perditi homines vana praesumptione confidunt . . .'

[45] Ibid., 301 ff. For a recent discussion, see C. Leyser, 'Cities of the Plain: The Rhetoric of Sodomy in Peter Damian's "Book of Gomorrah"', *Romanic Review*, 86 (1995), 191–211. See also introduction, *Book of Gomorrah: An Eleventh Century Treatise on Homosexuality*, ed. P. J. Payer (Waterloo, Ontario, 1982); Payer's translation (based on Migne) has been superseded by O. Blum, *The Letters of Peter Damian*, 3 vols. (The Fathers of the Church, Medieval Continuation; Washington, DC, 1989–92). L. K. Little, op. cit., sees Damian's reaction in relation to his own experience with homosexuality.

[46] Reindel, I, no. 31, p. 300: ' . . . ex ipsis aliqua hic apponimus, ut non solum eas, sed et omnes alias sibi similes scripturas, *ubicunque repertae fuerint*, falsas et omnino apocrifas liquido demonstremus. [et infra] . . . et multa alia mendosa atque sacrilega versutia dia-boli sacris canonibus reperiuntur inserta, quae nobis magis libet obliterare quam scribere, magis conspuere quam tam vana ludibria scedulis inculcare' (my italics).

weight of antiquity: only the edicts of the Fathers, and the decrees of the sacred councils were to be held as authentic canons.[47] Although he expressed some reservations over the authenticity and value of some of the papal decretals (it seems his concern was with Ps.Isidorian decretals), Damian none the less believed that they should be given precedence in canonical terms out of respect for the infallible position of the vicar of St Peter. Damian, however, was not a rigid papalist who insisted upon specific papal confirmation of any given canon. Unlike his contemporary Humbert, and the later canonists Cardinal Atto and Deusdedit, Damian was prepared to accept among others, transalpine conciliar canons, provided that these were not in conflict either with canons or doctrinal positions sanctioned by Rome.[48]

What Damian revealed here, however, was a deeper deficiency in the reformers' attempts at defining a new constitution for the Church and Christian society. Not only was there a lack of any explicit articulation of the appropriate mechanism by which a new code of behaviour could be established, not much thought had been given to the principle by which the different legal responses of the past could be reconciled. Whether consciously or not, Damian's crusade for moral purity led him to realize the need to find a way of harmonizing canon law. Although a long way from the more sophisticated ideas of Bernold of Constance, Ivo of Chartres, and Gratian, what it entailed was a significant step towards a doctrine of sources.[49]

In an effort to work out the complexities of harmonizing the law and especially the needs of day-to-day justice, Damian ultimately fell back on the principle of papal discretion as the definitive, though not wholly satisfactory, principle of conciliation. Recognizing that there were practical circumstances which on occasion made rigorous observation of the canons impossible, Damian underscored the need for some principle or

---

[47] Reindel, I, no. 31, p. 304: '. . . sequitur ergo, ut nequaquam inter canones habeantur, quae nec a decretalibus patrum edictis nec a sacris videntur prodire conciliis. Quicquid enim inter species non annumeratur, a genere proculdubio alienum esse decernitur.'

[48] e.g. Humbert, *Responsio in Libellum Nicetae*, c. 24 (*PL* 143, 983–1000), 955; Atto, *Breviarium*, prologus, ed. A. Mai (Scriptorum veterum nova collectio et vaticanis codicibus, 10 vols.; Rome, 1825–38), 6/2, p. 61: '. . . ita apud nos locus est ad faciendam hanc monetam, ut non sit scriptum authenticum quod a Romano pontifice non fuerit confirmatum'; and *Die Kanonessammlung des Kardinals Deusdedit*, ed. V. Wolf von Glanvell (Paderborn, 1906), prologue, p. 3, where Deusdedit accepted the first four ecumenical councils, but stipulated that other conciliar canons had to be sanctioned by Rome.

[49] See Ryan, 147–9.

person to make the necessary interpretations.[50] The theory which he was beginning to articulate was that which later would be identified—as jurisprudence began to influence developments in canon law—as '*aequitas–iustitia*': the latter being the ideal of justice, the former the ideal of justice in practice. *Aequitas*, however, was not a familiar concept to Damian and the reformers, who continued to counterpoise their understanding of Christian charity, of benignity, and especially of *misericordia* against the full rigour of the canons. Lacking both the ideology and the terminology of jurisprudence, Damian effectively conceded *misericordia* to papal discretion.[51]

Although Damian's canonical ideas posed important questions, these ideas need to be seen, like his concept of reform, in the wider context of his understanding of Rome's unique place within the universal Church. In 1059, he was sent by Pope Nicholas II together with Bishop Anselm I of Lucca (later Pope Alexander II) as a papal legate to Milan to investigate the problems created by the Patarenes' attempts to impress reform upon a large part of the Milanese clergy who were unwilling to break with simony, clerical marriage, and their unique Ambrosian independence.[52] Damian wrote an account of the legation in a letter to Hildebrand, including a sermon he had preached in Milan.[53] Known as *De privilegio Romanae ecclesiae*, it contained a powerful

---

[50] e.g. Reindel, II, no. 67, esp. pp. 288–9; and Reindel, II, no. 89, pp. 569–70 where Damian referred to famous examples when the canons regulating episcopal elections had been relaxed. Cf. Ryan, text no. 172, p. 90. See also Reindel, III, no. 112, p. 267: 'Concilium, inquam, vestrum, quodcunque vultis, nomen optineat, sed a me non recipitur, si decretis Romanorum pontificum non concordat. Aucupantur enim quaedam quasi canonum adulterina sarmenta, eisque praebent auctoritatem, ut autenticam canonum valeant vacuare virtutem.'

[51] Reindel, I, no. 31, p. 304: ' . . . nec cuiquam soli homini licet canones edere, sed illi tantummodo hoc competit privilegium, qui in beati Petri cathedra cernitur praesidere.' Cf. Reindel, III, no. 96, p. 64: 'Sedis apostolicae qui vult retinere vigorem,| Aequa libret rigidae pondera iustitiae.| Iuris enim pariles nescit suspendere lances,| Quem favor inflectit, spes vel avara trahit|.' In general, see 'Equité', in *Dictionnaire de droit canonique*, 5 (Paris, 1953), 394–410; C. Lefebvre, *Les Pouvoirs du juge en droit canonique* (Paris, 1938), 164–70; and S. Kuttner, *Harmony from Dissonance: An Interpretation of Medieval Canon Law* (Latrobe, Penn., 1961).

[52] On the dating of the legation, see Reindel, II, p. 230, note 10. See also *Arnulfi gesta archiepiscoporum Mediolanensium*, III, cc. 13–14 (*MGH, SS*, 8), 20–1; Andreas of Strumi, *Vita sancti Arialdi*, c. 7 (*MGH, SS*, 30/2), 1054. On the Patarene movement in general, see C. Violante, *La pataria milanese e la riforma ecclesiastica (1048–57)* (Rome, 1955); and B. Stock, *The Implications of Literacy: Written Language and Models of Interpretation in the Eleventh and Twelfth Centuries* (Princeton, 1983).

[53] Reindel, II, no. 65, pp. 228–47. Damian here acknowledges Hildebrand's famous request that he compile a small collection of decrees pertaining to the authority of the Apostolic See.

statement of Roman primacy, and, consequently, of Rome's right to set the norms of clerical life. While the text contains no explicit appeals to canonical authorities, there are telling allusions which demonstrate that the weight of the canons was never far from Damian's mind.[54]

Damian opened his sermon with pacifying remarks that he had not come to enhance the honour of Rome, but from concern for the interests of his audience. The main premise of his argument, however, was the declaration of the universality of jurisdiction—from which no one was exempt—of the *ecclesia Romana*, which had been founded by Christ alone.[55] Damian believed that Christ, through his exclusive foundation, had conferred the *privilegium* of jurisdiction upon St Peter.[56] He had explored this idea previously. In an letter to Hildebrand, and the elected, though as of then unconsecrated, Pope Nicholas II, Damian had explicitly made the point that St Peter, the pope, and the *ecclesia Romana* were one.[57] In Damian's understanding, the unique privilege that had been given to Peter—the universality of jurisdiction—was indubitably continued in his true successors at Rome.

Damian then considered the repercussions of any failure to acknowledge Rome's authority. The issue was explicitly dogmatic. Anyone who attempted to deny or disregard this divinely-conferred right fell into heresy.[58] Although with the advent of Gregory VII, the term *hereticus* would lose its specific link with doctrine, and be increasingly equated with any situation of disobedience to the Apostolic See, Damian's use of the term remained more restricted. The fault (and heresy) of the Milanese was less their failure to be obedient to Rome than the denial of Rome's right to overlordship implicit in that disobedience. Faithful to the meaning, and intention of Anastasius Bibliotecarius—almost certainly his source, as Ryan suggested—Damian saw the issue as a denial

---

[54] See Ryan, text no. 106 ff. The only non-scriptural quotation was from St Ambrose.

[55] Reindel, II, no. 65, pp. 232–3. Cf. Ryan, no. 106–14, pp. 60–8.

[56] Reindel, II, no. 65, p. 233: 'Non ergo quaelibet terrena sententia, sed illud verbum, per quod constructum est coelum et terra, per quod denique omnia condita sunt elementa, Romanam fundavit ecclesiam. Illius certe privilegio fungitur, illius auctoritate fulcitur.'

[57] Reindel, II, no. 57, pp. 165–6: 'Et quia vos apostolica sedes, *vos Romana estis aecclesia*, ad deponendum reddendumque, quod baiulare nequiveram, integrum mihi visum est non adire fabricam lapidum, sed eos potius in quibus viget ipsius aecclesiae sacramentum. . . . vos Petrus vobiscum fugiens attrahit, illic esse Romanam aecclesiam omnibus indubitanter ostendit' (my italics).

[58] Reindel, II, no. 65, pp. 233–4: 'Unde non dubium, quia quisquis cuilibet aecclesiae ius suum detrahit, iniustitiam facit, qui autem Romane aecclesiae privilegium ab ipso summo omnium aecclesiarum capite traditum auferre conatur, hic proculdubio in heresim labitur . . . hic est dicendus hereticus.' Cf. II, no. 88, p. 521: 'Praeterea si eos sacri canones hereticos notant, qui cum Romana aecclesia non concordant . . . '

of orthodox faith.[59] Rome's universal *privilegium* was more than a point of legalistic dominion; rather it was a question of orthodoxy.

Damian, however, moved the narrative forward: offering some important vindications for the primacy of Rome as a principle of unity and for the universality of her jurisdiction as a prerequisite of orthodox faith. Damian clearly envisaged the Roman Church as personified by the papacy as being both the legislator for reform, and the ultimate arbitrator of authenticity regarding canon law. Yet, while he saw the papacy and the law as needing to come together, his inability to recognize, or come to terms with, the increasingly discordant relations of *regnum* and *sacerdotium* meant that his somewhat roseate view would need further sharpening.

The first crisis arose in 1058. Following the sudden death of Pope Stephen IX at Florence on 29 March, the Tusculum nobility, probably with a measure of support from lesser clergy and laity, disregarded the express wishes of the deceased pontiff and hastily elevated Bishop John of Velletri as Pope Benedict X.[60] When the reformers refused to accept Benedict, five cardinal-bishops along with Hildebrand met in Siena, sometime after October, and elected Bishop Gerard of Florence as Pope Nicholas II. With the aid of Duke Godfrey of Lower Lotharingia, Nicholas was enthroned at Rome on 24 January 1059.

The election of Nicholas II presented the reformers with an immediate and serious problem of legitimacy. Not only had the election of Benedict X taken place at Rome, in technical accordance with the requirements of the canons (though the traditional imperial rights had been disregarded), but it was also hard to paint Benedict as a schismatic usurper. As Cardinal-bishop of Velletri, he had been a member of the reforming circle, and his election probably enjoyed large support in Rome. The delayed election of Nicholas II, on the other hand, with its provincial setting of Siena, its small clerical audience, and the delay of enthronement, must have seemed to many people to bear all the hallmarks of a schismatic election.

Potentially more troubling, the contested papal election not only revealed that ideas about reform were changing, but also that relations

---

[59] Ryan, no. 107, p. 63.

[60] With a premonition of his impending death, Stephen had sworn the Romans to refrain from electing a new pope until Hildebrand returned from his legation to the German court. See Reindel, II, no. 58, pp. 193–4; *Leonis Marsicani et Petri diaconi Chronica monasterii Casinensis*, II, c. 98 (*MGH, SS*, 7), 694; and L. G. Meyer von Knonau, *Jahrbücher des deutschen Reiches unter Heinrichs IV. und Heinrichs V.*, 7 vols. (Leipzig, 1890–1909), I, 674–7.

within the leadership were becoming strained. The fourteenth-century account in John of Bayon's *Historia Mediani monasterii* is instructive.[61] It states that, following the election in Rome, Hildebrand had urged Humbert either to take the Apostolic See for himself or to yield it to him. Humbert, according to John of Bayon, preferred to give it to Nicholas. While the value of this scenario is debatable, it none the less points to the wider problems facing the reformers: the lack both of indisputable leadership, and a clear plan of action. Not having been presented with such a potentially dangerous situation since the time of Sutri, when the Roman Church had had a pious king to intervene, the reformers demonstrated a not unsurprising inability to deal with the crisis. Other events confirm the confusion. Peter Damian, although he in no way supported Benedict X, seems to have taken the opportunity of the upheaval to resign the Cardinal-bishopric of Ostia to which he been appointed in 1057.[62] Although what was seen as his reluctance towards the reformers' candidate may have been more apparent than real (i.e. personal doubts as to the propriety of a hermit's adopting the active life of pastoral care), Damian was none the less obliged to protest his loyalty to Nicholas II and the reformers.[63] Whether Damian may have feared, in the light of Nicholas II's connection with Duke Godfrey, that political rather than reform agendas were at work remains a matter for speculation.[64] In any event, the contested election not only made man-

---

[61] John of Bayon, (partly edited) in H. Belhomme, *Historia Mediani in monte Vosago monasterii O.S.B. ex congregatione SS. Vitoni et Hidulfi* (Strasbourg, 1724), p. 249.

[62] See Reindel, II no. 58, p. 193 for his refusal to consecrate Benedict. According to the *Liber censuum*, c. 58, 81, if the Bishop of Ostia was unavailable, an archpriest either from Ostia or Velletri was to preside at papal consecrations: see P. Fabre, *Étude sur le liber censuum de l'église romaine* (Bibliothèque des écoles françaises d'Athènes et de Rome, 62; Paris, 1892), 312. Benedict was consecrated by an unknown archpriest of Ostia. Cf. *Chron. Casinensis*, II, c. 99, p. 695.

[63] See Reindel, II, no. 57, pp. 162–90. It is unlikely that Damian was concerned about the taint of simony upon Nicholas—a charge levelled in an imperial *damnatio* of 1060?—who had been consecrated by Gregory VI, as he insisted upon the validity of *gratis* ordinations by simonists. There is no evidence that he acquired the See of Florence by simoniacal means, though the *Annales Romani* noted that money had been paid by both Hildebrand and Nicholas II for the Apostolic See. *Annales Romani* (1044–73) in *Le Liber Pontificalis*, II, ed. L. Duchesne (Paris, 1892), 334–45. On the German condemnation of Nicholas II, see Meyer von Knonau, I, 180–1, and Excurs VIII, 684–7.

[64] Godfrey had figured in his brother, Stephen IX's, plans to exert papal influence in southern Italy. Hildebrand's legation to the German court had been aimed, at least in part, at obtaining sanction for Godfrey's proposed acquisition of Camerino-Spoleto. Since, after his enthronement in January 1059, the pope initially tried to enforce this lordship, Godfrey may in some way have influenced, or at the least looked to reap the benefits of, a decision in favour of Nicholas. See *Chron. Casinensis*, III, c. 12, pp. 704–5. On Nicholas's support of Godfrey, see Reindel, II, no. 60, pp. 203–5, where Damian petitioned for the

ifest the relative lack of coherence among the reformers, but also underscored the inadequacy of existing arrangements for dealing with papal elections. To many, only an appeal to canon law might provide an answer.

The task which faced them was not simply that of nullifying the election of Benedict X and legitimizing that of Nicholas II. That might solve the immediate crisis, but the larger problem would remain: that of discovering which factors would determine who was the true pope. The first task was to dispense with the idea that election at Rome, and possession of Rome, in some way conferred papal privileges. Damian had addressed this issue in his letter of atonement to Nicholas, emphasizing that the true pope drew upon himself the powers of St Peter, and exhibited to all the world the true Roman Church.[65] What lay behind this was the concept that a true *electus* was in full jurisdictional possession of his office, and exercised all of its prerogatives even before consecration.[66] There was, in addition, the problem of defining who actually conveyed legitimacy on the pope, that is, who was empowered to elect him. In his condemnation of Benedict, Damian had insisted on the constitutive role of the cardinal-bishops in papal elections.[67] He had first identified this role for them at his elevation to the Cardinal-bishopric of Ostia in 1057, at which time the privileges of the Lateran bishops were largely liturgical or sacramental in character. In an interesting, if complex, theological discussion, Damian used the unique situation of the Lateran Basilica, and the universality it conferred upon the cardinal-bishops, as a bridge from a liturgical domain towards an electoral one. In so doing, he had effectively derived a political role for the cardinal-bishops: if they alone could consecrate a new pope, then they must also be instrumental in his election.[68] Such ideas would leave their imprint on the decisive action subsequently taken by the reformers.

The retrospective seal of legitimacy for Nicholas II came from the papal election decree of 1059.[69] The decree seems ultimately to have

---

removal of papal ban placed on Ancona for its failure to accept Godfrey's overlordship. On Hildebrand, and his legation to the German court, see G. B. Borino, 'L'archidiaconato di Ildebrando', *SG* 3 (1948), 463–516. Cf. Meyer von Knonau, I, 91–2.

[65] Reindel, II, no. 57, pp. 165–6 (for text see above, note 57).

[66] See R. L. Benson, *The Bishop-Elect: A Study in Medieval Ecclesiastical Office* (Princeton, 1968), 6–10, 35 ff.

[67] Reindel, II, no. 58, pp. 191–2.   [68] Reindel, II, no. 48, pp. 52–61, esp. 55–7.

[69] *Concilium Romanum 1059, Decretum electionis pontificae* (*MGH, Const.* 1), no. 382, pp. 538–41; H. G. Krause, *Das Papstwahldekret von 1059 und seine Rolle im Investiturstreit* (*SG* 7; Rome, 1960), text 271 ff.; D. Jaspar, *Das Papstwahldekret von 1059: Überlieferung und Textgestalt* (Beiträge zur Geschichte und Quellenkunde des Mittelalters, 12; Sigmaringen,

been designed to re-secure the hold upon the Roman Church which the reformers had almost lost during the brief, but significant, schism. The *narratio* of the decree was explicit: the regulations had been made necessary by the confusion that had arisen following the death of Stephen IX.[70] The primary role in papal elections, therefore, was confined to the cardinal-bishops; their decision was to be confirmed by the clergy and people of Rome.[71] It also fell to the cardinal-bishops to ensure the moral probity and worthiness of the person elected as pope. This was justified by a somewhat tendentious argument that, as the Apostolic See, unlike episcopal sees, had no superior or metropolitan to provide oversight, those to whom the task of election was given were the only possible '*vice metropolitani*'.[72] Election by the cardinal-bishops outside Rome was also sanctioned, even if only with a small audience of clerics and laymen, when circumstances such as war or intimidation might hinder a free and canonical election.[73]

The most striking canon, however, was the explicit affirmation of the dispositive powers of a legitimate papal *electus*.[74] It was, in effect, an attempt to distinguish between the jurisdictional and the other powers of papal office. According to the decree of 1059, a legitimate papal *electus* obtained the *auctoritas regendi et disponendi*. These represented the non-priestly powers of the pope: jurisdictional and administrative headship over the Church, and, more important, dispositive stewardship of ecclesiastical properties and rights. This distinction is all the more important, as Benson noted, for its implicit acknowledgement that, prior to 1059, enthronement had been the constitutive factor in the election of a pope.[75] Not surprisingly, the ramifications of this, especially in terms of Nicholas II's exercise of office prior to enthronement, were

---

1986), text 98 ff. K. M. Woody, '*Sagena piscatoris*: Petrus Damiani and the Papal Election Decree of 1059', *Viator*, 1 (1970), 33–54, argued that Damian was directly responsible at the least for the decree's *narratio*. Krause, 257–70, was more cautious.

[70] *Decretum electionis pontificae*, c. 2 (*MGH, Const.* 1), 539. On the stylistic similarities of this to Damian's letter (Reindel, II, no. 57), see Woody, '*Sagena piscatoris*', 36–8.

[71] *Dec. elect. pont.*, c. 3, p. 539.

[72] Ibid., c. 4, p. 539.   [73] Ibid., c. 7, p. 540.

[74] Ibid., c. 8, p. 540: 'Plane postquam electio fuerit facta, si bellica tempestas vel qualiscunque hominum conatus malignitatis studio restiterit, ut is qui electus est in apostolica sede iuxta consuetudinem intronizari non valeat, electus tamen sicut papa auctoritatem obtineat regendi sanctam Romanam ecclesiam et disponendi omnes facultates illius, quod beatum Gregorium ante consecrationem suam fecisse cognoscimus.' The reference to Gregory I was correct, as Benson showed (p. 42, note 38), as there had been a delay of some seven months between Gregory's election and enthronement.

[75] Benson, *The Bishop-Elect*, 42–3.

conveniently glossed over.[76] The clause, moreover, was an exceptional one. Only when a situation of war or unrest prevented enthronement at Rome did the *electus* exercise the *auctoritas regendi et disponendi* prior to consecration.[77] Under normal circumstances, enthronement would remain the jurisdictionally constitutive factor.[78]

In 1061, the papal election decree had its first test, becoming the principle of legitimacy to which the reformers turned in the face of the ensuing schism. For, following the death of Nicholas II in July, the Roman opposition, mindful perhaps of the failure of their earlier attempts, sent envoys to the young king, Henry IV, asking him to designate a new pontiff.[79] Meanwhile, the reformers led by Hildebrand (Humbert having died on 5 May 1061) elected Bishop Anselm I of Lucca as Pope Alexander II at Rome on 30 September. He was quickly enthroned the following day, with the aid of Richard of Capua.[80] At the German court in late October, however, Bishop Cadalus of Parma was chosen as Pope Honorius II. When the struggle between the two claimants to possess Rome proved indecisive, both parties were prevailed upon to retire to their respective sees until a decision could be rendered by a synod to be held in the presence of the king at Augsburg.[81] Cadalus' support initially seemed substantial, but a number of events, including the coup at Kaiserwerth which placed the young Henry IV in the powerful hands of the reform-minded Archbishop Anno of Cologne, favoured the ultimate victory of Alexander II.[82] In October 1062, the synod at Augsburg

---

[76] Sources for Nicholas II's activities prior to enthronement are scanty. He consecrated Jullita, daughter of Marquis Ugo, as abbess of St Hilary, sometime in December 1058, and also confirmed St Hilary's immunity: *Regesta pontificum Romanorum*, I, JL no. 4392, ed. P. Jaffé; 2nd edn. by S. Loewenfeld, F. Kaltenbrunner, and P. Ewald (Leipzig, 1885). This would have been in accordance with his episcopal powers. If Bonizo is to be trusted, Nicholas was present (though was not described as presiding) at a synod in early January at which Benedict was condemned as a perjuror and usurper: Bonizo, *Liber ad amicum*, lib. 5 (*MGH, LdL*, 1), 593. Baronius, however, described Nicholas as presiding: *Annales ecclesiastici*, 11, cols. 324–5.

[77] *Dec. elect. pont.*, c. 8, p. 540.   [78] See Benson, *The Bishop-Elect*, 43.

[79] *Bertholdi Annales a. 1061* (*MGH, SS*, 5), 271. Cf. *Chronici Herimanni continuatio (codicis Sangallensis)* (*MGH, SS*, 13), 731–2; *Annales Altahenses maiores a. 1061* (*MGH, SS*, 20), 811; and Meyer von Knonau, I, 217–18.

[80] On Alexander II, see T. Schmidt, *Alexander II. (1061–73) und die römische Reformgruppe seiner Zeit* (Päpste und Papsttum, 11; Stuttgart, 1977).

[81] On Augsburg, see *Annales Altahenses maiores a. 1061*, 811, though the synod was mistakenly dated as August 1061, when it took place in October 1062. Cf. Schmidt, 119ff.; and Meyer von Knonau, I, 296ff.

[82] On Kaiserwerth, and the situation in the Reich, *Lamperti annales a. 1062*, 79–81; *Annales Altahenses maiores a. 1062*, 811; *Bertholdi annales a. 1062*, 272; and *Brunonis Saxonicum bellum*, c. 1, in F. J. Schmale, ed. *Quellen zur Geschichte Kaiser Heinrichs IV.* (Darmstadt, 1974), 194. Cf. Meyer von Knonau, I, 267ff.

provisionally accorded recognition to Alexander, though a final decision was reserved to a later time, pending further inquiry. Bishop Burchard of Halberstadt, who had been charged with investigating the accusations of simony made against Alexander, travelled to Rome, ultimately confirming him as legitimate pope. Yet after Alexander had been reseated on the papal throne, Cadalus' forces once again attacked Rome.

There followed a curious set of events. In a letter to Anno of Cologne which he wrote while on legation to France, Damian seems to have rekindled the issue of Alexander's legitimacy by calling for a new council to deliberate on the schism.[83] Using Gelasian texts, Damian stressed the ideal relationship which had once existed between *regnum* and *sacerdotium*. Their obligation was to come to the aid of one another.[84] Damian then considered the ways in which the sacerdotal power had upheld the royal one in recent times, referring to Anno's preservation of the king and his realm through the coup at Kaiserwerth. His appeal to Anno, as regent of Henry IV, was an appeal that the 'royal' power assume its burden, and come to the aid of the beleaguered Church. With the letter, which reopened old and nagging wounds, Damian again showed himself to be more the conscientious pastor of souls, and less the 'politically-minded' figure which other reformers might have preferred.[85]

Damian's *Disceptatio synodalis*—written in anticipation of the synod at Augsburg—is an important source for the papal schism of 1061. Based upon the papal election decree of 1059, the treatise was presented as a legal debate between a fictitious royal *advocatus* and a papal *defensor*. While the rhetoric is typically extreme, Damian clearly sought in the text to restrict the conflict to boundaries within which compromise might be possible. He in no way denied the rights of the king, whom he described as having been misled.[86] Nor did he refer in any way what-

---

[83] Reindel, III, no. 99, pp. 97–100.

[84] Reindel, III, no. 99, p. 99: 'Sciebat enim, quoniam utraque dignitas alternae invicem utilitatis est indiga, dum et sacerdotium regni tuitione protegitur, et regnum sacerdotalis officii sanctitate fulcitur.' See Ryan, text no. 181; and R. L. Benson, 'The Gelasian Doctrine: Uses and Transformations', in *La Notion d'autorité: islam, byzance, occident*, ed. G. Makdisi (Colloques internationaux de la napoule, 2; Paris, 1982), 13–45.

[85] Though Alexander was allowed to preside at the subsequent synod held at Mantua in 1064, he was humiliatingly forced to respond to the charge of simony with a sacred oath. On Mantua, see *Annales Altahenses a. 1064*, 814; Sigebert of Gembloux, (with the wrong date) *Chronica a. 1067* (*MGH, SS*, 6), 361–2; and Meyer von Knonau, I, 380–1. Alexander's letter to Bishop Rainald of Como shows that he was presiding: see *Epistolae Alexandrini*, no. 63, in *Collectio Brittanica*, Brit. Lib., MS Addit. 8873, fo. 49ʳ: 'Unde in Mantua sinodo te admonuimus . . . ' (cf. JL no. 4558).

[86] Reindel, II, no. 89, pp. 549, 552.

soever to the papacy's secular allies, the Normans, who seem to have weighed against Alexander at Augsburg, and later at Mantua.[87] For Damian, the issue was the religious and moral crisis of schism, and the danger presented to the Church by Cadalus.

The treatise is also a significant witness to more ominous issues underlying the schism, and the problematic clash with the German court. With its insistence that the schism be resolved 'sub canonici iuris auctoritate', Damian's treatise was perhaps as much directed at the Roman circle of reformers as it was towards promoting a favourable decision for Alexander II at Augsburg.[88] The text reveals a new sense of obduracy among the Roman reforming circle, and, above all, their increasing unwillingness to compromise on any level. Damian's continual emphasis upon the need for orderly conciliar debate would suggest that he sought to counter those, like Hildebrand, who were perhaps unwilling to submit the issue of the contested election to an imperial council, and who were perhaps also tempted to summon their Norman allies to fight to bring the schism to an end.[89]

Damian also reveals his concern at the widening rift between the Roman Church and the German court, and at what he understood as the consequent danger to the divinely-established order of the world. It is a perception of change, a learned but nostalgic appeal of a man who felt himself to be living in a time of crisis. It is not surprising, therefore, that he concluded his treatise with a resounding appeal for unity, supported by Gelasian texts on the two powers.[90] As in the letter to Anno of Cologne, he emphasized the Gelasian ideal of co-operation between the two powers, and he underscored its importance for the events of the day. Damian's aim was not to press for a distinction between the respective functions of *regnum* and *sacerdotium*. On the contrary, he looked to find shared ground, to emphasize what he believed to be the essential, yet practicable, ideal of unity between the two spheres.[91] It was a unity

---

[87] *Annales Altahenses a. 1061*, 811 (Augsburg, though erroneously dated); *a. 1064*, 814 (Mantua). Cf. Meyer von Knonau, I, 300–1, 381, and notes 126, 129.

[88] Reindel, II, no. 89, p. 541, where Damian alluded to Daniel 7: 9–10, to emphasize the importance of scholarly, rational judgement as opposed to one forged by force. See also K. M. Woody, 'Damiani and the Radicals' Ph.D thesis (New York, 1966), 122–3.

[89] For the fighting in Rome, *Annales Altahenses a. 1062*, 812; *Bertholdi Annales a. 1062*, 272; and *Annales Romani*, 356. In a letter written in early 1062 to Bishop Olderic of Fermo (Reindel, II, no. 67), Damian vehemently condemned clerics who had involved themselves in active battle. It was surely a theme still foremost in his mind when compiling the *Disceptatio* some time just after mid-April. Cf. Ryan, text no. 150, pp. 81–2.

[90] Reindel, II, no. 89, pp. 571–2. See Ryan, texts no. 174–5, pp. 90–2.

[91] Ryan, texts no. 174–5, pp. 90–2.

which Damian surely, if somewhat naïvely, believed could still hold good. What he failed to realize was that the stakes were now higher. By articulating their position in the hope of eradicating immorality and simony, the reformers had moved onto a new, and necessarily uneven playing field, where *sacerdotium* would need to be exalted above *regnum*.

Immediately following the death of Pope Alexander II, the most passionate advocate both of reform and the superiority of the sacerdotal order was swept onto the papal throne in a tumultuous election on 22 April 1073. More than any of his predecessors, Gregory VII had a sense of mission: he lived, and he acted, with an unshakable conviction of his divine vocation. And perhaps more than his predecessors, Gregory VII was preoccupied with canon law. For him, it was inextricably linked with his understanding of the papal office.

Gregory believed that, as it fell to every cleric to be conversant with the sacred canons, this was all the more necessary for the Roman pontiff, who, as the earthly representative of St Peter, stood as the ultimate upholder of *iustitia*. Writing to the bishops and abbots of Brittany in August 1074 about the synod to be held at Rome the following year, Gregory clearly expressed his conception of the papal office and its unique connection with canon law. The burden of office, he wrote, compelled that he both inquire persistently, and teach, with vigilance in order to ensure that all churches correctly maintained the documents of faith and the rules of sacred scripture.[92] He then insisted that all the abbots and bishops of the region attend the coming synod, as he was aware that they were not as diligent as they should be in the observance of the decrees of the holy fathers and the ideal of religion.[93] The burden of office in essence required that Gregory be not only the arbiter of true faith but also the validator of canonical norms.

Gregory constantly reiterated that everything he did, and enjoined others to do, was in accordance with time-honoured ecclesiastical authorities and statutes.[94] Writing to Siegfried of Mainz in February 1075 of his injunction that the laity 'boycott' the ministrations of simoniacal and unchaste clergy, Gregory insisted that this derived not from

---

[92] *Reg.* II: 1, p. 124: 'Suscepti nos officii cura compellit omnium ecclesiarum sollicitudinem gerere et, ut fidei documenta ac sacrae scripturae regulas teneant, vigilanti circumspectione perquirere ac docere.'

[93] *Reg.* II: 1, p. 124: 'Quoniam igitur inter vos sanctorum patrum decreta et ecclesiasticae religionis statum non ea qua oportet aut observari diligentia aut studio tractari intelligimus . . .'

[94] e.g. *Reg.* I: 56, 57; II: 15, 20, 25; III: 10; V: 12; VI: 26; IX: 29, 35.

his own authority, but from that of the Fathers.[95] Otto of Constance was also sharply brought to task, and was sternly reminded that the decrees of the Lenten council of 1075 were made under the authority of the holy Fathers, not Gregory's.[96] The pope's aim here, as elsewhere, was to demonstrate that it was not he, but rather the force of divine principles, which worked through him as an unworthy instrument, and which provided the basis of the decrees and judgements he promulgated.[97]

Yet while his letters and decrees were replete with insistence upon the *decreta sanctorum patrum* and the authority of the sacred canons, Gregory VII was neither a jurist, nor a canon lawyer. While seldom failing to refer his addressees' attention to the burden of proof afforded by the authorities, he rarely cited a specific text. Although his detractors complained that Gregory manipulated and violated the sacred texts (either indicating a great deal of canonistic erudition, or none at all), Gregory's knowledge of canon law, beyond general principles, remains suspect.[98] Gregory, in fact, relied almost entirely upon vague appeals to the authority of canon law, coupled often with thunderous and more

[95] *Ep. vag.*, no. 6, p. 14: 'Cum apostolica auctoritate et veridicis sanctorum patrum sententiis incitati ad eliminandem simoniacam heresim et praecipiendam clericorum castitatem pro nostro officii debito exarsimus . . . [et infra] Statuimus etiam ut si contemptores fuerint nostrarum immo sanctorum patrum constitutionum . . . '

[96] *Ep. vag.*, no. 8, p. 16: ' . . . nos iuxta auctoritatem sanctorum patrum in eadem synodo sententiam dedisse . . . '

[97] e.g. Gregory to Burchard of Halberstadt in March 1075, *Reg.* II: 66, p. 222: 'Denique novit fraternitas tua quas proponimus regulas a sanctis patribus esse prefixas tantoque venerabilius observandas, quanto constat non suo libitu sed Spiritus sancti promulgasse afflatu'; Gregory to Anno of Cologne in March 1075, *Reg.* II: 67, p. 223: 'Novit enim fraternitas tua, quia precepta haec non de nostro sensu exculpimus, sed antiquorum patrum sanctiones Spiritu sancto predicante prolatas officii nostri necessitate in medium propalamus . . . ' Cf. *Reg.* II: 68, p. 226; III: 10, p. 266; and *Ep. vag.*, no. 9, p. 20; no. 10, p. 22; and no. 14, p. 40.

[98] e.g. *Benonis aliorumque cardinalium schismaticorum contra Gregorium VII. et Urbanum II. scripta* (*MGH, LdL*, 2), 380. See also 392, where he was criticized for his perversion of Gregory I: ' . . . beati Gregorii, cuius doctrinam crudeliter detraxisti . . . ' Cf. *Wenrici scolastici Trevirensis epistola sub Theoderici episcopi Virdunensis nomine composita* (*MGH, LdL*, 1), 282–99; Liemar of Bremen to Hezilo of Hildesheim, in *Briefsammlungen der Zeit Heinrichs IV.*, no. 15, pp. 33 ff.; and Udo of Trier to Gregory VII, ibid., no. 17, pp. 39 ff. Gregory's surprisingly limited canonical sources testify to this sparse knowledge. Apart from Gregory I with 58 citations, there are extremely few papal decretals cited in Gregory's letters: some seven texts from Leo I, two from Innocent I, and two from Gelasius. Other sources were also noticeably lacking, patristics being the most conspicuous: just five texts from Ambrose, two from John Chrysostom, and only one from Augustine. See Caspar, Index 3, 649–50; and Cowdrey, *Ep. vag.*, 169–70. Gregory's sources were often not explicitly identified: e.g. Leo I, ep. 166 [*PL* 54, 1191; JK no. 544 (ex Ps.Isidore?, p. 617)] in *Reg.* IV: 6, p. 304 (source is not explicit: 'sententia sanctorum patrum'); Leo I, ep. 166 [ibid.; JK no. 544 (ex Ps.Is?, p. 616)] in *Reg.* IV: 8, p. 307 (source not explicit: 'sicut in sacris statutum est canonibus').

explicit scriptural citations.⁹⁹ Though he granted to himself the right both to make new laws, and to temper and change existing law, Gregory was clearly happier with a precedent.¹⁰⁰ He turned above all to what he perceived as the higher authority: the indisputable sanction of *apostolica auctoritas*. While he sought where possible to strengthen his position with the *consona sanctorum patrum vox*, thereby avoiding charges of novelty, Gregory had the utmost confidence in the Petrine powers of binding and loosing, the foundation of all papal authority.¹⁰¹

Only the pope's second letter to Bishop Hermann of Metz in 1081 contained any significant and explicit appeals to canon law. Since Gregory would later note in a letter to the Bishop of Cambrai that he was unaccustomed to providing such a prolific justification of his policy except in matters of grave importance, the letter to Hermann, quite apart from its content, stands as a unique treatise.¹⁰² Despite the range of canonical sources employed, however, the bias of the letter remained scriptural, and indeed, hyperbolic, what with Gregory virtually labelling kings the descendants of robbers and murderers, and with the long passage regarding the superiority even of the exorcist (the lowest clerical office) over kings. The letter, none the less, did display some interesting interpretations of canonical texts. One of the most significant is

---

⁹⁹ e.g. *Reg.*, I: 60, p. 88; *Ep. vag.*, no. 11, p. 26. Gregory's most vehement intermingling of law and scripture was his use of Samuel (I Reg.15: 22–3) with the gloss of Gregory I: *Reg.* II: 66, p. 222: 'Melior est oboedientia quam victimae; quasi enim scelus idolatrie est non auscultare, et quasi peccatum ariolandi est nolle acquiescere. Quod beatus Gregorius in moralibus exponens dicit: Oboedientia ergo est, sine qua, quamvis fidelis quique videatur, infidelis convincitur.' Cf. *Reg.* II: 45, 75; IV: 1, 2, 11, 23, 24; VI: 10, 11; VII: 14a, 16, 24; VIII: 15, 21; IX: 20, 35; and *Ep. vag.* 11, 32. It might be argued that Gregory used Jer. 48: 10: 'Maledictus homo, qui prohibet gladium suum a sanguine . . . .' as a quasi-legal source; cf. *Reg.* I: 9, 15, 17; II: 5, 66; III: 4; IV: 1, 2; VII: 23; VIII: 21.

¹⁰⁰ See *Reg.* II: 68 to Werner of Magdeburg, where, though Gregory denies that the decrees are his own creations, he none the less insists upon his right to create law, p. 226: 'Non nostra decreta, quamquam licenter, si opus esset, possemus, vobis proponimus . . .'; cf. II: 55a, *Dictatus papae*, c. 7: 'Quod illi soli licet pro temporis necessitate novas leges condere . . .'

¹⁰¹ It is scarcely surprising, therefore, that most of Gregory's overt authorities were scriptural, predominantly from the New Testament. For the scriptural citations, see Caspar, index 2, 644–8.

¹⁰² *Reg.* IX: 35, p. 626: ' . . . non est consuetudinis nostrae alicui tam prolixam epistolam facere, nisi res magna sit valde.' The letter to Hermann (*Reg.* VIII: 21) was Gregory VII's greatest contribution to canon law: see J. T. Gilchrist, 'The Reception of Pope Gregory VII into the Canon Law (1073–1141)', *ZSSRG, kan. Abt.* 90 (1973), 35–82, continued 97 (1980), 192–229, now also in *Canon Law in the Age of Reform, 11th–12th Centuries*. The letter was well-known at the time, as the writings of the schismatic cardinals demonstrated: see *Benonis aliorumque cardinalium scripta*, 366–422, esp. 380–403.

Gregory's use of the Gelasian text on the two powers. By omitting Gelasius' acknowledgement of the divine origin of the imperial office (although without explicitly denying its divine origin), the pope radically transformed the intention of the original text, setting himself apart from previous usage. Unlike Peter Damian and the earlier reformers who used the text to emphasize the ideal state of mutual co-operation, Gregory pressed home a distinction between the ecclesiastical and secular spheres to the detriment of the latter.[103]

While his knowledge of canon law may have been less than penetrating, Gregory was not unaware of the significance of the law. Even before his elevation as pope in 1073, he felt the need for new and better canonical collections. His request that Peter Damian compile a small collection of decrees pertaining to the authority of the Apostolic See is a pointed reminder of how essential an element the papacy was seen to be in the attainment of the reformers' goals.[104] The pope needed indisputable authority to do what was, or might be, necessary. Once he was pope, Gregory both envisaged, and used, the law as a means to specific ends, as the legislation from his many reforming synods demonstrates.[105] Gregory, in fact, had a keen understanding of the law in relation to the Church over which he presided. As the protocol of the Lenten synod of 1078 indicates, he viewed his position as the definer of canonical norms, correcting what needed to be corrected, confirming what needed to be confirmed.[106] Like Leo IX, his task was to provide, through legislation, for the *utilitas* of the holy Church.[107]

Gregory's intentions were perhaps nowhere more apparent than in the twenty-seven titles of the *Dictatus papae*.[108] One of the most striking aspects of *Dictatus papae* is that, with only a few exceptions, the

[103] See R. Benson, 'The Gelasian Doctine: Uses and Transformations', 13–44, esp. 25–7.

[104] See Reindel, II, no. 65, pp. 228–47, where Damian acknowledges Hildebrand's request.

[105] For a recent discussion, see R. Somerville, 'The Councils of Gregory VII', in *La riforma gregoriana e l'Europa* (*SG* 13; Rome, 1989), 33–53.

[106] *Reg.* V: 14a, p. 368: 'In qua apostolica constituta corroborans multa, quae corrigenda erant, correxit et, quae corroboranda, firmavit.'

[107] *Reg.* VI: 5b, p. 401: 'Constituta etiam sunt illic ad utilitatem sanctae ecclesiae quaedam capitula . . . '

[108] *Reg.* II: 55a. For a recent survey, see H. Fuhrmann, 'Papst Gregor VII. und das Kirchenrecht: zum Problem des *Dictatus Papae*', in *La riforma gregoriana e l'Europa*, 123–49. See also H. Mordek, '"*Dictatus Papae*" e "*Proprie Auctoritates Apostolica Sedis*": intorno all'idea del primato pontificio di Gregorio VII', *Rivista di storia della chiesa in Italia*, 28 (1974), 1–22, who suggested that Gregory or a few of his canonistic collaborators at an early stage (perhaps pre-1073) compiled a decisive compendium of canonical texts supporting Roman primacy, which Gregory himself may have later encapsulated with the *Dictatus papae* sentences.

principles embodied therein were supported by long-standing canonical tradition. No objections could be made regarding the premise that the Roman Church had been founded by God alone (*Dp* 1), or to the unique papal right to depose and reconcile bishops (*Dp* 3), or to the premise that no one could retract papal sentences (*Dp* 18), or with the immunity of the pope from judgement (*Dp* 19), or with the immunity of him who appealed to the Apostolic See (*Dp* 20). Such were the cornerstones of the Church's legal tradition.[109] It was only with selected issues that the charges of novelty, or of disregard of the sacred canons, could truly be applied. Texts that flew in the face of canonical tradition were: *Dp* 2, which permitted the pope to be called universal; *Dp* 5, which gave him the right to judge the absent; *Dp* 12, the right to depose emperors; *Dp* 24, that with his leave, inferiors could accuse their superiors; and *Dp* 27, that the pope could absolve sworn oaths of fidelity.

Many of these 'novel' principles for the most part remained merely that: claims that were rarely exercised or invoked. One of the most important of these was the right to judge the absent. As can be seen in his dealings with the German episcopate, Gregory resorted to judgement *in absentia* only in cases of extreme contumacy.[110] Although as some German bishops complained, Gregory did accept the accusation of inferiors, by and large, as Gilchrist showed, the pope acted largely within canonical norms.[111] Even *Dp* 12 and *Dp* 24 were not without canonical precedents. Gregory I, Ambrose, and Stephen—as the letter to Hermann of Metz showed—provided concrete, if different, justifications for imperial deposition, as well as the absolution of sworn oaths of fidelity. Nevertheless, Gregory VII undeniably acted in a far different, and far more final spirit, in his depositions of Henry IV than had been the case with these canonical precedents.[112]

---

[109] For instance, Gelasius (JK no. 611), among others, supported the premise of *Dp* 3; Nicholas I (JE no. 2879), that of *Dp* 18; the *Constitutum Silvestri*, that of *Dp* 19. For other texts supporting these premises, see below, Table IV: Anselm's '*Dictatus papae*' Texts.

[110] e.g. *Ep. vag.* no. 10, where Gregory makes it clear that it is the contumacy of Otto of Constance which is responsible for the judgement *in absentia*. Cf. *Reg.* II: 28, where Liemar of Bremen is suspended until he accounts for his failure to co-operate with, and accept, legatine authority.

[111] A case in point is that of Pibo of Toul, who was suspended from office following an accusation made by one of his cathedral clerics. See *Reg.* II: 10, to Udo of Trier (as Pibo's metropolitan), and Udo's response, in *Briefsammlungen der Zeit Heinrichs IV.*, no. 17, p. 39. Cf. J. T. Gilchrist, 'Gregory VII and the Juristic Sources of his Ideology', *Studia Gratiana*, 12 (1967), 1–37.

[112] See *Reg.* VIII: 21, pp. 550, 554. There was a vast difference between the temporary privation of the Eucharist advocated by Gregory I, or Ambrose's excommunication of

It is here that the novelty, and perhaps the true import, of *Dictatus papae*, and with it Gregory's entire position regarding canon law, lies. It was not in the novelty of the canonistic positions, nor in the acumen with which sources were or were not exploited, but in the rigid, uncompromising, and unequivocal language with which apostolic prerogatives were enunciated, and papal decisions treated as canonical principles. As Karl Leyser wrote, 'Gregory was the sternest, most unrelenting, exponent of the ideas which his measures sought to impose.'[113] His conciliar legislation of 1078–80 is instructive in this respect. Many of these decrees were not new in themselves. It was their 'Gregorian' formulation that is the significant factor. While still pinpointing the particular and ongoing reform issues of simony, chastity, investiture, and *libertas*, his legislation was promulgated above all with a higher agenda in mind. Gregory may have professed himself willing to work with others, to yield if the Fathers allowed, but he was seldom put to the test. His legislation was increasingly concerned with the 'political' and ecclesiological battles being waged between Gregory and his opponents in Germany and northern Italy.[114] The thundering and repetitive prohibitions of simony, the ban on lay investiture, the clauses of *Dictatus papae*, and indeed perhaps all of his papal judgements must not merely be seen as being aimed at establishing desired ends. They also reflect Gregory's understanding of his elevation to a unique position as the legal head of the universal Church.

John Gilchrist showed that Gregory VII's legislation was only patchily received into the subsequent canonical tradition; the texts which gave voice to the intransigent spirit, and ideological inflexibility, of Gregory's pontificate were 'quietly dropped'.[115] It would seem he has little direct significance for the study of canon law. Yet, Gregory is not entirely without significance. His impact, however, derives not from his knowledge of specific 'canon laws', but from his unique appreciation of the importance of canon law as a whole. It lies not only in the force with which Gregory VII set himself up as pope, the definer of canonical tradition, but also in the force with which he demanded adherence to that tradition. It would be the task of others to find the necessary authorities, and to provide the specific vindications for his revolution.

Theodosius, which had been a disciplinary measure levelled as a 'personal' rather than a 'political' excommunication, and Gregory VII's idea of complete separation and political deposition.

[113] K. J. Leyser, 'The Polemics of the Papal Revolution', p. 148.
[114] See R. Somerville, 'The Councils of Gregory VII', 45 ff.
[115] J. T. Gilchrist, 'The Reception of Pope Gregory VII', pp. 72–3; 223–6.

PART II

A Canonist in the Age of Reform

I

Anselm of Lucca:
A Sainted Gregorian Bishop

ANSELM of Lucca was born c.1040, most probably in Milan. He belonged
to the branch of a noble family that had its principal seat in that city
though it may also have had rights in Baggio, near Milan.[1] The family's
recorded history goes back to the ninth century. There are two notices
of a Tazo da Badaglo—a vassal of the monastery of St Ambrose in
Milan—in 873 and 876; he appears to be the ancestor of the family that
would become a century later the *capitanei de plebe*, possessing the *pieve*
of Cesano Boscone in which Baggio was situated.[2] During the tenth century, the original family split into three branches: one centring in Milan,
one in Vignolo, and one remaining in Baggio. The consciousness of the
original family, however, clearly remained strong, and probably intensified with every rise in status; both Anselm, and his uncle Anselm I (later
Pope Alexander II) were often identified as 'da Baggio'.[3]

The Milanese branch of the family belonged to the new class of nobility developing in the city in the late tenth and early eleventh centuries.
Apparently involved in the imperial service (*messo imperiale*) as part of the
newly-forming professional class of judiciaries and notaries, the family
was also clearly connected to the cathedral and canonry of St Ambrose.[4]

---

[1] *Vita Anselmi*, c. 17, p. 18: ' . . . indigena fuit, et nobilis prosapia.' See H. Keller, 'Le
origini sociali e famigliari del vescovo Anselmo', in *Sant'Anselmo vescovo di Lucca*, 27–50.

[2] M. L. Corsi, 'Nota sulla famiglia da Baggio (secoli IX–XIII)', in *Raccolta di studi in
memoria di Giovanna Soranzo* (Pubblicazioni dell'università cattolica del Sacro Cuore, ser.
3, vol. 10; Milan, 1968), 166–204.

[3] H. Keller, 'Le origini sociali e famigliari del vescovo Anselmo', 32.

[4] Ibid., 34 ff. Cf. H. Keller, 'Origini sociali e formazione del clero cattedrale dei secoli
XI e XII nella Germania e nell'Italia settentrionale', in *Le istituzioni ecclesiastiche della 'societas christiana' dei secoli XI–XII: diocesi, pievi e parrocchie* (Misc. del centro di studi
medioevali, 8; Milan, 1977), 136–86, esp. Table II, p. 181.

Anselm's grandfather Arderic was named both as a *missus regiae* and a *miles sancti Ambrosii*, and evidently belonged to a premier rank of the Milanese nobility.[5] The family may have achieved prominence in the city's rebellion against the family of Archbishop Landulf. It is also tempting to link the family with those juridic elements of the urban nobility who rose up in the Patarene crisis. It is important, however, not to overestimate the sympathy of the family, particularly Anselm I, for the Patarene movement. Landulf of Milan's description of Anselm I as a leader among them is misleading, and incorrect; only with ecclesiastical reform would his concerns have overlapped with those of the Pataria.[6]

There is little definite information regarding Anselm's early life.[7] It seems most probable that he was educated in Milan under the patronage of his family, particularly his uncle, and was perhaps made a canon at St Ambrose of Milan.[8] Testimony to Anselm's early studies in Milan in the ambiance of the cathedral, however, is provided by mention in the *Vita Anselmi* of a certain Lanzo Iudex—apparently a school comrade.[9]

Anselm's cultural and intellectual formation—like that of his uncle—took place in the increasingly chaotic, and progressively non-imperial, ambience of the social and urban 'revolution' beginning to take hold in northern Italy by the mid-eleventh century.[10] It seems quite obvious that, in spiritual terms, his social class on the whole was orienting itself away from the tendencies of the imperial court as early as the reign of Henry III, but especially during the minority of Henry IV.[11] Profound

[5] See Corsi, 'Nota sulla famiglia da Baggio', 203, and geneaological table; and Keller, 'Le origini sociali e famigliari del vescovo Anselmo', 38 ff.

[6] See Keller, 'Le origini sociali', 38–9; *Landulfi historia Mediolanensis usque ad a. 1075*, III, c. 5 (*MGH, SS*, 8), 76. Landulf may have been unhappy at Anselm I's support of the extension of Rome's authority over Milan in his legation with Peter Damian in 1059. On the Patarenes in general, see C. Violante, *La pataria milanese* (Rome, 1955).

[7] *Vita Anselmi*, c. 2, p. 13: 'A pueritia qualiter vixerit, tum quia pleniter non novimus, tum quia reticere in praesentiarum satius aestimamus, praetermittimus.'

[8] Cf. G. M. Fusconi, 'Anselmo II, vescovo di Lucca', *Biblioteca Sanctorum*, II, cols. 26–36; C. Violante, 'Anselmo da Baggio, santo', *Dizionario biografico degli Italiani*, 3 (1961), 399–407; here 399.

[9] *Vita Anselmi*, c. 74, p. 33: 'Erat vir quidam Lanzo Iudex nomine, Mediolanensis genere . . . coepit orare his verbis . . . Sancte confessor, memento familiaritatis, quae nos in scholis socios iunxerat . . .'

[10] See Keller, 'Le origini sociali', 42 ff. For urban revival and 'social revolution' in Italy, see C. Violante, *La società milanese nell'età precommunale* (Bari, 1955); B. Stock, *The Implications of Literacy* (Princeton, 1983); C. Wickham, *The Mountains and the City: The Tuscan Apeninnes in the Early Middle Ages* (Oxford, 1988); G. Tabacco, *The Struggle for Power in Medieval Italy* (Cambridge, 1990). See also the works cited above, Pt. I, notes 8–10.

[11] As can be seen in the opposition to Henry III's candidate, the imperial chaplain Guido of Velate as archbishop of Milan in 1045. Guido had no connection either with the

changes in urban life in northern Italy, particularly in Milan, were prompting new modes of thought, rhetoric, and action both in reform models or strategies, and in intellectual life in more general terms.[12] The text *De ordinando pontifice*, for instance, written in the aftermath of the synod of Sutri in 1046, reveals the cracks that were already appearing between imperial views of reform and those represented by the bishops of Francia, Lotharingia, and other circles.[13] Any attempt to understand the world in which Anselm grew to maturity is caught up in the larger problem of determining what precisely was occurring in northern Italy, especially in terms of intellectual developments. It seems indisputable that some dramatic transformation was taking place in the northern Italian cities in the eleventh century. Its catalyst, and its immediate effects are more difficult to measure.[14] How, for instance, are the migrations of Lombard scholars such as Lanfranc and Anselm of Aosta from Italy to Francia to be explained? That there were perceptions of profound changes is, at least, unchallengeable. Peter Damian's disgust at the 'iocosae urbanitatis suavitas' of Alexander II may very well represent discomfiture at new attitudes, or at some new type of education, the ramifications of which had as yet to be fully comprehended.[15] Even so, all we can do is speculate on how these great changes affected the young Anselm.

Milanese nobility or with the cathedral clergy, and was accepted only with reluctance. The supposed emnity between Guido and Anselm I, which according to Landulf's *Historia Mediolanensis*, III, c. 5, resulted in Anselm being appointed away to Lucca, is probably overstated. On the problems of Landulf, see Keller, 'Le origini sociali . . . ', 40–1; C. Violante, *La pataria milanese*; and H. E. J. Cowdrey, 'The Papacy, the Patarenes and the Church of Milan', *TRHS*, 5th ser. 18 (1968), 25–48. Anselm I had studied with Lanfranc at Bec, which may also have contributed to his orientation away from the imperial-minded milieu. See below.

[12] See e.g. C. Leyser, 'Cities of the Plain: The Rhetoric of Sodomy in Peter Damian's "Book of Gomorrah"', *Romanic Review*, 86 (1995), 191–211, esp. 210; and H. E. J. Cowdrey, 'Anselm of Besate and Some Northern Italian Scholars of the Eleventh Century', *JEH* 23 (1972), 115–24.

[13] *Der sogennante Traktat 'De ordinando pontifice'*, ed. H. H. Anton (Bonn, 1982). Other instances of this beginning alienation can be seen in Abbot Halinard of St Beninge de Dijon's refusal to offer the customary oath of fealty to Henry III at the time of his elevation to the archbishopric of Lyons; in Wazo of Liège's condemnation of Henry III's deposition of Archbishop-elect Widiger of Ravenna; and in Wazo's reaction to Sutri. See *Ex chronico s.Benigni Divionensis* (*MGH, SS*, 7), 235–7; *Anselmi Gesta episcoporum Leodiensium*, c. 58 (Widiger), c. 65 (Sutri), (ibid.), 224, 228. Peter Damian, however, had praised Henry III: see Pt. I, note 41.

[14] See Cowdrey, 'Anselm of Besate and Some Northern Italian Scholars', 118, 122–4; cf. *Landulfi historia Mediolanensis*, II, c. 35, p. 71.

[15] Reindel, IV, no. 156, p. 75; cf. Keller, 'Le origini sociali', 45.

Where and what Anselm studied are matters of much debate. The two *Vitae Anselmi* are largely silent on Anselm's early life and education, speaking only of his good knowledge of grammar, and acquaintance with dialectic.[16] The possibility exists, however, that like his uncle, Anselm studied under Lanfranc's auspices in Normandy. In an undated letter to Lanfranc—1061–70, but probably before 1065—Pope Alexander II expressed the desire to send 'quemdam nostrum fratruelem' to be instructed by Lanfranc.[17] A number of historians have believed that Anselm was that relative, but it has proved impossible to ascertain whether or not Anselm went to Normandy. This issue is complicated by a letter of Berengar of Tours, dated 1063–5 to St_____ (Cardinal-priest Stephan of Grisgogno?) in which Berengar commented upon reports that the Pope was planning to send a relative to Tours.[18] According to those who believed that Anselm was the *fratruelis* meant in Alexander's letter to Lanfranc, this was either a misunderstanding on Berengar's part, or else referred to some other agent of the pope.[19]

In his book on Alexander II, Tilmann Schmidt considered the issue of this *fratruelis*. He believed that this person was not Anselm, but rather another nephew of the pope, a certain P_____ (Petrus), whose name could be found in the early registers of Bec under Abbot Herluin, and who could also be placed in Tours in some connection with Berengar.[20] The studies described by Alexander's letter fitted well, in Schmidt's opinion, with what else is known of this Petrus, whom he also located as a papal arbitrator in a conflict between St Aubin, Anger, and St Trinité de Vendome.[21] Schmidt's argument, however, does not completely convince. In the first place, no 'Petrus' can be identified in any branch of the Baggio family, save once in the tenth century. Characteristic family names were Arderic, Ariald, Adelard, Anselm, and

---

[16] *Vita Anselmi*, c. 2, p. 13: 'Studiosum tamen iam tunc in scholasticis etiam legendis libris fuisse, ipso saepius referente, cognovimus; quod et rei evidenter probavit effectus; quia in arte grammatica et dialectica extitit peritus.'

[17] Alexander II, ep. 70 (*PL* 146), 1353: 'Huius itaque gratiae venerabilis fama, circumquaque diffusa, quia ab omnibus fere mundi partibus ad tuae fluenta eloquentiae multos allexit, quemdam nostrum fratruelem, quem paternis ut nosmetipsos diligimus affectibus, ad eiusdem tuae eloquentiae dulcedinem nimium gliscentem dirigere cupimus, qui tamen Deo gratias, grammaticae artis peritia bene instructus, dialecticae omnino non est alienus.'

[18] *Briefsammlungen der Zeit Heinrichs IV.*, no. 100, p. 168: 'Ceterum innotuit mihi frater ille Rahardus concepisse domnum apostolicum mittere in hos fines discendi causa quendam suum cognatum.'

[19] Ibid., 168, note 8.   [20] T. Schmidt, *Alexander II. (1061–73)*, 26–30.

[21] Ibid. 28–9; cf. B. de Broussillon, *Cartulaire de l'abbaye de St Aubin, Angers*, II (Angers, 1903), 215 ff.

Arnulf.[22] In the second place, Schmidt failed to value Lanfranc's own testimony on the matter. In a letter to Alexander II, dated between 25 December 1072 and 21 April 1073, Lanfranc, while seeking to obtain release from the unwelcome burden of the archbishopric of Canterbury, reminded the pontiff of the kindnesses done for him in the past, namely of receiving his *consanguineos*, and others, for instruction at the monasteries of Bec and St Etienne, Caen.[23] Schmidt had seized on the fact that Alexander's letter spoke only of one kinsman, whereas Lanfranc himself stressed the plural *consanguineos*.[24] Lanfranc's letter, however, raises another point. Schmidt did not appreciate the possibility that Alexander's 'relation' may have been sent, not to Bec, but rather to St Etienne, Caen, to which Lanfranc moved in 1063.[25] Schmidt's final contention against Anselm concerned the nature of the studies that were to be undertaken by the *fratruelis*. He compared the *grammaticae artis* found in Alexander's letter with the *divinarum litterarum scientiam et rationem* (his knowledge and understanding of divine letters) used later by Gregory VII in his letter to Beatrice and Matilda of Tuscany regarding Anselm's studies. This, in Schmidt's opinion, eliminated Anselm. Such evidence, however, is far from conclusive, partly because grammar was regarded as a stepping stone to theology, and especially as he dismissed the description of Anselm's skills in *arte grammatica et dialectica* in the *Vita Anselmi*.[26]

At present there is no definitive evidence that can either place Anselm with Lanfranc at Bec or Caen, or specify whether in fact sending him was ever considered. Both Schmidt and Borino, though for far different reasons, suggested that Anselm may have entered the Benedictine monastery at Polirone for instruction.[27] At the same time, the possibility that Anselm

---

[22] See Corsi, 'Nota sulla famiglia di Baggio', 173, and geneaolgical table; and Keller, 'Origini sociali e formazione', tables, 180–1.

[23] *Letters of Lanfranc, Archbishop of Canterbury*, eds. H. Glover and M. Gibson (Oxford, 1979), no. 1, p. 7: 'Meminisse siquidam debetis nec tradi oblivioni oportet, quam benigne consanguineos vestros aliosque a Roma scripta deferentes in prefatis adhuc coenobiis constitutus sepe recepi, quam studiose eos pro captu meo ingeniique ipsorum tam in sacris quam in secularibus litteris erudivi . . . '

[24] Corroborated by later sources: see A. Du Monstier, *Neustria Pia seu De omnibus et singulis abbatis et prioratibus totius Normanniae* (Rouen, 1663), 647, though speaking of Bec, notes Alexander II and 'eius nepotes'.

[25] M. T. Gibson, *Lanfranc of Bec* (Oxford, 1978), 103, stated that Alexander II's kinsman (she did not name him) was sent to Lanfranc at St Étienne, Caen.

[26] T. Schmidt, *Alexander II.*, 26. Cf. *Vita Anselmi*, c. 2, p. 13: ' . . . quia in arte grammatica et dialectica extitit peritus.'

[27] The possibility that Anselm was schooled at San Benedetto di Polirone remains tenuous. While silent on this, the *Vita Anselmi* noted that Anselm had been a monk under

received instruction from Lanfranc cannot be completely ruled out. The fact that his uncle Alexander II did study with Lanfranc would suggest at least a strong possibility that there were thoughts of sending Anselm to Normandy. Perhaps Alexander II sought to prepare Anselm with the legal and administrative training—for which Lanfranc and the school at Bec were renowned—that would enable his nephew to follow him in the bishopric of Lucca.[28]

Between 18 March and 21 April 1073, Anselm was designated as Bishop of Lucca by Pope Alexander II (who had retained the see during his pontificate), and was sent in the company of Bishop Meginhard of St Rufino to be invested by the king.[29] Yet according to his anonymous biographer, writing with the hindsight of the Investiture Contest, Anselm began to have doubts about the propriety of receiving investiture from the king, and decided to seize any opportunity to depart from the court without being invested.[30] Then, in the very next chapter, the *Vita Anselmi* offered an interesting contradiction to its earlier report by noting that following the death of Alexander II and the elevation of Gregory VII, Anselm was elected to the bishopric of Lucca, and was subsequently consecrated by Gregory VII.[31] The biographer then

the Cluniac custom at a monastery on the 'ripa fluminis Eridani', which has been identified as Polirone. Borino, examining this in light of Rangerius' text, which spoke of Anselm making a new vow and taking up a new habit after his crisis of conscience with investiture, believed that Anselm had been at Polirone before his episcopacy. Cf. Rangerius, vv. 1065 ff.; and G. B. Borino, 'Il monacato e l'investitura di Anselmo vescovo di Lucca', *SG* 5 (1956), 361–74, here 363–4. C. Violante, 'Anselmo da Baggio, santo', 399–407, believed that there was no foundation in the theory that Anselm had studied at Polirone. On Anselm's investiture and monastic seclusion, see below.

[28] See S. N. Vaughn, 'Lanfranc, Anselm and the School of Bec: In Search of the Students of Bec', in *The Culture of Christendom: Essays in Medieval History in Commemoration of Denis L. T. Bethell*, ed. M. A. Meyer (London, 1993), 155–81. While Alexander appears on the lists of students (appendix, pp. 176 ff.), Anselm does not. Anselm's letter to William in 1085 notes his recollection of the king's kindnesses to him, *Briefsammlungen der Zeit Heinrichs IV.*, no. 1, p. 16: 'Ego autem memor beneficiorum, quae in me tua benivolentia contulit . . . ' It is tempting to see this as a possible proof of Anselm having been at Bec or St Etienne—two of the king's favourite monasteries.

[29] *Vita Anselmi*, c. 2, p. 13: 'Dum autem videretur iam idoneus, immo meritis, moribus ac scientia dignus, ut in honorem sublimaretur episcopatus, mittitur a reverendissimo papa Alexandro ad regem, dato sibi comite, religioso episcopo sanctae Rufinae, nomine Meginardo.'

[30] Ibid., c. 2, p. 14: 'Sed quia iam perfecte coeperat odisse, ut sacri ordines ecclesiastici a secularibus darentur potestatibus, quecunque vel occasione, vel ratione potuit, absque dignitatis investitura discessit, quamquam ea intentione domnus papa illum direxit.'

[31] Ibid., c. 3, p. 14: 'Defuncto itaque predicto papa Alexandro, dum sanctissimus Gregorius VII. in Romanum pontificem Spiritu sancti instigatione ac voto communi clericorum et laicorum diu renitens, esset electus, ut sequeretur eum iste in omnibus, in Lucanam ecclesiam est et ipse electus episcopus, atque ab illo postmodum religiose consecratus.'

recorded that Anselm, after perusing books of diverse authorities, began to consider himself damned for having received his office at the hands of a king. Finding the situation thoroughly insupportable, Anselm used the pretext of a visit to Rome to leave his bishopric, and became a monk under the Cluniac custom. A short time after, so this text says, Anselm was recalled by Gregory VII, who restored him to the bishopric of Lucca, but allowed him to carry on wearing the monastic habit.[32]

The story of Anselm's election, his investiture by a layman, his consecration at the hands of a pope, his monastic profession, and subsequent return to Lucca narrated by the *Vita Anselmi* makes for good reading. Unfortunately, it dramatically distorts events which in fact persisted for at least two years. While accurate only in the broadest terms, the account is obviously faulty in detail. Apart from the repetition, and outright contradiction of the circumstances of Anselm's election, the author provides no information regarding Anselm's actual investiture. There is only a brief notice of his apparent crisis of conscience that supposedly followed this investiture.[33] No information is provided regarding the monastery into which Anselm retired. Chronological details fall foul of the author's undeniable polemical intentions.

Fortunately there are other sources which help to determine the probable circumstances and events. In the first place, the contradictions in the report of Anselm's election to Lucca were clearly a product of the anonymous author's overriding concern to portray Anselm as following Gregory VII, both figuratively and literally, in all things.[34] Anselm had been elected, though not consecrated, prior to Alexander's death. Whether or not Alexander II did send Anselm to the king for investiture is a more difficult question. It is clear that investiture itself was not an issue. Lucca, after all, was within what would have been recognized as 'imperial' territory. The real issue was Henry IV's status following the Lenten synod of 1073, at which Alexander II excommunicated several of the king's advisers. (The subsequent prohibition of Gregory VII regarding Anselm's investiture stemmed from the fact that the king was

---

[32] Ibid., c. 4, p. 14.

[33] Ibid., c. 4, p. 14. The editor of the *Vita Anselmi*, R. Wilmans (p. 14, note 1), taking the account rather too literally, stated that the first election by Alexander noted in c. 2 must have referred Anselm's election to some other bishopric, and not that of Lucca, noted in c. 3.

[34] *Vita Anselmi*, c. 3, p. 14: ' . . . ut sequeretur eum iste in omnibus . . . ' Cf. G. B. Borino, 'Il monacato e l'investitura di Anselmo', 368, note 29. Gregory VII's letter to Beatrice and Matilda (*Reg.* I: 11) makes it clear that he had not appointed Anselm to Lucca.

tainted by his continuing communion with these excommunicated advisers, not because of any objection to investiture in itself.) It would be curious, though not improbable, that Alexander would have sent a bishop-elect, who was also his own nephew, to receive investiture from a king who was possibly communicating with excommunicates.[35] Both lives, however, were clearly reflecting a later time when lay investiture was prohibited.[36]

In a letter to Beatrice and Matilda of Tuscany dated 24 June 1073, which names Anselm '*electus*', Gregory VII responded to their concerns by saying that he hoped that the bishop-elect's knowledge of divine literature, and his own reason, would enable him to distinguish between the correct and incorrect paths.[37] It seems that Gregory was referring to the question of whether or not Anselm would go to receive investiture from Henry IV. Some time after this letter, Gregory was apparently in communication with Anselm about such matters.[38] In a letter of 1 September 1073, however, there is clear evidence of Gregory's understanding of the problem. It was not investiture itself but rather what Gregory obviously believed to be the corrupted status of Henry IV which might be harmful to Anselm and to the assumption of high ecclesiastical office. Gregory specifically prohibited Anselm from receiving investiture from the king until such time as the question of Henry IV's status had been resolved.[39] He likewise requested that Anselm come to Rome where the matter could be better discussed.[40]

---

[35] As Rangerius complained, vv. 603–7 (p. 1169): 'O quid agis, Petri successor, tunc cruentes| Arbitrare manus haec sacra posse dare?| Quis te pontificem Romana sede locavit?| Nunquid non clerus qui solet, et populus?| Si licuit, proprium noli dampnare nepotem| Et si non licuit, quid Cadulo nocuit?'

[36] See E. Pasztor, 'Sacerdozio e regno nella *Vita Anselmi episcopi Lucensis*', *AHP* 2 (1964), 91–115; cf. E. Pasztor, 'Una fonte per la storia dell'età gregoriana: la *Vita Anselmi episcopi Lucensis*', *Bull. Ist. Stor. Ital.*, 72 (1960), 1–33.

[37] *Reg.* I: 11, pp. 18–19: 'De electo vero Lucensi non aliud vobis respondendum esse pervidimus, nisi quod in eo tantam divinarum litterarum scientiam et rationem discretionis esse percepimus, ut, quae sinistra quae sit dextra, ipse non ignoret. Quodsi ad dexteram inclinaverit, valde gaudemus; sin vero, quod absit, ad sinistram, utique dolemus; sed nullius personae gratia vel favore impietati assensum dabimus.'

[38] This letter is no longer extant. There is a reference to an earlier letter in *Reg.* I: 21.

[39] *Reg.* I: 21, p. 35: 'Ut enim viam, qua ambules, postulasti tibi notificaremus nullam novam, nullam expeditiorem scimus ea, quae nuper dilectioni tuae significavimus, videlicet te ab investitura episcopatus de manu regis abstinere, donec de communione cum excommunicatis Deo satisfaciens rebus bene compositis nobiscum pacem possit habere.'

[40] Ibid., p. 35: 'Quodsi prefati operis perfectio dilationem quacunque occasione contigerit habere, interea nostrae familiaritati poteris adhaerere Romae ut nobiscum seu adversitatem seu prosperitatem communicare.'

Borino made some interesting propositions regarding this letter to Anselm. He noted that at the time of its composition Gregory VII had not as yet received a response from Henry IV regarding either the situation at Milan or the problem of his excommunicate advisers. According to Borino, Gregory did not receive Henry's letter—which hinted at the possibility of being able to come to terms with the pontiff's demands—until between 24 and 27 September 1073. This, he believed, had accounted for Gregory's unequivocal stand on the question of Anselm's investiture in the letter of 1 September.[41]

There is little record of Anselm's actions or movements throughout the summer of 1073 until the first half of August, when he can be located at the monastery of St Zeno in Verona with Beatrice and Matilda, as a witness to a charter.[42] The next clear mention of Anselm comes from the chronicle of Hugh of Flavigny, which placed Anselm in Rome sometime around late December 1073–January 1074. According to Hugh, Anselm had come to Rome at the same time as Hugh of Die for them both to be consecrated by Gregory VII.[43] (This journey occurred just prior to Henry IV's second letter to Gregory VII.[44]) Anselm and Hugh, however, apparently requested that their consecrations be delayed until such time as they could be invested by the king.[45] Although the consecration of Hugh went ahead on 16 March 1074, this may have been a result of the somewhat turbulent situation in Die which demanded the bishop's presence, and not necessarily a reflection of a hardening of Gregory's attitude.[46] As Gregory apparently acquiesced in the case of Anselm, it seems that there had been definite progress in relations between himself and Henry IV during the beginning of 1074.

[41] Borino, 'Il monacato e l'investitura di Anselmo', 370 and note 42. Henry's letter was written between Aug. and Sept. 1073. *Die Briefe Heinrichs IV.*, ed. C. Erdmann (*MGH, Deutsches Mittelalter*, 1), no. 5, esp. p. 9. The grovelling tone of Henry IV was a product of the tense situation between the king and the Saxons. The letter in no way represented Henry's true views, but had the effect of winning him time to manoeuvre. On these aspects, see C. Erdmann, *Studien zur Briefliteratur Deutschlands im elften Jahrhundert* (Schriften des Reichsinstitut für ältere deutsche Geschichtskunde, 1; Leipzig, 1938), 228 ff.

[42] F. M. Fiorentini, *Memorie della Gran Contessa Matilda* (Lucca, 1756), 98–9: 'Anselmus episcopus Lucensis huic facto interfuit . . . '; cf. L. A. Muratori, *Antiquitates Italicae Medii Aevi*, I (Milan, 1783), 591–2; and A. Overmann, *Gräfin Mathilde von Tuscien, ihre Besitzungen, Geschichte ihres Gutes von 1115–1230 und ihre Regesten* (Innsbruck, 1895), *Regesta*, no. 14.

[43] Hugh of Flavigny, *Chronicon*, II (*MGH, SS*, 8), 411–12.

[44] Borino, 'Il monacato e l'investitura', 371. There is a reference to this letter, which is not extant, in *Reg.* I: 39.

[45] Hugh of Flavigny, *Chronicon*, II, 412.

[46] Cf. Borino, 'Il monacato', 371–2. Cf. *Reg.* I: 69.

In other words, the deferral of Anselm's consecration may have been part of peace considerations with Henry IV. It is known that in late February–early March 1074 Gerald of Ostia and Hubert of Palestrina had been sent as papal legates in an attempt to reconcile the king. In April, their efforts were successful. They imposed penance and reconciled Henry IV to Gregory and the Church.[47] For Anselm, royal investiture and papal consecration could now proceed.

When precisely this occurred is difficult to determine. Anselm was in Pisa from 21–24 April with Beatrice and Matilda for Easter, and may have travelled in their company from Rome after the Lenten synod of 1074.[48] He is next found active in Lucca in August 1074, presiding over and witnessing grants, notably one which gave a portion of the *castello* of Montecatino from a certain Ildebrando di Maona to the episcopate of Lucca.[49] In these charters, Anselm was still described as *electus*, as he was in a charter of 29 September 1074.[50] In fact it was not until the following year, on 28 April 1075, that Anselm is named simply as *episcopus* in a charter stipulating the contract of purchase of the *corte* and *castello* of San Gervasio.[51] It would appear then that he had been both invested and consecrated sometime between late April 1074 and 28 April 1075: invested in October 1074, according to Barsocchini, and between April and August 1074 according to Borino. Anselm, therefore, was probably consecrated by Gregory VII in late 1074–early 1075.

[47] This reconciliation was part of a wider attempt by the papacy to deal with outstanding issues between itself and the German episcopate, in particular the charges of simony against Bishop Hermann of Bamberg. On the complicated sequence of events, see Erdmann, *Studien zur Briefliteratur Deutschlands*, 232 ff.

[48] See *Chronicon sancti Huberti Andaginensis (MGH, SS,* 8), 583–4, which noted that Beatrice and Matilda had originally planned to go to Rome in the company of Hermann of Metz for Easter, but that delays forced them to divert to Pisa, where they met Anselm. Cf. Overmann, *Regesta,* no. 20e. It is not clear, despite reports from Bonizo, whether Matilda and Beatrice were present at the synod in Rome, though it seems likely that Anselm was. Cf. Baronius, *Annales ecclesiastici,* 11, 589.

[49] *Raccolta di documenti per servire alla storia ecclesiastica lucchese (Memorie e Documenti per servire all'istoria del principato Lucchese),* ed. D. Barsocchini, V, pt. I (Lucca, 1844), contains editions and excerpts of documents from the Archivio Arcivescovale in Lucca. The charters here are Lucca, Archivio Arcivescovale, tt C. 75; and tt S. 76: see excerpts, p. 321 and note 1. Hereafter, citations will be: Barsocchini, page, archive number.

[50] See notice in Borino, 'Il monacato', p. 372, note 55, referring to Archivio Arc. di Lucca, AB 19. There is no reference to this in Barsocchini.

[51] Barsocchini, V, pt. I, pp. 325–7, and note 2: Archivio Arc. di Lucca, tt R. 70. This charter escaped the notice of Borino who referred (p. 372) to Archivio Arc. di Lucca, * F. 71, dated 7 May 1075, which noted that Anselm was in Florence with Beatrice and Matilda at the confirmation of the portion of the *castello* and *corte* of Montecatino donated the previous year by Ildebrando of Maona. Cf. Barsocchini, V, pt. I, p. 327; Muratori, cols. 969–72; Fiorentini, 116–17.

There remains the question of Anselm's crisis of conscience over investiture and his consequent retirement into a monastery. Why, when, and where Anselm retired are difficult questions, due in large part to conflicting sources. The specific issues of why and when, however, seem to be entwined with the wider problem of clarifying the reformers' campaign against investiture. Much seems to depend on the problem of whether or not a prohibition of investiture was issued by Gregory VII at the Lenten synod of 1075. While no decree is extant, many historians, citing the *Gesta archiepiscoporum Mediolanensium* of Arnulf of Milan, have subscribed to the view that investiture was in some way banned in 1075.[52] If such legislation was enacted, it was undeniably not a universal prohibition, but rather a specific injunction aimed at Milan and the northern Italian bishoprics.[53]

If some prohibition or injunction was promulgated at the Lenten synod of 1075, it would go a long way towards explaining Anselm's supposed crisis of conscience and the chronology of his monastic seclusion. The *Vitae Anselmi*, again, are of mixed assistance. The discussion of Anselm's crisis in the anonymous Life was clearly part of the author's polemic intent to establish Anselm as the perfect Gregorian bishop.[54] Rangerius, however, specifically made the prohibition of investiture at the Lenten synod of 1075 the *sine qua non* of Anselm's crisis.[55]

Both Lives agree that Anselm retired into a monastery after his consecration. As has been seen, this consecration probably took place sometime in late 1074–early 1075. There is, however, no specific information regarding Anselm's whereabouts until 28 April 1075, when he can be placed at San Gervasio near Lucca, and then again on 7 May, when he was in Florence with Beatrice and Matilda.[56] There is no further notice of him until 25 November 1075, when a charter placed him at San Miniato in the Lucchesia.[57] Anselm is next mentioned in a charter of 21

---

[52] *Gesta archiepiscoporum Mediolanensium*, lib. IV, c. 7 (*MGH, SS*, 8), 27: ' . . . papa habita Romae synodo palam interdicit regi, ius deinde habere aliquod in dandis episcopatibus, omnesque laicas ab investituris ecclesiarum summovet personas.' For a survey of the debate, see R. Schieffer, *Die Entstehung des päpstlichen Investiturverbots für den deutschen König* (*MGH, Schriften*, 28; Stuttgart, 1981), 114–32. Though Schieffer argues against the 1075 decree, Gregory's letter to Henry in Dec. 1075 (*Reg.* III: 10) weighs against his argument.

[53] Despite the subsequent imposition of the royal candidate Tedald in Milan, Gregory VII did not protest the royal appointments and investiture of either Huzmann to Speyer in February, or Henry to Liège in the early summer.

[54] Cf. E. Pasztor, 'Una fonte della storia dell'età gregoriana', 1–33.

[55] Rangerius, vv. 819–38 (p. 1174); vv. 915 ff. (p. 1176).

[56] See above, note 51.

[57] Barsocchini, V, pt. I, 330, 337: Archivio Arc. di Lucca, tt Q. 29*.

December 1075, in which he was resolutely called *monachus et episco-pus*.[58] It would follow, therefore, that if his crisis was brought on by the prohibition of investiture, Anselm must have retired to a monastery either between late February 1075 (that is, after the Lenten synod, 24–28 February) and 28 April 1075, or between 7 May 1075 and 25 November 1075.[59]

Although the latter seems more probable, the question of where may shed more light on the problem of when. Wherever Anselm went, he was clearly not there for long.[60] From the *Vita Anselmi*, which noted Anselm's wish to be buried at the monastery on the river Po where he had been a monk, some historians have proposed that it was to that place, San Benedetto di Polirone, that Anselm retired.[61] Rangerius, however, who provided more, though suspect, detail regarding Anselm's retirement, stated that he fled across the Alps to St Gilles.[62] It is hard to say whether or not more credence should be given to the report of Rangerius, who at the least furnished a specific place. St Gilles, how-ever, may simply have reflected Rangerius' own nationality, or national pride.[63]

Both biographers emphasized the fact that Anselm had entered the Cluniac obedience. This is still problematic. While Polirone did not assume Cluniac obedience until between 27 June 1076 and 7 April 1080 (although probably at the beginning of 1077), the fact that St Gilles had become Cluniac in 1066 does not ensure that it was the site of Anselm's brief seclusion. The 'Cluniac' description put forward by the anony-mous (and likely taken up by Rangerius) may simply represent the author's understanding at the time, writing as he did, after Polirone had assumed such obedience.[64]

---

[58] Barsocchini, V, pt. I, 330, note 1: Archivio Arc. di Lucca, B81.

[59] Violante, 'Anselmo da Baggio, santo', 400, believed the latter. According to Barsocchini (p. 337), Anselm was making a pastoral tour of his diocese around 25 Nov.

[60] *Vita Anselmi*, c. 4, p. 14: 'Qui non post multa . . . '

[61] *Vita Anselmi*, c. 40, p. 24: 'Rogavit itaque, quoad vixit, quatenus in capitulo monas-terii sancti Benedicti, quod est in ripa fluminis Eridani sub obedientia sacri Cluniacensis coenobii, unde frater ipse ac monachus fuit, sepulturae commendaretur . . . '

[62] Rangerius, vv. 1000 ff. (p. 1178) : ' . . . et peregrinus abit.| Alpibus emensis preceps torrente profundo| Offertur Rodanus, post vada cuius eum| Respirare iubet patris grat-tissima sedes/ Egidii, multis amata domus,| Et miranda satis virtutum nobilitate . . . '

[63] See P. Guidi, 'Della patria di Rangerio . . . ', *SG* 1 (1947), 263–80; H. E. J. Cowdrey, *The Cluniacs and the Gregorian Reform* (Oxford, 1970), 250, note 5; and id., 'Anselm of Besate and Some Northern Italian Scholars ' 127.

[64] See Gregory VII to Hugh of Cluny, in *Italia Pontificia*, ed. P. Kehr (1923), 329, note 5; and Borino, 'Il monacato', 361. Charter for St Gilles, dated 15 Dec. 1066, *Recueil des chartes de l'abbaye de Cluny*, IV, no. 3410, eds. A. Bernard and A. Bruel (Collection de documents inédits sur l'histoire de France, 6 vols.; Paris, 1888), 517–19; and L. Santifaller

In the end, Anselm's monastic retirement, although brief, was evidently an important event. Anselm wore the monastic habit for the rest of his life, and both Lives agree that he devoted himself to ascetic practices. In less personal terms, however, Anselm's investiture crisis effectively made him a prototype and a conscience-prodder to many of his contemporary bishops about the grave error of accepting royal investiture. At the same time, it provided a valuable guide to how one could be reconciled with the Church. Most important of all, the crisis provided Anselm's biographers with the story of a man whose desire for a secluded contemplative life was outweighed by his obedience to Gregory VII, and by his acceptance of the burden of an active life in the cause of righteousness.

The consideration of the remainder of Anselm's career presents almost as many difficulties as did that of his early life. The *Vitae Anselmi* remain of rather mixed assistance. Both increasingly focused upon the clash between Gregory VII and Henry IV, only making reference to Anselm insofar as his actions reflected the wider struggle for reform. The details of his episcopacy, in particular, are few and far between. It is principally known for his violent contest with the canons of the cathedral, San Martino, in Lucca. Yet even this can only be imperfectly assessed. There is no mention whatsoever of Anselm in any of the charters of the cathedral chapter, possibly as a product of this clash and the resulting alienation between the bishop and the canons.[65] Anselm's consequent expulsion from Lucca to the entourage of Countess Matilda in late 1080, the papal schism and the ensuing war between the supporters of Henry IV, and the Matildine *fideles sancti Petri*, all make it exceedingly difficult to be specific about the bishop's later career.

Anselm was probably in Lucca during the early part of 1076. It is unclear, as some would have it, whether or not he attended the Lenten

---

(ed.), *Quellen und Forschungen zum Urkunden-und Kanzleiwesen Papst Gregors VII.* (Studi e testi, 190; Vatican City, 1957), no. 110 (St Gilles), and no. 125–6 (Polirone). The 17th cent. Benedictine Benedetto Bacchini, in his *Dell'istoria del monastero San Benedetto di Polirone*, for obvious reasons, believed that Anselm went to Polirone after his investiture crisis. One point (which remains to be explored) that weighs in favour of Polirone is that its library possessed a number of compilations of canonical sources, particularly patristic texts. It is tempting to speculate that these may have influenced Anselm in his canonical work. On the library, G. Motta, 'I codici canonistici di Polirone', in *Sant'Anselmo, Mantova*, 349–74; and P. Golinelli and B. Andreolli, *Storia di San Benedetto di Polirone* (Bologna, 1983), 222–58.

[65] *Regesto del Capitolo di Lucca*, ed. P. Guidi and O. Parenti, 3 vols. and index (Regesta Chartarum Italiae, 6, 9, 18, 18*; Rome, 1910–39). The charters refer to Anselm I, to the schismatic bishop Peter, and after him, to Rangerius.

synod at which Henry IV was excommunicated.[66] While no direct evidence exists of his presence, subsequent events, including the intervention of Gregory VII in Anselm's attempts to reform the canons in Lucca, would indicate a strong possibility that Anselm attended the synod. If he had journeyed to Rome, it is probable that he returned quite quickly to northern Italy, for the death of Beatrice of Tuscany on 18 April at Pisa would surely have brought Anselm to Matilda's side. Nothing specific, however, can be established until June 1076 when Anselm can be located at San Miniato, granting portions of a previously donated estate as benefices.[67] After the document of June 1076, there is no further mention of Anselm in the charters of Lucca until 23 February 1077—a charter which does not necessarily ensure that Anselm was in Lucca on that specific date.[68] Anselm's whereabouts after June 1076 become linked with the mounting crisis between Gregory VII and the excommunicated Henry IV. In late 1076, Gregory VII was in Florence, on his way to meet the German princes headed by Rudolf of Rheinfelden and settle the outstanding issues between them and the king.[69] At some point during this trip, Gregory went to Lucca to support Anselm's efforts to enforce the communal life on the canons of the cathedral.[70] Although it is not precisely clear when Matilda joined this struggle, she was with, or at least was in contact with, both Gregory and Anselm during this time.[71]

While the events that turned on Canossa captured the interest of Anselm's biographers, the question remains whether Anselm was present.[72] Although there was no mention of him in any of the reports of

---

[66] As Barsocchini, V, pt. I, pp. 340–1, believed.

[67] Ibid., V, pt. I, pp. 337–8; Archivio Arc. di Lucca, t C, 74.

[68] Ibid., V, pt. I, p. 341: Archivio Arc. di Lucca, tt L. 16. The document was a simple donation to the bishopric. Other sources indicate that Anselm was not, nor could possibly have been, in Lucca at that time.

[69] Bull, 28 Dec. 1076, Santifaller, *Quellen*, no. 122; JL no. 5015. Barsocchini erroneously dated this bull 1077: see V, pt. I, p. 355.

[70] Cf. *Vita Anselmi*, c. 8; and *Reg.*, V: 1; VI: 11. It is unclear whether Gregory went to Lucca before or after his meeting with the king at Canossa.

[71] Overmann, *Regesta*, 27f–g; cf. *Vita Anselmi*, c. 7. Matilda was definitely with Gregory by 8 Jan. 1077 in Mantua, and probably remained with him until the meeting at Canossa. She subsequently toured Lombardy with Gregory, while working in conjunction with Empress Agnes to secure the release of the captured legate Gerald of Ostia. Cf. Santifaller, *Quellen*, no. 126 to Hugh of Cluny, which mentions Matilda's familial associations with Polirone, and no. 127, a privilege for S.Apollonio at Canossa, made at the request of Matilda; Overmann, *Regesta*, 27l–m, and Gregory's letter to Udo of Trier, *Reg.* V: 7, pp. 356–8.

[72] The interest in Polirone evinced by Gregory VII in the early part of Jan. 1077 may have been prompted by Anselm's petitions, though the requests may have come from Matilda.

Canossa, one important result of the encounter between Gregory and Henry IV was agreement on the need to resolve the situation in Milan. Anselm and Gerald of Ostia were sent to Milan as papal legates towards these ends immediately following the reconciliation of the king. The closeness in time of that legation, together with the accounts of the *Vita Anselmi* and Bernold of Constance, would strongly indicate that the two legates had been at Canossa.[73] The legation, unfortunately, ended in disaster when Anselm and Gerald were taken prisoners by the schismatic bishop, Denis of Piacenza. Anselm, however, was quickly released, apparently on account of his native race and noble lineage.[74]

After that, there is no further mention of Anselm until 21 June 1077, when he can be located at Pavia with Matilda, who had been travelling with Gregory VII's entourage in Lombardy following the meeting of pope and king at Canossa.[75] It is unclear whether Anselm had again met or toured with the pontiff following his release from captivity. It is equally unclear whether, during his tour of northern Italy after Canossa, Gregory VII stopped again in Lucca.[76] Anselm's exact whereabouts following this time are difficult to ascertain. From this point forward to 1080, there are only sporadic notices of Anselm in the extant charters from the *Archivio Arcivescovale*, and in Matildine documents.[77]

Precisely how Anselm exercised his episcopal functions largely remains a mystery. There is little that can be said regarding Anselm's administrative and economic activity as bishop, and even less concerning his pastoral role.[78] One is probably not wrong, however, to envisage a continuation of Alexander II's policies, especially as regards the recovery and conservation of the diocesan patrimony. Like that of his predecessor, Anselm's episcopacy was overshadowed by a variety of local situations and forces.

---

[73] Bernold stated that Henry IV, who had sworn at Canossa to safeguard papal legations, did not even keep his promise for 15 days: *Chronicon a. 1077*, 433: 'Hoc autem iuramentum nec XV dies observavit, captis venerabilibus episcopis, Geraldo Ostiensi et Anselmo Lucensi.' Cf. *Vita Anselmi*, c. 16, p. 18.

[74] *Vita Anselmi*, c. 16–17, p. 18.   [75] See Barsocchini, IV, pt. II, doc. 106.

[76] No evidence exists of such a visit. The possibility stems from Barsocchini's erroneus dating of Gregory VII's bull of 26 Dec. 1076. It could be that Gregory's visit to Lucca did not take place until after Canossa.

[77] e.g. 24 July 1077, Anselm granted a *corte* and *castello* near the parish of San Gervasio to Tegrimo and Udo, sons of Azio: Barsocchini, IV, pt. II, doc. 107 (cf. V, pt. I, p. 347); 26 Sept. 1078, he received a *castello* Diecimo from Matilda: Barsocchini, IV, pt. II, 112; 17 Sept. 1079, he received a grant from Matilda: Fiorentini, II, 7.

[78] A. Spicciani, 'L'episcopato lucchese di Anselmo II da Baggio', in *Sant'Anselmo vescovo di Lucca*, 65–112, here 66 ff.

In the eleventh century, the city of Lucca was rich and prosperous. As a major centre on the Via Francigena, a principal route between Rome and France, Lucca's economy benefited from its provision of services to travellers. Situated in a fertile plain which, unlike similar Tuscan regions, was almost completely reclaimed and cultivated, Lucca and its environs, the Lucchesia, were able by the eleventh century to support a stable population.[79] Landholding in the Lucchesia, however, was extraordinarily fragmented, even by Italian standards, where partible inheritance was the norm.

Hans Schwarzmaier distinguished two levels of aristocratic society in the Lucchesia. First was the 'diocesan aristocracy', who owed their position (and had done so for over two centuries) primarily to grants of land, and pieval tithes, from the bishops of Lucca. The second group, who were more firmly based in the city, included the judiciaries, notaries, cathedral canons, and so on, who began to develop as a social class in the late tenth century. It was this latter group who, after 1080, would govern the slow movement of the city towards autonomy and communal identity.[80]

Throughout the eighth and ninth centuries, the bishopric of Lucca had been considerably enriched by extensive lay donations, especially from small and medium-sized landholders.[81] Yet by the end of the tenth century, large parts of the bishop's total landed property had been effectively lost to episcopal control.[82] As Wickham has documented, the diocesan aristocracy had effectively become episcopal tenants, and they derived the bulk of their power from ecclesiastical property and lordships held on lease, often at the expense of episcopal authority.[83] The bishops of Lucca had been driven to leasing their resources in an attempt both to establish their own kin, and to create new military and even administrative power bases. In large part, however, such alienations had been made necessary by their increasing relative political weakness both in the city, and in the Lucchesia at large. In the second half of the tenth century, for instance, it was not uncommon to find the leasing of

---

[79] C. Wickham, 'Economia e società rurale nel territorio lucchese durante la seconda metà del secolo XI: inquadramenti aristocratici e strutture signorili', in *Sant'Anselmo vescovo di Lucca*, 391–422; and id., *The Mountains and the City* (Oxford, 1988).

[80] H. Schwarzmaier, *Lucca und das Reich bis zum Endes des 11. Jahrhunderts* (Tübingen, 1972), esp. 246–61, 284–334, and 374–412. Cf. Wickham, 'Economia e società', 400 ff.

[81] C. Wickham, *The Mountains and the City*, 39 ff.; D. J. Osheim, *An Italian Lordship: The Bishopric of Lucca in the Late Middle Ages* (Berkeley, 1977), 11 ff.

[82] C. Violante, 'Pievi e parrochie dalla fine del X secolo all'inizio del XIII secolo', in *Le istituzioni ecclesiastiche della 'societas christiana'*, 643–799, here 657–69.

[83] Wickham, *The Mountains and the City*, 85 ff.; cf. Osheim, *An Italian Lordship*, 11.

fractions of a *pieve* rather than the leaving of the church under the jurisdiction of a single *plebano*. Such leases were obviously an attempt to maximize income from local churches.

By the mid-eleventh century, the episcopal patrimony was in a dire state. Alexander II was clearly suffering from the alienations of his predecessors.[84] The need for cash was particularly pressing. Alexander frequently requested, unlike his predecessors, that the *census* be paid in money rather than in cultivated or raw products.[85] The extremely poor state of Lucca's patrimony at the outset of his episcopate is made clear in an undated papal bull (1070–1072?). Decrying the vast alienations of his predecessors at Lucca, and the depleted resources which had made simony rampant, Alexander prohibited further alienation of ecclesiastical property save in cases of extreme need.[86] Since Alexander remained bishop of Lucca after his elevation as pope in 1061, this clearly facilitated his efforts to recover and preserve the patrimony. The fact that he was able to begin reconstruction of the cathedral would seem to indicate that he achieved some amelioration, or at least had introduced a measure of fiscal consistency.[87]

While there is not a great deal of evidence for Anselm's handling of ecclesiastical property, there are indications that during the period 1077–1080 Anselm had a significant interest in the defence, recovery, and acquisition of various *castelli*. This activity was undoubtedly connected with his attempts to foster tighter bonds with some of the local nobility. In June 1076 at San Miniato, for instance, Anselm tried to settle a question that had been outstanding for some 50 years, granting one portion of the estate *in hereditatem* and one *in beneficium*.[88] He laboured intensively for the episcopal rights of hospitality (*receptum*), and in 1077 at San Gervasio, clearly sought to elicit judicial and military assistance.[89] He endeavoured to strengthen ties with known episcopal supporters and

---

[84] Spicciani, 'L'episcopato lucchese di Anselmo II', 76 ff. Cf. Kehr, *Italia pontificia*, III, p. 389, note 6; and Barsocchini, V, pt. III, pp. 666–8 and note 185.

[85] C. M. Angeli, 'L'episcopato lucchese di Anselmo I da Baggio: l'amministrazione delle finanze e del patrimonio della chiesa', *Actum Luce: rivista di studi lucchesi*, 15 (1986), 95–117, here 101, note 15. Cf. Spicciani, 'L'episcopato lucchese di Anselmo II', 81.

[86] *PL* 146, cols. 1388–91. Cf. Spicciani, 83–4, and Angeli, 106. The bull noted that only 5 *pievi* out of some 50 were under the complete authority of the bishop.

[87] See Angeli, 104. Cf. R. Silva, 'La ricostruzione della cattedrale di Lucca (1060–1070): un esempio precoce di archittetura della riforma gregoriana', in *Sant'Anselmo vescovo di Lucca*, 297–309.

[88] Barsocchini, V, pt. I, pp. 337–8: Archivio Arc. di Lucca, t C, 74. Cf. Spicciani, 91–2.

[89] On 24 July 1077, Anselm granted a *corte* and *castello* near the parish of San Gervasio to Tegrimo and Udo, sons of Azio with conditions: Barsocchini, IV, pt. II, doc. 107, (cf. V, pt. I, p. 347). Cf. Spicciani, 94–5.

families linked with Matilda, for instance the de Maona family, who may well have come to his support in 1080. All of these actions surely must be seen in light of his attempts to counter and deal with the deteriorating situation between himself and the canons of San Martino.

The reform of the cathedral canons was a protracted, if ultimately unsuccessful affair, despite the assistance and intervention of Gregory VII and Countess Matilda. Matilda provided the material support: many of her donations to Lucca during this period were put at the discretion of the bishop, instead of being made to the cathedral chapter.[90] Gregory VII, who joined the struggle as early as December 1076, brought to bear all the authority of Rome.[91] In a letter of 21 August 1077, Gregory demanded that the canons acquiesce in the communal life, warning of dire consequences if they disobeyed.[92] In late November 1078, the pope again wrote to the canons bitterly complaining of their failure to attend the November synod as summoned.[93] Finally in October 1079, he took decisive action. With reference to canonical texts, Gregory excommunicated the canons for their persistent contumacy, their conspiracy against their bishop, and their failure to respond to the second synodal action taken against them, presumably at the Lenten synod of 1079.[94]

The matter did not end there, however. After the second excommunication of Henry IV and the election of Wibert of Ravenna as antipope, the canons took advantage of the possibilities offered by the schism. The reformers' response was a council under the headship of the papal legate, Cardinal-bishop Peter of Albano, at San Ginesio near Lucca in late June–early July 1080. According to the *Vita Anselmi*, the canons and their conspirators were again excommunicated.[95] Yet the canons were able to muster significant local support against Anselm and Matilda, and with the aid of Henry and Wibert's partisans succeeded in expelling Anselm from Lucca.[96] The remainder of his life would be

---

[90] *Vita Anselmi*, cc. 7–9, pp. 15–16; cf. Matildine donations in *Italia Sacra sive De episcopis Italiae*, I, ed. F. Ughelli (Rome, 1644), col. 869 ff.

[91] See *Vita Anselmi*, c. 8; *Reg.* V: 1, p. 348: 'Meminisse debetis, quotiens et cum quanta cura vos monuerimus apud vos manentes . . . '; Cf. *Reg.* VI: 11, p. 412.

[92] *Reg.* V: 1, pp. 348–9.   [93] *Reg.* VI: 11, pp. 412–13.

[94] *Reg.* VII: 2, pp. 460–2. Cf. *Vita Anselmi*, c. 8, p. 16. It is not clear whether Anselm was at the Lenten synod of 1079 (no mention in the protocol). According to Barsocchini, Anselm was present to testify to Berengar of Tours' abjuration, see p. 349, note 3.

[95] *Vita Anselmi*, c. 8–9, p. 16; Barsocchini, V, pt. II, pp. 351 ff.

[96] *Vita Anselmi*, c. 9, p. 16. Anselm initially removed himself to the *castello* Moriano on the Serchio about four kilometres from Lucca, remaining there until spring 1081 at which point he apparently joined Matilda's entourage.

spent in exile in the entourage of Matilda of Tuscany, waging war against the Henrician-Wibertine supporters.

Anselm's desire to reform the canons of San Martino seems to have been motivated by a number of factors. The struggle provides, in the first place, an important example of his uncompromising reform sensibilities, and his equally stringent views on canon law. In his struggle to reform the canons, Anselm's ambitions clearly went beyond simply demanding and effecting adherence to the communal life imposed on them by Leo IX in 1051.[97] The core of his understanding was the belief that personal poverty, as exhibited by the apostolic community, was an integral aspect of canonical discipline, and one that ensured a high level of morality in the clergy. Unlike other reform canonists, Anselm's interpretation of the communal life took a most rigid view: that of the Augustinian rule, where all private benefices were nullified, and property was held communally at the discretion of the bishop.[98] It was an interpretation with which Gregory VII most emphatically concurred.[99] Anselm's vehemence in this undertaking is shown in the *Vita Anselmi*, which reported that the bishop would have preferred to see all of the churches utterly empty than to be filled with irregular canons.[100]

Behind an evidently sincere desire to promote a high level of morality in the secular clergy, also lay the delicate issue of property. The canonry of San Martino had existed since the eighth century. During the course of the tenth century, the chapter had become a well-defined structure increasingly distinct from the episcopate. Like the episcopate, the chapter had benefited from extensive gifts and donations of land. Jurisdiction was held in common, but agricultural rents had probably

---

[97] For Leo IX's imposition of the communal life in 1051, see Barsocchini, V, pt. III, Appendix, doc. 1590.

[98] The 74T was not concerned with the issue of communal life, and later canonists, i.e. Bonizo, Deusdedit, and Ivo, did not follow Anselm's example regarding strict poverty, insisting only upon the aspects of the communal life stipulated by the Rule of Aix. Anselm, for whom the Rule of Aix was insufficient, took into consideration the views of Gregory I and Peter Damian on the communal life presented in the Acts of the Apostles, which, particularly in Damian's case, called for personal poverty. See C. Dereine, 'Le Problème de la vie commune chez les canonistes d'Anselme de Lucques à Gratien', *SG* 3 (1948), 287–98, here 295–6; and C. D. Fonseca, 'Il capitolo di San Martino e la riforma canonicale nella seconda metà del secolo XI', *Sant'Anselmo vescovo di Lucca*, 51–64.

[99] For Gregory VII's views, see *Reg.* V: 1; and esp. VI: 11, p. 413: ' . . . id est, ut omnia ecclesiae bona in communem utilitatem redigantur et communiter, sicut supra dictum est, expendantur, aut si id facere recusatis, ecclesiae prebendas in manu episcopi ad ecclesiae utilitatem reddatis.'

[100] *Vita Anselmi*, c. 31, p. 22: ' . . . inquit, ut in ecclesia nullus esset vel clericus vel monachus, quam irregularis, ut ita dicam, et irreligiosus.'

been divided into individual benefices by the early eleventh century.[101] More potentially damaging, these benefices were increasingly bound up with, and seen to be, familial property. It is obvious that the issue of property offered an important motivation to Anselm in his struggle to reform the canons. Rangerius, in particular, makes it clear that Anselm was interested not merely in 'collegiality', but in the renunciation of personal property.[102] Rangerius' version, though, is problematic. In his opinion, what was at stake was simony. His account of the council at San Ginesio in 1080, with its depiction of a trial by fire involving Anselm's champion, Cardinal-bishop Peter of Albano, was effectively that of a struggle against Simon Magus.[103]

While simony may well have been a factor, it was the issue of property and its disposal which appears to have been the principal reason for the prolonged struggle. On the one hand, the insistence upon the communal life should be seen as an attempt on Anselm's part to avoid further alienation of ecclesiastical property, an effort to retain at least some degree of supervision by the bishop. Gregory VII's excommunication of the canons in 1079 called upon those who refused to be 'corrected' to give up canonical property.[104] The pope's letter, at the same time, seems to have implied an eventual renunciation of familial property as well. It is in this light that one can easily see how the entire conflict quickly became caught up in the tensions and partisan politics of the local society. The notice in the *Vita Anselmi* of Matilda's apparent promise of grants and money to the families of those canons who agreed to be reformed shows the ramifications of the struggle.[105] If the report is to be believed, one must see Matilda's actions as an attempt to defuse a dangerous situation by offering compensation for the loss of income derived from canonical property.

In the end, Anselm's episcopacy, and the entire conflict with the canons, was a struggle of a bishop looking to recover and stabilize his position, both in financial and pastoral terms, *vis-à-vis* an increasingly well-connected and powerful chapter. It is difficult to assess the range of local forces opposed to Anselm and Matilda in 1080. Schwarzmaier believed that the ambitions of the canons should be seen in the light of the nascent communal aspirations of the class to which they belonged.

---

[101] See Osheim, *An Italian Lordship*, 14 ff.

[102] Rangerius, vv. 5415–16; vv. 1511–14; v. 1524; vv. 1551–2; v. 1559. Cf. Fonseca, 'Il capitolo di S. Martino', 59.

[103] Rangerius, vv. 1811–12, 1817–18.

[104] *Reg.*VII: 2, pp. 460–2; cf. Spicciani, 66, and Osheim, 16.

[105] *Vita Anselmi*, c. 7, p. 15.

That their desire was for a measure of autonomy is at least clear. Henry IV's privilege to Lucca in 1081 must surely be seen as a reward at least in part for their efforts.[106]

Anselm's biographers were concerned, on the most basic level perhaps, to demonstrate the ways in which Anselm's life had been devoted to the promotion of ecclesiastical reform. While Anselm, unlike Gregory VII, was perhaps not a revolutionary, he was none the less one who demanded immediate action.[107] Yet whereas Gregory 'effected a revolution in the name of tradition',[108] Anselm attempted to vindicate that vision, or at the least was portrayed as such. As the *Vita Anselmi* noted:

'[Gregory] was the source; [Anselm] was the good stream that flowed from him and watered the arid ground. [Gregory] was the head that governed the entire body; [Anselm] was the zealous hand that executed what had been imposed.'[109]

As will be seen in the following pages, Anselm, unlike his reformist predecessors, was not merely a canonist who sought to reform canon law. The salvation of all of western Christendom lay behind Anselm's consecration to the task of refashioning the law of reform.

---

[106] *Heinrici IV. Diplomata*, no. 334 (*MGH, Diplomatum*, 6), 437–9.

[107] Anselm of Lucca, *In libro secundo super Matthaeum*, (*PL* 149), 476–7: 'Unde multum tremenda sunt haec, dilectissimi, et digno expavescenda timore, sedulaque praecavenda industria, ne veniens improvisus, perversum quid in nobis unde merito flagellari ac de ecclesia eiici debeamus, inveniat.'

[108] T. F. X. Noble, review of Gerd Tellenbach, *The Church in Western Europe from the Tenth to the Early Twelfth Century*, in *American Historical Review*, 100 (1995), 146–7.

[109] *Vita Anselmi*, c. 32, p. 22: 'Ille fons erat, hic quasi rivus bonus ab illo fluebat, et aridam irrigabat. Ille caput totum corpus gubernabat, iste quasi manus studiosa quod iniunctum est peragebat.'

2

Anselm and His Canonical Sources*

1. ANSELM AND THE 'REFORM' COLLECTIONS: NEW SOURCES AND NEW METHODS

DRIVEN by the need to devise strategies for the renovation of the Church and Christian society, the reformers of the mid-eleventh century had turned their attention, first and foremost, to the reaffirmation and strengthening of existing ecclesiastical law. At Rome, at Rheims, and again at Rome, successive reforming popes solemnly opened their councils with insistence upon the traditional and sacred canons before embarking on their own legislative agendas.[1] Hand in hand with these endeavours, men like Peter Damian were also anxious to identify and eradicate dubious or doubtful canonical texts which undermined the sacred law. Although 'on the eve' of the Gregorian revolution, their concerns had been reflected in a variety of ways, these reformers had not produced the canonical collections which spelled out their aspirations regarding ecclesiastical law. Such ambitions only began to be articulated purposefully when the collections of the 1070s and 1080s, the *Diversorum patrum sententie sive Collectio in LXXIV titulos digesta* [here-

---

* *A Note on Terminology*: In this chapter, 'independent', 'genuine', and 'original' are used with certain connotations. Unless otherwise specified, 'independent' refers to canons which seem to have been taken directly from a source (e.g. from *Decretales Pseudo-Isidorianae*), and not through the medium of another intervening collection (e.g. *Decretum Burchardi* or the *Diversorum patrum sententie*); 'genuine' is used loosely to refer to all canons *except* Ps.Isidorian ones (though there are texts in the Decretals which are not spurious—these will be specified as ex Ps.Isidore); 'original' refers to what can be approximated of the text as initially written.

[1] See above Part I: Papacy and Law on the Eve of the Gregorian Revolution. In general, see R. Knox, 'Finding the Law: Developments in Canon Law during the Gregorian Reform', *SG* 9 (1972), 419–66.

after 74T] (*c.*1075), the *Breviarium* of Cardinal Atto (*c.*1075), the *Collectio canonum* of Anselm of Lucca (*c.*1083), and the *Collectio canonum* of Cardinal Deusdedit (*c.*1083–1087), were promulgated and diffused.[2] On the one hand, these collections offer testimony of the extent to which ideas or strategies regarding the law had been devised and consolidated. More important perhaps, such collections allow us to gauge the ways in which the movement for reform was making an impact on canon law.

The collections of the 1070s and 1080s, although dissimilar in many ways, had two features that distinguished them from earlier collections, quite apart from their polemical or selective qualities. The new collections all to a greater or lesser extent reveal that there had been some conscious attempts to eliminate dubious or contradictory texts. In addition, they disclose that equally deliberate efforts had been made to introduce a variety of new canonical texts. Despite such innovations, it is clear, however, that these so-called reform canonists did not envisage their collections as having any intrinsic value in themselves. Their canonical compilations were simply the vehicles by which the authentic and sacred canons were to be transmitted. Polemical interests aside, it was the authority of the canonical text itself which was of paramount concern to these canonists.[3]

Tracing the formal sources of these 'new' texts, however, continues to be a troubling matter. The problem lies in detecting, and establishing, a particular textual dependency. Unfortunately, what survives of the canonical collections compiled during the half century between the promulgation of the *Decretum libri XX* of Burchard of Worms (*c.*1023), and the first known use of the 74T (*c.*1076) does not sufficiently account either for the new sources, or for the polemical quality that is to be

---

[2] The *Breviarium* of Cardinal Atto, ed. A. Mai (Scriptorum veterum nova collectio et vaticanis codicibus edita, 10 vols.; Rome, 1825–38), vol. VI, pt. II, pp. 60–100, though an extremely short-lived collection, pointed to the insufficiency of existing collections and made a strong case for Roman sanction of any given canon. *Diversorum patrum sententie sive Collectio in LXXIV titulos digesta*, ed. J. T. Gilchrist (Monumenta Iuris Canonici, Ser. B: Corpus Collectionum, 1; Vatican City, 1973). The relationship between Anselm and the 74T will be discussed in Sect. 3 below. *Die Kanonessammlung des Kardinals Deusdedit*, ed. V. Wolf von Glanvell (Paderborn, 1905). The connections between Anselm and Deusdedit will be discussed in Sect. 5. On the 'reform collections' in general, see P. Fournier, 'Les Collections canoniques romaines à l'époque de Grégoire VII', *Mémoires de l'académie des inscriptions et belles-lettres*, 41 (1920), 271–395; P. Fournier and G. Le Bras, *Histoire des collections canoniques en occident depuis les fausses décrétales jusqu'au décret de Gratien*, 2 vols. (Societé d'histoire de droit; Paris, 1931–2), II, 5 ff.; and A. M. Stickler, *Historia iuris Canonici Latini*, I: *Historia fontium* (Rome, 1974), 166 ff.

[3] S. Kuttner, '*Liber canonicus*: A Note on *Dictatus papae* c. 17', *SG* 2 (1947), 387–401, here 398.

found in these 'reform' collections.[4] Often, one can only guess at the research which must have taken place in medieval libraries and archives in order to extract ancient (or what appeared to be ancient) texts. Regrettably, there is little indication of how, when, to what extent, and by whom this process was carried out. It is clear that 'intermediate' compilations of canonical sources, particularly patristic texts, were being produced, and that they were to be found in monastic and other libraries. These compilations—such as those from the library of the Benedictine monastery San Benedetto di Polirone, now in Mantua—may offer an important clue towards resolving this problem.[5]

The bulk of the newly-disseminated material sources were papal decretals, and included previously unknown or uncirculated texts from Gregory I, Honorius I, Martin I, Gregory II, Gregory III, and fragments from Nicholas I, John XII, Stephen V, Nicholas II, and Gregory VII.[6] There was also a growing number of conciliar texts relative to the Eastern councils, largely via Anastasius Bibliotecarius, although there was generally in the new collections a preponderance of papal texts.[7]

---

[4] For a description and source analysis of these minor collections, most of which were either local in essence or penitential in character, and almost all of which are unedited, see Stickler, 154, 159, and Fournier/Le Bras, I, 431–53.

[5] Fournier was one of the first to formulate this theory of the existence of rudimentary 'intermediate collections': see 'Un tournant de l'histoire du droit (1060–1140)', *Nouvelle revue historique de droit française et étranger*, 41 (1917), 129–80, esp. 131–54; cf. Fournier/Le Bras, II, 9 ff. The text known as the *Collectio Brittanica*, British Library, MS Addit. 8873, seems, in some aspects, to have been the end product of one of these 'intermediary collections'. See R. Somerville, 'Note on Paris, Bibl. de l'Arsenal, MS 713', *BMCL*, n.s. 17 (1987), p. xxi; id., 'The Letters of Pope Urban II in the *Collectio Brittanica*', in *Proceedings of the Seventh International Congress of Medieval Canon Law*, ed. P. Linehan (MIC, Ser. C: Subsidia, 8; Vatican City, 1988), 103–14; and id. with S. Kuttner, *Pope Urban II, the Collectio Brittanica, and the Council of Melfi (1089)* (Oxford, 1996). H. Mordek, however, remains more cautious on this issue: 'Dalla riforma gregoriana alla *Concordia discordantium* di Graziano: osservazioni marginali di un canonista su un tema non marginale', in *Chiesa, diritto e ordinamento della 'societas christiana' nei secoli XI e XII* (Misc. del centro di studi medioevali, 11; Milan, 1986), 89–112, here 100 and note 39. Anselm's possible use of the exemplar or 'intermediary collection' which resulted in the *Collectio Brittanica* will be noted in Sect. 4. On the library of San Benedetto di Polirone, see P. Golinelli and B. Andreolli, *Storia di san Benedetto di Polirone*, 222–58; and G. Motta, 'I codici canonistici di Polirone', in *Sant'Anselmo, Mantova*, 349–74. Whether these compilations were used by Anselm remains to be fully explored.

[6] Fournier/Le Bras, II, 9 ff.

[7] The 74T, for instance, had only two conciliar texts, one from the fourth Council of Toledo, c. 49 [= 74T c. 312], and one from the eighth Council of Toledo, c. 3 [= 74T c. 136], which the compiler erroneously attributed to Ambrose. Anselm correctly identified the text. Two conciliar texts are found in the Swabian Appendix to the 74T (not completed before 1086), one from the Council of Antioch a. 341, c. 4 [= 74T c. 316], and one from the fourth Council of Carthage, c. 29 [= 74T c. 317].

One finds, at the same time, an increasing number of patristic texts, indicating that the formerly distinct branch of biblical exegesis was finding a more prominent, if still secondary, place in canon law. In similar fashion, texts from the *Liber pontificalis*, from Cassiodorus, and especially from Anastasius Bibliotecarius were increasingly being deployed to impart legal precedent in historical terms. Secular law was likewise acquiring a more significant role, and was being used principally to bolster privileges conceded by emperors and kings to the Roman Church.[8] The most important development in terms of secular texts, however, was the rediscovery and use of the authentic version of Justinian's *Novellae*, replacing the previously used and somewhat suspect *Epitome Juliani*.

In addition to the elimination of contradictory canons and the introduction of new texts, the reform collections also demonstrated that significant developments in the organization and handling of the canonical sources were taking place. One finds greater precision and care both in textual identification with the *inscriptio*, and in authorial direction or interpretation with the rubric titles. Developments with the rubric were of particular significance. The rubric offered the compiler (or his recensor) an important opportunity to put forward his own opinion or interpretation of the canonical text in question, techniques which later would play an important role in the concordance of texts that would triumph with Gratian. This is not to say that reform collections such as the 74T or Anselm's *Collectio canonum* were responsible for these two features. Rubric titles and inscriptions of a sort were more or less present in the *Dionysio-Hadriana*, the *Anselmo Dedicata*, Regino of Prum's *Libri duo de ecclesiasticis disciplinis et religione christiana*, and Burchard of Worms's *Decretum libri XX*, although the Pseudo-Isidorian Decretals did not contain rubric titles *per se*.[9] In these collections, however, though some identification was indispensable in order to provide authoritative value for the canon in question, such elements were generally far less significant or durable. This was particularly the case with the rubric title,

---

[8] In general, the reformers used the pseudo-*Constitutum Constantini* to support papal claims to temporal privileges and supremacy in the West.

[9] The *Dionysio-Hadriana*, the *Hispana*, and the Pseudo-Isidorian *Decretals* were not 'systematic' collections. They were organized into sections according to genre (i.e. conciliar texts, papal decretals) and usually chronologically within each section (something also found in Deusdedit). The texts were generally preceded by a brief resumé in the form of a rubric or by a *capitulatio*. The *Anselmo Dedicata*, Regino's *Libri duo*, and Burchard's *Decretum*, however, were 'systematic' collections. On this, see G. Fransen, *Les Collections canoniques* (Typologie des sources du moyen âge occidental, fasc. 10; Turnhout, 1973), 17 ff.

which in essence was often little more than a facile summary, or the first line of the subsequent canonical text. Even in the 74T, the rubrics rarely offered more than a mere encapsulation of the text, and thus afford little insight into the compiler's intention. This was perhaps due in part to the collection's 'sentence-like' structure with its one, more generalized, title encapsulating a series of canons. The collection of Cardinal Deusdedit, as will be seen, was a special case.

In the *Collectio canonum* of Anselm of Lucca the rubric was to become a complementary, almost intrinsic element of the canonical text itself. Many of the rubrics, particularly in Books I and II, seem to be 'original' ones; that is, they were not copied from the exemplar or formal source along with the canonical text. Clearly, there are tremendous problems with seeing the rubric as a definitive statement of Anselm's (or in fact any compiler's) opinion, particularly in the light of the collection's evolving tradition. The variations in the different recensions make it difficult to state unequivocally that these represent his own opinion. In spite of this, and because of textual and thematic similarity to other of his works, it is not wholly unreasonable to see Anselm using the rubric as a means of underscoring essential reform objectives, of sharpening generalities, of lending universality to localized issues and sanctions, and, especially, of updating ancient texts to current ecclesiastical and reform concerns. Particularly with his Ps.Isidorian texts and those taken from the 74T, Anselm (or at least his recensor) can be seen to use the rubric in an effort to avoid the ambivalent attitude of these compilers towards the issue of papal primacy.

Greater precision in the identification of texts, the *inscriptio*, was another important characteristic of the new collections. Certainly this too was not a radical innovation. In the pre-reform collections, texts were generally identified to a greater or lesser extent, the authority provided by the inscription being indispensable to the canon's value. Yet, false inscriptions and attributions proliferated. Most of these were clearly due to misascription, scribal error, and erroneous past transmission.[10] There are, however, numerous instances where it can be shown that they resulted from deliberate falsification. The *Decretum libri XX* of Burchard of Worms is a noteworthy example in this respect. Although some of his errors were probably due to inaccurate past transmission, it seems clear that on occasion Burchard deliberately falsified inscriptions in an effort to give greater authority to canons from regional

---

[10] Fransen, *Les Collections canoniques*, 33, noted that the *inscriptio* was the most vulnerable part of any canonical text.

councils, or to capitulary texts which had not been sanctioned by Rome, and which he certainly knew were of somewhat suspect value.[11] The same can be seen with respect to his patristic texts. With many of these, Burchard seems to have knowingly but erroneously cited the authority of Augustine, thereby achieving greater sanction for his texts.[12]

While there are erroneous attributions in Anselm's collection, especially in Book XI, the penitential, it is apparent that Anselm (or his recensor) took considerable care to be as accurate as possible. It is clear that he did not always accept the attribution of his exemplar even though he did use its transmission of the canonical text in question. This would indicate a strong possibility that some form of comparative work took place during the course of his compilation, or in its subsequent transmission. This can clearly be seen with respect to his use of the Pseudo-Isidore. On occasion, it seems almost as if texts were 'cross-referenced' independently in order that the correct, and, in many cases, entire inscription might be cited, whereas the exemplar had only contained a partial one.[13] The relatively few false attributions in his collection stemmed for the most part from erroneous past transmission. Others resulted from attributions which were widely acknowledged as accurate at the time, for instance the attribution to Augustine of the false *Gravi de pugna* text, and to Augustine of Gennadius' *De dogmatibus ecclesiasticis*.[14]

The *Collectio canonum* of Anselm of Lucca had pretensions to being a comprehensive work. It addressed itself to a variety of ecclesiastical concerns by means of appeals to a wide range of canonical sources.[15] The collection comprised some 1149 chapters of varying length, subdivided

---

[11] A few of these false attributions passed into Anselm. See Table I, under Book X.

[12] Regino of Prum was equally at fault in this respect, and may account for a number of Burchard's errors. For Burchard's false Augustinian attributions, see C. Munier, *Les Sources patristiques du droit de l'église du VIIIe au XIIIe siècles* (Mulhouse, 1957), 213. Burchard's erroneous attributions none the less testify to the growing authority of Augustine in canon law, whereas in earlier collections patristic texts, and especially Augustine, had been employed in subordinate positions primarily for moral and penitential issues.

[13] See below, Sections 2 and 3.

[14] Anselm, VII: 22; and XIII: 5. The inscription 'Item ad eundem' carries over from XIII: 4 'Augustinus Bonifacio illustri viro'. The text is actually Ps.Augustine to Boniface [*PL* 33, 1098]. The text went into Gratian, C. 23 qu. 8, c. 17, under the same inscription.

[15] Not all of the concerns in the *Collectio canonum* necessarily represented reformist issues or principles. A case in point is Book XI, the penitential; an issue which appears not to have been a matter of serious interest to most 'Gregorians', apart from Peter Damian.

into thirteen books of unequal scope, though the number of chapters
varies in different recensions of the collection.[16] Book I (89 chapters)
addressed the power and primacy of the Apostolic See; Book II (82
chapters), the liberty and right of appeal; Book III (114 chapters), the
order of accusing, testifying, and judging; Book IV (55 chapters), the
authority of privileges; Book V (64 chapters), the ordination of churches,
their rights and status; Book VI (190 chapters), the election, ordination,
and powers of the episcopate; Book VII (174 chapters), the communal
life of clerics; Book VIII (34 chapters), the lapsed; Book IX (49 chapters), the sacraments; Book X (45 chapters), marriage; Book XI (151
chapters), penance; Book XII (72 chapters), excommunication; and Book
XIII (29 chapters), lawful coercive power (*de iusta vindicta*).[17]

Anselm's known formal sources included the *Collectio Hadriana*
(probably the *Dionysio-Hadriana* version), the *Collectio Hispana*, the
Ps.Isidorian Decretals, the *Anselmo Dedicata*, the *Capitula Iudiciorum*,
the *Decretum* of Burchard of Worms, and the 74T.[18] Of these, the
Ps.Isidorian Decretals, which accounted for some 263 texts, and the
74T, with some 237 texts (excluding the Swabian Appendix), were of
the greatest significance, although, as will be seen, Anselm was
extremely cautious in his approach to these two collections.[19] Anselm
was also wary about relying upon Burchard, and he used the *Decretum*
primarily for texts on marriage and penance, although ignoring all penitential texts of Celtic or insular origin. In terms of conciliar canons,
Anselm was apparently not attached to any particular version. The bulk
of his conciliar texts were provided primarily by the *Dionysio-Hadriana*,

[16] The varying number of *capitula* is often due to scribal misnumeration, as well as to
additions and omission of texts within the books themselves—as one finds particularly in
the 'B' recension. Thaner's edition often fails to clarify these variations. For instance, he
fails to note the three texts at the end of Book I which are characteristic of the 'A' recension: MS Vat. lat. 1363, fos. 26ᵛ–27ʳ: *Codex Iustinianus* 1. 3. 30, given as canon 90 (a text
which corresponds to Anselm's own VI: 4 which occurs on fo. 103ʳ of the Vatican MS);
fo. 27ʳ–ᵛ: Stephen III, Lateran council a. 769, excerpt from third and fourth actions (cited
as: Ex concilio Stephani in actione tercia), given as canon 91; and fo. 27ᵛ: *Liber pontificalis*, excerpt. The last two are in a contemporary but different hand. Cf. *A Catalogue of
Roman and Canon Law MSS in the Vatican Library*, I, for Vat. lat. 1363 and 1364.

[17] Calculations based upon Thaner's edition together with MS Vat. lat. 1363. The 'A'
recension has 72 cc. for Book XII, and 29 for XIII, while the 'B' version, due to misnu-
merations and additions, has 77 for Book XII and 30 for XIII.

[18] On Anselm's sources, see P. Fournier, 'Les Collections canoniques', 294–327; and
Fournier/Le Bras, II, 25–35.

[19] See below, Tables II and III. This 263 also includes Ps.Isidorian texts via the 74T,
which accounted for some 102 Ps.Isidorian texts. Gilchrist, the editor of the 74T, put the
entire number of Anselm's texts taken directly from the 74T at 247. For reasons which
will be explored in Section 3, I would hesitate to concur completely with this number.

the *Hispana*, with some by the Ps.Isidore, the *Capitula Angilrammi*, and the *Versio Prisca*. Civil (Roman) legislation texts were provided by the *Codex Iustinianus*, the *De institutionibus*, and the *Novellae*. Other sources included excerpts from the *Liber pontificalis*, the *De ordinibus Romani*, and Anastasius' *Historia ecclesiastica sive Chronographia tripertita*.

The majority of Anselm's material sources were papal decretals and accounted for some 679 texts.[20] About 269 of these were false texts (or else came via the Ps.Isidore (263/266), which did not automatically mean that they were forged), with about 410 being genuine. Gregory I accounted for some 133 of these decretals, with another 16 in patristic texts, and 3 from John the Deacon's *Vita Gregorii Magni*. Conciliar canons accounted for some 134 texts. The use of conciliar canons, however, was uneven, the bulk being concentrated in Books VI and VII. Secular law sources accounted for some 42 texts, the bulk of which were from the *Codex Iustinianus*. Patristic sources accounted for some 164 texts, Augustine being the most prominent with 101.

Anselm also benefited from the 'new' texts being brought into wider circulation in the second half of the eleventh century.[21] Whether these were the product of his own research, or from intermediate collections, is less clear. Among the most significant of these were papal decretals from Gelasius I, Pelagius I, Nicholas I, John VIII, and Stephen V. In terms of new conciliar texts, Anselm's collection is noteworthy for its use of canons from the seventh and eighth universal councils via Anastasius Bibliotecarius. Apart from Justinian's *Novellae*, other new texts included various imperial privileges from the Ottonians and others, the *Liber pontificalis*, the *Chronographia* of Anastasius, the *Gesta Liberii*, the *Vita Silvestri*, and the *Vita s.Iohanni Chrysostomi*.

The following consideration of Anselm's canonical sources is aimed not only at establishing what can be gleaned of his attitude towards his sources, but also his fidelity, or lack thereof, to them. Stickler believed that Anselm had neither arbitrarily nor systematically altered the texts of his collection.[22] Although, as will be seen, there are some notable examples to the contrary, only after an exacting and thorough comparison of all the texts in each of the various recensions of the collection would it be possible to make a definitive statement. Even so, it would be difficult to ascribe all these alterations or modifications specifically to

---

[20] See below, Table I. [21] P. Fournier, 'Les Collections canoniques', 311 ff.

[22] Stickler, *Historia iuris canonici*, 172. In the following sections, the principal test case will be Books I–III. Though there will be examples from other books, these will not be examined systematically. A more thorough examination of Books XII and XIII, however, will take place in Chapter 4. See also Appendix II.

Anselm. It does not seem possible, though, to characterize Anselm as arbitrary in this respect. Equally, it cannot be denied that he was both polemical and selective in his compilation. By tempering certain canonical texts, by removing canons from the wider context of their formal source, and by employing pointed rubrics, Anselm was able to focus, in the collection, upon the ideas he believed to be of crucial importance. The rest of this chapter, while considering some of Anselm's principal material, and formal sources, will attempt to explore those instances which offer an insight into his attitude, and consequently his fidelity, towards those sources. Only with this established, is it then possible to consider the ways in which the collection may have been aimed at providing a manual for reform.

2. ANSELM AND THE PSEUDO-ISIDORE

THE single most important of Anselm's formal and material sources, not merely in numerical terms, was the Pseudo-Isidorian Decretals.[23] Indeed, Anselm's collection seems to have played a significant role in the spread and popularization of these texts in Italy. Of some 1149 *capitula* in the collection, some 263(266) were Ps.Isidorian.[24] The formal sources of these Ps.Isidorian texts varied. Their selection, however, offers some important insights. One is occasionally able to discern not only Anselm's dissatisfaction with the canonical collections of the recent past as vehicles of transmission in general, but also his critical attitude towards their handling of papal decretals. The choice of formal source, at the same time, reveals Anselm's concern with textual precision. It can sometimes be suggested that he sought out those sources which he believed would provide uncorrupted, unadulterated, or at least unbiased texts of the revered early pontiffs.

An important source of Ps.Isidorian texts was the 74T, which accounted for some 101 texts.[25] It will, however, be seen in the exami-

---

[23] *Decretales Pseudo-Isidorianae et Capitula Angilrammi*, ed. P. Hinschius (Leipzig, 1863), though somewhat imperfect. The text consists of three parts: (1) forged papal letters from Clement I (before 90–99?), Anacletus I (79–90?) to Melchiades (311–14), closing with the pseudo-*Constitutum Constantini*, (2) genuine conciliar canons (with some interpolations) taken from the *Hispana Gallica Augustodunensis*, and (3) papal decretals (mostly genuine) from Silvester to Gregory II (314–731), based probably on the *Hispana*. The essential work on the Ps.Isidore is H. Fuhrmann, *Einfluss und Verbreitung der pseudoisidorischen Fälschungen*, 3 vols. (*MGH, Schriften*, 24/1–3; Stuttgart, 1972–4). Vol. III provides extensive tables and itemization of the Ps.Isidorian Decretals in the collections from *Anselmo Dedicata* to Gratian.

[24] See below, Table II.

[25] This is a provisional number, see below, Section 3. Cf. Fuhrmann, II, 512–13.

nation of the transmission of Ps.Isidorian texts from the 74T that Anselm modified, sharpened, or even went elsewhere for his text. Fuhrmann believed that approximately 96 texts had been taken from the 74T.[26] What is striking, however, is the fact that the bulk of Anselm's Ps.Isidorian *capitula*—some 157—were provided by an 'independent' text or texts of the Decretals. Indeed, according to Fuhrmann, Anselm must have had several recensions of the Decretals at his disposal.[27]

Another source of Ps.Isidorian texts, though of considerably less significance, was the *Decretum libri XX* of Burchard of Worms. This accounted perhaps for some five *capitula*.[28] There are, however, no convincing examples of the *Anselmo Dedicata* having been a similar formal source in this respect for Anselm, though it had previously been an important vehicle of Ps.Isidorian texts.[29] In some cases, it is impossible to ascertain Anselm's formal source. At least three Ps.Isidorian texts are of unknown or unclear provenance.[30]

The majority of Anselm's Ps.Isidorian texts—some 163 *capitula*—as demonstrated in Table II, were concentrated in the first three books of the collection. Of these 163, some 106 were provided by an independent source of the Ps.Isidorian Decretals. The significance of these texts, however, does not lie solely in number, but also in the ends towards which they were employed. Many of them were used, somewhat ironically as will be seen, towards the crucial assertion of an absolute Roman primacy. While the first book was the only one to address itself explicitly to Roman primacy—Books II and III concerning themselves with the right of appeal, and the procedures for accusing, testifying, and judging—the issue was, in effect, the underlying theme of all three

---

[26] Fuhrmann, II, 512, note 235. See below, Section 3.

[27] On the diverse recensions and possible manuscript sources, see Fuhrmann, II, 514–15.

[28] Anselm I: 1 = Burchard, *Decretum libri XX* I: 1; I: 52 = *Decr.* I: 42; III: 77 = *Decr.* XVI: 6; III: 81 = *Decr.* I: 132; V: 37 = *Decr.* XI: 27. Cf. Fuhrmann, II, 516, note 246.

[29] Fuhrmann, II, 516–17.

[30] (1) Anselm V: 21 = *Decretum* III: 32 or an independent Ps.Isidore ? (cf. Hinschius, 696). Anselm follows both versions of the text for the first line, and then abbreviates the substance of what follows in both. The only clue lies in the fact that Anselm uses the phrase 'absque ulla mora consecrate' found in Burchard, where the Ps.Iohannes text reads 'absque ulla mora consecrare'. (2) XI: 77 = *Decr.* VII: 1 or an independent Ps.Isidore? (cf. Hinschius, 140). Anselm's text is an abbreviated version of both of the others. (3) VI: 139 = 74T c. 225 or an independent Ps.Isidore? (cf. Hinschius, 145): Anselm follows both versions, save where he uses the phrase 'illis quibus', whereas both the 74T and the Ps.Urban use 'quibus illi'. The only clue lies in the fact that Anselm uses 'Deum veneretis' as does the 74T, whereas the Ps.Urban uses 'Deum veneremini'. Though as Fuhrmann noted (II, 517), there was a parallel of this in Deusdedit, it is clear that he was not dependent upon Anselm, and that the two compilers used the same (perhaps 'intermediate') source.

books. Anselm, as will be seen, by means of some subtle manipulation of his texts, was in fact underscoring the supremacy of the Roman Church, and consequently, of the Roman pontiff.

The Ps.Isidore (and indeed the compiler of the 74T) set out above all with the intention of protecting and safeguarding the rights of the episcopate.[31] By setting in the distance a pontiff to whom the right of final judgement in all episcopal matters was reserved, the Ps.Isidore in essence made effective judgement of the episcopate impossible. These decretals stipulated that a bishop could not be accused or judged by his inferiors, save in those cases where he deviated from the faith. Even there, however, the decretals hedged the question by stipulating that his fellow bishops should first approach him 'unofficially'.[32] Other safeguards were unequivocal. A bishop could not be accused by immoral or unvirtuous people.[33] A bishop could not be despoiled, nor could any procedures be taken against him while he was not in full possession of his office together with all its appurtenances.[34] A bishop could not even be judged by a council which was convened without apostolic knowledge or sanction.[35] A bishop maintained at all times the right to appeal to Rome, and the right to enjoy full status while that appeal was taking place.[36] A bishop was to be granted the indulgence of 'suitable' time to prepare his defence when an accusation or charge was brought, especially if he had been despoiled.[37] These are indeed but a few examples. Yet it quickly becomes apparent that when all else failed, the Ps.Isidorian texts ensured the immunity of the episcopate by pointing to that distant guarantee of episcopal liberty: the Apostolic See. Yet the Apostolic See was a guardian, at least in the Ps.Isidore's view, who was expected not to intervene unless called upon.

Anselm, however, approached the Ps.Isidorian Decretals from the opposite perspective.[38] He made the implicit, if vague, acknowledgement of the papal role in the protection of the episcopate a manifest declaration of the supremacy of the pontiff at the top of the ecclesiastical

---

[31] See Fuhrmann, I, 137–50. Cf. R. Knox, 'Accusing Higher Up', *ZSSRG, kan. Abt.* 108 (1991), 1–31, here 3–5.

[32] e.g. Ps.Calixtus, c. 3 ff. (ed. Hinschius), p. 136; Ps.Anacletus, c. 19, pp. 76 ff.; Ps.Fabianus, c. 23, p. 166; Ps.Iohannes, p. 694.

[33] e.g. Ps.Anacletus, c. 21, pp. 77 ff.; Ps.Fabianus, c. 13, p. 162.

[34] e.g. Ps.Sixtus, c. 6, pp. 108–9; Ps.Fabianus, c. 20, p. 165.

[35] e.g. Ps.Julius, p. 471; Ps.Damasus, c. 11, p. 503.

[36] e.g. Ps.Sixtus I, c. 5, p. 108; Ps.Victor, c. 5, p. 128; Ps.Fabianus, c. 29, p. 168.

[37] e.g. Ps.Eusebius, c. 11, p. 237.

[38] See Fuhrmann, II, 520–2. Cf. R. Knox, 'Accusing Higher Up', 7 ff.; and id., 'Finding the Law', 449.

hierarchy. While there are few instances where it can be shown that Anselm *dramatically* altered a given Ps.Isidorian text, it can be seen that, with careful excerpting and pointed rubrics, Anselm was intent upon 'overcoming' Ps.Isidore, and finding authorities that would contribute to an increasing centralization both of the Church, and of papal supervision over the episcopate.[39] He set about transforming the expression of episcopal guarantees into universal and all-encompassing stipulations of apostolic powers. To a considerable extent, this reflects within a legal framework the reformers' need to devise and articulate strategies: to provide an authoritative basis with which to transform the papacy from passively providing a 'customer's service' into a pro-active force. Some examples seem warranted.[40]

In Book I, textual transmission was largely consistent, although one finds a number of changes in word order, in spelling, and similar minor variants. For the most part, Anselm adhered to the text of the Ps.Isidore (if not always the context), and let the rubrics do the work of emphasis. Although the Ps.Isidore certainly conceded supremacy to the Apostolic See by virtue of the Petrine commission, his texts most assuredly did not always provide the forceful and succinct message which Anselm sought. Two of the most striking examples are found in texts from the Ps.Clement. In the Decretals, these were identified as being part of Clement's 'speech' to the people. The first of these, *Collectio canonum* I: 5, was encapsulated by the rubric 'Quod Christum non recipit qui papam contristaverit'. What is striking is not the fact that Anselm altered the actual text, but rather that there was no reference in that text to the Roman pontiff. The Ps.Clement's text actually said that he who saddens Christ is not received by God![41] The second example, *Collectio canonum* I: 6, again with practically no textual alteration, was also from the Ps.Clement's 'speech'. It was introduced by the rubric 'Quod nec loqui debemus, cui papa non loquitur'. Again there was no reference in the original text to the Roman pontiff. For the Ps.Clement, it was Christ himself who defined relations in Christian society: that is, that no one

---

[39] Fuhrmann noted (II, 521) the case of XII: 8, where Anselm modified the Ps.Silverius text (p. 709) 'apostolica et synodali auctoritate' to simply 'apostolica auctoritate'. This was the only example he noted. Cf. R. Knox, 'Accusing Higher Up', 7, and 'Finding the Law', 449.

[40] For more detailed documentation of Anselm's manipulation of Ps.Isidorian texts, see Appendix Ia. The following examples are taken only from those texts which have been identified as being 'independent' Ps.Isidore. Ps.Isidorian texts via the 74T will be discussed in Section 3.

[41] See Appendix Ia, A, no. 1.

should associate with him who is an enemy of Christ. The Ps.Clement text had little to do with the rubric's undeniable exaltation of the Roman pontiff, which set the pope in Christ's place as definer of relations within Christian society.[42]

In Books II and III, however, modification and adaptation become more apparent. Again it is not so much that Anselm radically altered the existing text, but rather that he transformed its original emphasis. What one discovers most often is that Anselm's text has been removed from the context it had in the Ps.Isidore. For instance, a text which set the Apostolic See as the final but distant guarantor for resolving issues concerning the episcopate was modified by its removal from the Ps.Anacletus' far more wide-ranging discussion of how such issues are to be resolved. This change in context had the effect of conveying that *all* of the more difficult *causae* had to be brought to Rome. The original guarantee of the Ps.Isidore had thus been transformed into an unequivocal expression not only of the power of the Apostolic See, but also of its unique right to intervene in those difficult *causae*.[43]

Frequently the original intention of the Ps.Isidorian text was altered by a particularly pointed rubric title. Not only did the rubric generalize and, as it were, universalize a given local injunction, but often it sharpened ideas regarding the hierarchy of the ecclesiastical order. For instance, an original text which sought to protect the episcopate from local judgement was transformed by Anselm's rubric which distinguished between the lesser rights of the episcopate to scrutinize and debate issues, and the Roman pontiff's all-encompassing and divinely conferred right of definitive judgement.[44] The original safeguard for the episcopate had thus been transformed into an expression of the fullness of apostolic authority in a hierarchical sense.

Some of the most interesting alterations of the original text in the Ps.Isidore are found in those cases where Anselm omitted local or outdated details. The removal of references to apparently obsolete issues, such as the reprehension of Arian bishops or the clash between orthodox and Arian doctrines, gave Anselm the opportunity to use indisputable 'ancient' canons while at the same time signalling their continuing relevance. This, of course, was a task which faced anyone

---

[42] See Appendix Ia, A, no. 2.

[43] See Appendix Ia, B, nos. 1, 4. The role of Anselm as well as that of the 74T in insisting upon the referral to Rome of all of the difficult *causae* was an important one, emphasizing the 'caput et cor' quality of the Roman See. See below, Ch. 3.

[44] See Appendix Ia, B, nos. 3, 5.

appealing to earlier authorities: to effect a meaningful dialogue with the past in the context of the present. Modifications of this sort can also be found in Books XII and XIII where Anselm employed texts written to combat fifth-century heresies to support his condemnation of eleventh-century schismatics whom he identified as heretics. Here, Anselm can be seen almost groping for categories to describe these 'new' heresies which were effectively the product of the need to vilify the opponents of reform. With such modifications, he created universal, and relevant canons, from what were specific and perhaps out-dated injunctions.[45]

This is not to say that Anselm was always 'creative' with his Ps.Isidorian texts. Elsewhere in Book II, and particularly in Book III, Anselm remained true to the 'episcopal' tenor of his Ps.Isidorian sources. In these instances, the textual transmission was in general accurate and consistent. The context was often not corrupted, and the rubrics were far less pointed, and even, on occasion, were simple summaries.[46] Perhaps as a reflection of his own experience, Anselm was certainly aware of the immense disadvantages of placing the episcopate at the mercy of local forces. As will be seen, however, Anselm on the whole followed the pro-episcopal quality of the Ps.Isidore only with texts chosen from the 74T.[47]

Although dramatic alteration occasionally occurred,[48] a true appreciation of Anselm's adaptation of his Ps.Isidorian texts depends in the end upon seeing those texts as Anselm may have understood them. He viewed the Ps.Isidorian texts not as manifestations of a robust episcopate protected by a barrier of complicated canonical procedure, which in times of local crisis, could none the less summon the papacy for help.

---

[45] See Appendix Ia, B, nos. 9 and 10. There are, however, many instances where Anselm maintained the references (not only in the text itself) to outdated or local issues, for instance, I: 15, Ps.Marcellus, c. 1, 2, p. 223 under the rubric 'Ut Antiocena ecclesia Romanae sit subiecta nec ab eius dissentiat dispositione'. Though by the 11th cent. the hierarchy of the early sees was not exactly a burning issue, this may reflect tensions resulting from the schism of 1080.

[46] See Appendix Ia, C, nos. 1, 3.

[47] There are in addition a number of what have been termed 'genuine' texts, not noted by Fuhrmann, which may have been provided through the Ps.Isidorian Decretals. As noted above, the collection contained a number of genuine texts, notably Gelasius. While the Ps.Isidore's transmission did not differ radically from independent transmission of these sources, there are a few important variants. Though excerpts from some of these are found in the 74T, it became clear during the examination of Anselm's 74T texts that the 74T may have been at best a guide in this respect, as it can be shown that Anselm looked to other sources, notably independent Ps.Isidorian transmission of Gelasius and Felix. See below, Section 3, and Appendix Ib and Ic.

[48] e.g. Appendix Ia, B, no. 4.

Rather, he saw them from the papal end, as indicating that the bishop of Rome not only held sway over other, merely local, bishops, but that it was also his right and duty to bring them into line. Anselm effectively reversed the emphasis, transforming the Ps.Isidore's final guarantor for the episcopate into the head of the universal and ordered Church. Whether used in isolation, or, as frequently was the case, in conjunction with each other, these various modifications suggest not only that Anselm knew precisely towards what ends the Ps.Isidorian texts were aimed, but how he wanted to transform them.

3. ANSELM AND THE 74T

THE *Diversorum patrum sententie sive Collectio in LXXIV titulos digesta* [74T] was one of the earliest, and one of the most significant of the 'reform collections'. Both with, and without, the so-called Swabian Appendix, the 74T was widely diffused. It served as a formal source not only for Anselm and Deusdedit, but also for a number of post-Gregorian collections.[49] Unlike Anselm's compilation, however, the 74T had no pretensions towards being a comprehensive collection. Much smaller in scale, the 74T was organized somewhat like a sentence collection: the basic form being seventy-four titles, each supported by varying numbers of chapters, totalling 315.

The principal material, and formal source of the 74T was the Ps.Isidorian Decretals, which provided some 250 texts—146 of which were false—according to Gilchrist, the collection's editor.[50] While in terms of genre the sources were varied, the compiler showed an unde-

---

[49] *Diversorum patrum sententie* (as above no. 2); English translation as *The Collection in Seventy-Four Titles: A Canon Law Manual of the Gregorian Reform* (Medieval Sources in Translation, 22; Toronto, 1980); on the dating see *Div. pat. sent.*, pp. xxvii ff. On the 74T in general, see P. Fournier, 'Le premier manuel canonique de la réforme du XIe siècle', *Mélanges d'archéologie et d'histoire*, 14 (1894), 142–223, though his contention that the 74T was a papally-oriented collection has largely been dispelled. On the MSS and their diffusion, see *Div. pat. sent.*, pp. xvii–xxxii. Gilchrist believed that Anselm used the so-called Montecassino recension. The Swabian Appendix—an addition of 15 titles concerning excommunication compiled probably by Bernold of Constance, was begun perhaps as early as 1077, but was not completed before 1086. On Bernold, the Swabian recension, and the Swabian Appendix, see *Div. pat. sent.*, pp. xxvii ff., lxxviii ff., and J. Autenrieth, 'Bernold von Konstanz und die erweiterte 74T', *DA* 14 (1958), 206–38. See also below, Appendix Id. The 74T was the basis for the Collection in 2 Books (MS Vat. 3832) (1085?), the Collectio Tarraconensis (1085–90?), and the Collection in 3 (4) Books (1085?). On these, see Stickler, *Historia*, 175–7.

[50] See *Div. pat. sent.*, pp. lxxxix ff. Cf. below, Tables II and III. According to Gilchrist, it is doubtful that the compiler consulted any other 'original' formal source apart from the Ps.Isidore.

niable preference for papal decretals. Gregory I figured prominently, providing some 47 texts (40 of which are found in the Register) with an additional two from John the Deacon's *Vita Gregorii Magni*. Leo I accounted for 29 texts, Innocent I for 16, and Gelasius for 13. Conciliar texts, however, were of little significance to this compiler, providing only two chapters.[51] Civil law texts, largely from the Theodosian Code—via Hincmar of Rheims's *Pro ecclesiae libertatum defensione*—made a modest contribution, accounting for some six texts.[52] Patristic sources, however, were on the whole noticeably lacking: among them, only five from Cyprian, one from Isidore of Seville, and notably, none from Augustine.[53]

First used *c*.1076, the 74T, while technically responding to the reformers' desire for new canonical compilations, none the less cannot be seen as being a special product of the Gregorian camp in the way that Anselm's collection can.[54] Its emphasis upon judicial rights and procedures, however, does demonstrate the important link in general terms between ecclesiastical reform and the surge in the production of canonical collections. Yet like his Ps.Isidorian exemplar, the compiler of the 74T was concerned above all with the criminal, judicial, and other legal aspects which affected the secular clergy, particularly the episcopate.[55] Another prominent issue was the worthiness of candidates for clerical office, and the criteria by which they were to be selected.[56] The powers of the ministers of the Church were also set out, as were stipulations regarding their liturgical, and sacramental functions.[57]

Somewhat surprisingly, perhaps, the issue of Roman primacy occupied a relatively small percentage of texts. A mere seven titles with a total of 37 *capitula* considered the Roman pontiff and the primacy of the Apostolic See.[58] A closer examination of these, however, reveals that for the compiler of the 74T, Roman primacy was essentially conceived in

---

[51] 74T c. 136 [Council of Toledo VIII c. 3]; and c. 312 [Council of Toledo IV, c. 49], wrongly attributed to Ambrose. See above, note 7.

[52] 74T cc. 33–8. These passed into Anselm IV: 13–18.

[53] 74T c. 137 is attributed erroneously to Augustine; the text is Leo I, ep. 12, c. 2. Anselm correctly identified the text in VI: 29.

[54] A survey of the controversy surrounding the compiler, the origin, the date and the aims of the collection is found in H. Fuhrmann, 'Über den Reformgeist der 74-Titel Sammlung', in *Festschrift für Hermann Heimpel zum 70. Geburtstag*, 2 vols. (Veröffentlichen des Max-Planck-Instituts für Geschichte, 36; Göttingen, 1972), II, 1101–20. See also Gilchrist, *The Collection in Seventy-Four Titles*, 29 ff.

[55] 74T tits. 5–14, cc. 44–110 (a total of 67 chapters).

[56] 74T tits. 15–21, cc. 111–73 (63 chapters).

[57] 74T tits. 25–8, cc. 186–202 (17 chapters); tits. 29–37, cc. 203–21: liturgical/sacramental functions (19 chapters).   [58] 74T tits. 1, 2, 22–4, 43, 44.

terms of being a more strictly judicial supremacy, and not a doctrinal or theological one. For instance, Title 1, with twenty supporting canons (eight of which were Ps.Isidorian) addressed the primacy of the Roman Church. Yet the emphasis of these chapters centred upon the notion of Rome—herself unable to be judged—as the final court of appeal.[59] A more encompassing Roman primacy was indicated only by virtue of Christ's personal commission to Peter, and, significantly, accounted for a mere five chapters.[60] Title 2, supported by only three canons, confirmed Roman primacy over the other sees in terms of the double apostle factor, i.e. that Sts Peter and Paul suffered at Rome on the same day. Title 22, supported by four canons, addressed itself to the moral character of the Roman pontiff, emphasizing that he was obliged to act in a way that would not desecrate the sanctity of the Holy See. Title 23, supported by six canons, demanded observance of papal decrees. One of its texts from Leo I, however, did note the pontiff's discretionary power to modify outdated decrees.[61] Title 24, with only two texts, introduced the negative issue that no one was to be called universal. It was a canon in direct contradiction of Gregory VII's arrogation of universality, though not of other reform collections.[62] Titles 43 and 44 completed the specifically papal consideration on a more mundane note each with one chapter, one dealing with the cantors of the Roman Church, and the other concerning the arrangements for the pope's funeral bier.

The 74T was an important formal source for Anselm in a strictly textual sense, transmitting Ps.Isidorian and other texts.[63] These were usually incorporated into Anselm's collection in small groupings.[64] It should, however, already be clear from the above that there was a wide divergence in opinion and intention between Anselm and the compiler of the 74T. It is therefore of tremendous importance that the ends towards which Anselm used texts from the 74T are carefully considered. Although there are a number of instances where transmission was identical, closer scrutiny of the evidence suggests that Anselm envisaged the 74T as little more than a guidebook or compendium of canonical texts, to be altered, re-ordered and, especially, re-directed towards different ends.[65]

---

[59] 74T cc. 1–3, 6–8, 11, 17.   [60] 74T cc. 3, 4, 9, 12, 18.

[61] 74T c. 180, Leo I, ep. 167 [*PL* 54, 1202].

[62] *Reg*.II: 55a, c. 2 Quod solus Romanus pontifex iure dicatur universalis. Anselm followed the 74T, using its transmission of Ps.Pelagius II and Gregory I in VI: 117–18.

[63] e.g. Anselm IV: 1–9; 13–18 = 74T cc. 24–32; 33–8.   [64] See below, Table III.

[65] See Fuhrmann, II, 513. The insufficiency of the 74T in general terms is apparent in the addition of the Swabian Appendix, which should be seen as a deliberate corrective to the original collection.

As Table II shows, the bulk of Anselm's Ps.Isidorian texts from the 74T are found in Books III and VI of the *Collectio canonum*. It seems well worth noting that it was in these two books that Ps.Isidorian texts coming from the 74T substantially outnumber those identified as being independent Ps.Isidore. Book III is perhaps of greater significance, not least in numerical terms.[66] In both cases, however, the selection of the 74T as a principal formal source is unsurprising. These two books addressed the very issues which had also been of paramount importance to the compiler of the 74T: judicial procedures, and the status of the episcopate.

It has already been seen that while many of the independent Ps.Isidorian texts were modified beyond an implicit acknowledgement of the judicial primacy of Rome in order to convey a more encompassing primacy, Anselm often remained faithful to the Ps.Isidore's intentions, above all in Book III. Anselm's adherence to the 74T's transmission of Ps.Isidore in Books III and VI should perhaps be seen in a similar light. This fidelity not merely reflects his interest in providing a comprehensive collection, but also seems to emphasize Anselm's very deliberate attitude towards his sources. That is to say, Anselm seems to have read quite clearly the tone of the 74T, and saw its value in terms of being a formal source for *selected* issues. Its insufficiency as a comprehensive source for Anselm is demonstrated in the first place by this very selectivity. It is also apparent in those instances where it can be suggested that Anselm may have ignored, or better still, rejected, the 74T's transmission of a Ps.Isidorian text in favour of an independent one. Some examples seem warranted.[67]

In the broadest terms, Anselm generally adhered to the intention and tenor of his 74T exemplar regarding its transmission of Ps.Isidorian texts. One does, however, often find a more exacting interpretation of the text in question in Anselm's collection, as was the case with the independent Ps.Isidorian texts. As before, this was achieved largely by means of authorial re-direction in the rubric title.[68] For instance, in a text of Ps.Calixtus found under title 1 of the 74T, *De primatu Romanae ecclesiae*, Anselm carefully re-directed attention towards the issue of judicial supremacy which the text actually addressed with the rubric

---

[66] See below, Table II.   [67] For more detailed documentation, see Appendix Ib.
[68] Rarely did Anselm use the 74T's title, e.g. title 4 De monachorum monasterio-rumque libertate (V: 54); title 48 De ieiunio clericorum ante pascha (VII: 156). The only title of significance used by Anselm was title 24: Ne universalis quisquam vocetur (VI: 117).

'Quod a regulis Romanae ecclesiae nullatenus convenit deviare'. Texts which figured in the 74T under its assertion of Roman primacy were often employed by Anselm in a more narrow judicial sense.[69]

Elsewhere, and particularly in Book III, Anselm did remain almost entirely faithful to his exemplar.[70] A large proportion of these texts were taken from title 5 of the 74T, which considered the procedures for accusation and for those bringing accusations. Anselm's rubrics were not quite as interpretative as has been seen on other occasions, textual transmission being almost identical. Of course, insistence upon rigorous adherence to judicial procedure was an important aim of reform, and one which Anselm most definitely supported.

In other places, however, Anselm seems to have judged that the 74T's transmission of a given Ps.Isidorian text was inadequate or insufficient for his purposes. In such instances, he seems to have turned to one of his 'independent' Ps.Isidorian formal sources, favouring its transmission over that of the 74T for reasons at which we can often only guess. It is a puzzling phenomenon, not least because there is little information about how the collection was compiled or by what procedures texts were selected. Yet when considering those texts where Anselm seems to have rejected a 74T transmission in favour of an independent Ps.Isidorian source, one occasionally finds significant evidence to indicate that it was done purposefully, and not at random.[71] A striking example is a text of Ps.Vigilius, found in *Collectio canonum* I: 9. Fuhrmann believed that it was an independent Ps.Isidore, although Gilchrist identified it as being from the 74T.[72] The text in question concerned the issue of Roman primacy. Both in Anselm, and in the 74T, it was found under this heading. Yet the 74T, which had a much fuller citation of the Ps.Vigilius text, stressed that this primacy was contingent upon the supremacy of Rome over the other churches in a judicial sense: the fact of Rome's primacy in terms of being the appropriate venue for cases involving bishops. Anselm, whose text omitted this final section, noted primacy in a more complete and doctrinal sense: namely that of her *plenitudo potestatis*.[73] Other cases, however, where an independent Ps.Isidore was used as opposed to one in the 74T, offer less conclusive justifications.[74]

Turning to Anselm's use of the 74T as a formal source of genuine texts, one finds a somewhat different picture. The 74T was an important source for genuine texts, accounting for some 136 *capitula*. (This

---

[69] See Appendix Ib, A.   [70] See Appendix Ib, B.   [71] See Appendix Ib, C.
[72] Fuhrmann, II, p. 513 and note 236. Cf. apparatus for 74T c. 12, p. 25.
[73] See Appendix Ib, C, nos. 1–2.   [74] See Appendix Ib, C, nos. 3 ff.

does not include the texts that are found both in Anselm and in the Swabian Appendix.) The most important of these were texts from Gregory I, Leo I, Innocent I, and Gelasius I, who together accounted for 105. It is important, however, to recognize here that these, along with all of the genuine texts from the 74T, accounted for only a small percentage of Anselm's genuine texts. Anselm clearly had a variety of other sources at his disposal.[75]

The majority of Anselm's genuine texts from the 74T were concentrated in Books VI and VII, with texts predominantly from Gregory I and Leo I. These popes offered formidable support for the overriding concern of the compiler of the 74T—the episcopate—and were used as such.[76] As was seen with the Ps.Isidorian texts from the 74T, Anselm used the 74T's transmission of such texts to support his own books on the same subject. Somewhat surprisingly however, at least at first glance, texts from the 74T also figured prominently in Book VII, supporting Anselm's consideration of the *vita communis*—an issue which was not of particular interest to the compiler of the 74T. The title of Book VII, however, is somewhat deceptive. It contained, in fact, a myriad of often very brief texts concerning clerical morals, behaviour, promotion, and not simply texts stipulating the full-blown communal life favoured by Anselm. Book VII was in essence almost a practical compendium of texts on the relations between the lower orders of clergy. It offered advice on more mundane and even trivial concerns. While it is perhaps unfair to regard rules on the reception of pilgrims and unknown persons into holy orders (VII: 21), and the promotion of laymen in general to orders, as trivial, it does seem significant that Anselm selected a number of texts concerning these more practical, less partisan issues, from the 74T. Its noticeable preoccupation with procedure and the firm establishment of the relations between the ecclesiastical orders clearly made it the appropriate formal source.[77] This is not to say, of course, that these matters were of little significance to Anselm. On the contrary, the length of the book suggests the opposite. Yet it is interesting to see

---

[75] See Fournier, 'Les Collections canoniques', 310–17; Fournier/Le Bras, II, 28–33; and Stickler, 171.

[76] See Table III. It is important to remember, however, that there were in all some 106 genuine decretals in Book VI, and some 80 in Book VII. Cf. Table I.

[77] e.g. a number of Anselm's texts were taken from tit. 16, on the issue of to whom sacred orders are to be given and denied. Others were taken from tit. 17, on the premise that holy orders should not be given to those who are unknown; from tit. 19, on the ordination of priests and deacons; and from tit. 47, that clerics and priests should not be acquisitive.

another example of Anselm's selectivity in his formal sources having, as it were, a thematic justification. Needless to say, Anselm went elsewhere for texts specifically advocating the extremely strict interpretation of the communal life which he advocated.[78]

Anselm's transmission of genuine texts from the 74T tends, on the whole, to be far more faithful, and far less capricious, than was the case with his Ps.Isidorian ones. In Book VI, in particular, transmission was accurate in almost every sense: the tenor was not modified by pointed rubrics, nor was the wording altered in any substantive sense. Leo I and Gregory I were consistently used within the spirit intended by the compiler of the 74T.[79]

Among the most interesting of Anselm's 'genuine' texts from the 74T were those from Gelasius, who will serve as the example for more detailed consideration. Although Anselm's Gelasian texts from the 74T were not significant in strictly numerical terms, his transmission of these texts offers a pointed example of why he may have regarded the 74T as being insufficient as a comprehensive source. At the same time, his transmission offers evidence of some important developments in the use of Gelasian texts generally.[80]

As was the case with his Ps.Isidorian texts, Anselm made a number of modifications to the 74T's transmission of Gelasian texts. In fact, those texts which were modified, or re-directed, actually equal in number those which were uniformly taken from the 74T.[81] Again, however, there is evidence that Anselm seems to have rejected, or ignored the 74T's transmission in favour of another Gelasian source.[82] Yet even where the 74T's transmission had been largely preserved, significant modifications, whether from rubrics or omissions, are apparent. What is striking about this, as was the case with his Ps.Isidorian texts, is the fact that Anselm's 'independent'

---

[78] E.g. Anselm VII: 3: De communi vita clericorum et eorum qui se continere non possunt [Gregory I, *Reg.* XI: 56a]; VII: 5: Augustinus in sermone suo de communi vita clericorum [Augustine, Sermo 355]. Cf. C. Dereine, 'Le Problème de la vie commune chez les canonistes d'Anselme de Lucques à Gratien', *SG* 3 (1948), 287–98.

[79] Hence the title of book VI: De electione et ordinatione ac de omni potestate sive statu episcoporum.

[80] For more detailed documentation, see Appendix Ic. This only notes Gelasian texts which are, at least in part, found in the 74T. Anselm's other Gelasian texts will be considered in Section 4. In general, see R. L. Benson, 'The Gelasian Doctrine: Uses and Transformations', 13–44.

[81] See Appendix Ic. It must be conceded that there are minor variants, even in those which largely adhered to the 74T's transmission.

[82] See Appendix Ic, A, nos. 2, 3, 5. As indicated in Appendix Ic, Anselm's formal Gelasian source often may have been Ps.Isidore, the most important vehicle for Gelasian texts.

or modified Gelasian texts can be divided from those uniformly transmitted from the 74T in thematic terms. That is to say, there seems to have been significant justification in terms of content, and/or emphasis, either for Anselm's modification, or for his rejection, of the 74T's transmission. Indeed, the Gelasian texts which Anselm more or less identically transmitted from the 74T addressed the relatively speaking more basic, more mundane, and more procedural considerations such as the laying of charges, that no one could retain the servant of another, and so on.[83]

This is not to imply that Anselm considered such issues unimportant. But if, as has been argued throughout this discussion of Anselm's sources, it was among his chief priorities to stress the hierarchical nature of the Church as the necessary starting-point for reform, then textual transmission and modification towards these ends must be significant. The fact that Anselm introduced the famous Gelasian letter to the Emperor Anastasius under a rubric referring to the *auctoritas pontificis*, while the 74T used the more generic, and conservative, *auctoritas sacerdotalis* in its heading, cannot simply be regarded as fortuitous.[84] Likewise, when Anselm did not use the 74T's version of Gelasius on the consecration of basilicas, it cannot be mere coincidence first that his rubric demanded apostolic sanction for the consecration of *any* basilica, and second that he proceeded to quote from the Gelasian text, thus implying that this was merely one aspect of Rome's control over every facet of ecclesiastical life.[85]

The 74T was undoubtedly an important guide for Anselm. Unfortunately, there is no information as to when or how he used it during the compilation of the *Collectio canonum*. The answers to all these questions would be extremely helpful in establishing Anselm's attitude towards the 74T as a formal source. John Gilchrist argued that Horst Fuhrmann had overemphasized those few instances where Anselm had not always maintained the full 74T text.[86] In light of what has been said above, this view perhaps needs to be challenged. Anselm's numerous modifications, and not simply those where he omitted part of the 74T text, cannot all be due to chance, faulty texts, or scribal negligence. Some, if not most, must be understood as deliberate correctives on the part of Anselm to what he perceived as the inadequacies of the 74T's transmission of texts and, more important, as the insufficiency of that collection in general as a guide to papally-inspired reform.

---

[83] See Appendix Ic, B.   [84] See Appendix Ic, A, no. 3.
[85] See Appendix Ic, A, no. 5.
[86] J. T. Gilchrist, *The Collection in Seventy-Four Titles*, 32, note 49.

4. SOME OTHER GENUINE AND PATRISTIC SOURCES

WHILE many of Anselm's texts ultimately derived from a Pseudo-Isidorian source, most of the *capitula* in the collection were genuine ones. The *Dionysio-Hadriana*, the *Anselmo Dedicata*, the *Collectio Avellana*, Burchard, and the 74T, among others (including the Ps.Isidore) provided Anselm with many of his genuine texts. A number of these, according to Fournier, may have come from original sources, or intermediate compilations which are no longer extant.[87]

The vast number of genuine texts in the collection prohibits here any consideration of transmission along the lines previously used in connection with Anselm's Ps.Isidorian sources. The texts are so widely varied that it is difficult to classify them in a more manageable fashion than that attempted in Table I. Yet even classification in this manner results in categories so large that it is difficult to deal with them in any systematic way. On the whole, Anselm's transmission of genuine texts seems to have been accurate or faithful.[88] There can be no doubt that modification, generalization, and different emphasis by means of the rubrics in particular, such as has been seen with the Ps.Isidorian texts, occurred in the transmission of the genuine ones. It would, however, be an impossible task to check the transmission of all of Anselm's genuine texts, provided of course it was actually possible to identify the precise formal source for every text. Since our principal aim is to explore what can be known of Anselm's attitude towards his sources, and whether an agenda was being set, we can perhaps be more selective.

As previously noted, Anselm preferred papal decretals as the clearest and most authoritative sources, turning especially to Gregory I, Leo I, Nicholas I, Innocent I, and Pelagius I, among other early pontiffs, for many of his texts. Gregory I was perhaps Anselm's single most important material source. As was the case for many of the eleventh-century canonists, Gregory I was a comprehensive authority. His letters provided important texts on episcopal matters, on moral concerns of the clergy, and on the ordering of the ecclesiastical hierarchy in general.[89]

---

[87] See Table I. On the new sources, see Fournier, 'Les Collections canoniques', 311 ff.; and Fournier/Le Bras, II, 28 ff.

[88] See Fournier, 'Les Collections canoniques', 317 ff., and Fournier/Le Bras, II, 28 ff.

[89] While texts from Gregory I are spread throughout the collection, the majority are found in Books V, VI, and VII, which addressed episcopal matters, and the clergy in general. Many of these came from the 74T. *Book V*: De ordinationibus ecclesiarum: 17 texts [Anselm 12, 22, 24–6, 28 (= 74T c. 128), 30, 34 (= 74T c. 269), 35 (= 74T c. 270), 44,

Gregory, however, also offered important comments on what is perhaps the most innovative element of Anselm's collection: the recognition that coercive action might be needed against those who dissented from the Church.[90]

Pelagius I was another crucial source in this respect. Even more than Gregory I, Pelagius actually advocated the use of coercive action to maintain unity.[91] Anselm's formal source for these texts is somewhat unclear, although they certainly were texts only recently coming into

49, 54 (= 74T c. 39), 55 (= 74T c. 41), 56 (= 74T c. 42), 57, 60, 61]. *Book VI*: De electione . . . episcoporum: 46 texts [Anselm 10, 11, 22, 23, 25, 26, 49, 50, 67 (= 74T c. 125), 68 (= 74T c. 126), 69 (= 74T c. 127), 71 (= 74T c. 131), 72 (= 74T c. 133), 73 (= 74T c. 132), 78 (= 74T c. 134), 79 (= 74T c. 135), 81–4, 85 (= 74T c. 235), 86–8, 94–6, 118 (= 74T c. 185), 119, 120, 128 (= 74T c. 246), 130, 131 (= 74T c. 259), 132 (= 74T c. 261), 133, 147, 148, 151, 161, 170–3, 179, 180, 184 (= 74T c. 173)]. *Book VII*: De communi vita: 27 texts [Anselm 3, 6, 21 (= 74T c. 159), 35, 39, 60 (= 74T c. 233), 64–70, 87, 94 (= 74T c. 258), 106, 111, 127, 129, 151, 163 (= 74T c. 43), 164 (= 74T c. 40), 165 (= 74T c. 232), 171–4]. Somewhat surprising perhaps, there are only 11 texts from Gregory in the first three books: Anselm I: 25, 56, 70; II: 68; III: 30, 69, 85 (= 74T c. 102), 90, 100, 101, 110.

[90] Anselm XII: 11 Quod non debet quis ei communicare quem sedes apostolica repellit nisi ab illatis se mundaverit [Gregory I, *Reg.* VI: 26]; XII: 12 ⟨no rubric⟩ [fo. 210ᵛ] 'Pervenit ad me quosdam vestrorum ignorantia vel necessitate deceptos his qui ab apostolica sede culpa, sicut nostis, exigente communione privati sunt, communicasse, quosdam vero se salubri discretione protegente Domino suspendisse . . . Ne inde reus ante conspectum eterni iudicis unde poterat salvari consistat' [*Reg.* VI: 46]; XII: 22 (cf. 74T c. 314) Ut propter propriam iniuriam nullus excommunicare quemquam presumat [*Reg.* II: 47]; XII: 23 (cf. 74T c. 315) Quod pastores dum pro suis voluntatibus iniuste solvunt vel ligant, ipsa se potestate privant [*Homilies*, II, 126, 5].

XIII: 6 De persequendo hostes [*Reg.* II: 7]; XIII: 7 Item de eadem re [*Reg.* II: 32]; XIII: 8 De predando hostes [*Reg.* II: 33]; XIII: 9 De habenda oboedientia [*Reg.* II: 34]; XIII: 20 Quando mali sunt tolerandi, vel quando deserendi [*Vita s. Benedicti*, II, c. 3]; XIII: 23 ⟨no rubric⟩ (Cambridge, Corpus Christi 269 = Quod reginae corrigendi malefactores potestas datur) [*Reg.* VIII: 4]; XIII: 25 ⟨no rubric⟩ (Corpus 269 = Ut rectores ecclesiae et iudices saeculares non temere proferant sententiam) [*Moralia in Job*, Lib. 19, c. 23]; XIII: 28 ⟨no rubric⟩ (Corpus 269 = Quod christianus princeps sicut terrenum peragit bellum, sic contra hereticos aecclesiasticum peragit praelium) [*Reg.* I: 72]; XIII: 29 ⟨no rubric⟩ (Corpus 269 = Quod victoria religiosi principis non ex opinione humana sed ex Deo disponente proveniat) [*Reg.* I: 73]. See Appendix II for more details.

[91] Anselm XII: 41 Quod non est consecratio sed execratio quae extra aecclesiam sit [Pelagius, JK no. 983]; XII: 42 Quod papa Aquileiensem et Mediolanensem episcopum ad principem sub custodia dirigi praecepit, et quotiens de universali synodo dubitatur, ab apostolica sede veritas requiratur [Pelagius, JK no. 1018]; XII: 43 Quod scismaticus non conficit corpus Christi cui catholici non debent sociari [Pelagius, JK no. 994]; XII: 44 Quod aecclesia non persequitur sed diligit cum punit vel prohibet malum, et divisi a sede apostolica scismatici sunt, et comprimendi sunt a saecularibus iniusti episcopi [Pelagius, JK no. 1018]; XII: 45 Quod nullis [nullum] sacrificium Deo a potestatibus gratius est quam ut scismatici episcopi ab [ad] obediendum coerceantur [Pelagius, JK no. 1024]; XII: 46 De scismaticis coercendis a secularibus [Pelagius, JK no. 1012]. See Appendix II for more details.

circulation. Here again, there is the convenient, if not wholly satisfactory, explanation of intermediate collections. Yet the presence of some
of these Pelagian texts in the *Collectio Brittanica* may indicate the existence of some intermediary collection or source used by Anselm.[92]
These texts are of particular significance, as they are not found in
Burchard, the *Collectio V. librorum*, the 74T, or in Ps.Isidore.

Like Gregory I, Gelasius was another important authority, offering
meaningful statements on the issues of papal primacy, relations within
the hierarchy, and especially on the increasingly critical issue of the relationship of the Church with secular powers.[93] In general terms, moreover, Anselm's transmission of Gelasian texts reveals that some quite
innovative interpretations were taking place in certain circles. This is
most apparent in the use of the *Duo sunt* letter to the emperor
Anastasius, and the *Tomus* on Christ's separation of the two powers.
Anselm's version, in essence, transforms the traditional Gelasian ideal
into a ringing statement of ecclesiastical superiority. Whereas men like
Peter Damian and the compiler of the 74T had used the texts to underscore the functional separation and distinction of the two powers while
emphasizing their interdependence and the obligation to co-operate,
Anselm employed them more narrowly, to postulate what he believed to

---

[92] *Collectio Brittanica*, British Library, MS Addit. 8873: Epistolae Pelagii, fos. 21ʳ–38ᵛ.
Some of the early fragments are under false inscriptions to Gelasius. Though *Coll. Britt.*
does contain some of the Pelagian texts on coercion used by Anselm in Book XII, a direct
dependence cannot be established between the two as they exist now, as the texts are not
identical. An intermediary source seems probable. Anselm XII: 41: cf. *Coll.Britt.*, Epist.
Pelagii, no. 11 [MS Addit. 8873, fos. 25ᵛ–26ʳ]; XII: 42: cf. no. 46 [fo. 32]; XII: 43: cf. no.
22 [fos. 27ᵛ–28ʳ]; XII: 44: cf. no. 46 [fo. 32]; XII: 45: cf. no. 52 [fo. 34]; XII: 46: cf. no.
40 [fo. 31ʳ].
    See Fournier, 'Les Collections canoniques', 311 ff. On *Coll. Britt.*, see above, note 5,
and Fournier/Le Bras, II, 155–63.
[93] And as with Gregory I, texts from Gelasius were spread relatively uniformly
throughout the collection, addressing a variety of issues. Only Books III and VIII had no
Gelasian texts (in III, one is cited as Gelasisus, but is actually Ps.Pelagius II). Unlike
Gregory, Gelasius did figure in Book I on papal primacy. Anselm I: 31 [Epist. 14 ad uni-
versos episcopos per Lucaniam, Brutios et Siciliam constitutis (Thiel, p. 366 or
Ps.Isidorian?); 46 [ibid., p. 356]; 47 [epist. 26 ad episcopos Dardaniae (forma brev.), p.
416]; 48 [ibid., p. 416]; 49 [ibid., p. 415]; 50 [cited as Gelasius, but Symmachus, synod a.
502]; 52 [cited as Gelasius, but Ps.Isidore, preface]; 67 [epist. 42: *De recipiendis et non recipiendis libris*, p. 455 (cf. 74T c. 22)]; 68 [ibid., p. 454 (cf. 74T c. 22)]; 71 [epist. 12 ad
Anastasium, p. 351 (cf. 74T cc. 227–8)]. Others are found at Anselm II: 16 (= 74T c. 10),
24, 32, 56; IV: 27, 51; V: 4 (cf. 74T c. 209), 5–7, 11, 15, 19, 64; VI: 35, 41–2, 109–10,
134, 144, 187; VII: 15 (cf. 74T c. 155), 24–5, 32, 38 (cf. 74T c. 166), 53, 76, 79, 85, 109,
144, 145 (= 74T c. 182), 170 (= 74T c. 231); IX: 11 (= 74T c. 219); X: 9; XI: 5 (cf.
Swabian Appendix c. 320), 78(?), 80 (= 74T c. 254); XII: 20 (= 74T c. 256), 21 (cf. Swab.
App. c. 327, no. 12), 28 (cf. Swab. App. cc. 323–4); 29, 37 (apocryphal), 67; XIII: 22.

be the correct order of the world.[94] In addition, though Gelasian texts were not specifically used in the collection to support the lawfulness of coercive action, Gelasius' injunctions concerning excommunication were clearly of importance. Anselm notably included the famous Gelasian text on the futility of ostracizing heretics, if those who communicated with them were not similarly penalized.[95]

Redirection, however, was not only limited to older texts, and sources. One of the most interesting transmissions in the collection occurred with a near-contemporary text from Peter Damian's *De privilegio Romanae ecclesiae ad Hildebrandum*—his report of the legation to Milan undertaken with Anselm's uncle, Anselm I, at the request of Pope Nicholas II in 1059.[96] The text in Anselm's collection, identified as *ex epistola Nicolai papae iunioris Mediolanensibus missa*, claimed first of all, in the rubric, that the Roman Church had instituted all ecclesiastical dignities, though she alone was the product of divine foundation.[97] In the original text however, Damian had pointed to the *agency* of Rome, through which all ecclesiastical dignities had been divinely founded. Whereas Damian had stressed the instrumentality of Rome because of her special status, Anselm's version severely narrowed the sense by insisting upon Rome's *direct* institution of all ecclesiastical dignities. Although, as in cases earlier examined, it cannot be said unequivocally that Anselm was directly responsible for these alterations, this was, in effect, a 'new' source that had not appeared in any previous collection.

---

[94] Anselm I: 71 Quod auctoritate pontificum et potestate regum mundus regitur et regalis tamen potestas subiecta esse debet pontificibus [Gelasius, epist. 12 (via Ps.Isidore?); cf. 74T cc. 227–8; and Appendix Ic, A, no. 3]; Gelasius, *Tomus de anathematis vinculo* via Nicholas I, in I: 72: Quod sacerdotibus imperatores obedire debent non iubere [Nicholas I, JE no. 2796]. See Benson, 'The Gelasian Doctine: Uses and Transformations', 24 ff.

[95] Anselm XII: 21 Quod par culpa est communicare heretico vel ei qui coniunctus est illi [Gelasius, epist. 27, c. 11, ex Ps.Isidore?, p. 649 (cf. Swab. App. c. 327, no. 12)]; XII: 28 Quod audientiam denegatur excommunicatis post annum, et de eadem ut supra [Gelasius, frag. 37 (cf. Swab. App. cc. 323–4)]; XII: 29 Quod absolutionem quam superstes non quaesivit mortuus impetrare non potuit [epist. 18]; XII: 37 Si quis audet transmutare quod sancti patres et universales synodi statuerunt condemnatus est [apocryphal Gelasius, see Thiel, p. 612, no. 7]; XII: 67 Quod Acacius iuste et canonice sit damnatus [epist. 26, probably not ex Ps.Isidore, see pp. 641 ff.]; XIII: 22 Quod non putetur fallax qui quod promisit superna dispositione praeventus adimplere praetermisit [epist. 30, c. 11 ff.]. This does not include XII: 20, which was taken from the 74T; see Appendix Ic, B, no. 6. See also E. Vodola, 'Sovereignty and Tabu: Evolution of the Sanction against Communication with Excommunicates', in *Studia in honorem eminentissimi cardinalis A. M. Stickler*, ed. R. J. Card. Castillo Lara (Rome, 1992), 581–98.

[96] Reindel, II, no. 65, pp. 228–47.

[97] Anselm I: 63 Quod Romana ecclesia omnes instituit dignitates ecclesiasticas, ipsam autem verbum illud fundavit, per quod creata sunt omnia.

The more hierarchical view supported by this modified text in Anselm's collection clearly suggests both a deliberate agenda, and a deliberate adjustment which to some might appear to be deliberate falsification.[98]

One surprising feature of Anselm's genuine material sources is the extreme paucity of texts from Gregory VII. Although, as has been noted, Gregory can hardly be seen as a forerunner of the lawyer-popes of the twelfth century, his preoccupation with the law is indisputable.[99] Gregory VII, however, provided Anselm with only six texts.[100] The majority of these came from the pope's reforming councils. In broad terms, they concerned the relations of the Church with the secular world, and in particular the *res ecclesiae*. Two of them came from the Lenten synod of 1080, and focused upon the issue of investiture.[101] The first of these—a confirmation of the pontiff's earlier legislation of 1078— was the outright prohibition of the lay investiture of bishops and abbots (VI: 63). The second stipulated anathema for those laymen who presumed to confer ecclesiastical dignities (VI: 62). Anselm, not surprisingly, wholly adhered to the text as well as the tenor of Gregory's stipulations. In the case of VI: 62, he also seems to have reinforced, by means of the 'audiantur' in his rubric, Gregory's connection of obedience and faith: those clerics who received their dignities from laymen would be judged as no longer numbering among true catholics.[102] Three other texts from Gregory VII addressed the issue of infringement upon ecclesiastical property and rights.[103] All were drawn from the legislation of the November synod of 1078.[104] The texts addressed the inviolability of the patrimony of St Peter [IV: 37], that laymen were not to possess tithes [V: 45], and that an abbot was not to retain the *primitiae*

---

[98] *Reindel, II, no. 65, p. 233:*
'Omnes autem sive patriarchivi cuiuslibet apicem, sive metropoleon primatus, aut episcopatuum cathedras, vel aecclesiarum cuiuscumque ordinis dignitates sive rex sive imperator, sive cuiuslibet conditiones homo purus instituit, et prout voluntas aut facultas erat, spetialium sibi praerogativarum iura praefixit Romanam autem aecclesiam solus ille fundavit . . . '

Anselm, I: 63, p. 31:
'Omnes autem sive patriarchae in cuiuslibet apicem sive metropoleon primatus aut episcopatuum cathedras vel ecclesiarum cuiuscumque ordinis dignitatem ipsa instituit; illam vero solus ipse fundavit . . . . '

[99] See above, Pt. 1, esp. note 102.

[100] Anselm I: 80 = *Reg.* VIII: 21, pp. 547 ff.; IV: 37 = *Reg.* VI: 5b, c. 11, p. 405; V: 45 = *Reg.* VI: 5b, c. 7, p. 404; V: 48 = *Reg.* VI: 5b, c. 9, p. 405; VI: 62 = *Reg.* VII: 14a, c. 1, p. 480; and VI: 63 = *Reg.* VII: 14a, c. 2, p. 480.

[101] Anselm VI: 62–3 = *Reg.*, VII: 14a, cc. 1–2, p. 480.

[102] Anselm VI: 62 Ut inter episcopos vel abbates non habeantur nec *audiantur* qui de laicis hanc susceperint dignitatem, et idem de inferioribus dignitatibus (my italics).

[103] Anselm IV: 37; V: 45, 48.   [104] Cf. *Reg.* VI: 5b, cc. 7, 9, 11, p. 405.

without the consent of the Apostolic See, or his own diocesan bishop [V: 48].

Anselm also included the important second letter to Bishop Hermann of Metz, Gregory VII's most important contribution to canon law.[105] Anselm placed the text under the uncompromising rubric 'Quod apostolico licet imperatores excommunicare ac deponere, quod etiam aliqui fecerunt episcopi'. Though the text was excerpted, Anselm included most of Gregory's salient points. It should be noted, however, that Anselm's text focused especially upon the precedental cases of excommunication and deposition, rather than upon Gregory's deposition of Henry IV, which had figured prominently in the letter to Hermann as contained in the pope's Register.[106] The care with which Anselm transmitted this important document was very much apparent, though this of course may be due to his exemplar: the letter was widely diffused, and any variation would have been quickly picked up. It is made clear none the less in Anselm's version that the text had been excerpted. Phrases such as 'post pauca' and the rather telling 'et post quasdam optimas interpositiones' revealed an appreciation of the immense significance of the entire text of the letter. It was, after all, one of the most resounding statements of the supremacy of the Roman pontiff that had ever been articulated.

Among the most interesting of Anselm's genuine sources are his patristic texts. Anselm's collection in fact marks the beginning of a dramatic transformation in the use of patristic texts as sources of law. While they had figured in canonical collections since the time of the *Collectio Hibernensis* in the eighth century, patristic texts had, on the whole, been used sporadically as auxiliary sources for issues of penance, and for moral and eschatological matters.[107] The use of patristic texts had increased dramatically by the time of Burchard's *Decretum*, but even there, they still had been used primarily to support penitential or eschatological concerns.[108] In fact, as he had made expressly clear in his preface, Burchard had ranked patristic texts second to last in his 'hierarchy of sources', barely ahead of penitential texts.[109] Yet with the ongoing

---

[105] See Gilchrist, 'The Reception of Pope Gregory VII', 35–82.

[106] Anselm I: 80. Anselm did follow the beginning of Gregory's letter: 'Quod autem postulasti . . . ', and included Gregory's examples of Gregory I, Innocent I, Zachary, and Ambrose as precedents.

[107] C. Munier, *Les Sources patristiques*, 27–31.

[108] Most of Burchard's patristic texts were in Book XIX: *Corrector*, and in Book XX: *Speculator*.

[109] Burchard, prefatio ad *Decretum*, 540: 'Porro legentibus, etiam id persuasum esse cupimus, nihil de meo in hoc opere additum esse, sed ex divinis testimoniis scripturarum

popularity of the *Decretum* (it must be remembered that the reform collections never quite eclipsed Burchard's compilation), Burchard was none the less responsible for a widespread diffusion of patristic texts. He was also responsible, as noted above, for the diffusion of a number of false attributions.[110]

Although there is not an explicit hierarchy or doctrine of sources in Anselm's collection, his patristic texts cannot simply be regarded as auxiliary sources of law. The redirection of these sources towards new ends stemmed in part perhaps from the reformers' general lack of interest (Peter Damian excepted) in eschatological matters. For Anselm, patristic sources were true *auctoritates*. He used them to support Roman primacy and 'political' issues, as well as questions of sacramental theology, familial concerns, and clerical morality. They not only imparted precision to juridical terminology, at the same time they provided new material from which universal proclamations could be derived.[111] Most often, such texts were used to transform the ideal of clerical life described by the Fathers—towards which men should aspire—into actual binding requirements and obligations. Anselm in particular used patristic sources to recommend, and indeed demand, that clerics practice humility, that they display no interest in the world or secular affairs, and most of all, that they be submissive to their superiors.[112]

Anselm's patristic material sources included 12 texts from Cyprian, 13 from Ambrose, 16 from Jerome, 16 from Gregory I, 4 from Isidore of Seville and, notably, 101 from Augustine. The formal sources of these texts present some problems. Some texts from Cyprian were provided by the 74T, and Burchard clearly accounted for some of the Augustinian texts.[113] Yet while the collection did not in itself introduce new patris-

---

singula esse decerpta, ea sane fide, ut perpetuam auctoritatem habitura non dubitem. Ex quibus autem scriptis selegerim *ordo sequens indicat* . . . '

[110] See above, notes 11–12.

[111] e.g. though Anselm used Jerome's distinction between heresy and schism: XII: 48 Quod heresis perversum dogma habet, scisma vero dissensionem [Jerome, *Comment. in epist. ad Titum*, c. 3], he continued to use the two terms somewhat indiscriminately.

[112] e.g. Anselm VI: 27 Quod secundum proprietatem nominis episcopus non est, qui dilexerit preesse non prodesse [Augustine, *De civitate Dei*, lib. IX, c. 19]; VI: 135 De tribus personis: pastoris, mercenarii et furis [Augustine, *Sermo* 137, c. 5].

[113] The 74T accounted for five of Anselm's Cyprianic texts. Anselm I: 10 = 74T c. 18 [Cyprian, *Liber de catholicae ecclesiae unitate*, cc. 4, 5]; V: 1 = 74T c. 19 [ibid., c. 5, 6]; V: 2 = 74T c. 20 [ibid., c. 6]; IX: 4 = 74T c. 207 [Cyprian, epist. 63, c. 13]; IX: 5 = 74T c. 208 [epist. 63, c. 14]. The 74T, however, was not the source of the important text in XII: 40 Quod heretici in aecclesia nichil habeant potestatis et iuris [epist. 69 to Magnus]. On Anselm's 'new' Cyprianic texts, see Fournier, 'Les Collections canoniques', 311 ff. On the Augustinian texts from Burchard, see above, notes 10–11, and below, Table I.

tic texts, with the exception of several from Cyprian, Anselm was none the less exploiting known patristic sources, particularly Augustine, in extremely innovative ways. A number of these texts, which often figure in the collection in a series, including some from Ambrose, and from Augustine, had not appeared in any of the canonical collections of the recent past. Charles Munier noted that such series generally indicated that the textual order of the original source was being followed. That is to say, a series of canons often followed the order of the work consulted.[114] The ends towards which Anselm applied some of his patristic sources would seem to indicate that these may well have been the product of his own research, possibly in the library of San Benedetto di Polirone, or, and perhaps more likely, the product of those 'intermediate compilers'.[115]

Augustine was by far the most important of Anselm's patristic sources, and he ranks among the most important of his sources in general. The greatest of the Latin Fathers, Augustine was an indisputable authority for matters of sacramental theology and familial concerns, as well as quasi-political questions. Although there were surprisingly few Augustinian texts in the first eight books of Anselm's collection, those that did figure often addressed issues of importance.[116] Yet neither

[114] e.g. Augustine, *De baptismo contra Donatistas* = Anselm IX: 29–40; Augustine's correspondence = Anselm IX: 41–8; Augustine, *De bono coniugali* = Anselm X: 10–12; Jerome = Anselm XII: 48–9; Cyprian = Anselm VI: 56–7 and VII: 25–7. Munier, *Les Sources patristiques*, 37, believed that an 'intermediate researcher' was responsible.

[115] As noted above (note 5), the existence of compilations, particularly of patristic texts, in the library at Polirone, may offer clues as to Anselm's formal sources, as well as to the larger problem of 'intermediate' collections. New texts from Ambrose included: *Comment. s. Lucam*, *De officiis*, and *De excessu fratris*. New Augustinian texts included: *In Iohannis evangelium*, *De fide et operibus*, *De utilitate credendi*, *De baptismo contra Donatistas*, and *Contra Faustum*. See Fournier/Le Bras, II, 9 ff. I hope to explore further the textual similarities between Anselm's collection and the so-called *Collectio altera in V. libris* [MS Vat. lat. 1348], especially the Augustinian coercion texts.

[116] There are only eleven texts from Augustine in Books I–VIII: no texts in Books I, II, and IV, and just one apiece in Books III and VIII. This compares with some 90 in Books IX–XIII. The early ones are not without significance: e.g. Anselm III: 67 Quod sacerdos non debet iudicare quemquam nisi confessum aut convictum [Sermo 351, no. 10, 11]; V: 3 Quod ecclesia vel domus Dei columba appellatur et sponsa, et quod potestatem accepit ligandi et solvendi [*De baptismo contra Donatistas*, lib. 7, c. 51]; V: 29 Qualiter ecclesiastica pecunia sit servanda [*In Iohannis evang.*, tract. 62, c. 13]; VI: 27 Quod secundum proprietatem nominis episcopus non est, qui dilexerit preesse non prodesse [*De civitate Dei*, lib. IX, c. 19]; VI: 135 De tribus personis: pastoris, mercenarii et furis [Sermo 137, c. 5]; VI: 145 Quod petendum est auxilium ab imperatore, quando fuerit necesse [Epist. 185 ad Bonifacium, c. 7 (28)]; VI: 177 Quod nichil facilius sed apud Deum dampnabilius, quam sacri ordines si secundum homines agantur, si vero secundum Deum nichil difficilius et beatius [Epist. 21 ad Valerium]; VII: 5 Augustinus in sermone suo de communi vita clericorum [Sermo 355]; VII: 137 Quod prepositi sua quaerentes mercennarii

should the preponderance of Augustinian texts in the final books qualify or limit their significance; location, after all, is sometimes deceiving. In Book IX, with Augustinian texts primarily from the *De baptismo contra Donatistas*, Anselm reaffirmed the mainstream reformist view of the disturbing issue of the validity of the sacraments and orders of unchaste, simoniacal, or even schismatic or heretical clergy, which had divided the reformers since the time of Leo IX. By means of universalizing rubrics, Anselm in effect supported what would become the classical doctrine on the ministry and on the efficacy and economy of the sacraments.[117] In Book X with texts from the *De bono coniugali*, Anselm seems to reflect the reformers' increasing preoccupation with defining rules for Christian marriage.[118] In Book XI, he seems to foreshadow twelfth-century developments, using Augustine on one occasion in an attempt to define the moral intentionality of true penitence.[119]

sunt [*In Iohannis evang.*, tract. 47, c. 10]; VII: 160 Quibus defunctis sacrificia vel orationes prosint viventium [*Enchiridion*, no. 29]; VIII: 3 ⟨no rubric⟩ (MS Vat. lat. 1364 = Quod nemo post poenitentiam sit clericus rigore disciplinae non indulgentiae desperatione statutum est) [Epist. 185, c. 10 (45)].

    [117] Anselm held that such orders were valid but technically illicit, thus distinguishing between the intrinsic value of the sacrament and its lasting effect. As gifts of Christ, they could not be contaminated. Even the contentious point regarding sacraments administered by heretics did not seem to trouble him: the recipient would find upon his return to the flock that that sacrament, whose intrinsic value had not been corrupted, would be corrected in terms of lasting effect. (Anselm rejected the notion of reconsecration, VII: 87 Quod reconsecrari nullus possit, from Gregory I.) Anselm IX: 32 Quod sacramenta tam per malos quam per bonos administrantur [*In Iohannis evang.*, tract 5, c. 1]; IX: 33 Quod sacramentum baptismatis apud hereticos haberi et dari potest [*De baptismo*, lib. 1, c. 1 (2)]; IX: 34 Quod eadem sacramenta ubique sunt integra [ibid., lib. 3, c. 15]; IX: 36 Quod heretici sacramenta et scripturas habent ad speciem non ad salutem [ibid., lib. 3, c. 19 (27)]; IX: 38 Quod mali sacramentum Christi maculare non possunt [ibid., lib. 4, c. 12 (18)]; IX: 39 Quod Dei sacramenta ubique recta sunt [ibid., lib. 5, c. 20]; IX: 40 Quod sacramentum apud hereticos et haberi et dari potest, effectus vero sacramenti minime [ibid., excerpts from lib. 1, 5, and 6]; IX: 46 Quod mater ecclesia etiam invitos sanat [Epist. 89, num. 6]. Cf. Anselm IX: 10, 18, 26, 29–31, 35, 37, 41, 43–5, 47–9. In general, see J. T. Gilchrist, '*Simoniaca haeresis* and the Problem of Orders from Leo IX to Gratian', *Proceedings of the Second International Congress of Medieval Canon Law*, ed. S. Kuttner and J. J. Ryan (MIC, Ser. C: Subsidia, 1; Vatican City, 1965), 209–35; now also in *Canon Law in the Age of Reform*.

    [118] Anselm X: 10 [*De bono coniugali*, c. 4]; 11 [ibid., cc. 14,15]; 12 [ibid., c. 34]; 13 [*De bono viduitatis*, c. 11]; 14 [*Sermo* 392, c. 2]; 39 [epist. 228 ad Honoratum, no. 7]; 40 [epist. 11 ad Nebridium]; 41 [*De adulterinis coniugiis*, lib. 2, c. 6]; 42 [ibid.]; 43 [ibid., c. 9]; 44 [*De fide et operibus*, c. 7]. In general, see R. I. Moore, 'Family, Community and Cult on the Eve of the Gregorian Reform', *TRHS*, 5th ser. 30 (1980), 49–69; J. A. Brundage, *Law, Sex and Christian Society* (Chicago, 1987); and id., 'Sexuality, Marriage, and the Reform of Christian Society in the Thought of Gregory VII', in *La riforma gregoriana e l'Europa* (*SG* 14/2), 69–73.

    [119] e.g. Anselm XI: 137 Quod non sunt peccata nescientium nisi volentium [*Questionum*, lib. III (*Quest.de numeris*), num. 24, c. 15] [fos. 202ᵛ–203ʳ]: 'Merito quaeritur quae sunt

The use of Augustine was not limited to such specific matters. Anselm found in Augustine the substance, and the authority, by which he could advocate and justify the use of coercive action against schismatics, heretics, or other internal enemies of the Church. He sought not only to justify the use of force on behalf of the Church, but also to legitimize force directly exercised by the Church. In this way, he sought to provide the Church with the ability to continue, and fulfil her earthly mission even when her traditional defender—the Emperor—had proved himself unwilling or had indeed fallen into heresy or schism.[120] The greatest of the Latin Fathers was, in short, mustered to support an innovative canonical agenda.

5. ANSELM AND DEUSDEDIT

THE *Collectio canonum* of Cardinal Deusdedit has been called the second of the major 'Gregorian' collections.[121] Compiled between 1083 and 1087 by Deusdedit, Cardinal-priest of San Pietro in Vinculo, the collection, as with its predecessors, was fundamentally pro-reform. While it is clear that there is little direct connection in terms of textual dependency between the collections of Anselm and Deusdedit (except for their possible direct or indirect use of an 'intermediate' collection of northern Italian origin, the so-called *Collectio canonum Barberiana*), a brief

---

peccata nolentium utrum quae a nescientibus committuntur, an etiam possit recte dici peccatum esse nolentis, quod facere compellitur. Nam et hoc contra voluntatem dici solet . . . ' There are some 26 (?) texts from Augustine in Book XI, some of which cannot be identified, others that were erroneously attributed to Augustine. As this book remains unedited, a complete list of material sources seems warranted. Anselm XI: 1 [epist. 265 ad Seuleucianam, no. 7 (Vat. 1363 = Felicianum)]; 4 [*Sermo* 351, no. 12]; 24 [*Sermo* 82, no.10]; 28 [*Enchiridion*, c. 70, no. 19]; 38 [excerpts: *De consensu evangelistarum*, c. 13; *Enarratione* in Ps. 56, no. 63; *In Iohannis evangelium.*, tract. 114 and 115]; 61 [cited as Augustinus, but actually Council of Toledo X, c. 2]; 62 [epist. 47 ad Publicolam, c. 2]; 64 [*De sermone Domini in monte*, lib. 1, c. 17, no. 51]; 66 [*Enarratione* in Ps. 5, no. 7]; 73 [*Sermo* 392, no. 3]; 90 [*Questionum*, lib. II (Quest. de Exodo), no. 39]; 93 [epist. 153 as Macedonium, c. 20]; 94 [*In Iohannis evang.*, tract. 50, no. 10]; 119 [*Homilies*, lib. 50, hom. 41]; 120 [Augustinus ??—unknown]; 124 [*Liber de continentia*, c. 6, no. 6]; 126 [*Enchiridion*, c. 65, no. 17]; 137 [*Questionum*, lib. II (Quest. de Numeris), no. 24]; 138 [cited as Augustinus, but Jerome, ad cap. 3 Michae]; 139 [cited as Augustinus, but Gregory I, *Moralia*, IX: 27]; 140 [*De peccatorum meritis et remissionis*, XI, c. 34 (55)]; 142 [Augustinus, in libro de trinitate ??—unknown]; 144 [Augustinus, in genesi ad litteram ??—unknown]; 145 [Augustinus ??—unknown]; 146 [Augustinus, in Psalmis ??—unknown]; 147 [Sermo 41]; 148 [epist. 93 ad Vincentium, c. 53]; 149 [Augustinus, in libro retractionum ??—unknown].

120 Anselm XIII: 14 Quod ecclesia persecutionem possit facere. See App. II and Ch. 4.
121 *Die Kanonessamlung des Kardinals Deusdedit*, ed. V. Wolf von Glanvell (Paderborn, 1905). On the collection, see Fournier/Le Bras, II, 37–51, and Stickler, 173.

examination of Deusdedit serves to place Anselm in greater relief.[122] More important, it also serves to underscore the different responses to the call for canonical works stimulated by Gregory VII and earlier reformers, as well as the quite diverse positions that were animating the reformers of the time.

Little is known of Deusdedit's life and career. Identified by Berengar of Tours as a monk from Tulle in the diocese of Limoges, Deusdedit seems to have come to Rome to join the reform entourage during the earlier part of Gregory VII's pontificate, ultimately being installed, *c.*1078, as Cardinal-priest of St Peter in Chains. It is known that he spent some time in Saxony—perhaps on a papal mission with Odo of Ostia in 1084–5— where he found some materials for his collection.[123] In addition to his canonical work, Deusdedit composed around 1097 a scathing treatise against Wibert of Ravenna, and against the validity of the sacraments of simonists, entitled *Libellus contra invasores et simoniacos*.[124] He died shortly thereafter, between 1098 and 1100.

The canon law collection was divided into four books with a total of some 1220 *capitula*.[125] Book I, *De privilegio auctoritatis ecclesiae Romanae* (284 chapters), addressed the authority of the Roman Church. Book II, *De clero Romanae* (163 chapters), paid specific attention to the Roman clergy, but was also understood by Deusdedit as being appropriate for the clergy of other churches. Book III, *De rebus ecclesiae* (289 chapters), was specifically aimed at the Roman Church's temporalities. Book IV, *De libertate ecclesiae et rerum eius et cleri* (487 chapters), was somewhat of a catch-all, addressing not merely the liberty of the Church regarding her personnel and properties, but also including texts on the functioning of ecclesiastical authority, the Church's role in administrative matters, and the exercise of her judicial and repressive powers.

Despite Deusdedit's protestations, the collection was not rigorously or systematically ordered, although there is a method behind the ordering of the sources. Themes often overlap, however, especially in Books III and IV. Then there are problems with the rubric titles and the tex-

---

[122] See the detailed comparison of the two collections in Fournier, 'Les Collections canoniques', 365–95, and more recently in U.-R. Blumenthal, 'Rom in der Kanonistik', in *Rom in hohen Mittelalter*, ed. B. Schimmelpfennig and L. Schmugge (Sigmaringen, 1992), 29–39. On the *Collectio canonum Barberiana* (MS Barberini lat. 538), see Fuhrmann, II, 529 ff. and note 281.

[123] Deusdedit, IV: 240, where he notes that he obtained this text in Germany.

[124] *Libellus contra invasores et simoniacos*, ed. E. Sackur (*MGH, LdL*, 2), 292–365.

[125] Deusdedit's collection has suffered from many interpolations over the course of time; only two manuscripts have the entire collection. On this and on the numbering problem, see Wolf von Glanvell, pp. xix–xliv, and Fuhrmann, II, 524 ff.

tual inscriptions. The collection does not have individual rubric titles preceding each text. Deusdedit devised an index of four *capitulationes* to address this problem. The title of each *capitulum* in the index is followed by the numbers of the texts which correspond to the respective issue both in that book and in any of the other three. Deusdedit obviously saw this as a means of avoiding repetition. In practice, however, the system is quite unwieldy. Deusdedit's warning to future scribes regarding the necessity of being attentive to the numbering has clearly broken down over the passage of time.[126] The lack of many inscriptions, along with numerous errors in the identification of texts, may also be due to this.[127]

Deusdedit's canonical sources were considerably more varied than he had indicated in his prologue.[128] Material sources included conciliar canons, both universal and otherwise, papal decretals and other documents, patristic texts, especially Augustine, Ambrose, Jerome, Cyprian, and Gregory I. Roman law was also a source, with texts coming from the *Codex*, *De Institutionibus*, and the *Novellae*. There are also some civil law texts from German capitularies. Known formal sources included Dionysius Exiguus, the *Collectio Hispana*, Pseudo-Isidore, and to a lesser extent the collections of Burchard, Cardinal Atto, and the 74T.

The inclusion of new canonical sources is among the most notable features of Deusdedit's collection.[129] Deusdedit clearly widened his search to include a number of new types of sources, among the most outstanding of which are fragments of papal letters to secular princes, including texts from Nicholas II, Alexander II, and Gregory VII, and the privileges of secular princes to the Roman Church. There are, in addition, a number of new excerpts from other sources, including texts from *De ordinibus Romanis*, the *Liber Diurnus*, the *Liber pontificalis*, along with new texts from Cyprian. It should be noted here that, unlike Anselm, Deusdedit was an important transmitter of Gregory VII, as he incorporated some 39 texts on a variety of issues.[130]

Among the most striking of the new sources, however, were the extracts from the Lateran archives and the *tomi*—the papyrus rolls of

---

[126] Prologus, p. 3; cf. Wolf von Glanvell, pp. xii–xiii; Fournier, 'Les Collections canoniques', 333.

[127] See Wolf von Glanvell, pp. xii–xiv and note 37, for examples.

[128] For a detailed discussion of his sources, see Fournier, 'Les collections canoniques', 336 ff. On his Ps.Isidorian texts, see Fuhrmann, II, 522–33; III, 1036–8. Deusdedit used a more extensive version of Atto's *Breviarium* than is represented in Mai's edition.

[129] Fournier, 'Les Collections canoniques', 342 ff.; and Fournier/Le Bras, II, 37 ff.

[130] See J. T. Gilchrist, 'The Reception of Pope Gregory VII', 38 ff.

early papal correspondence—which included texts from Honorius I, Nicholas I, and Stephen V. These were clearly the product of Deusdedit's own research in the Roman archives.[131] His activity must surely be seen as concrete evidence of the care with which those in Gregory VII's entourage sought to provide indisputable authorities in support of their call for reform.

In his preface, Deusdedit was explicit about what he considered to be authoritative among canonical sources.[132] Roman sanction, for him, was clearly an important guarantee of canonical authenticity.[133] At the same time, he was clear in his own mind why certain sources were preferable to others.[134] These factors, together with the actual ordering of his texts in the collection, offer some important insights not merely into the general development of canon law, but also into how Deusdedit viewed the organizational structure of the Roman Church.

Above all, Deusdedit's collection provides evidence of the strong beginnings of a carefully thought-out hierarchy of sources. Deusdedit states quite simply in his prologue that certain canonical sources were to give way to more authoritative ones.[135] And this notion of hierarchy continued in the collection. Texts were ordered according to their respective types or genres.[136] Book I provides the best example. It begins with a series of canons from the universal councils, for instance, Nicaea, Chalcedon. These were followed by papal decretals—most of which were from the Pseudo-Isidore—in more or less chronological order from Clement to Gregory VII. Then came texts of a more biographical nature, largely from the *Liber pontificalis*. After these, there was a series of patristic texts, which were grouped according to their

---

[131] Deusdedit, III: 191 ff., pp. 353 ff.: 'Haec itaque, quae secuntur, sumpta ex tomis Lateranensis bibliothecae.'; III: 207 ff., pp. 363 ff.: 'Haec ex tomis patriarchii Lateranensis'. On these, see Fournier, 'Les Collections canoniques', 342 ff.; and Fournier/Le Bras, II, 37 ff. Cf. I. S. Robinson, *Authority and Resistance in the Investiture Contest* (Manchester, 1978), 41, who suggested that there may have been another depository of papal documents, that of the *turra cartularis*, near the Arch of Titus on the Via Sacra. B. Schimmelpfennig, *The Papacy* (New York, 1992), 138, indicated that Anselm, like Deusdedit, was working in the archives at the papal court appropriating Roman texts. No evidence is cited to support this.

[132] Deusdedit, prologus, p. 3.   [133] Ibid., pp. 3–4.

[134] Ibid., p. 5: 'Porro de modo ducendi subditos pauca hic inserta sunt, quoniam et laboriosum et alterius operis arbitratus sum ad hoc sacram deflorare scripturam. Potissima autem ad id operis mihi visa sunt evangeliorum et apostolorum epistolae et Clementis et pastoralis Gregorii et super evangelia omeliae eiusdem XL et VIII et VIIII et X et super Ezechielem.'

[135] Ibid., p. 3: 'Quod si patenter adversari contigerit, *inferior auctoritas potiori cedere debebit.*' (my italics)

[136] For the following, see Fournier, 'Les Collections canoniques', 334–5.

author. Book I concluded with historical texts, excerpts from Roman law, and capitulary texts.[137]

Like Anselm, Deusdedit was depicted by the schismatic cardinals as a 'discipulus Hildebrandi', that is, as being directed by Pope Gregory VII and his agenda.[138] This characterization, however, poses problems. Devoted as Deusdedit was to Gregory VII and the need for reform, he none the less was capable of an independence of mind. Both in his collection and in the *Libellus contra invasores*, he not only advocated a type of reform which differed in many respects from that envisaged by Gregory, but also espoused a quite unique view of the ideal structure of the Roman Church.

For present purposes, there is no need to go into detail regarding the connections, or rather, similarities, between the collections of Anselm and Deusdedit. The basic work of analytical comparison was done by Paul Fournier in 1920 and more recently has been supplemented by Horst Fuhrmann and Uta-Renate Blumenthal.[139] It should be noted, however, that while there are a number of common, and analogous sources—including a possible shared though independent use of the intermediate collection known as the *Collectio canonum Barberiana* (MS Vat. Barberini lat. 538)—the two collections were, in a strictly textual sense, compiled in complete isolation from each other. None the less, some general observations are called for.

Unlike Anselm's *Collectio canonum* with its pretensions towards collecting texts covering all aspects of ecclesiastical reform, Deusdedit's collection concentrated on the primacy of the Roman Church as a corporate institution. As is indicated in his prologue, Deusdedit selected his texts with a view towards buttressing the privileged status and the universal rights and responsibilities of Rome within the universal Church in order to further reform.[140] His intention was first to demonstrate the

---

[137] The same pattern is discernible in the other books, though to a lesser extent. Book III ends with a series of extracts from papal archives that interrupts the established hierarchy. In Book IV, it completely breaks down. See Fournier, 'Les Collections canoniques', 334–5.

[138] See below, Ch. 3. *Benonis et aliorumque cardinalium schismaticorum contra Gregorium VII. et Urbanum II. scripta* (*MGH, LdL*, 2), 366–422, esp. 399. See also U.-R. Blumenthal, 'Rom in der Kanonistik', 29–39; id., 'History and Tradition in Eleventh-Century Rome', *Catholic Historical Review*, 79 (1993), 185–96; and H. Mordek, ' "*Dictatus papae*" e "*Proprie auctoritates apostolicae sedis*": intorno all'idea del primato pontificio di Gregorio VII', *Rivista di storia della chiesa in Italia*, 28 (1974), 1–22, esp. 11 ff.

[139] Fournier, 'Les Collections canoniques', 365–95; Blumenthal, 'Rom in der Kanonistik:', 29–39; and Fuhrmann, II, 529 ff.

[140] Deusdedit, prologus, pp. 2–3. Cf. R. Knox, 'Finding the Law', 460 ff.

facts of Roman primacy by texts of a strictly ecclesiastical nature, and then to prove, by reference to the various acts of secular powers, that this primacy was universally recognized in the Christian world. Yet for Deusdedit, primacy was an issue concerning not so much the Roman pontiff but rather the whole *sancta Romana ecclesia*. As Peter's successor, the pope of course enjoyed the role of leader, but even he was always subservient to the wider Church. There is not the sense of the immediate identification of the Roman pontiff with the Roman Church which is to be found in Anselm's collection.[141] For Deusdedit, primacy had been given by Christ to the Roman Church in an almost institutional sense. For Anselm, however, it was the pope, as Peter's successor, who had inherited the fullness of power.[142]

These different emphases are reflected in the choice of language. Anselm entitled his first book: On the power and authority of the Apostolic See (*De potestate et auctoritate [primatu] apostolicae sedes*). Deusdedit, however, selected a slightly different focus, calling his first book: On the privilege of authority of the Roman Church (*De privilegium auctoritatis Romanae ecclesiae*). This difference in emphasis continued, especially in their respective first books. Anselm often referred directly to the pope in his rubrics, whereas Deusdedit mentioned the pope quite rarely.[143] Of the first 44 chapter titles in the index to Book I of the latter, only two actually referred to the pontiff, and neither was particularly significant for the exercise of papal authority.[144] The others referred either to the *sancta ecclesia*, or to the more generic *sedes apostolica*.[145]

Rome was clearly an important symbol for Deusdedit.[146] He had a strong feeling for the traditions of Rome as the city of the apostles. Blumenthal has recently shown how he made some modifications to his canonical texts, adding St Paul as a '*co-apostolicus*'.[147] This reflected a more conservative and perhaps historical consciousness on his part for

---

[141] e.g. Deusdedit, I: 2, 6, 28.

[142] See R. L. Benson, '*Plenitudo potestatis*: Evolution of a Formula from Gregory IV to Gratian', *Studia Gratiana*, 14 (1967), 193–217, here 208–9. Anselm incorporated Gregory IV and the Ps.Vigilius texts ' . . . in partem sollicitudinis, non in plenitudinem potestatis . . . .', the former to the episcopate, the latter to the pope, in Book II, 17–18, with a rubric that clearly emphasized papal superiority. Deusdedit summarized the Ps.Vigilius text with the simple statement that the Roman Church has bestowed its office, not the fullness of power, on all churches.: Deusdedit, I: 139 [Capitulum, p. 1: Quod (Romana ecclesia) omnibus ecclesiis largita suam vicem non potestatis plenitudinem].

[143] e.g. Anselm, I: 5, 6, 24, 28, 45, 49, 50.   [144] Deusdedit, I: 31, 35.

[145] See Deusdedit, capitula libri primi, pp. 6–15.

[146] See Blumenthal, 'History and Tradition in Eleventh-Century Rome', 185–96.

[147] Ibid., 187–8.

the city of the martyrs. Deusdedit referred to himself without fail as cardinal-priest of '*Apostolorum in Eudoxia*'—an ancient Roman name that had almost been completely forgotten even in his time. This reverence for the Rome of the Apostles, and his equation of the city with the whole of the Roman Church, produced in him a deep devotion to the idea of the Church as a corporate entity.

Much has been made in recent times of the difference between Deusdedit's 'conciliarism' and the hierarchical papalism of other reformers, notably that of Anselm of Lucca.[148] In many ways, Deusdedit is best known for his views on the role of the cardinals in the government of the Roman Church, views which clearly anticipated developments in the twelfth century.[149] Deusdedit insisted upon the dignity of all of the cardinals, and he was naturally solicitous of the status of the cardinal-priests. He borrowed the term *cardo* from Isidore of Seville's *Etymologies*, and with a personal interpolation made it into a celebration of the dignity of the Roman cardinals.[150] They were the 'hinges' (*cardines*) that ruled and guided God's people. For Deusdedit, their participation in the administration of the Church was both a canonical necessity and an obligation.

His unrelenting and utter rejection of the 1059 decree on papal elections, with its restriction of the primary role of the cardinals in the election of a pope to the cardinal-bishops, reflected these concerns.[151] Deusdedit did not cease to rail against the exclusion of the cardinal priests, and the expansion of the circle from which a pontiff was to be selected.[152] He ignored the 1059 decree when compiling his collection, preferring instead the papal election *ordo* of 769. Deusdedit expressed himself forcefully in his prologue, noting that he had included the ancient decree as certain persons had recently had the temerity to write an abominable new election decree.[153]

Like Anselm, Deusdedit was both polemical and selective in his canonical work. His collection, like that of Anselm, offers many

---

[148] e.g. Robinson, *Authority and Resistance*, 48–9; U.-R. Blumenthal, 'Fälschungen bei Kanonisten der Kirchenreform des 11. Jahrhunderts', in *Fälschungen im Mittelalter* (*MGH, Schriften*, 33/1–6; Hanover, 1988–90), II, 241–2; id., 'Rom in der Kanonistik', 29–39, and 'History and Tradition in Eleventh-Century Rome', 185–96.

[149] Deusdedit, Book II: De Romanae Clero, e.g. II: 103–8, 109. See S. Kuttner, '*Cardinalis*: The History of a Canonical Concept', *Traditio*, 3 (1945), 129–214, esp. 172–8.

[150] Deusdedit, II: 109, 114–16.

[151] Deusdedit, II: 160. See Kuttner, '*Cardinalis*', 176–7 and notes 108, 110.

[152] *Libellus contra invasores*, 310, and 311 ff., where he used an interpolated reform decree to demonstrate the invalidity of the decree of 1059.

[153] Deusdedit, pp. 4–5: 'Preterea antiquum ordinem electionis seu consecrationis Romanai pontificis et cleri eius huic operi inserere libuit. Nam quidam olim in dei et

examples of canonical texts being modified in order to foster his own view of reform.[154] It has been asked recently whether Deusdedit should be seen as a forger or even a falsifier.[155] In one sense, he was. Deusdedit did modify and interpolate texts for his own ends. Yet he was at the same time a man both of great learning, and immense piety. It is a matter of choice whether we ought to accept the words of his prologue at face-value: Deusdedit may have been offering what he believed to be a more correct and authentic version of the truth for the Roman Church.

CONCLUSION

WHILE this must remain a preliminary examination of Anselm's canonical sources, a number of significant points have none the less been established. Whereas Alfons Stickler believed that Anselm had neither randomly nor deliberately altered his canonical authorities, it is now clear that this was not always the case. Although textual transmission in many cases was technically accurate, it is clear that Anselm was not always entirely faithful to the intention, and perhaps ambition, of the original text or its formal source. His attitude towards his canonical sources in the end, however, is somewhat difficult to define. It is clear that he regarded his canonical texts as enduring and unassailable authorities. Yet with his rubrics, his omissions, and his excerpts, he could also most effectively distort and transform those sacred authorities.

Yet Anselm cannot be seen as capricious. Granted, there are *lacunae*, repetitions, and contradictory canons in the collection, but these seem largely to be the exception, not the rule. Even a preliminary examination of the canonical sources indicates that Anselm set out to articulate a strategy for reform. He knew precisely what had to be achieved, and he selected, shaped, and ordered his sources accordingly. Anselm was more than a mere editor or a collector of texts; he was an interpreter, who, from a vast and inchoate body of texts and formal sources, fashioned a *collection* to meet the requirements of the Church in an age of reform and revolution.

---

sanctorum patrum scilicet ostentationem et adscribendam sibi ventosam auctoritatem, quae nullis canonicis legibus stare potest, scripserunt sibi novam ordinationem eiusdem Romani pontificis, in qua quam nefanda quam deo inimica stauterunt, horreo scribere. Qui legit intellegat.' Cf. Blumenthal, 'History and Tradition', 195.

[154] e.g. Deusdedit, I: 43, 162, 257; II: 103–4, 108–9, 111–13, 140, 160; III: 62, 107, 176; IV: 18, 22, 136, 184–5. Cf. Fournier, 'Les Collections canoniques', 353–8; and Blumenthal, 'Fälschungen bei Kanonisten', 241–62.

[155] Blumenthal, 'Fälschungen bei Kanoniste', 261–2.

3

Roman Primacy and
the Legal Vindication of Reform

IN the writings of Beno and the schismatic cardinals who defected from
Gregory VII in 1083, there is an interesting portrait of canonistic activity at Rome during Gregory's pontificate.[1] The depiction, however, is
far from flattering. They sharply criticized Gregory's 'exploitation' of
canon law, particularly his modifications of what are clearly Ps.Isidorian
documents, and complained that he had manipulated, disregarded, and
even violated the sacred texts.[2] The schismatic cardinals proffered an
imposing number of contradictory authorities, which none the less
revealed that they were not always surefooted in their understanding of
the canonical texts in question.[3] Yet, beyond the harsh critique of
Gregory himself, there were also pointed condemnations of the pontiff's
wicked co-disciples, *Anselmus, Turbanus, Deusdedit,* whose 'fraudulent'
compilations were seen as being equally at fault in the perversion of the
sacred canons.[4] The cardinals' description of the texts supposedly corrupted by these reformers presents a riveting image: that of Gregory VII

---

[1] *Benonis aliorumque cardinalium schismaticorum contra Gregorium VII. et Urbanum II.
scripta (MGH, LdL, 2),* 366–422; esp. 380–403: 'Contra Decretum Hildebrandi'.

[2] e.g. 380: 'Hoc est decretum Hildebrandi, in quo a doctrina et fide catholica erravit
. . .'; and 396: 'Non recte autem divisisti, dum te irrevocabiliter a fide catholica errantem
et a patribus sanctae sedis derelictum, sedem apostolicam esse reputasti, cum iam non
solum spiritualia, sed etiam secularia a te non possent iudicari.' See also 390, where
Gregory was berated for his modification of Ps.Clement texts, and above, Pt. 1, note 98.

[3] e.g. 393, where the writer, quite clearly ignorant of the sense of the text, set
Augustine's *Sermo 250,* no. 1, against Gregory VII's excommunication of those who had
communicated with the king.

[4] 399: 'Hildebrandus, Turbanus, Anselmus Lucensis episcopus, Deusdedit in compila-
tionibus suis fraudulentis . . .'

leading, and directing his canonistic associates, with *Dictatus papae* as their primary agenda.[5]

The question of a direct connection between Pope Gregory VII and the reform collections is a much debated issue. It has already been shown that Gregory strongly felt that there was a need for new canonical collections, and that he even asked Peter Damian to undertake such a work.[6] Unfortunately, there is no evidence to confirm that Gregory knew of the collections being compiled by Anselm or Deusdedit. Though he surely would not have been unaware of research undertaken in the papal archives such as that of Deusdedit, Gregory's involvement, direct or otherwise, in the production of these compilations cannot be demonstrated. Stickler viewed these collections, especially Anselm's, as being products of the pro-reform camp, and he grouped them under the heading of 'strict Gregorian collections'.[7] Though Anselm's collection has generally been seen to espouse the policies of Gregory VII, did it set out expressly towards these ends? Was it compiled under a watchful papal eye? Was the *Collectio canonum* truly intended to be a manual of, or, for reform?

The Bb recension of the *Collectio canonum*, Biblioteca Apostolica Vaticana, Barberini 535, contains an interesting inscription. It describes the collection as being the work of Anselm of Lucca, the zealous disciple of Gregory VII, at whose express request the compilation was undertaken.[8] While the actual value of this inscription is debatable, it none the less indicates that at least one near-contemporary viewed Anselm's compilation as an official collection emanating from the ambiance of Gregory VII. It is an opinion that is echoed elsewhere, even if we set

---

[5] 399–400: 'Hildebrandus, Turbanus, Anselmus, Deusdedit: Romanus pontifex absque dubio sanctus est, si canonice electus fuerit . . . . Titulus iste Hildebrandum et discipulos eius scripturarum perversores manifeste detegit. Ex toto enim est contrarius eidem capitulo, cui ab Hildebrando et discipulis eius preponitur; et unde ab Hildebrando falsa interpretacione falso confirmatur . . . '

[6] See above, Pt. 1. Also H. Fuhrmann, 'Das Reformpapstum und die Rechtswissenschaft', in *Investiturstreit und Reichsverfassung*, ed. J. Fleckenstein (Konstanzer Arbeitskreis für mitteralterliche Geschichte, Vorträge und Forschungen, 17; Sigmaringen, 1977), 175–204, esp. 201 ff.; and id., 'Papst Gregor VII. und das Kirchenrecht: zum Problem des *Dictatus papae*', *La riforma gregoriana e l'Europa* (*SG* 13), 123–49.

[7] Stickler, *Historia iuris canonici*, 160 ff. Stickler included among these the so-called *Redactio Gregoriana Decreti Burchardi* (MS Vat. lat. 3809), Atto, the 74, Anselm, Deusdedit, and the *Liber de vita christiana* of Bonizo of Sutri. Furhmann (as note 6) believed that there was perhaps not much more (at least at this time) than a shared understanding of 'Roman' ecclesiology which fed the new collections.

[8] Biblioteca Apostolica Vaticana, MS Vat. Barb. 535, fo. 14ᵛ, (for text, see above, Introduction, note 27). An additional attribution to Anselm is found at fo. 1ʳ.

aside the problematic identification of what the *Vita Anselmi* referred to as Anselm's 'apologeticum' with the collection.[9] For instance, the always well-informed Sigebert of Gembloux noted that Anselm had compiled a work which contained and confirmed the 'doctrinam Hildebrandi'.[10] Whether Gregory specifically requested that Anselm compile a canonical collection is, perhaps, of merely academic interest. It is clear that the collection was understood at least by some contemporaries as embodying Gregory's vision of reform.

Yet is this an accurate description, or characterization? As has been previously discussed, Gregory VII himself furnished Anselm with surprisingly few texts.[11] While these included important examples of the pontiff's thought, especially regarding papal privilege—notably a lengthy excerpt from the second letter to Hermann of Metz regarding the pontiff's right to excommunicate and depose emperors, as well as the prohibition of the lay investiture of bishops and abbots—such examples in themselves scarcely seem to justify Sigebert's use of the 'doctrinam Hildebrandi'.[12] The small number of texts from Gregory VII, however, does not necessarily mean that the collection did not embody the principles of that pontiff. As in many cases, omissions can often prove far more telling than inclusions.

One possible explanation is that Anselm, like others of his party, conceived of reform with the conviction, however anachronistic, that Gregory VII and his predecessors were restoring the authentic and ancient traditions of the Church. It was perhaps Anselm's task to associate, and even to vindicate, that 'revolution' *with* tradition. As is suggested by his not inconsiderable reliance upon Ps.Isidorian documents, Anselm perhaps set out to convey that historical weight and precedence underlay the reform principles he was advancing in the collection. Surely aware of the disparaging charges of novelty which were constantly being levied upon the reformers, and upon Gregory in particular, Anselm may have consciously avoided using him as a canonical source in favour of ancient, or what appeared to be ancient, texts. Gregory's statements that he was not an innovator, and was simply restoring the ancient principles of the Church of the Fathers, may find a corollary in Anselm's exploitation of 'ancient' sources as authorities to

---

[9] *Vita Anselmi*, c. 26, p. 21. Cf. C. Erdmann, *The Origin of the Idea of Crusade*, trans. M. W. Baldwin and W. Goffart (Princeton, 1977), 246, who identified the word with the collection, and saw it in terms of 'justifying the principles of Gregory VII'.

[10] *Chronica a. 1086*, 365; cf. *Catalogus Sigeberti Gemblacensis monachi*, no. 162, p. 100.

[11] See above, Ch. 2, Sect. 4.   [12] Anselm I: 80; VI: 62–3.

support Gregory's policies.[13] In this light, one must consider the more important issue of whether, and to what extent, Anselm may have conveyed the *essence* of Gregory VII's thought into canon law.

It is useful here to return to the reports of the schismatic cardinals. Was *Dictatus papae*, after all, a 'program for reform' used by the Gregorian canonists? On the face of it, at least with respect to Anselm, the answer seems to be no. After all, the cardinals noted only one topic in connection with Anselm that bore any reference to *Dictatus papae*. This was c. 23: 'Quod Romanus pontifex, si canonice fuerit ordinatus, meritis beati Petri indubitanter efficitur sanctus . . . '[14] Anselm dealt with this issue in Book VI of the collection under a similar, but different, rubric.[15] His source was Ennodius, as was explicitly the case in *Dictatus papae* too.[16]

A strong case, however, can be made for Anselm's incorporation of many of the themes found in *Dictatus papae*.[17] Anselm's own rubrics, for all their problems, occasionally used the same, or similar, wording as that found in Gregory VII's text. The more important issue, however, lies in the ways in which Anselm conveyed the essence of selected points from *Dictatus papae* into his collection with considerably more historical precedence. For instance, the sentence that the pope's legate presided over any council, and was thus able to pass judgement, even if he was inferior in grade (*Dictatus papae* 4)—an assertion which wrought havoc with episcopal and metropolitan jurisdiction—was included in

---

[13] e.g. *Reg.* I: 56, 57; II: 15, 20, 25; III: 10; V: 12; VI: 26; IX: 29, 35.

[14] *Benonis aliorumque cardinalium . . . scripta*, 399–400. On *Dp* 23, see W. Ullmann, '"*Romanus Pontifex indubitanter efficitur sanctus*": *Dictatus papae* 23 in Retrospect and Prospect', *SG* 6 (1959–61), 229–64.

[15] Anselm VI: 2 'Ut sanctum esse nemo dubitet quem apostolicae dignitatis apex iuste attollit'.

[16] Anselm VI: 2 'In eadem synodo Ennodio episcopo dictante'; *Reg.* II: 55a, c. 23: ' . . . testante sancto Ennodio Papiensi episcopo ei multis sanctis patribus faventibus sicut in decretis beati Symmachi papae continetur.'

[17] While to a certain extent comparisons can also be made between Anselm and the *Proprie auctoritates apostolicae sedis*, the similarities seem to be a result of correspondances between *Dictatus papae* and *Proprie auctoritates*. It should be noted that Deusdedit also seems to have incorporated some of the concepts of the *Dictatus* sentences. See H. Mordek, ' "*Dictatus papae*" e "*Proprie auctoritates apostolicae sedis*": intorno all'idea del primato pontificio di Gregorio VII', *Rivista di storia della chiesa in italia*, 28 (1974), 1–22, and id., '*Proprie auctoritates apostolicae sedis*: Ein zweiter *Dictatus papae* Gregors VII.?', *DA* 28 (1972), 105–27, (a German version, which has an edition of the text at 126–7). A table comparing texts of the *Dictatus papae*, *Proprie auctoritates*, and Deusdedit is included in both articles. Cf. Caspar's apparatus for *Reg.* II: 55a, pp. 201–8. See also H. Fuhrmann, 'Papst Gregor VII. und das Kirchenrecht: zum Problem des *Dictatus papae*', 123–49, who is more cautious.

Anselm's collection under the authority of Gregory I.[18] Anselm seems also to have taken great care with the important issue of papal immunity from judgement (*Dp* 19). The matter was considered on at least four occasions, each time from slightly different vantage points, and was supported by a variety of canonical sources. The initial reference, supported by the *Ps.Constitutum Silvestri*, declared that the first See could not be judged by anyone. The next, from Ennodius' *Libellus pro synodo*, stated that the pope could not be judged save by God. The same notion was conveyed by the positive rubric, supported by a text from Ps.Anterus, that the pope was to be judged by God alone. The idea of papal immunity could also be seen to be reinforced by a text from Nicholas I, under a rubric which prohibited judgement by inferiors.[19]

These examples can be multiplied.[20] Anselm conceded the pontiff's right to divide wealthy episcopates, and to unite poorer ones (*Dp* 7), with texts from Gregory I. He likewise insisted upon the pontiff's right to temper existing law according to necessity (*Dp* 7) with texts from Symmachus VI and Cyprian. He firmly incorporated the concept of non-communion with those excommunicated by the pontiff (*Dp* 6)—an issue of much and persistent significance—with texts from Ps.Clement, Ps.Calixtus and Gregory I.[21] Anselm also transmitted the essence of the important precepts: that the Roman Church has never erred (*Dp* 22), with texts from Ps.Lucius; that no synod is general or authoritative without the pontiff's order or consent (*Dp* 16), with texts from Ps.Julius and one, erroneously but perhaps significantly cited as Gelasius; that no book is canonical without his authority (*Dp* 17), with texts from Leo I, Gelasius, Origen, and Innocent I; that no one is able to retract his sentences (*Dp* 18), with texts from Nicholas I and Gelasius; that to him alone is granted the right of using the imperial insignia (*Dp* 8), with texts

---

[18] *Dictatus papae* c. 4 = Anselm I: 25. For the following, see below, Table IV: Anselm's '*Dictatus papae*' Texts

[19] See R. Knox, 'Accusing Higher Up', *ZSSRG*, kan. Abt. 108 (1991), 1–31, esp. 3 ff.

[20] For documentation, see Table IV.

[21] The question of communion with excommunicates, along with the troublesome issue of the absolution of sworn oaths, was a matter of much debate between the papal and imperial parties as the polemical tracts of Gebhard of Salzburg and Wenrich of Trier demonstrate. See *Gebhardi Salisburgensis archiepiscopi epistola ad Herimannum Mettensem episcopum*, c. 5, 265; *Wenrici scolastici Trevirensis epistola*, 289–99; and *Benonis aliorumque cardinalium . . . scripta*, 380–1, 390. Subsequent reforming pontiffs were forced to modify the stringent regulations of Gregory VII regarding communion with excommunicates, and take into consideration those like servants, who could not avoid contact. Gregory, however, had recognized the practical difficulties of such sweeping bans: e.g. *Reg.* V: 14a, no. 16. In general, see E. Vodola, 'Sovereignty and Tabu: Evolution of the Sanction Against Communication with Excommunicates', 581–98.

from the *Constitutum Constantini*; that his name is to be recited in the churches (*Dp* 10), with a text from Pelagius I; that the greater cases of any church are to be referred to the Roman pontiff (*Dp* 21), with texts from Ps.Anacletus and Ps.Felix I, among others; that no one appealing to the Apostolic See could be condemned (*Dp* 20), with texts from Ps.Eleutherus and Gregory I among others; that the pontiff alone was able to depose and reconcile bishops (*Dp* 3), even without a synod (*Dp* 25), with texts from Gelasius, Symmachus, and others; that the Roman Church was founded by God alone (*Dp* 1), with texts from Ps.Anacletus and Peter Damian among others; that he who did not concord with the Roman Church was not catholic (*Dp* 26), with a text from Ambrose; that the pontiff was made *sanctus* by the merits of St Peter (*Dp* 23), with a text from Ennodius; and that the pontiff could depose, and excommunicate emperors (*Dp* 12), and absolve subjects from their oaths of fidelity (*Dp* 27), with Gregory VII's letter to Hermann of Metz, among others.

While Anselm largely incorporated the concepts of *Dictatus papae* into his collection, there were some important discrepancies. The most significant divergence is the dramatic difference in tone. Anselm, or at least as the rubrics show, was far less unequivocal than Gregory VII had been in his unique claims. Although he was able to find considerable historical precedence for the papal claims in *Dictatus papae*, Anselm was either unable, or unwilling, to concede to the pope the comprehensive list of prerogatives contained in Gregory's text. Perhaps ironically, one of these concerned the issue of the pope's doctrinal supremacy as definer of canonical or orthodox norms (*Dp* 17). Another addressed the troublesome matter of the absolution of sworn oaths (*Dp* 27).[22]

There were also some outright contradictions. One of these concerned *Dp* 2: that the Roman pontiff alone by right was to be called universal. Anselm proffered the exact opposite with texts from Ps.Pelagius II and Gregory I, both of which came from the 74T.[23] More telling in some ways, however, was Anselm's opposition to *Dp* 5: that the pope could depose the absent. While he noted the extraordinary case from the Council of Chalcedon of the condemnation of Dioscorus—who had ignored a summons to the synod—as a legitimate example, elsewhere Anselm followed long-standing canonical tradition, and wholeheartedly prohibited the judgement of the absent.[24]

---

[22] See Table IV, Anselm's rubrics at *Dp* 17 and 27.   [23] See Table IV, at *Dp* 2.
[24] See Table IV, at *Dp* 5 and 24. Cf. Anselm III: 28 Ut clericus criminatus sua in provincia audiatur, et ut sententia iudicis, quae absente accusato datur, irrita sit, et proditoris calumnia non audiatur [Ps.Eleutherus, c. 4, p. 126]; III: 53 Ut nullius accusatio vel testimonium per scripturam recipiatur, sed propria voce presente eo qui pulsatur

Anselm's acknowledgement of the legitimacy of the case of Dioscorus was perhaps a far more accurate reflection of Gregory VII's own position regarding the deposition of the absent than was the claim in *Dictatus papae*. The case of Dioscorus was a question of prolonged disobedience, of persistent contumacy. Otherwise, for Gregory, the canonical principle seems to have stood firm. Indeed, as Gilchrist had shown, Gregory VII only resorted to the deposition of the absent when all other measures to bring the accused to judgement had proved ineffective.[25]

With *Dictatus papae* 24, however, which permitted inferiors to bring accusations against their superiors with the pontiff's leave, Anselm found no such mitigating circumstances. With Ps.Isidorian texts from the 74T among others, Anselm flatly rejected the concept that inferiors could accuse their superiors.[26] Although elsewhere he acknowledged that the upright may undertake to accuse a bishop, and did accept the long-standing principle of *nisi a fide*, it is clear that he held strongly to the Ps.Isidorian principle of *magis est tolerandus* when it came to ecclesiastical status.[27] The opposition to *Dp* 24 seems to suggest an important difference between Anselm and Gregory. Perhaps a reflection of his own experience with his cathedral canons at San Martino in Lucca, Anselm seems unwilling to tolerate any infraction regarding the ordering of the ecclesiastical hierarchy, even, it appears, when it occurred with the permission of the pontiff.[28] Though, as will be seen, this

[Ps.Calixtus, c. 17, p. 141 (= 74T c. 48)]; III: 57 Ut ea quae adversus absentes aguntur evacuentur [Ps.Cornelius, c. 6, 174 (= 74T c. 106)]; III: 86 Quod iniustum iudicium et diffinitio alicuius potentis metu vel iussu ordinata non valet [Ps.Calixtus, c. 6, p. 137 (= 74T c. 105)]. Cf. 74T, tit. 13: Ut nemo absens iudicetur et de iniustis iudiciis, cc. 103–7 (all Ps.Isidorian).

[25] e.g. *Reg.* I: 51, p. 78: ' . . . adeo ut contempta auctoritate apostolicae sedis neque tu venire neque alios iuste te excusaturos studeris mittere. Unde quia absentatio tua iudicium iniustitiae tuae clarissimum tribuit . . . ' See also *Reg.* III: 14, and J. T. Gilchrist, 'Gregory VII and the Juristic Sources of his Ideology', *Studia Gratiana*, 12 (1967), 1–37, esp. 20–4.

[26] See Table IV at *Dp* 24. Cf. 74T cc. 66–9. Peter Damian used this in 1067 in his confrontation with the Vallombrosans, who had tried to use their reputation for sanctity (which Damian labelled 'odiosa sanctitas') as a justification for their illicit accusations against Bishop Peter Mezzabarba of Florence. Damian was resolute that judgement of a bishop required synodal or papal action. See Reindel, III, no. 146, pp. 531–42, especially 541. Cf. P. Golinelli, '*Indiscreta sanctitas*: Sull'uso polemico della santità nel contesto del movimento riformatore', in '*Indiscreta sanctitas*': *studi sui rapporti tra culti, poteri e società nel pieno medioevo* (Rome, 1988), 157–98. On Damian's earlier clashes with the Vallombrosans, see K. M. Woody, 'Damiani and The Radicals', Ph.D. thesis (New York, 1966), 39 ff.

[27] Anselm III: 32–3. Cf. Knox, 'Accusing Higher Up', 9.

[28] e.g. Anselm III: 13 Quod episcopi a populis non sunt corrigendi, et de quibus non sunt iam accusandi [Ps.Telesphorus, c. 3, 4, p. 111]; III: 31 Quod episcopus, si in fide erraverit, primo est corrigendus; si non emendaverit, accusandus est ad apostolicam sedem

did not necessarily contradict his other more pointed pro-papalist convictions, the inviolability of ecclesiastical status, whether confronted by opposition from the lay or lesser clerical spheres, always came first.[29]

Anselm, however, seems to have viewed this issue from two standpoints: one strictly legal, and the other moral. In this respect, Anselm was possibly a more subtle canonist as regards papal primacy than we may give him credit for being.[30] Rather than speaking directly, and explicitly, of the papal right to override or modify old rules and to create new ones (as in *Dp* 7), or of the papal privilege to dispense people from rules as in *Dp* 24, ' . . . with the pope's license . . . ', Anselm emphasized first and foremost the pope's ultimate duty for the wellbeing of the Church. It was this duty from which that power (to modify, and to create), and that privilege (to dispense)—in short, *to do what was needful*—ultimately derived. To this more subtle, less specific, but no less forceful, articulation of Roman primacy we must now turn.

While the canonical collections in the era prior to Gratian can be characterized by certain conventional methodological principles regarding form and content, the so-called reform collections of the late eleventh century also had an undeniable polemical quality. The ease and flexibility with which canonical texts from such collections could be transferred into more strictly polemical treatises, thereby explicitly reflecting the particular partisan issues which preoccupied each compiler, demonstrate the close link between the polemical and the canonical literature of the period. For instance, Anselm's polemical treatise, the *Liber contra Wibertum*, uses a number of canonical sources almost identical, though much abbreviated, with those found in Book XIII of his collection. More

[Ps.Fabianus, c. 23, p. 166]; III: 36 Ut qui causas habet contra pastores vel ecclesias eorum primo caritative expectet emendationem, quodsi ante infestare presumpserit, excommunicetur [Ps.Anacletus, c. 20, p. 77]; III: 51 Ut accusatus legitime episcopus vocatus ad synodum veniat, si non potest, legatum pro se mittat, ipse vero a communione non prohibeatur, nisi sex vel plures menses venire distulerit [Ps.Felix II, c. 12, p. 486]; III: 56 Ut episcopus accusatus congregata legitime synodo ab omnibus comprovincialibus audiatur, si accusatores legitimi sunt, sin autem, non fatigetur accusatus [Ps.Felix I, c. 12, 13, p. 202]; III: 88 Ut qui habet negotium contra episcopum prius caritative conveniat, quam in querimoniam deducat [Capitula Angilrammi, pp. 757 ff.]. Anselm was particularly careful to guard the episcopate against the accusations of *infames*: e.g.III: 1–3, 6, 8, 12, 16–20, 60. In general, see O. Capitani, 'La figura del vescovo in alcune collezioni canoniche della seconda metà del secolo XI', in *Vescovi e diocesi in Italia nel medioevo (sec. IX–XIII)* (Italia Sacra, 5; Padua, 1964), 161–91, esp. 179–82. For the views of Ps.Isidore, see Ch. 1, Sect. 2.

[29] See Table IV at *Dp* 24. Cf. Appendix Ib, A, no. 8.
[30] Cf. Knox, 'Accusing Higher Up', 10 and note 26.

telling perhaps, these sources were used in both genres to similar effect. The same sort of connection can be found between Deusdedit's *Libellus contra invasores et simoniacos* and his *Collectio canonum*. Of course, canonical texts were a significant feature of the polemical literature of both parties during this period. Neither side had a monopoly on the rhetorical traditions of the past, and both often appealed to the same authorities to corroborate opposing positions. The treatises of Bernold of Constance for instance, such as *Pro Gebhardo episcopo Constantiensi epistola apologetica* and *De excommunicatis vitandis*, are noteworthy both for their highly developed canonical theory, and for their exploitation of canonical sources. The same can be found in more imperial polemic, particularly that in the writings of the schismatic cardinals, and to a lesser extent that in Petrus Crassus' *Defensio Henrici IV*.[31]

This polemical quality is an important feature of Anselm's *Collectio canonum*. Indeed, one must agree with Robinson when he describes the collection as being 'a valuable guide to the central preoccupations of the Gregorian papacy'.[32] For despite its conventional formal structure, and its customary consideration of issues such as Roman primacy, the relationship of papal and episcopal authority, and the correlation between ecclesiastical and secular powers, the collection has clear partisan overtones. The usual issues acquire a sharper urgency as a result of the unrelenting insistence upon the absolute supremacy of the Roman pontiff, the preoccupation with the issues of clerical obedience, and the reform of the clergy in general, but most especially perhaps, as a result of the discussion of those who were *extra ecclesiam*. Anselm's collection, therefore, is not merely a catalogue. It also has the function of articulating, defining, and even propagating doctrine. As such, one can scarcely avoid seeing it as an almost 'legal' justification of reform.

This agenda is nowhere more apparent than in the articulation of

---

[31] See K. J. Leyser, 'The Polemics of the Papal Revolution', 147–8, 155; and I. S. Robinson, *Authority and Resistance*, 39 ff., 75–83, and 163 ff.

[32] Robinson, *Authority and Resistance*, 164. H. Mordek, 'Dalla riforma gregoriana alla *Concordia discordantium canonum* di Graziano', 89–112, is more cautious, warning (p. 94) that because of so many variables, it is extremely difficult to pinpoint the specific conceptual fundamentals of the Gregorians about the law. Cf. O. Capitani, 'L'interpretazione "pubblicistica" dei canoni come momento della definizione di istituti ecclesiastici (sec. XI–XII)', in *Fonti medioevali e problematica storiografica*, 2 vols. (Rome, 1976–7), i, 253–82, who believed that it is impossible to see canonical collections as semantic expressions of ideologies. While to some extent I share Mordek's cautious attitude, particularly in light of the different recensions of Anselm's collection, it seems that a reasonable case can be made.

Roman primacy.[33] In Books I and II of the collection, Anselm in essence made the unity of the Church contingent upon obedience to Rome and the Roman pontiff.[34] He supported this consideration in part with Ps.Isidorian texts, although, as has been discussed above, he 'overcame' them, modifying their essentially limited or 'last-ditch' bias by stressing the papal privilege inherent in such definitive jurisdiction.[35] In Anselm's mind, Roman primacy went far beyond any mere jurisdictional supremacy which had devolved onto Peter by the consent of the other apostles. Whereas the Ps.Isidorian documents had stressed the parity of Peter and the other apostles, and consequently that of the pontiff and the episcopate (though the Ps.Isidore had accepted the need for an independent but far-off pontiff to guarantee episcopal liberty), Anselm, on the other hand, insisted upon Christ's special foundation of the Church

[33] On Roman primacy, see Robinson, *Authority and Resistance*, 163 ff.; and H. Fuhrmann, 'Widerstande gegen den päpstlichen Primat im Abendland', in *Il primato del vescovo di Roma nel primo millenio: ricerche e testimonianze*, ed. M. Maccarrone (Pontificio comitato di scienze storiche, Atti e documenti, 4; Vatican City, 1991), 707–36; and J. Gaudemet, 'La Primauté pontificale dans les collections canoniques grégoriennes', in *Cristianità ed Europa: Miscellanea di studi in onore di Luigi Prosdocimi*, ed. C. Alzati (Rome, 1994), 59–90.

[34] Anselm I: 5 Quod Christum non recipit qui papam contristaverit [Ps.Clement, c. 17, p. 35]; I: 6 Quod nec loqui debemus cui papa non loquitur [Ps.Clement, c. 17, p. 36]; I: 11 Ut nemo dissentiat a Romana ecclesia, quae est caput omnium ecclesiarum [Ps.Pius, cc. 1–2, pp. 116, 117]; I: 12 Quod a regulis Romanae ecclesiae nullatenus convenit deviare [Ps.Calixtus, cc. 1–2, p. 136]; I: 16 Quod prima salus est regulas rectae fidei custodire et a statutis patrum non deviare, sicut Romana permansit ecclesia beati Petri sacerdotio ditata [Ps.Eusebius, cc. 15, 19, pp. 238, 239]; I: 20 Ut sacerdotes sive omnes ecclesiae statuta conservent sanctae Romanae ecclesiae, si nolunt eius communione carere [Gregory IV, JE no. 2579 (spurious)]; I: 31 Ut omnes catholici sequantur quod sedes apostolica docet, cui principatum Dominus dedit totius ecclesiae [Gelasius, ep. 14, p. 366]; I: 34 Item de eodem, et ut omnes qui veri filii volunt esse sciant et sequantur quae in Romana ecclesia sacro ritu aguntur [Ps.Fabianus, c. 1, p. 156]; I: 41 Quod traditionem Romanae ecclesiae debent reliquae observare, quia principium ab ipsa acceperunt [Innocent I, JK no. 311]; I: 42 Non aliter de scripturis sentiendum preterquam sancti patres docuerunt [Leo I, ep. 82 (JK no. 462)]; I: 44 Quod non sit recedendum ab apostolicis institutis [Leo I, ep. 16 (JK no. 414)]; I: 56 Quod in una ecclesia catholica, apostolicae sedi subiecta, vera Christi hostia immolatur [Gregory I, *Moralium*, lib. 35, no. 13]; I: 57 Quod ab apostolica sede fidei veritas est inquirenda tamquam ab ipso Petro, qui fidei plenitudinem breviter complexus est dicens: 'Tu es Christus' et cetera [Leo I, ep. 33]; I: 62 Ut nulli fas sit temerare divina et apostolicae sedis instituta [Hilary, synod a. 465 (Thiel, p. 161)]; II: 2 Edictum imperatoris, ut omnes eam sequantur religionem quam divinus Petrus apostolus edocuit [Codex Iustinianus, I, 1, 1]; II: 44 Ut omnes observent quod apostolica sedes observat [Ps.Julius, c. 9, p. 461]; IV: 47 Ut constituta sedis apostolicae et sanctorum patrum inrefragabiliter observentur [Ps.Damasus, c. 22, p. 507]; XII: 2 Quod omnes violatores decretorum Romanorum pontificum sint anathema [Capitula Angilrammi, cor. 20, p. 769]; XII: 47 Non esse veram fidem quae cum Romana ecclesia non convenit [Ambrose, *De excessu fratris*, I, no. 47].

[35] See above, Ch. 1, Sect. 2, and Appendix Ia, A.

upon Peter.[36] The sacerdotal *ordo* had sprung from Christ through the Petrine commission. This personal empowerment was not only the source of the legitimate pontiff's authority, but one that at the same time confirmed his position at the apex of the ecclesiastical hierarchy.[37] Peter's primacy, and consequently that of his legitimate successor, was not a nominal headship of one among equals. Not only could no one judge the pope; no one could judge what the pope was to judge.[38]

Behind Anselm's assertion of an absolute papal primacy lay a thoughtful, and essentially reform, ecclesiology. His text known as the *Sermo de caritate* is particularly instructive. Although written late 1085–early 1086, in the final months of his life, it seems clear that the same ecclesiology underlay his consideration of Roman primacy, and other issues, in the *Collectio canonum*.[39] The occasion of the sermon is

[36] Anselm I: 7 Quod Christus sancto Petro concessit volentibus apostolis, ut primus esset inter illos [Ps.Anacletus, c. 33, p. 83]; I: 8 Quod ad formam apostolorum facta est quaedam distinctio episcoporum, quibus tamen omnibus beati Petri sedes preminet [Ps.Julius, c. 9, p. 461]; I: 9 Quod ecclesia Romana omnibus preest ecclesiis, sicut beato Petro datum est preminere ceteris apostolis [Ps.Vigilius, c. 7, p. 712]; I: 10 Quod super unum, id est Petrum, aedificavit Dominus ecclesiam suam [Cyprian, *De catholicae ecclesiae unitate*, cc. 4, 5]; I: 18 Quod ecclesiae columpnae, qui sunt episcopi, confirmatae sunt super firmamentum Petri, quod est sedes apostolica [Ps.Damasus, c. 8, p. 502]; I: 51 Quod Petrus accepit claves regni caelorum, ut aliis aperiret [Ambrose, *Expositio evang. secundum Lucam*]; I: 55 Quod sanctus Petrus ius ligandi atque solvendi Lino et Cleto non tradiderit, licet eos sibi associaverit [Ps.John III, p. 716]; I: 63 Quod Romana ecclesia omnes instituit dignitates ecclesiasticas, ipsam autem verbum illud fundavit, per quod creata sunt omnia [Peter Damian, epist. 65]; I: 65 Quod pro fide Petri specialiter supplicatus est Christus [Leo IV, Sermo IV]; I: 66 Quod Romana ecclesia ab ipso Domino primatum obtinuit, et quod ambo apostoli Petrus et Paulus una die sua eam morte consecraverunt, et quod ipsa prima sedes est, secunda Alexandrina, tertia Antiocena [Ps.Anacletus, cc. 30–3, 34, pp. 83–4]; I: 67 Quod evangelica auctoritate prima omnium est Romana ecclesia, ubi Petrus et Paulus una die mortui sunt [Gelasius, ep. 26 (form. brev.), p. 454]; I: 68 Quod Romana ecclesia non synodicis sed evangelicis institutis primatum obtinuit, et quod sanctus Petrus et Paulus una die in urbe Roma coronati sunt [Gelasius, ep. 26 (form. brev.), p. 454]. The parity of the episcopate with the Roman pontiff was a predominant theme of anti-papal polemic of the late 11th cent. which (e.g. *Liber de unitate ecclesiae conservandae*) relied upon the Cyprianic *textus receptus* as opposed to the 'primacy' version favoured by papalists.

[37] e.g. Anselm I: 1 Quod in novo testamento post Christum dominum a Petro sacerdotalis coepit ordo [Ps.Anacletus, c. 24, p. 79]; I: 3 Ubi beatus Petrus concessum sibi ius ligandi ac solvendi in suos transponit successores [Ps.Clement, c. 2, p. 31]; I: 17 Quod Romana ecclesia omnibus est prelata non tantum canonum decretis sed voce ipsius Salvatoris [Ps.Julius, c. 6, p. 459]. Cf. I: 7, 10.

[38] For documentation of Anselm's understanding of Roman primacy, see App. Ia and Ib. See above, notes 34 and 36, for texts indicating more obvious doctrinal or moral supremacy. In general, see Knox, 'Accusing Higher Up', 1–31.

[39] *Sermo Anselmi episcopi de caritate*, ed. E. Pasztor, in 'Motivi dell'ecclesiologia di Anselmo di Lucca in margine a un sermone inedito', *Bull. Ist. Stor. Ital.* 77 (1965), 45–95; text, 96–104.

not without significance. As with the collection and the *Liber contra Wibertum*, the *Sermo de caritate* was composed after the schism of 1080, and therefore can, and should, be seen as responding to the upheaval created by that event. The *Sermo de caritate* was not merely a refutation of Wibert and his schismatic supporters, but also an impassioned appeal to the flagging spirits of the reform party. The text surely sought to revitalize and reunite the reformers following their leader's poor and perhaps bitter end in exile at Salerno.[40]

The *Sermo de caritate* was a thoughtful exposition of what the bishop believed to be the fundamental principle of *caritas*.[41] It was a topic, moreover, that offered Anselm an opportunity to unite his theological, ecclesiological, and 'political' thought, while specifically addressing the issues of Roman primacy, the dignity of the sacerdotal order, the position of excommunicates and schismatics with regard to the Church, and the role of secular princes in general within the life of the Church. These were, of course, standard issues, and had figured prominently in the *Collectio canonum*. In the collection, however, the consideration of these topics had lacked the pastoral urgency or immediacy with which they were infused in the *Sermo de caritate*.[42] It is useful here, therefore, to consider this text in more detail before returning to the collection.

The sermon opened with a consideration of Augustine's definition of *caritas*, and quickly switched to a somewhat plaintive appeal, reminiscent of Gregory VII's famous *milites* metaphor, regarding the dearth of initiative, enthusiasm, and even action on the part of the sacerdotal order.[43] Like Gregory, Anselm was indignant at those among the clergy

---

[40] See Pasztor, 'Motivi dell'ecclesiologia di Anselmo', 47–8. On Gregory VII's so-called 'last words', (*Briefsammlungen der Zeit Heinrichs IV.*, no. 35: 'Dilexi iustitiam et odivi iniquitatem, propterea morior in exilio') , see P. Hübinger, *Die letzen Worte Papst Gregors VII.* (Oppladen, 1973).

[41] Though Anselm began with Augustine's standard definition: 'Radix est et fundamentum virtutum omnium caritas . . . ' [Augustine, ep. 167, c. 5], his understanding of *caritas* leaned more towards the idea of 'mutual charity', a pastoral concern for the things of others. Cf. Anselm to Abbot Ponzio of Frassinoro (*c.*1078), in Hugh of Flavigny, *Chronicon* (*MGH*, *SS*, 8), 444: 'Tolerabilius est enim ut tu solus pereas, quam tecum pariter sicut hactenus omnes tibi commissos in discrimen adducas.'; and G. Fornasari, 'Sant'Anselmo e il problema della *caritas*', in *Sant'Anselmo, Mantova*, 301–12. St Bernard would echo this pastoral quality, seeing *caritas* as the duty even of contemplatives towards others. On this, see H. Mayr-Harting, 'Two Abbots in Politics: Walla of Corbie and Bernard of Clairvaux', *TRHS* , 5th ser. 40 (1990), 217–37, 231 ff.

[42] See Pasztor, 'Motivi dell'ecclesiologia di Anselmo', 48–9.

[43] *Sermo de caritate*, 98: 'Omnes quidem Deum Patrem presumimus invocare et celestis regni gaudia sanctorumque omnium communionem et consortium postulare non timemus, per viam tamen sanctorum, per artam et angustam viam que ducit ad vitam, ambulare nolumus, Redemptoris nostri vestigia sequi contempnimus, mandata regis eterni superbiendo,

who, in the light of the potentially tremendous eternal rewards, were not mindful of their pastoral obligations, and did not act from a spirit of *caritas*.[44] In Anselm's understanding, though, *caritas* was far more than the theoretical 'root of all virtues' of Augustine's definition. *Caritas* had a particularly practical manifestation. It represented for Anselm the quintessence of the entire pastoral life of the Church in the world. *Caritas* had entered the world with the birth of Christ and had been made manifest in his Passion.[45] *Caritas*, therefore, was simultaneously the obligation, and the motivation, of all ecclesiastical activity.[46]

The true import of *caritas* for Anselm, however, lay in the structure through which it operated in all of its many forms and expressions. This was the *ecclesia Romana*. It is this conviction that reveals the most basic element of Anselm's ecclesiological vision: the identification of the Apostolic Church with the Roman Church. From this, he was able to forge a definitive link between Apostolic prerogatives and the privileges of the Roman pontiff. By affirming the divine institution of the Church, Anselm drew attention to the perpetual stability which inhered in the Apostolic foundation, and which continued in the legitimate successors to that Petrine establishment. Roman primacy, therefore, entailed the Roman Church *together* with the Roman pontiff. The powers of the two were indistinguishable and could not be divorced. Everything hinged upon Peter; for in essence, Peter had become synonymous with the Roman Church.[47] The authority of the legitimate successor to Peter was, therefore, that of the Roman Church.

In the *Sermo de caritate*, by means of lengthy Petrine citations and exegesis, Anselm had not only justified primacy as a particularly Roman

inobediendo concalcamus.' Cf. Gregory VII, *Reg.* IX: 21, p. 602: 'Et tamen adhuc usque ad sanguinem rari ex nostris impii restiterunt et, quod omnino erat optandum, paucissimi nostrum pro Christo mortem subierunt. Pensate, carissimi, pensate, quot cotidie milites seculares pro dominis suis vili mercede inducti morti se tradunt. Et nos quid pro summo rege et sempiterna gloria patimur aut agimus?'

[44] Ibid. 98: 'Concupiscit anima nostra in atria Domini, sed deficere recusat a vanitatibus huius seculi. Sedere ad dexteram Patris cupimus, sed calicem Christi bibere nolumus. Vocat ipse et renitimus, pulsat ad ostium nostrum et aperire negligimus. Cum eo esse et regnare desideramus, sed tamen vana et caduca huius seculi gaudia toto affectu amplectimur. Consolationis eius participes fieri volumus, sed societatem passionis eius abhorremus. Delectat eternum in sublimitate glorie pondus, sed momentaneum et levis tribulationis subire refugimus.'

[45] Ibid. 97: 'Diligamus ergo nos invicem, quia caritas Deus est, ut per hanc supereminentem scientie caritatem Christi, que nunquam excidet, possimus comprehendere.'

[46] Anselm also used *caritas* with those who were *extra ecclesiam*. See below, Ch. 4.

[47] In the *Sermo de caritate*, the Church is indiscriminately called 'ecclesia Romana' and 'ecclesia Petri'.

attribute, but at the same time had testified to the utter lack of power of those who, voluntarily or otherwise, were *extra ecclesiam*. Most important, however, Anselm seemed to separate, and as a consequence revealed, the unique jurisdictional powers of the Roman Church, and consequently of the Roman pontiff, as against the more obvious moral ones.[48] It is an ecclesiology with important ramifications. By equating the Roman Church with Peter, and with Peter's authority, Anselm not only nullified the claims and powers of *any* schismatic hierarchy, but at the same time affirmed the institutional framework of the *ecclesia Romana* through which *caritas* operated. At the top of this hierarchy was the all-important Roman pontiff: the expression, the symbol, and the guarantee of the faith. Those who did not participate in the fellowship of Peter, who did not obey his precepts, but dissented from him, lay outside the faith of which Peter himself was the foundation.[49]

Within this articulation of the supremacy of the Roman pontiff lies an urgent moral imperative. It was essentially a summons to the pope to action, an appeal that he be ever-vigilant on behalf of the Church.

[48] *Sermo de caritate*, 100–1: 'Romana namque Ecclesia non ab homine, neque per hominem, sed ipso capite nostro fundata est. [. . .] Romana siquidem Ecclesia princeps est omnium ecclesiarum, magistra et domina, cui ligandi solvendique principaliter a Domino est concessa potestas. Nam sicut beato Petro non solum agnos verum etiam oves pascendas commisit, sic Ecclesiae in Petro fundate non solum populorum gregem, sed ipsos insuper gregum pastores ubique terrarum subiecit, quod evidentibus argumentis approbamus: Si Ecclesia Romana sponsa Christi est, immo quia est, et de sponso et sponsa scriptum est: erunt duo in carne una—sacramentum hoc magnum est, dicit apostolus, ego autem dico, in Christo et in Ecclesia—qui in corpore Christi non sunt membra, utique Christi esse non possunt, et si Filio subiecit Pater omnia, que in celis et que in terra sunt, eadem procul dubio omnia sponse eius subiecta sunt et per eam multiformis sapientia Dei principibus et potestatibus innotescit etiam in celestibus. Pro cuius fide rogavit Christus ut non deficeret et Petro precepit ut fratres suos confirmaret. Unde colligi potest, quod sicut Romana Ecclesia nunquam erravit, sic usque in finem seculi Deo protegente in fide perserverabit. Cum enim clavigero Petro a Domino dictum sit: quecumque solveris super terram erit soluta et in celis et tibi dabo claves regni celorum, cum Petrus in ea usque in finem seculi, per fidem quae non deficiet, presideat, patet profecto quod qui extra Ecclesiam Petri est, ligandi et solvendi potestatem habere non potest. Et cum a Petro sacerdotalis ordo ceperit et propter illum in Ecclesia eius principium novi sacerdotii sit, constat procul dubio quod veri sacerdotii locus extra hanc esse non possit.' Cf. Pasztor, 'Motivi dell'ecclesiologia', 56 ff.

[49] *Sermo de caritate*, 101: 'Quicumque ergo istius membrum non est, istius precepto non obedit, istam non sequitur, ab ista dissidet, fidei exors est, quia eius fundamentum fides est.' Cf. Anselm IV: 26 Qui promulgata ab Apostolico pro catholica fide et ecclesiastica disciplina contempserit, anathema sit [Nicholas I, in synodo a. 863, c. 5, JE post 2747]; IV: 27 Item de eadem re, et quod hoc privilegium statutum Christi est [cited as Gelasius, but according to Thiel, Gelasius for Felix III, p. 287]; VI: 57 Qui ab unitate ecclesiae recesserit, nec episcopi potestatem habere potest nec honorem [Cyprian, ep. 55, c. 24]; XII: 41 Quod non est consecratio sed execratio quae extra ecclesia sit [Pelagius I, JK no. 983].

(This, of course, was something that Gregory himself had constantly stressed.) In Anselm's view, the moral duty or obligation to act was as significant as the pontiff's actual legal right to do so, if not more so.[50] Effectively, it was from this that the rest of the pontiff's authority derived. This moral imperative, moreover, when combined with the doctrine of *plenitudo potestatis*, presented the Roman pontiff with a mandate *to do what was needful*—effectively a legal mandate for reform.[51]

This is a subtle, but critical, concept which reveals a certain amount of tension, although not necessarily contradiction, in Anselm's thought. The stewardship of the Church by the Roman pontiff not only epitomized for Anselm the pastoral life of the Church, but also provided the model of the true pastor. Not only was the Roman pontiff technically, and legally, above reproach and judgement, he was obliged always to act in such a fashion as morally to justify that unique legal position.

This, of course, was a customary point of canon law. It was made in the 74T, and was repeated by Anselm with the same canonical source, although under a more exacting rubric.[52] Anselm, however, seems to have had an even more vigorous and practical idea of the ramifications of moral rectitude on the part of the pontiff. He was to be the reformer *par excellence*. It was incumbent upon him to defend the Church, and to act quickly to correct or check any malicious force. The Roman pontiff was not to be seen as a pastor who did not love Christ, and who did not attend to his flock.[53] The obligation of the Church, and especially the

---

[50] Anselm I: 26 Quod papae non licet tacere, quod in querelam potest venire [Syricius, JK no. 263]; I: 28 Quod papa pro universis ecclesiis principaliter curare debeat [Leo I, ep. 14]; I: 29 Item de apostolicae sedis auctoritate, et quod pro necessitate temporis adhibenda est curatio vulneratis [Leo I, ep. 159]; I: 32 Quod pro omni statu ecclesiae papa debet curam habere [Ps.Sother, c. 3, p. 124]; I: 33 Ut omnibus ecclesiis papa provideat et succurrat [Ps.Zepherinus, c. 10, p. 133]; I: 39 Quod habet Apostolicus a beato Petro fiduciam defendendi fidem rectam in omni ecclesia [Ps.Liberius, c. 1, p. 476]; I: 49 Quod nullus magis debeat observare canones quam Apostolicus [Gelasius, ep. 26, p. 415]; IV: 6 Quod papa sicut suae ecclesiae privilegia, ita singularum debet ecclesiarum iura defendere ac servare [Gregory I, *Reg.* II: 52].

[51] Anselm I: 14 Quod per universam ecclesiam quicquid nocivum in ea est debet papa corrigere et emendare [Ps.Dionysius, c. 2, p. 195]; I: 40 Quod papae maior cunctis necessitas corrigendi incumbit [Syricius, JK no. 255]; VIII: 27 Quod vigor antiquitatis servetur in lapsis usque ad auctoritatem et consilium papae [Cyprian, ep. 30]; XIII: 19 Qui potest perturbare perversos et non facit eorum impietati consentit [Ps.Damasus, p. 508].

[52] 74T, tit. 22, cc. 174–17. Cf. Anselm VI: 1 Ut papa incolumi nullus ambiat papatum, et de electione alterius, si ipse adhuc vivens nichil inde disposuit [Symmachus, synod of Rome a. 499, Thiel, p. 645].

[53] Anselm I: 43 Quod papa ipsius sedis reverentia cogitur studiosus pro omnibus esse, ut non videatur pastorem Christum non amare [Leo I, ep. 16].

Roman pontiff, was for *all* of the flock, and under all circumstances.[54] Reform was presented not only as the legal right of the Roman pontiff, but in fact his overriding duty. Conversely, this duty presented him with a legal right to act. In so doing, Anselm underlined perhaps the most basic aspect of the pontificate of Gregory VII: it was a papacy on the offensive, a papacy going against the current, a papacy unwilling to tolerate the status quo.

The tension between the legal right and the moral obligation of the Roman pontiff to act—what Ovidio Capitani viewed in terms of a struggle between *diritto* and *dovere*—had far-ranging ramifications for Anselm's view of the relations within the ecclesiastical hierarchy.[55] Capitani used the terms only in connection with the relations between the Roman pontiff and the episcopate, particularly in respect to Gregory VII. As has been suggested, however, this concept had a far wider applicability for Anselm since he considered both the Roman pontiff in his own right and in regard to his position *vis-à-vis* the entire Church. For, by insisting upon both the legal right and the moral obligation of the Roman pontiff to ensure that correct faith and doctrinal norms were maintained in all churches, Anselm underlined the vast chasm that separated papal and episcopal authority. The fullness of power lay with the Roman pontiff; but it was his task to exercise that authority for the good of the entire Church. Anselm was, in essence, recognizing that tighter jurisdictional control needed to be exerted over the episcopate. This intensified jurisdiction was essential not only to the success of reform, but also for the preservation of the faith.

The inevitable consequence of this concept of papal jurisdiction was the beginning, in theoretical terms, of a dramatic centralization of the Church upon Rome and upon the Roman pontiff. This idea was expressed particularly in Book II, where, as has been seen, Anselm had modified his Ps.Isidorian texts by stressing the papal privilege inherent in the judgement of the episcopate. Yet his concept went beyond mere emphasis of papal privilege, and thus seems to have reflected the narrower, and more immediate, situation of Gregory VII. The numerous complaints voiced by the German episcopate over Gregory's incessant commands, his frequent calls for them to come *ad limina apostolorum*, together with the regular synods held at Rome (undeniably, a practical manifestation of centralization) indicate the extent to which it was

---

[54] This appears to be the primary motivation behind Anselm's call for schismatics and other *errantes* be coerced, if necessary, to return to true obedience. See below, Ch. 4.

[55] O. Capitani, 'La figura del vescovo in alcune collezioni canoniche', 186 ff.

already becoming a reality.[56] Anselm was in essence providing a *de facto* justification. By ignoring, superseding, and even nullifying the jurisdiction of the metropolitan, Anselm sought not only to reinforce the already-existing hierarchic lines between the pontiff and the episcopate, but also to emphasize the pope's dominion over *each* individual sector of the ecclesiastical hierarchy.[57] The clash between Siegfried of Mainz and Gregory VII over the dispute between the sees of Prague and Olmütz (Moravia), in which Siegfried believed that his metropolitan rights had been infringed when John of Prague was accused without his knowledge, is a case in point. Gregory responded by remarking how little Siegfried and his *confratres* knew of canonical tradition and the decrees of the Fathers.[58]

Anselm also sought to place restraints upon the jurisdiction of the episcopate as a whole. For instance, stipulations that the greater *causae* (which went unspecified) of all churches terminate at Rome were significant extensions of papal authority over the episcopate's right of self-regulation.[59] While the basic principle of matters being settled within

[56] e.g. Liemar of Bremen to Hezilo of Hildesheim, *Briefsammlungen*, no. 15, p. 34: 'Periculosus homo vult iubere, quae vult, episcopis ut villicis suis; quae si non fecerunt omnia, Romam venient aut sine iudicio suspenduntur.' Cf. I. S. Robinson, '*Periculosus homo*: Pope Gregory VII and Episcopal Authority', *Viator* 9 (1978), 103–33.

[57] Anselm II: 12 Ut primates accusatum episcopum discutiant, sententiam vero damnationis sine apostolica auctoritate non proferant [Ps.Felix I, c. 4, p. 198]; II: 51 Ut apostolicam sedem appellet qui metropolitanum suum vel ceteros episcopos habet suspectos et quod ipsa potestatem habet iniuste dampnatos et excommunicatos restituere et sua eis reddere, quia caput omnium est [Ps.Athanasius, c. 4, p. 480]; II: 59 Ut pregravati a comprovincialibus episcopis vel metropolitano sedem appellent apostolicam et nullam interim molestiam patiantur, donec ibi res finiatur [Ps.Felix II, c. 12, p. 488]; II: 60 Quod metropolitano cum omnibus comprovincialibus episcopis summas ecclesiasticas causas licet discutere, sed non diffinire, nec episcopum dampnare nec synodum congregare absque apostolicae sedis auctoritate [Ps.Damasus, c. 8, 9, p. 502]; II: 65 Sicut inter apostolos fuit discretio potestatis, ut unus aliis premineret, sic inter episcopos ordinatum est, ut in singulis provinciis singuli presint et desub primates, quibus tamen omnibus Romana preest ecclesia [Nicholas I, JE no. 2785]; II: 66 Invectio papae contra Remensem archiepiscopum, qui Rothardum episcopum appellantem apostolicam sedem dampnare ausus est [Nicholas I, JE no. 2784]. Cf. Appendix Ia, B for additional documentation.

[58] Siegfried of Mainz to Gregory VII, in *Codex Udalrici*, no. 40 (Biblioteca rerum Germanicarum, 5), 84–7. For Gregory's response, see *Reg.* I: 60, and I: 61 to Wratislaw II, Duke of Bohemia.

[59] e.g. Anselm II: 4 Ut difficiliores causae et maiora negocia ad sedem apostolicam, si appellatum fuerit, deferantur [Ps.Anacletus, c. 17, p. 74]; II: 6 Quod ad Romanam ecclesiam ab omnibus oppressis appellandum est, ubi etiam omnes ecclesiasticae causae maiores sunt terminandae [Ps.Zepherinus, c. 6, p. 132]; II: 13 Quod dubiae ac maiores causae ab apostolica sede debent terminari [Ps.Felix I, c. 17, p. 204]; II: 39 Ut difficiliores singularum provinciarum quaestiones ad sedem apostolicam referantur [Ps.Gaius, c. 7, p. 218]; II: 53 Ut contentiones inter clericos et laicos a comprovincialibus episcopis terminentur, maiores vero ad sedem Romanam transferantur [Innocent I, JK no. 286]; II: 58 Ut

the confines of the diocese or *provincia* in question was acknowledged, the unique local authority of the episcopate did not go unchallenged.[60] The pope could not only empower a legate with superior jurisdiction, but he could also appoint external judges.[61] While Anselm did insist upon the right of the episcopate to scrutinize and debate lateral issues, he effectively contrasted this more limited right with the definitive judgement of the Roman pontiff.[62]

Like the compiler of the 74T, Anselm sought to construct a solid constitution for ecclesiastical society. Yet whereas the 74T had focused upon the episcopate, and had not envisaged that any opposition would arise between the respective claims of Roman primacy and the rights of the bishops, for Anselm even the possibility of conflict was unimaginable. In Anselm's vision, the framework for ecclesiastical society was one which took its reference directly from Rome. His blueprint involved a narrow chain of obedience that bound the various clerical orders in a vertical, hierarchic structure. Though the episcopate was to remain immune from attack from below, absolute obedience to the higher level was unchallengeable, and not to be questioned. While Anselm was particularly solicitous of the position and the rights of the episcopate, reference to the centre, to the Apostolic See, was the best insurance for them—a theme reminiscent of the 74T.

Yet Anselm was equally insistent about the reverse: the necessary scrutiny of the Apostolic See over the episcopate, those vital and essen-

---

difficiliores quaestiones ad sedem apostolicam referantur [cited as Gregorius, but Ps.Pelagius II, pp. 722–4].

[60] Anselm II: 21 Ut nullus metropolitanorum causas episcoporum sive aliorum agere presumat, nisi quae ad propriam pertinent parrochiam [Ps.Annicius, c. 4, p. 121]; but also III: 80 Ut provinciae suos habent iudices, nisi papa aliter voluerit [Ps.Anacletus, c. 15, p. 73].

[61] See texts, Table IV at *Dp* 4. Legatine authority probably did the most to impede local monopolies regarding jurisdiction. For instance, the consecration of Gebhard of Constance in 1084 by the papal legate Odo of Ostia, which was an important triumph for the reformers, was, according to the *Liber de unitate ecclesiae conservandae*, an unprecedented infringement of the metropolitan rights of Mainz. Cf. Bernold, *Chronicon a. 1084*, 441. It is not without significance that Urban II abandoned the practice of standing legates in his efforts to create better relations both with the cardinals and with the episcopate.

[62] Anselm II: 9 Quod absque auctoritate apostolica nulli licet episcoporum causas diffinire, quamvis scrutari liceat comprovincialibus episcopis [Ps.Victor, cc. 4–6, p. 128]; II: 30 Ut ad apostolicam sedem referatur, si qua dissensio inter fratres oriatur [Leo I, ep. 14, c. 11]; II: 31 Ut causae ecclesiarum ab episcopis ventilatae corroborentur ab apostolicae sede, si ratae debuerint permanere [Leo I, ep. 12, c. 13]; II: 37 Ut accusatus episcopus alieno iudice non constringatur, sed apud suos episcopos causa eius rationabiliter discernatur; finis vero ad apostolicam sedem referatur [Ps.Zepherinus, c. 5, p. 131]; II: 81 Ut accusatus vel iudicatus a comprovincialibus episcopis licenter papam appellet, qui eius causam retractet, et in loco eius interim alius non ordinetur [Ps.Victor, c. 5, p. 128].

tial men who were to be the local agents and implements of reform.[63]
The idea of primacy, the centralization under Rome, advocated by
Anselm was perhaps not so much the consequence of a particular religious ideal or strategy, but rather an institutional necessity and even
inevitability. In the end, therefore, Anselm evinced a legal and an institutional awareness of the need for the Church to be guided by a single
figure with the authority to do what was needful. This person, the
Roman pontiff, would be the unchallengeable figure who would be able
to discipline, order, and reform the ranks of the Church from within,
without recourse to any external, local, or especially secular, force.
Whether or not *Dictatus papae* set his agenda, the interests of reform
drove his articulation of papal primacy. Whether or not he specifically
set out to do so, in the end he provided a vindication for Gregory VII's
revolution based on both moral and legal tradition.

---

[63] As Anselm was depicted as being: *Vita Anselmi*, c. 32, p. 22. Cf. Gregory to Siegfried
of Mainz, *Ep. vag.*, no. 6, p. 14: ' . . . hoc obedientiae munus iniungere decrevimus, ut
tam per te quam per coadiutores tuos hoc Romanae ecclesiae decretum universo clero stu-
diosius inculcares et inviolabiter tenendum proponeres'; and Anselm II: 19 Ut quisquis
sacerdotum apostolicae sedis non obedierit preceptis, a ministerio deponatur et excommunicetur, quia non solum obedire debuit, sed et aliis ut obedirent insinuare [Gregory IV,
JE no. 2579 (spur.)].

4

Anselm and Coercion:
A Legal Form of Persuasion

In the spring of 1085, Anselm wrote to Bishop Hermann of Metz, commending him, at a time when the *caritas* of many was growing cold, for his willingness to persevere and to risk even death in the cause of the Lord.[1] The imperialists, Anselm wrote, seemed to re-crucify Christ and his heir, the universal Church of Peter, and were contending with new and unheard of blasphemies even against the prince of the Apostles himself.[2] Schism had left the reform movement in a dire climate of crisis: Christ, as Anselm stirringly and significantly noted, stood alone on the field of battle.[3]

There can be little doubt that the schism of 1080 was a thorough disaster for the papacy of Gregory VII. Of course, schism at any time represented a serious danger, not least because of the creation of rival hierarchies from whom great benefits could be reaped. Yet the schism

---

[1] *Briefsammlungen*, no. 21, p. 50: 'Quia animam tuam pretiosiorem quam te non fecisti et usque ad sanguinem pro testamento Domini resistere tempore, quo iniquitate multiplicata caritas multorum refrigescit, sicut nobis relatum est, disposuisti.' This probably refers to Hermann's refusal to attend the imperial council at Mainz in early May 1085, held as a reaction to the reform synod at Quedlinburg at Easter; it was a refusal for which Hermann was subsequently deprived of his see. On Mainz, see M. E. Stoller, 'Schism in the Reform Papacy: The Documents and Councils of the Anti-Popes, 1061–1121', Ph.D. thesis (New York, 1985), 241–67, esp. 245–6; and Meyer von Knonau, IV, 21–5, 547–50.

[2] *Briefsammlungen*, 51: 'Nonne tibi videntur Christum crucifigere et contemptui habere, qui hereditatem eius, vineam Domini Sabaoth, universalem videlicet Petri ecclesiam, conculcantes adversus ipsum apostolorum principem novo et inaudito blasphemiae genere insurgunt . . . ?' Cf. Anselm's commentary on Psalm II (fragments), in Paul of Bernried, *Vita Gregorii VII.*, c. 112, in *Pontificum Romanorum Vitae*, I, ed. J. M. Watterich (Leipzig, 1862), 541: ' . . . non solum venerunt, sed et adstiterunt et exercitu suo Romanam obsederunt . . . [et infra] Nonne iterum Barabbas eligitur et Christus sub Pilato morti addicitur, cum Ravennas Guibertus eligitur et Papa Gregorius reprobatur?'

[3] *Briefsammlungen*, 50: 'Ecce enim Christus solus in campo est . . . '

which followed from Gregory VII's second excommunication of Henry IV at the Lenten synod of 1080 was particularly bitter, provoking a climate of seemingly insurmountable intransigence whose effects would linger well into the following century, until the Concordat of Worms in 1122, if not beyond.[4] The reasons for this stemmed in part from Henry IV's three-year campaign of military operations and attacks upon Rome, from the resulting defection of hitherto pro-papal bishops and Roman cardinals, from the ensuing and prolonged state of open war between the royal and papal supporters in the Reich and in Italy, and from the destruction of the material resources of the Church. Regionally, of course, the impact of the schism varied. Clement III enjoyed little if any sustained support in France, the Iberian peninsula, and England. But in the Reich and in Italy, the position both of Gregory VII and his supporters was severely undermined.

In the climate of recrimination and partisan obstinacy that followed, a number of disturbing and problematic issues—many of which had been simmering under the surface since 1076, if not earlier—quickly rose to the forefront. For by bitterly intensifying both the rhetoric and the debate over the relationship between secular and ecclesiastical authority, the schism had brought two diametrically opposed, and seemingly irreconcilable, concepts of the 'right order of the world' to a point of no return. Unlike the earlier excommunication of the king, the papal sentence of 1080 did not appear to have a single or easily identifiable motive. It was viewed, not without some justification perhaps, as a personal attack on the king. Henry IV and his supporters, particularly among the episcopate, labelled Gregory a dangerous man who subverted the traditional order in favour of a quasi-autocratic hierarchy with himself at the apex.[5] Gregory VII and his supporters, for their part, continued to insist upon not merely the right, but the overwhelming

---

[4] The events that led from the synod of Worms in 1076 to the second excommunication of Henry IV in 1080, the clash between Gregory VII and Henry IV, its background and ongoing manifestations, are enormous topics with vast amounts of literature. An excellent discussion is U.-R. Blumenthal, *The Investiture Controversy: Church and Monarchy from the Ninth to the Twelfth Century* (Philadelphia, 1988), esp. ch. 3 with its bibliography.

[5] e.g. *Vita Heinrici IV. imperatoris*, c. 6 (*MGH, SRG*; Hanover, 1899), 22: 'Ad quorum criminationem apostolicus eum iterum banno, ut ipsi iactabant, illigavit; sed non magni ponderis ille bannus habebatur, eo quod non rationis, sed arbitrii, non amoris, sed odii esse videretur.' Cf. *Wenrici scolastici Trevirensis epistola*, 297: 'Quis enim videat, non ex religionis zelo, sed ex principis odio . . . ' See also the letters of Huzmann of Speyer, Egilbert of Trier, and Theoderic of Verdun, written in an effort to elicit support for a new papal election in *Codex Udalrici*, nos. 60–2, pp. 126 ff.; M. E. Stoller, 189–218; and Meyer von Knonau, III, 277 ff.

duty, of the pope to direct Christian society at all levels.[6] Events had in essence outstripped contemporaries' capacity to understand them. Theoretical issues such as rival obediences, the nature of sworn oaths, the relationships between catholics and schismatics, and the validity of the sacraments and orders of those who were *extra ecclesiam* quickly became pressing and practical concerns as the two hierarchies vied for authoritative position. As the rapid proliferation of polemical treatises indicated, each side felt a need to justify policy by firmly portraying it as ancient tradition. As such, the schism had a profound impact upon canon law.

While it is unwise to be too rigorous in insisting that the schism dictated the development or incorporation of certain themes in canon law, neither can one overlook the ways in which the law seemed to reflect, or at least respond to, the problems made manifest by the schism. This is perhaps nowhere more apparent than in the two final, and still unedited, books of Anselm's *Collectio canonum* (Book XII: *De excommunicatione*, and Book XIII: *De iusta vindicta*), where he considered the status of those who contended against the Roman Church, and then discussed the methods by which such persons should be handled.[7] Although the canonical authorities used to justify coercion were familiar ones, and had been employed in previous collections (though not in the immediate past), both in this particular formulation and in the broader context of events, they found a new, pointed, more stringent and uncompromising expression. Indeed, the preoccupation with the canonical definition and the status of excommunicates, schismatics, and heretics,[8] the strict injunctions regulating the contact and relations of

---

[6] e.g. *Reg.* VIII: 21; *Ep. vag.*, nos. 51, 54; *Gebhardi Salisburgensis archiepiscopi epistola*, 261–79. See also K. J. Leyser, 'The Polemics of the Papal Revolution', 138–60.

[7] As indicated above, Introduction, pp. 7–8 note 29, all subsequent references will be to MS Vat. lat. 1363, with reference to the variant Vatican, Paris, and Cambridge MSS where appropriate. See Appendix II for more detail. In general, see A. M. Stickler, 'Il potere coattivo materiale della chiesa nella riforma gregoriana secondo Anselmo di Lucca', *SG* 2 (1947), 235–85, which explores the ecclesio-political aspects of Anselm's doctrine of coercion, and remains indispensable. Stickler provides a useful table at 248–9, listing the texts that specifically address coercion in Books XII and XIII, along with a brief incipit/explicit, the inscription, and location in Gratian. See also E. Pasztor, 'Lotta per le investiture e *"ius belli"*: la posizione di Anselmo di Lucca', in *Sant'Anselmo, Mantova*, 375–424.

[8] Anselm XII: 1 Quod excommunicati sunt omnes qui contra sanctam Romanam ecclesiam superbiendo se erigunt [Ps.Boniface II, p. 704]; XII: 2 Quod omnes violatores decretorum Romanorum pontificum sint anathema [Capit. Angilrammi, cor. 20, p. 769]; XII: 3 Ut anathema sit quicunque praecepta sedis apostolicae contempserint [Nicholas I, Council of Rome a. 863, JE post no. 2747]; XII: 31 Ut nomina excommunicatorum publicentur [John VIII, Council of Ravenna a. 877, c. 10]; XII: 32 Si quis presbyter contra episcopum suum inflatus scisma fecerit anathema sit [Council of Carthage (II), c. 8]; XII: 37 Si quis

catholics and schismatics,[9] the insistence upon the permissibility and even the obligation of compelling *malos ad bonum*,[10] the corresponding emphasis upon the benevolent aspects of coercion,[11] the contingent quality of the distinction between strictly secular coercion executed on behalf of the Church, and *persecutio* directed by the Church,[12] together with the hitherto unnoticed consideration of who in such situations was

audet transmutare quod sancti patres et universales synodi statuerunt condemnatus est [apocryphal Gelasius, cf. Thiel, 612, no. 7]; XII: 40 Quod heretici in aecclesia nichil habeant potestatis et iuris [Cyprian, epist. 69, c. 1 ff.]; XII: 41 Quod non est consecratio sed execratio quae extra aecclesiam sit [Pelagius I, JK no. 983]; XII: 47 Non esse veram fidem quae cum Romana ecclesia non convenit [Ambrose, *De excessu fratris*, I, no. 47]; XII: 59 Quod separatus ab ecclesia quantumcumque laudabiliter vivat non tamen habebit vitam aeternam [Augustine, epist. 141, c. 5]. See also XII: 5–7, 10, 25–8, 30, 43, 48, 50–2, 61, 68–71 (see App. II).

[9] Anselm XII: 11 Quod non debet quis ei communicare quem sedes apostolica repellit nisi ab illatis se mundaverit [Gregory I, *Reg*. VI: 26]; XII: 13 Ut excommunicatis nemo communicet in oratione, cibo, potu, osculo, nec ave eis dicat alioquin similiter excommunicatus est [Ps.Calixtus, c. 10, p. 138]; XII: 18 Quod cum excommunicatis non sit communicandum et qui fecerit excommunicetur [Ps.Fabianus, c. 6, p. 159]; XII: 20 Quod excommunicatus et communicator eius aeque debent refutari et puniri [Gelasius, ep. 12, cc. 7, 8]; XII: 63 Quando mali tolerandi sunt et quando separandi a nobis [Augustine, *De fide et operibus*, 6 ff.]. See also XII: 12, 14–17, 19, 21, 64, 65 (see App. II).

[10] Anselm XII: 55 De malis cogendis ad bonum [Augustine, epist. 173, cc. 1 ff.]; XII: 60 De scismaticis ad correctionem cogendis [Augustine, epist. 185, cc. 6 ff.]; XIII: 4 Quod militantes etiam possunt esse iusti [Augustine, epist. 189, cc. 4, 6]; XIII: 13 Quod inobedientes severius sint corrigendi [Ps.Calixtus, p. 138]; XIII: 19 Qui potest perturbare perversos et non facit eorum impietati consentit [Ps.Damasus, p. 508]. See also XIII: 5–7, 20 (see App. II).

[11] Anselm XII: 44 Quod aecclesia non persequitur sed diligit cum punit vel prohibet malum, et divisi a sede apostolica scismatici sunt, et quod comprimendi sunt a saecularibus iniusti episcopi [Pelagius I, JK no. 1018]; XIII: 1 Quod Moyses nichil crudele fecit quando praecepto Domini quosdam trucidavit [Augustine, *Contra Faustum*, lib. XXII, c. 79]; XIII: 2 De vindicta non odio sed amore facienda [Augustine, *De sermone Domini in monte*, I, cc. 64–5]; XIII: 3 Quod bella cum benivolentia sunt gerenda [Augustine, epist. 138, cc. 12 ff.]; XIII: 10 Ut temperetur vindicta [Augustine, epist. 133, cc. 1 ff.]; XIII: 12 Ut mali non occidantur sed corrigantur [Augustine, epist. 100, cc. 1 ff.]; XIII: 21 Quod homini misericordia peccatis persecutio debeatur [cf. App. II]; XIII: 27 ⟨no rubric⟩ (cf. App. II) [Ambrose, *Libri de officiis* I, cc. 30 ff.; II, cc. 15, 21, 28].

[12] Anselm XII: 45 Quod nullis [nullum] sacrificium Deo a potestatibus gratius est quam ut scismatici episcopi ab [ad] obediendum coerceantur [Pelagius I, JK no. 1024]; XII: 46 De scismaticis coercendis a saecularibus [Pelagius I, JK no. 1012]; XII: 53 De hereticis per saeculares potestates coercendis [Augustine, *In Iohannis evang.*, Tract. XI, 13 ff.]; XII: 54 Ut excommunicati cohibeantur a saecularibus [Augustine, epist. 93 (excerpts)]; XIII: 23 ⟨no rubric⟩ (cf. App. II) [Gregory I, *Reg*. VIII: 4]; XIII: 28 ⟨no rubric⟩ (cf. App. II) [Gregory I, *Reg*. I: 72]. Compare with Anselm XIII: 14 Quod aecclesia persecutionem possit facere [Augustine, epist. 185, c. 11]; XIII: 15 De eadem re [Augustine, epist. 185, c. 19]; XIII: 16 Item ad eundem de eadem re [Augustine, epist. 185, cc. 22 ff.]; XIII: 17 De eadem re [Augustine, epist. 185, cc. 36 ff.].

to maintain control over the *res ecclesiae*,[13] make it extremely difficult not to envisage these two books as a product, or at least a reflection, of the period of crisis initiated by the schism.

That such a reading is permissible is borne out by a number of factors. On the one hand, there is the argument that the texts and the themes in Books XII and XIII are also to be found in Anselm's polemical treatise, the *Liber contra Wibertum*, which was most clearly a *piece d'occasion*.[14] More telling, however, is the absence of any mention of coercion, of the legitimate use of force, or indeed of any significant consideration of how excommunicates are to be handled in either the 74T or the *Breviarium* of Cardinal Atto, apart, that is, from the wholly unexceptional view that they were to be excluded from the body of the faithful.[15] Only the Swabian Appendix to the 74T was noticeably preoccupied with the issue of excommunication. Yet even here the compiler largely adhered to the traditional ideas of exclusion and separation.[16]

While Anselm's collection does insist upon the traditional practices of complete separation and exclusion, it is also clear that he was advancing an active policy of incorporation. In his view, the Church was obliged to confront, persuade, and comprehend dissident or separated forces in order to fulfil her mission. What we effectively have here is a new articulation of the role of the Church; in short, a new ecclesiology that was perhaps an inevitable product of the schism. In the face of schism, the reformers' earlier insistence upon separation from the world, their call

---

[13] Anselm XII: 56 Quod scismatici nec divino iure nec humano res ecclesiarum debent possidere [Augustine, *In Iohannis evang.*, Tract. VI, 25–6]; XII: 57 Ut catholici res possideant excommunicatorum usque ad conversionem illorum [Augustine, epist. 185, cc. 35–6]; XII: 58 Quod qui extra ecclesiam sunt nullo iure possidere possunt bona aecclesiae [Augustine, epist. 93, c. 50]. There are additional texts where these issues, though not made explicit in the rubrics, are also addressed. Cf. XII: 54 Ut excommunicati cohibeantur a saecularibus [Augustine, epist. 93]; XII: 60 De scismaticis ad correctionem cogendis [Augustine, epist. 185, cc. 6 ff.]; XIII: 6 De persequendo hostes [Gregory I, *Reg.* II: 7]; XIII: 8 De predando hostes [Gregory I, *Reg.* II: 33]; XIII: 17 De eadem re [Augustine, epist. 185, cc. 36 ff.]; and XIII: 27 ⟨no rubric⟩ (cf. App. II) [Ambrose, *Libri de officiis*, I 30 ff., etc.].

[14] *Liber contra Wibertum* (*MGH, LdL*, 1), 517–28. As noted above, Introduction, Fransen opposed this view in 'Anselme de Lucques, canoniste?'. Cf. R. Somerville, 'Anselm of Lucca and Wibert of Ravenna', *BMCL*, n.s. 10 (1980), 1–13.

[15] The 74T did note that there should be no communion with excommunicates: title 68, c. 309 with a text from Ps.Fabianus, p. 159 (= Anselm XII: 18).

[16] The Swabian Appendix shows, however, the extent to which excommunication as the strictly spiritual sanction of the early Church had also become an important weapon in secular matters. See E. Vodola, *Excommunication in the Middle Ages* (Berkeley, 1986), esp. 1–27, and more recently 'Sovereignty and Tabu: Evolution of the Sanction against Communication with Excommunicates', 581–98. Cf. A. Murray, 'Excommunication and Conscience in the Middle Ages' (The John Coffin Memorial Lecture; London, 1991).

for the Church to be unencumbered by worldly ties and polluted elements in order to effect reform and fulfil her pastoral mission, had to
be abandoned for a new rhetoric or discourse of pro-active and just
force. It was also too weak, and too novel, a force to be anything other
than benevolent. Anselm's advocacy of coercion, therefore, is not merely
an expedient and practical measure specifically related to the crisis of
schism. While it undeniably marks a significant stage in the gradual but
radical transformation of the ecclesiastical position regarding warfare
that was taking place in the eleventh century, the doctrine of coercion
also reveals an important and subtle shift in the Church's (and the
reformers') attempts at self-definition.[17]

While Anselm was rigorous in his definition of those who were
excommunicate and schismatic, perhaps partly in an effort to attest to
the complete lack of authority of any schismatic/excommunicate hierarchy, it seems clear that his main concern lay not just with the evil of
schism and its perpetuation, but also with the schismatics themselves.[18]
This concern, however, was not translated merely into an injunction
that such persons simply be excluded from the body of the faithful, as
had been the case with previous canonists. On the contrary, such persons had to be returned, forcibly if necessary, to the flock.[19] For Anselm

---

[17] Erdmann believed that during the course of the 11th cent. the Church began to
transform warfare in its behalf into an ethical activity, most significantly with Gregory VII
and the *fideles* or *milites sancti Petri*. In canonical terms, however, the persistence of a more
conservative, and frankly negative, attitude on the part of clerics cannot be denied.
Burchard of Worms exemplified this sentiment in his influential and widely-diffused
Decretum (II: 211), reiterating vehemently the traditional prohibition for clerics of any
order to bear arms, with the clause that 'they cannot fight for both God and the world'.
Burchard also demanded penance for killing even in a just war, via Hrabanus Maurus
(though he cited the Council of Mainz, c. 2). The text is indicative of the prevailing eccle-
siastical characterization of soldiers, mentioning 'those who from greed . . . deliberately
slay . . . ' (IV: 23). See C. Erdmann, *The Origin of the Idea of Crusade*, trans. M. W.
Baldwin and W. Goffart (Princeton, 1977), esp. 241–8. For a reappraisal of Erdmann, see
J. T. Gilchrist, 'The Erdmann Thesis and the Canon Law, 1083–1141', in *Crusade and
Settlement*, ed. P. W. Edbury (Cardiff, 1985), 37–45, who believed that Erdmann had
underestimated the persistence of the conservative tradition represented by Burchard, and
had overemphasized Anselm as a significant precursor to theories of crusade. In general,
see F. H. Russell, *The Just War in the Middle Ages* (Cambridge, 1975).

[18] See above, notes 8–9. Cf. *Sermo de caritate*, 101; and *Liber contra Wibertum*, 522,
where Anselm cites Cyprian: 'Ecclesia una est, quae intus et foris esse non potest . . . '

[19] Anselm XII: 60 De scismaticis ad correctionem cogendis [Augustine, epist. 185, cc.
6 ff.]; XIII: 13 Quod inobedientes severius sint corrigendi [Ps.Calixtus, p. 138]. Cf. *Liber
contra Wibertum*, 525: 'Haec et his similia praedicamus et cum multo dolore cordis ab his
necessitatibus nostris eripi laboramus et ad dominum Deum nostrum de ista tribulatione
clamamus, ut vos humiles sub manu sua diesque nostros in sua pace disponat. Cum multo
siquidem dolore secat pius medicus, ni secaret, moriturum; cum multis lacrimis ligat pater
filium freneticum.'

believed that it was not enough simply to extirpate evil. Evildoers had to be corrected.[20]

Anselm was clearly influenced in this overriding duty of action by the doctrine of Augustine, and, perhaps more immediately, by Gregory VII himself. While there was nothing particularly new in this, he was clearly anxious to provide appropriate and acceptable motivation. Coercive force under such circumstances was not a matter of personal will or arbitrary discretion, but the duty of a true *pastor ecclesiae*.[21] The obligation to correct evil or evildoers was all-encompassing, for inaction in essence entailed tacit acquiescence.[22] Although Anselm did note occasions where forbearance might be required, unceasing vigilance was the overwhelming theme.[23] It was only with *caritas* that Anselm justified coercive action, transforming it into an expression of pastoral concern.[24] For

[20] Anselm XII: 55 De malis cogendis ad bonum [Augustine, epist. 173, cc. 1 ff.] (fos. 217ᵛ–218ᵛ): 'Displicet tibi quod traheris ad salutem, cum tam multos nostros ad perniciem traxeritis. Quid enim volumus, nisi te comprehendi et, praesentari et reservari ne pereas? [et infra] . . . quantomagis vos ab errore pernicioso, in quo vobis inimici estis, trahendi estis et perducendi ad veritatem vel cognoscendam vel eligendam, non solum ut honorem salubriter habeatis, sed etiam ne pessime pereatis! Dicis Dominum dedisse liberum arbitrium, ideo non deberi cogi hominem nec ad bonum.' Cf. XIII: 12 Ut mali non occidantur sed corrigantur [Augustine, epist. 100, cc. 1 ff.]; and *Lib. c. Wib.* 522: ' . . . et cum catholica matre nostra ecclesia persequar inimicos eius nec convertar, donec deficiant.'

[21] e.g. *Sermo de caritate*, 103–4: 'Pastores enim Ecclesiae nullum temporale commodum, nullius timorem, nullius amorem transitorium saluti animarum debent preponere, sed tam per sacerdotalis officii vigorem quam per principum fidelium fortitudinem, errantes ad ovile Domini instantissime reducere.'

[22] Anselm XII: 5 Qui consentit peccanti aut defendit maledictus erit [see Appendix II]; XII: 64 Quomodo recedere debeamus a malis [Augustine, *Sermo* 88, no. 23, 25] (fo. 221ᵛ): ' . . . Quid est enim tangere immundum, nisi consentire peccatis? Quid est autem exire inde, nisi facere quod pertinet ad correctionem malorum, quantum pro uniuscuiusque gradu atque persona salva pace fieri potest?'; XIII: 19 Qui potest perturbare perversos et non facit eorum impietati consentit [Ps.Damasus, p. 508]. Cf. *Lib. c. Wib.* 526–7 (which contains several canonical texts, see Table V. The Canonical Sources of the *Liber Contra Wibertum*): 'Si ergo Christum causam perditionis eorum, ad quos missus est, et vocem eius non audierunt, dicere non praesumis, nec Paulo audes asscribere stultitiam gentium et scandalum Iudeorum, a nostra quoque detractione linguam compesce, qui compellimur dicere veritatem, sicut per prophetam Dominus comminatur: Sacerdos ingrediens et regrediens nisi sonitum dederit, morte morietur. Item: Maledictus qui prohibet gladium suum a sanguine. . . . [et infra] Leo: Qui alios ab errore non revocat, se ipsum errare demonstrat . . . '

[23] Anselm XII: 63 Quando mali tolerandi sunt et quando separandi a nobis [Augustine, *De fide et operibus*, 6 ff.]; XIII: 20 Quando mali sunt tolerandi vel quando deserendi [Gregory I, *Vita s. Benedicti*, II, c. 3] Cf. however *Lib. c. Wib.* 522; and *Sermo de caritate*, 103–4. Stickler noted (252–3) Anselm's reliance upon the gerundive and 'debere' as further indications of the obligation to correct the erring.

[24] Anselm XII: 55 De malis cogendis ad bonum [Augustine, epist. 173, cc. 1 ff.] (fo. 218ᵛ): 'Quia etsi non ad salutem, non ad ecclesiae pacem, non ad Christi corporis unitatem, non ad sanctam et individuam caritatem, sed ad mala aliqua cogereris, nec sic tibi

Anselm as well as for Augustine, St Paul was a crucial figure: one who is compelled to the truth.[25]

The doctrine of coercion presented Anselm with a particular problem. If the Church was to exercise its coercive right, the *ius belli*, then he needed to find, or construct, a secure legitimate base. After all, there was the long-standing tradition which prohibited clerics from engaging in warfare and the effusion of blood. It was a doctrine, however, as Alfons Stickler noted, which required more than mere harmonization of war-like practices and the military profession with a Christian ethos, as Gregory VII had done with the *fideles sancti Petri*.[26] It demanded not only an exhaustive justification of the *ius belli*, and the *ius gladii* in general, but also a stringent reinterpretation of the role of secular power in the service of the Church. Anselm's consideration, thus, contained two distinct aspects: the legitimacy of the *ius gladii* in general, and the legitimacy of the *vis armata* of the Church in particular.

Anselm's first task was to demonstrate that war could be legitimate, and even 'just' provided that circumstances were right.[27] Towards this end, he followed Augustine by stressing that such action was not necessarily unpleasing to God. Here, using perhaps significantly the term *ministrare* as opposed to the customary *militare* of Augustine's text, Anselm wrote: 'Do not think that one who *ministers* with war-like arms

ipse mortem inferre debuisti.'; XIII: 1 Quod Moyses nichil crudele fecit quando praecepto Domini quosdam trucidavit [Augustine, *Contra Faustum*, lib. XXII, c. 79] (fo. 231ᵛ): 'Nam cum nulla crudelitate, sed magna dilectione fecisse quod fecit, quis non in verbis agnoscat orantis pro peccatis eorum et dicentis: "Si dimittis illis peccatum, dimitte; sin autem dele me de libro tuo? (Exod. 23: 22)." Sic plane et apostolus crudeliter sed amabiliter tradidit hominem in interitum carnis ut spiritus salvus sit in die Domini Ihesu. Tradidit et alios, ut discerent non blasphemare.' Cf. *Lib. c. Wib.* 528: 'Cum fiducia veni ad pingue[tu]dinem matris ecclesiae, a cuius utero errasti, ut coalescas ei'; and *Sermo de caritate*, 103: ' . . . sed utinam ad misericordiam eius confugiant, qui non vult mortem peccatoris sed ut convertatur et vivat, et redeant ad sinum Ecclesiae, de qua miserabiliter exierunt.'

²⁵ Anselm XII: 54 Ut excommunicati cohibeantur a saecularibus [Augustine, epist. 93 (excerpts)] (fo. 217ᵛ): 'Cum legas etiam ipsum primo Saulum, postea Paulum, ad veritatem cognoscendam et tenendam magna violentia Christi cogentis esse compulsum'; XII: 55 De malis cogendis ad bonum [Augustine, epist. 173, cc. 1 ff.] (fo. 218ʳ): 'Si voluntas mala suae permittenda est libertati, quare Paulus non est permissus uti pessima voluntate, qua persequabatur ecclesiam, sed prostratus est, ut cecaretur et cecatus est, ut mutaretur mutatus est, ut mitteretur, missus est, ut qualia fecerat in errore, talia pro veritate pateretur?'; XIII: 16 Item ad eundem de eadem re [Augustine, epist. 185, cc. 22 ff.] (fo. 235ʳ): 'Ecce habent Paulum apostolum; agnoscant in eo prius cogentem Christum et postea docentem, prius ferientem et postea consolantem.' Cf. *Lib. c. Wib.* 523.

²⁶ Stickler, 'Il potere coattivo', 266 ff.

²⁷ Anselm XIII: 4 Quod militantes etiam possunt esse iusti [Augustine, epist. 189, cc. 4, 6]; XIII: 5 De eadem re. Item ad eundem [Ps.Augustine, epist. 13]. Cf. *Lib. c. Wib.* 523–4.

is unable to please God.'[28] In so doing, Anselm implicitly emphasized both the spirit in which war should be waged (as a 'minister') and the ends towards which war was just. There were, after all, circumstances in which war was both necessary and unavoidable. Again following Augustine, Anselm conceded that it was not licit to kill for personal ends, but only for the objective of peace.[29] Furthermore, following Augustine's justification, Anselm noted that the physical prowess which manifested itself in war was, after all, a gift of God.[30]

With warfare and the military profession at least tacitly sanctioned, Anselm was obliged to justify the involvement of Christians. Here the theme of *caritas*, and the fraternal desire for salvation came into play as Anselm distinguished between the just and the unjust uses of force.[31] Legitimate coercive force was an expression of pastoral concern for salvation, a just endeavour in which the enemies of the truth were constrained into accepting the truth.[32] It did not take much to conclude that war conducted for the preservation of the Church was a service to God. Anselm did not stipulate in any place that *ius belli* was actually a pre-

---

[28] Anselm XIII: 4 (fo. 232ᵛ): 'Noli existimare neminem Deo placere posse, qui armis bellicis ministrat.' Cf. *Lib. c. Wib.*, 524, where Anselm also used *ministrare*.

[29] Anselm XIII: 3 Quod bella cum benivolentia sunt gerenda [Augustine, epist. 138, cc. 12 ff.] (fo. 232ᵛ): 'Nam si christiana disciplina omnia bella culparet, haec potius militibus consilium salutis petentibus in evangelio diceretur, ut abiecerent arma seque militiaque [*sic*] omnino subtraherent. Dictum est autem eis: "Neminem concusseritis, neque calumniam feceritis, sufficiat vobis stipendium vestrum" (Luke 3: 14). Quibus proprium stipendium sufficere debere praecipit, militare utique non prohibuit'; XIII: 4 (fo. 232ᵛ): 'Non enim pax quaeritur, ut bellum excitetur, sed bellum geritur, ut pax adquiratur. Esto ergo bellando pacificus, ut eos, quos expugnas, ad pacis utilitatem vincendo perducas.' Cf. *Lib. c. Wib.* 523–4.

[30] Anselm XIII: 4 (fo. 232ᵛ): 'Hoc ergo primum cogita quando armaris ad pugnam, quia virtus tua etiam ipsa corporalis donum Dei est; sic enim cogitabis de dono Dei non facere contra Dominum.'

[31] Anselm XIII: 14 Quod aecclesia persecutionem possit facere [Augustine, epist. 185, c. 11] (fo. 234ᵛ): 'Si ergo verum dicere vel agnoscere volumus, est persecutio iniusta quam faciunt impii aecclesiae Christi. Ista namque beata est, quae persecutionem patitur propter iusticiam. Proinde ista diligendo; illi seviendo. Ista ut corrigat; illi ut illam evertant. Ista ut revocet ab errore; illi ut praecipitent in errorem.' Cf. *Lib. c. Wib.* 523, where Anselm used the same text, though omitted the final part: 'Proinde ista diligendo . . . '

[32] Anselm XII: 44 Quod aecclesia non persequitur sed diligit cum punit vel prohibet malum . . . [Pelagius, JK no. 1018] (fo. 215ʳ): 'Non vos hominum vaniloquia retardent dicentium, quia persecutionem ecclesia faciat, dum vel ea quae committuntur reprimat, vel animarum salutem requirit. Errant huiusmodi rumoris fabulatores[is] non persequitur nisi qui ad malum cogit. Qui vero malum vel factum iam punit, vel prohibet ne fiat, non persequitur iste, sed diligit. Nam si ut illi putant nemo nec reprimendus a malo nec retrahendus ad bonum est, humanas ac divinas leges necesse est evacuari quae et malis poenam et bonis praemia iusticia suadente constituit [constituunt].' Cf. XIII: 2 De vindicta non odio sed amore facienda [Augustine, *De sermone Domini in monte*, I, cc. 64–5].

rogative of the Church, but by linking *caritas* with war, and the need to preserve the Church, he had effectively demonstrated that it was not prohibited.

There remained, however, the problem of the actual exercise of coercive force. Following long tradition as well as his canonical authorities, Anselm had indicated on a number of occasions that coercive action was to be carried out by secular power.[33] Like Augustine, Anselm essentially believed that war was the prerogative and duty of secular authority. But was war strictly a matter for secular authority? Or did he seek to claim that the Church retained a 'material sword' independent of secular force?

Anselm seems to have believed that the Church possessed an intrinsic coercive right. This, though not consistently, was defined as *persecutio*, whereas the exercise of secular authority was generally conceived of as *vindicta*. Stickler believed that the distinction in Anselm's mind between the two, even if not always maintained, was an important one.[34] *Vindicta* tended to entail material coercion in general terms, that is, punishment on account of a (specific) crime. *Persecutio*, on the other hand, while still denoting material coercion, seemed to imply somewhat higher aims: to impede evil, or to compel towards good. *Persecutio* did not necessarily entail armed force, yet neither was such force ruled out.

The two terms also concealed a crucial distinction in Anselm's mind, one which did not necessarily follow from the different terms

---

[33] Anselm XII: 45 Quod nullis [nullum] sacrificium Deo a potestatibus gratius est quam ut scismatici episcopi ab [ad] obediendum coerceantur [Pelagius I, JK no. 1024] (fo. 215ᵛ): 'Hoc enim et divinae et mundanae leges statuerunt, ut ab ecclesiae unitate divisi et eius pacem iniquissime perturbantes, a secularibus etiam potestatibus comprimantur. Nec quicquam maius est unde Deo possitis sacrificium offerre, quam si id ordinetis, ut hi qui in suam et aliorum perniciem debacchantur cum potenti debeant vigore compesci'; XII: 46 De scismaticis coercendis a secularibus [Pelagius I, JK no. 1012] (fo. 216ʳ): 'Quamvis igitur vestra per illorum scelus utilitas facta sit, nolite tamen impunitam praesumptionem iniquiorum hominum crassari permittere. Si enim hoc quod in vestram gloriam praesumpserunt, non fuerit vindicta compressum, quod in minoribus valeant ambigi ultra non debet. Exercete igitur in talibus auctoritatem, et ne eis amplius talia committenda crescat, Spiritus vestris coercionibus recomprima[n]tur'; XII: 53 De hereticis per saeculares potestates coercendis [Augustine, *In Iohannis evang.*, Tract. XI, 13 ff.] (fo. 217ʳ): 'Mirantur autem quia commoventur potestates christianae contra destandos dissipatores ecclesiae. Si non moverentur, quomodo redderent rationem de imperio suo Deo? Intendat caritas vestra quid dicam, quia hoc pertinet ad reges saeculi christianos, ut temporibus suis pacatam vellent matrem suam aecclesiam unde spiritaliter nati sunt'; cf. XII: 54 Ut excommunicati cohibeantur a saecularibus [Augustine, epist. 93 (excerpts)]; XIII: 23 ⟨no rubric⟩ (cf. App. II) [Gregory I, *Reg.* VIII: 4]; and XIII: 28 ⟨no rubric⟩ (cf. App. II) [Gregory I, *Reg.* I: 72].

[34] Stickler, 'Il potere coattivo', 239 ff. In Vat. lat. 1364, Book XII is entitled: *De vindicta et persecutione iusta*. See App. II for the use of '*vindicta*' and '*persecutio*' in the rubrics.

themselves, but rather from their point of reference. For Anselm, there seems to have been a fundamental distinction between the jurisdictional right of coercive action, and the actual exercise of that force. As he wrote to William I of England, the king was a *minister Dei* to whom the material sword had been yielded for the purpose of repressing the impiety of the people.[35] Although there was nothing new in the concept of kingship as a *ministerium*, by emphasizing all of the implications of ecclesiastical concession and guidance, Anselm was clearly relegating secular authority to a subservient level. The preoccupation of the reformers with notions of *utilitas* helps to clarify this point. As Anselm would note in the *Sermo de caritate* where he distinguished between *principes fideles* and *principes saeculi*, secular princes were *fideles* when they fulfilled their appointed task, which was the material defence of the Church.[36] Theirs was a task conceded by God and his Church, the most important part of which was to constrain the enemies of the truth (*inimicos veritatis*).[37] Secular authority was therefore understood by Anselm in terms of having a coercive *function* regarding the Church and her interests, and not (necessarily) a specific right. It was, moreover, a function which carried with it a strong implication of direct tutorial guidance or supervision.[38]

There remains the problem of Anselm's apparent assertion that the Church was able to exercise this right *directly*. Having, at least tacitly, established that the right of coercion was essentially within ecclesiastical jurisdiction, Anselm simply averred via Augustine that the Church had the power to persecute her enemies with little concern for the practical ramifications. But how could this be justified in the face of his stipulations regarding the exercise of force by secular powers, and the

[35] *Briefsammlungen*, no. 1, p. 17: 'Non sine causa gladium portas, Dei enim minister es ad vindictam malorum, ad laudem vero bonorum.'

[36] See *Sermo de caritate*, 104. Cf. Pasztor, 'Motivi dell'ecclesiologia', 88; and O. Capitani, '*Ecclesia Romana* e riforma: *utilitas* in Gregorio VII', in *Chiesa, diritto e ordinamento della 'societas christiana' nei secoli XI e XII*, 89–117.

[37] Cf. *Lib. c. Wib.* 525–6.

[38] Anselm to William I, *Briefsammlungen*, no. 1, p. 17: 'Dispensationem itaque tibi a Deo creditam in exhibendo cognosce et ad gloriam et laudem eius ministerium tuum imple.' Cf. *Sermo de caritate*, 104: 'Quibus tamen libertatem non concedimus seviendi vel rapiendi vel iniuste vivendi, sed impietati illorum, qui verum sibi crucifigunt et ostentunt habent Filium Dei, istorum sanctae intentionis opponimus desiderium, illorum sevitiam horum clementia temperantes, et sicut Moyses legislator oculum pro oculo, dentem pro dente etcetera huiusmodi, ad reprimendam impietatem gentium populo Dei divina inspiratione concessit, sic istos in inimicos veritatis vindictam exercere pro zelo, divini amoris proposito, pietatis officio volumus et laudamus'; and Anselm XII: 45, 46, 53, 54; XIII: 23, 28 (for texts, see above, note 33), where the concession of the function seems to be emphasized.

tradition which prohibited clerics from fighting? Can the exceptional situation of the time—the crisis of schism—be seen as providing the justification? Anselm does seem to have been looking to support a position by means of his authorities, especially Augustine and Pelagius, that the Church had the right to act independently of secular power in those circumstances when that power was either in contention with the Church, or had fallen into schism or heresy.[39] This covered contingencies such as those faced by the reformers when the 'normal' secular defender, Henry IV, was not only a schismatic and an excommunicate, but was also physically contending against the Roman Church and her supporters. The implicit point seems to be that under ordinary circumstances, the Church would act through the normal channels of secular authority while still retaining *ex professo* the jurisdictional right of coercive action.

It is important to stress, however, that Anselm was not in favour of clerical participation in coercive warfare. On the contrary, he was suggesting that under certain circumstances the Church would specifically direct the action, and would specify the aims of that action. What is significant is the insistence upon the Church's right of self-determination, especially in crisis, an insistence upon her right not only to define and name the objectives, but also to designate her own defender. It is further indication, as Erdmann noted, of the ways in which the Gregorians were transforming notions of kingship.[40] The role of the defender of the Church was legally being extended to a wider, and widening circle.

It is perhaps useful here briefly to examine this doctrine as developed in Anselm's *Liber contra Wibertum*. Written after the death of Pope Gregory VII in the last year of his own life, the *Liber contra Wibertum* represented Anselm's second attempt at compelling Wibert and his partisans to penance and reconciliation through vehement rhetoric and a barrage of canonical authorities.[41] Though Anselm addressed other concerns such as the sacraments and his own connection with Matilda of Tuscany—issues apparently raised by Wibert—the main purpose of the

[39] Anselm XIII: 14–17; *Lib. c. Wib.*, 524. Cf. Stickler, 263–4.

[40] C. Erdmann, *The Origin of the Idea of Crusade*, 57 ff.

[41] The *Liber contra Wibertum* makes it clear both that Anselm had written an earlier letter, and that Wibert had responded. Though Wibert's response is not extant, his text can be reasonably approximated both from the *Liber* itself and from Wido of Ferrara's *De scismate Hildebrandi* (*MGH, LdL*, 1), 529–67. For the earlier letter, and Wibert's response, see *Lib. c. Wib.* 520: 'Scripsi tibi pauca cum multo dolore et sincerae caritatis affectu . . . '; and 525: ' . . . et te pro superbia in reprobum traditum sensum sancto patri nostro crimen inposuisse et dicta sanctorum patrum, quae in epistola tua posuisti, non intellexisse.' Whether or not the text known as Ans.1 contains part of the earlier letter, remains unclear: see above, Introduction, note 14.

treatise was an authoritative rebuttal of the Wibertine position on the Church, the papacy, and war.[42] It is clear that the treatise also had a wider ambition: the justification of coercion in the face of strenuous objections not merely from Wibert, but perhaps also from Anselm's own party.[43] As it responds to Wibertine accusations concerning the war being waged against them by the *fideles sancti Petri*, the text therefore offers testimony of the extent to which Anselm envisaged this doctrine of coercion not merely as abstract theory, but also as having applicability in concrete situations.

Relying upon a number of the canonical authorities found in Books XII and XIII, although often much abbreviated, the treatise essentially followed the plan in the collection: the definition and consideration of those who contended against the Church, and the legitimacy of coercion. In the *Liber contra Wibertum*, the authorities, though, were arranged in a more systematic way, as required by Anselm's argument. As a result, it is a concise distillation of Anselm's doctrine of coercion.[44]

Anselm began the treatise by assessing the status of Wibert in order to justify his thorough condemnation. The first set of canonical authorities attested to the invalidity of Wibert and his hierarchy, by demonstrating that secular power could not subject divine things.[45] Wibert's claim to universality was then countered by a text from Cyprian, reinforced and updated by the modification of 'Fabianus' to 'Alexander' (meaning Alexander II).[46] These texts were obviously directed at Wibert's involvement with Henry IV, and with what Anselm envisaged as the consequent enslavement of the Church.[47]

---

[42] e.g. *Lib. c. Wib.* 522; and 527, where Anselm responded to accusations of impropriety in his relations with Matilda. His vehemence may have stemmed in part from misgivings about his role with the Matildine *fideles*.

[43] *Lib. c. Wib.* 522–3: 'Sanctum quippe suum, quod foris habetis, quod malo vestro accepistis, quia bono odore peristis, veneratur ecclesia, sed vos persequitur, ut Sara ancillam, quae tamen de semine Abrahae concepit et peperit. Intellege itaque, quomodo persequatur adhuc ancillam domina, ut docearis, quae sit persecutio beata, et scias, quomodo nec pro iusticia christianis iurgandum sit, cum competenter exponi tibi permiseris, ut addatur adversus catholicos, et non redarguas Christum, qui dixit: "Compellite intrare", et alia multa, quae in consequentibus posita audies.' Cf. Wido of Ferrara, *De scismate Hildebrandi*, 541: [Wibert's words] 'Sed hoc quis excusabile faciet, quod Teutonicos ad bella commovit vel saltim cum Heinrico pugnare permisit, et quod viris religiosis minime convenit, persecutionem tantam in iam dictum regem exercuit? Et docere est christianorum virorum non bella movere, pati aequanimiter iniurias aliorum, non ulcisi. Nichil tale Iesus, nichil tale quisquam legitur fecisse sanctorum.'

[44] See below, Table V.   [45] *Lib. c. Wib.* 520–1.   [46] Ibid. 521.

[47] Ibid. 520 ff., and 522, where Anselm castigated Henry IV about investiture.

Anselm began his vindication of coercion with the Augustinian distinction between just and unjust persecution, as illustrated by the story of Sarah and the slave, concluding with Augustine that coercion or persecution on account of excessive pride was justifiable.[48] Interestingly enough, however, the text did not include here the final part as found in the collection. Anselm was content simply to concentrate on unjust persecution, that is, what the impious do to the Church of Christ. This he did by omitting the references found in the text in the collection, where emphasis had been placed upon the differing characteristics of those who waged just wars, and those who persecuted the Church.[49] Perhaps uneasy about the Church's right in practice to persecute her enemies, Anselm was obviously anxious here to concentrate on the illegitimacy of the actions of the supporters of Wibert and Henry IV.

Using his Augustinian texts to imply that coercion and correction were the duties of the pious ruler, Anselm first described how the impious were to be corrected by imperial laws.[50] He then referred to the example of Christ and St Paul—one compelled to the truth—as a testimony to the ways in which such activity was to be undertaken. Unlike the text in the collection, Anselm here avoided the explicit connection with *caritas*.[51] He then addressed the circumstances in which war was licit. Although he again acknowledged the problem of the involvement of Christians in warfare, he again carefully followed Augustine's commentary on Luke, which at least tacitly legitimized warfare. In so doing, Anselm again achieved what he had done in the *Collectio canonum*: the tacit acknowledgement that the *ius belli* was a prerogative of the Church without actually stipulating that this was the case. Subsequent emphasis upon divine dispensation, victory to the just, and the legitimacy of the military profession in general rounded out his testimony.[52] It was only then that Anselm effectively introduced the motivation of *caritas*,

---

[48] Ibid. 523: 'Si autem melius discutiamus, magis illa persequebatur Saram superbiendo quam illam Sara coercendo; illa enim dominae faciebat iniuriam, ista inponebat superb[i]ae disciplinam.'

[49] See above, note 31. Anselm XIII: 14, however, omitted the final part as in the *Liber*, at 523: ' . . . illi vero miseri, qui persecutionem patiuntur propter iniusticiam.'

[50] For the following sources, see Table V.

[51] The omission of the phrase 'liberum est credere vel non credere?' as found in Anselm XIII: 16 (fo. 235ʳ) 'Ubi est quod isti clamare consuerunt, liberum est credere vel non credere? Cui vim Christus intulit?', makes the text in the *Liber* (523) incomprehensible, as Pasztor noted (p. 395).

[52] The Ps.Augustine text in the *Liber* continued, unlike that in Anselm XIII: 5, by stressing that God not only defended the just, but also gave them victory, 524: 'Deus apertis caelis spectat et partem, quam aspicit iustam, defendit *et ibi dat palmam*' (my italics).

arguing that coercion was both an expression of love and an unavoidable duty.

It seems clear that the justification of coercion in the *Liber contra Wibertum* had a more urgent purpose than the mere presentation of abstract theory. As has been suggested, the treatise also appears to have been the medium by which Anselm sought to demonstrate that the reformers' armed struggle against Wibert and Henry IV was a wholly just undertaking. The treatise is, therefore, not only indicative of those areas of the doctrine of coercive action where Anselm felt himself to be vulnerable to Wibertine accusations and even perhaps to those from his own party. Rather, it also may reflect Anselm's concerns about the legitimacy of the reformers' armed struggle in the field.

The crucial problem for Anselm seems to have been the conflict between the respective claims of armed warfare and the ideals of Christian morality or behaviour. There are a number of rejections of clerical participation in warfare. In one of the most striking of these, we almost hear Anselm himself denying any participation in the effusion of blood.[53] This with other instances where Anselm somewhat weakly implied that it was licit to fight against Wibert and his supporters precisely because they were no longer catholics—obviously an attempt to refute the tradition which prohibited catholic from killing catholic— indicate some wavering in his mind as to the legitimacy of the action. Indeed here it becomes apparent that Anselm's doctrine of coercion may have been as much a product of a life lived, as a theory worked out.[54]

While Anselm vehemently condemned Wibert and his supporters in the *Liber contra Wibertum*, he cannot simply be seen as being interested in exalting the Gregorian cause to the exclusion of all else. Behind the condemnation, there seems to lie a genuine desire to restore what he

---

[53] *Lib. c. Wib.* 525: 'Nos vero in nullius sanguine miscuimus nec protegente Deo miscebimus nec de perditione morientium exultamus.'

[54] Ibid. 522. Following his expulsion from Lucca sometime in Oct. 1080, Anselm joined the entourage of Matilda of Tuscany, and appears to have played an integral part in the resistance to Henry IV. As spiritual adviser to the Countess (perhaps from as early as 1074), and papal vicar for Lombardy (if the sources are to be trusted), Anselm probably travelled with the Matildine troops. While his biographers stopped short of portraying him as a 'fighting bishop', he may have been present at a number of battles, notably that at Sorbaria in 1084. For Anselm as Matilda's spiritual adviser: *Vita Anselmi*, c. 12, 20, p. 17, 19; Rangerius, *Vita Metrica*, vv. 3659–64, 6511–14; *Vita Matildis*, II, c. 2, pp. 65–6. For Anselm as vicar for Lombardy: *Vita Anselmi*, c. 24, pp. 20–1; *De thesauro Canusinae ecclesiae Romanam transmisso, et de compensatione ecclesiae canusinae facta* (RIS, n.s. 5, pt. II), 109–10. For Anselm with Matilda and the troops: *Vita Anselmi*, cc. 23–4, 29–31, pp. 20–1, 22; *Vita Matildis*, II, c. 2, pp. 65–6. In general, see Meyer von Knonau, III, 393 ff., 454 ff.; and Overmann, *Regesta*, 42d–44i.

believed to be the vital unity of the Church.[55] The way, or so Anselm seems to have hoped, if not believed, was open, if not for Wibert, at least for his supporters to return in penitence to the Church.[56] The desire for unity lay at the heart of his doctrine of coercion. This was apparent even when he somewhat surprisingly conceded that it was not perhaps licit after all to take up arms even on behalf of justice—a concession which seemed effectively to nullify his entire justification of coercion.[57] Yet this was not quite the case. Anselm seems here to return to the notion that duty somehow provides legitimacy for whatever action may be needed. For he then stipulated that war was to be waged on behalf of the *errantes*, in order that they be led *ad iustitiae perfectionem*.[58] Although this somewhat conveniently served to strengthen the justification for coercive warfare, it likewise resolved, if not wholly satisfactorily, the tension between warfare and the involvement of Christians. War was waged to constrain the *errantes* to the perfection of justice which effectively resided only in the *domus Dei*, which for Anselm was the Roman Church. It was a position which at the same time relieved the problem for the actual constrainers. They in effect 'perfected' themselves in their service of coercion, which, after all, was a duty of *caritas*.

One final aspect of the doctrine of coercion deserves a brief notice: the problem of the *res ecclesiae*. It is an issue that quite surprisingly has gone all but unnoticed, particularly when one remembers that the clash of the later reformers with Henry V would revolve almost exclusively around the issue of property. Yet it is not at all surprising that Anselm did address the issue in this context. For schism entailed disunity not merely in a spiritual sense, but also in a temporal one. It not only undermined the authority of the pope as the spiritual head of the Church, but likewise severely tested his position as the steward of the Church in temporal matters, thereby challenging the *auctoritas regendi et*

---

[55] *Lib. c. Wib.* 527: 'Veni ad dolentem et pro te gementem matrem ecclesiam, ut ipsa pro te offerat sacrificium acceptum Domino. Sola enim est, per quam sacrificium Dominus libenter accipit, sola quae pro errantibus fiducialiter intercedit, extra quam quicunque inventus fuerit, peribit regnante diluvio, extra quam quicunque agnum comederit, profanus est, de cuius carnibus lex efferri foras prohibet.' Wibert, however, is called 'sceleratissime omnium' in the *Liber*, and in Ans. 1, he is named antichrist: Brit. Lib. MS Harley 3052, (fo. 123ʳ): 'Anselmus L. gratia Dei (sic) Lucensis episcopus Wiberto praevaricatori antichristo.'

[56] *Ibid.* 528: 'Cum fiducia veni ad pingue[tu]dinem matris ecclesiae cuius utero errasti, ut coalescas.'

[57] *Ibid.* 525: 'Verum quidem est, quia nec pro iusticia ferrea arma corripi concessum est . . .'

[58] *Ibid.* 525: ' . . . sed propter se, quantum ad iusticiae perfectionem, quantum spectat ad domus Dei decorem.'

disponendi. Indeed, one of the most dangerous aspects of schism was not simply the loss or destruction of ecclesiastical property, but the loss of the dispository control of valuable rights and assets.

The effects of the schism resulted in a serious drain on resources for Gregory VII and his supporters. Revenue for Rome, in particular, facing ongoing attacks and siege from Henry IV, seems to have been a tremendous problem.[59] In May 1082, Gregory VII had convened a council at Rome, seeking approval for the alienation of ecclesiastical property in order to provide resources to defend Rome against the onslaught of Wibert and Henry IV. Those present at the synod, however, rejected the alienation on the canonical principle that ecclesiastical plate and resources were to be alienated solely for ransoming captives and providing for the poor.[60] It is worth noting here that Anselm and Matilda came to Gregory's support in 1082, causing church plate from Canossa to be 'loaned' for the purposes of defending Rome. This may not have been a solitary incident; Anselm was accused on several occasions of inciting Matilda to strip monasteries and to disperse her own goods in vain.[61]

---

[59] Bernold of Constance is an important source for the destruction in northern Italy: *Chronicon a. 1084, a. 1085*, 441 ff. While he glossed over the specific problem of ecclesiastical property, when he noted that the deaths of the anti-bishops of Modena, Reggio, and Pistoia in the battle of Sorbaria had permitted the reintroduction of 'catholic' bishops, the recovery of the episcopal estates and rights was obviously an added bonus. Cf. *Vita Anselmi*, cc. 23–4, pp. 20–1, and Gregory VII's testimony, *Ep. vag.* no. 55, p. 134: ' . . . et in religione friguit et terrenas opes maiori ex parte amisit. Nonnulli enim imperatores reges et principes aliorumque ordinum personae misera cupiditate capti, maternam maledictionem incurrere non timentes, eius possessiones invaserunt, distraxerunt, et in proprios usus redegerunt . . . ' Cowdrey (p. 135, note 1) suggested that this referred to the apostasy of the curia and 13 cardinals in 1084. It could quite as easily refer to simple material loss.

[60] *Concilium Romanum a. 1082*, in Z. Zafarana 'Sul "conventus" del clero romano nel maggio 1082', *Studi Medievali*, ser. 3, 7 (1966), 399–403, here 402: ' . . . convenientibus simul episcopis, cardinalibus, abbatibus, archipresbiteris, ut dicerent utrum bona ecclesiarum possent poni in pignore pro pecunia colligenda ad resistendum Wiberto archiepiscopo Ravennati Romanam sedem invadere conanti, quaesitis auctoritatibus exemplisque sanctorum, unanimiter laudaverunt sacras res ecclesiarum nullatenus in militia seculari expendendas, nisi in alimonia pauperum, in sancto usu rerum divinarum et in redemptione captivorum.' Cf. Wido of Ferrara, *De scismate Hildebrandi*, 526, who protested the misuse of such resources: 'De sacrilegio nichil iam dubito, quin sacrilegium dici possit, si quis aecclesiae pecuniam, cum sit pauperum, non pauperibus effudit, ac per hoc sacrilegum illum dixerim, si pecuniam aecclesiae missam ab oratoribus Teutonicis ducibus direxit.'

[61] *De thesauro Canusinae ecclesiae Romanam transmisso*, 109: 'Anno domini MLXXXII Comitissa Matildis cum episcopo Anselmo, qui et vicarius eius erat papae Gregorii VII. in illis diebus in Longobardiae, thesaurum ecclesiae Canusinae postulavit abbati Gerardo qui tunc preerat praefatae ecclesiae, ad dirigendum papae pro defensione Romanae

Throughout the *Collectio canonum*, Anselm had exhibited concern for the issue of ecclesiastical property and the material well-being of the Church.[62] The majority of his texts, however, had addressed the customary concerns: despoliation of the episcopate, the violation of ecclesiastical property and rights, the restitution of property and rights, the status of those invading ecclesiastical property, and the inalienability of ecclesiastical resources.[63] Yet in the final two books, as in the *Liber contra Wibertum*, Anselm turned, if briefly, to the issue of catholic property in the hands of schismatics. Using Augustine and Gregory I as authorities, he stipulated that schismatics and excommunicates had no right whatsoever to possess ecclesiastical goods, and that the possessions held by such persons were to be transferred to true catholics until such time

ecclesiae, quae illo tempore persecutionem grandem habebat a Guiberto heresiarcha . . . ' Cf. *Vita Matildis*, II, c. 2, p. 66; Benzo of Alba, *Ad Heinricum IV. imperatorum libri VIII* (*MGH*, *SS*, 11), 663; and *Lib. c. Wib.* 527: ' . . . serviens die ac nocte in custodiendo illam Deo meo et sanctae matri meae ecclesiae, cuius praecepto mihi commissa est; et spero, quod multa mihi retributio per gratiam Dei in eius custodia excrescat, *quae non in vanum, sicut tu dicis*, sua dispergit, sed indeficientem in caelo thesaurizat sibi theasurum, quem tinea non demolitur, ubi fures non effodiunt nec furantur, parata pro defensione iusticiae non solum terrena omnia distribuere, sed usque ad sanguinem pro vestra confusione et reverentia ad sanctae ecclesiae gloriam et exaltationem certare, donec tradat Dominus inimicum suum in manu feminae' (my italics). This may also refer to Matilda's donation of her patrimony to the Roman Church, initially made during Gregory's pontificate and confirmed later. For Matilda's donation see *Cartula Comitissae Matildis super concessione bonorum suorum facta Romanae ecclesiae* (RIS, n.s. 5, pt. II), 107–8.

[62] Though the 74T provided Anselm with several texts regarding the invasion of ecclesiastical property, there were no stipulations about the alienation of ecclesiastical property. Nor was Burchard terribly interested in such matters, although it seems that he regarded all donations to the Church as inviolate, and probably inalienable. Cf. 74T tit. 60: Ne laicis facultates commitantur ecclesiasticae (cc. 260–2); and tit. 61: De damnatione invasorum ecclesicorum prediorum (cc. 263–70). It should also be noted that there are no texts on the *res ecclesiae* in the Swabian Appendix.

[63] e.g. Anselm IV: 28 Ut non liceat Apostolico predia ecclesiae perpetualiter alienare vel commutare, nisi forte domus urbis pro clericis et captivis et peregrinis [Symmachus, synod a. 502, c. 4, 5 (cf. 74T c. 266)]; IV: 31 Ut nemo patrimonia Romanae ecclesiae petat, et si quis quomodolibet subtraxerit, anathema sit [John VIII, Council of Ravenna a. 877, c. 15]; IV: 37 Ut nemo beati Petri proprietatem usurpet vel sciens ocultet vel debitum non reddat servitium [Gregory VII, *Reg.* VI: 5b, c. 11]; VI: 132 Ut episcopus res ecclesiae saecularibus viris non committat [Gregory I, *Reg.* IX: 204]; XII: 4 Quod raptores et alienatores rei ecclesiasticae excommunicati sunt et illis qui consentiunt [Ps.Lucius, p. 179 (= 74T c. 265)]. Cf.I: 82; III: 49, 50; IV: 22, 32–3, 43, 44, 53; V: 27, 31–8, 40, 41, 43–6, 48, 52, 60; VI: 62, 63, 67, 149, 153, 156, 162; VII: 5, 67, 139, 155. See also M. C. De Matteis, 'Tematica della povertà e problema della *res ecclesiae*: notazione ed esemplificazione campione su alcuni collezioni canoniche del periodo della riforma ecclesiastica del sec. XI', *Bull. Ist. Stor. Ital.* 90 (1982–3), 177–226. De Matteis missed Anselm's texts on the *res ecclesiae* in Books XII and XIII, due perhaps to his reliance upon Thaner's incomplete edition.

as the former were reconciled.[64] Although there are not many of these texts—just three where the issue is made explicit in the rubric title—the implications are significant.

It is, though, the connection with coercion that is clearly the most important—a connection also made in the *Liber contra Wibertum*.[65] The texts in which Anselm, by means of careful, not to say dubious, editing had raised the issue of ecclesiastical property without making it explicit in the rubrics, were also all unequivocal justifications of coercion.[66] Yet even in those texts where the issue was explicit, there is an implicit connection which goes beyond the unequivocal demand for the restoration of property found in their rubrics. This connection is crucial. Anselm is in effect acknowledging that the transfer or restoration of ecclesiastical property will not happen without some forceful persuasion or coercive action. Yet he was not, as Wibert seems to have complained, advocating a rapacious seizure of property and goods from schismatics (which, in any event, was highly improbable). Anselm was at pains to insist upon the same ambitions for the restoration of property as for coercive action. As he insisted with Augustine, it is the schismatics, and not their goods which are the ultimate goal; both they, and their goods, had to be justified through *caritas*, that is justified through the true Roman Church.[67]

---

[64] For texts, see above, note 13.

[65] See *Lib. c. Wib.* 524–5, where Anselm seems to respond to Wibert's complaints regarding seizures: 'De depraedatione autem eorum, qui ab ecclesia praecisi sunt, respondeant patres nostri . . . ' Anselm used three texts to support his defence, all of which are found in Book XIII: Augustine, epist. 185, cc. 36 ff. (= XIII: 17); Gregory I, *Reg.* II: 7 (= XIII: 6); and Gregory I, *Reg.* II: 33 (= XIII: 8). Cf. *De scismate Hildebrandi*, 544, 555–6.

[66] Anselm XII: 54 Ut excommunicati cohibeantur a saecularibus [Augustine, epist. 93, excerpts] (fo. 217ᵛ): 'Constantinus imperator constituit ut res convictorum et unitati pervicaciter resistentium fisco vendicarentur.' This clause followed a lengthy discussion of the *caritas* aspects of coercion, e.g. (fo. 217) 'Meliora sunt vulnera amici quam oscula inimici; melius est cum severitate diligere quam cum lenitate decipere.'; XII: 60 De scismaticis ad correctionem cogendis [Augustine, epist. 185, cc. 6 ff. (excerpts)] for text, see note 67; XIII: 17 De eadem re [Augustine, epist. 185, cc. 36 ff. (excerpts)] (fo. 235ʳ): 'Si autem consideremus, quod scriptum est in libro sapientiae: "Ideo iusti tulerunt spolia impiorum [Wis. 10: 19]"; item quod legitur in proverbiis: "Thesaurizant autem iustis divitiae impiorum [Prov. 13: 22]", tunc videbimus non esse quaerendum, qui habeant res hereticorum, sed qui sint in societate iustorum. *Item post aliqua.* Si corpus Christi tollit spolia impiorum et corpori Christi thesaurizant divitiae impiorum, non debent impii foris remanere, ut calumnientur, sed intrare potius, ut iustificentur.' Cf. XII: 68, 70; and XIII: 8, 27.

[67] Anselm XII: 60 (fo. 220ᵛ): 'Verum in huius modi causis, ubi pro graves discessionum scissuras, non huius aut illius hominis est periculum, sed populorum strages iacent, detrahendum est aliquid severitati, ut maioribus malis sanandis, caritas sinceri [sincera] subveniat. Habeant ergo isti de praeterito detestabili errore, sicut Petrus habuit, de mendacii morte, amarum dolorem, et veniant ad ecclesiam Christi veram, id est matrem catholicam. Sint in illa clerici, sint episcopi utiliter, qui contra illam fuerunt inutiliter. Non

How do we account for this concern with the *res ecclesiae* in the midst of a justification of coercion? Does it further support the contention that the entire doctrine was a product of the schism? After all, this was an issue that was not taken up in the earlier reform collections. It gradually began to appear in collections after that of Anselm, ultimately finding a place in Gratian, who may have incorporated these texts from Anselm's compilation. There is an alternative viewpoint, however.

However much a personal affront to his beloved Gregory VII, it is quite clear that the schism, for Anselm, was a situation in which the very existence of his Church was in peril. Anselm's interest with ecclesiastical property in these final books of the collection seems to have stemmed from this concern: material resources were being unjustly seized, or appropriated from true catholics, with the effect of leaving them, and ultimately the Church, debilitated. More to the point, he feared that the Church's resources were being used not to preserve the Church but rather to destroy her.[68] Whether in his doctrine of coercion he was simply looking for an ethical covering or moral justification for a practical scheme to deal with harsh political, and especially economic, realities is another question. Yet Anselm's theory was not without a certain logic: for the Church in full possession of her resources would be able both to defend herself in the face of schism, and, at the same time, to restore, by force if necessary, the unity that was the objective of Anselm's entire doctrine of coercion.[69]

---

invidemus, immo amplectimur, optamus, hortamur, et quos in viis aut in sepibus invenimus, intrare cogimus, et sic nondum quibusdam persuademus, *qui iam non res eorum, sed ipsos querimus*' (my italics). Cf. *Lib. c. Wib.* 525–6: 'Pecuniam eorum et terras non concupiscimus, sed ut thesaurizent impiorum divitiae iustis et spolia impiorum tollant iusti, ea tamen intentione, ut eos lucrari possint et conversis non solum quae illorum sunt, sed omnia etiam sua in caritate distribuant, summopere satagimus et desideramus.'

[68] Cf. Anselm's Commentary on Psalm II in Paul of Bernried, *Vita Gregorii VII.*, c. 112, p. 541: 'Si enim dimiserimus eum sic, venient Romani et tollent nostrum locum et gentem: id est si Papa Gregorius vixerit, mittet contra nos praedicatores veritatis, qui discutientes vitam et actus nostros, eripient oves Christi de manibus nostris, et iusti diripient spolia nostra et committent ecclesiam facientibus fructum in ea.'

[69] Anselm XIII: 17 (fo. 235): 'In Christi ergo compagem corporis veniant et labores suos non dominandi cupiditate sed bene utendi pietate possideant. Nos autem voluntatem nostram, ut iam dictum est, ab huius cupiditatis sordibus quolibet inimico iudicante purgavimus, quando eos ipsos, quorum labores dicuntur, ut nobiscum et illis et nostris in societate catholica utantur, quantum valemus, inquirimus.' Cf. *Lib. c. Wib.* 525–6.

Conclusion: A Canonist of Reform

WHILE it has not been the ambition of this work to consider the complex evolution of the *Collectio canonum* of Anselm of Lucca, it still remains to place the collection in the wider developments in canon law during the eleventh century. The collection was reasonably well diffused in Italy during the late eleventh and early twelfth centuries, albeit without achieving the ongoing popularity of Burchard's *Decretum libri XX*, the diffusion of the 74T, or even the influence of Ivo of Chartres. Although it was an important formal source for subsequent collections, its existence as a unique and independent compilation was relatively short-lived. With the appearance of Gratian's *Concordia discordantium canonum* around 1141, Anselm's collection was in itself virtually forgotten, apart from a brief resurgence of interest by the *Correctores Romani* in their preparation of a new edition of Gratian in the sixteenth century.

The integrity of the collection, however, was not even rigidly maintained in its own time. While the unrelenting insistence upon absolute Roman primacy was preserved, interpolations and changes to the internal ordering, as well as other modifications were made almost immediately. Many of these additions were not broad statements of principle, but specific practical measures. They were oriented towards a less large-scale, and even more moderate, reform programme, whereby the clergy would be protected from any rash intrusions and could therefore get on with their principal business of pastoral care.

These modifications are important in two ways. On the one hand, they demonstrate that the deficiencies of the collection as a practical, day-to-day, working compendium were apparent almost immediately. On the other, they suggest that the strident tone and ideological inflexibility with which the collection was imbued and associated made its progressive abandonment almost certain. Gilchrist commented upon the

interpolations in the B recension of the collection (Berlin, Staatsbibliothek Preussicher Kulturbesitz 597) by noting that, while the recensor would do nothing to destroy the grand plans of the Gregorians,
neither would he do much to further them. This tendency is apparent
in the modifications of other recensions.

Significance cannot simply be measured in terms of lasting effect or
import, however. Coming as it did after a series of attempts to articulate a constitution for the Church, Anselm's collection stands as a concrete manifestation of the ways in which the reformers envisaged the law
as an aim, a means, and a justification of reform. Like the 74T, the
Collectio canonum of Deusdedit, and the many other small, short-lived,
collections compiled in the 1070s and 1080s, it answered on the most
basic level the reformers' call for new and better canonical collections.
With its emphasis upon judicial procedure, it, like the others, also attests
to the important connection between the generality of ecclesiastical
reform and the need for canonical collections.

Unlike these, however, Anselm's collection was not simply interested
in defining a new constitution, but also in providing the justification for
the papacy to articulate and effect those changes. Despite the many
problems of its evolution, it should be clear that Anselm's collection was
a book about 'principles'; and that it had an agenda which needs to be
seen in the context of its own time. The reform legislation and canon
law of this tumultuous period were above all an exercise in instruction.
They were a form of propaganda, indeed, an ideal postulation of what
the reformers desired for the Church and Christian society. They were
not simply an immediately binding set of regulations. Canon law did not
so much perhaps introduce a new mode of thinking as create a new force
by which that thinking could be spread.

Because of the many variables, one cannot always be sure that a
canonical collection represents the specific conceptual and fundamental
beliefs either of its compiler or of his party. It is, though, possible to
discern a perspective. The resolute insistence upon both the necessity
and the authority of the pope to steer the Church and Christian society
through troubled waters indicates that a deliberating mind lay behind
Anselm's compilation. The ability to justify 'Gregorian' ambitions by
appeal to the past, along with the competence to subordinate that past
to a general principle of papal discretion, and above all the capacity to
respond to the radically shifting circumstances of the time, suggest that
Anselm not only knew what was required, but also fashioned the law for
whatever might be necessary.

Appendices

APPENDIX I

Anselm's Canonical Sources:
Some Documentary Evidence

IA. ANSELM'S TRANSMISSION OF INDEPENDENT PS.ISIDORIAN TEXTS

The following examples are intended to demonstrate in greater detail the modifications which Anselm made to his 'independent' Ps.Isidorian texts. 'Independent' refers to those texts which Anselm took directly from a copy of the Ps.Isidorian Decretals, and not those which were provided through the 74T or Burchard. Each example notes: the location in the *Collectio canonum*, the Ps.Isidorian text in question [with reference to P. Hinschius, ed. *Decretales Pseudo-Isidorianae*]; Anselm's rubric title; the *incipit/explicit* of Anselm's text [identified from MS Vat. lat. 1363 by folio, or from Thaner's edition by page: Vat. lat. 1363 is used here in those instances where discrepancies were found in the text in Thaner's edition, and especially when noteworthy variations were found between Anselm and the Ps.Isidore; in such cases reference to Thaner is also provided]; the variations between Anselm's text and his Ps.Isidorian source (*only* where substantial); and finally a brief commentary on Anselm's transmission.

A. Ps.Isidore and Roman Primacy

These refer to those Ps.Isidorian texts which have been redirected, usually by the rubric title, away from the original intention, and towards an assertion of absolute Roman primacy.

(1) I: 5 Ps.Clement, c. 17 [Hinschius, 35]
  Quod Christum non recipit qui papam contristaverit

incipit/explicit: [pp. 8–9]
  Sed et vos, fratres karissimi et conservi mei, huic qui presidet vobis ad veritatem docendam in omnibus obedite . . . . . . et qui Christum non susceperit

nec Deum patrem suscepisse iudicabitur; et ideo nec ipse suscipietur in regno caelorum.

This text, part of Ps.Clement's 'speech' to the people, contains no reference whatsoever to the pope. The implication of the text suggests rather that he who saddens Christ will not receive, nor be received by God. Anselm has wholly altered the intention with his rubric, conveying that true faith is achieved only by those who are in complete concordance in every sense with the Roman pontiff.

(2) I: 6 Ps.Clement, c. 17 [Hinschius, 36]
  Quod nec loqui debemus cui papa non loquitur

incipit/explicit: [p. 9]
  Si ipse inimicus est alicui pro actibus suis, vos nolite expectare ut ipse vobis dicat: 'Cum illo nolite amici esse'. . . . . . . sed nec loqui his quibus ipse non loquitur.

This text, again part of Clement's 'speech' to the people, also has no reference to the pope. In fact, the text has little relation whatsoever to Anselm's rubric. Anselm has transformed the intention of the Ps.Clement text, which established Christ as the figure by whom one ought to judge one's relations with society, by proffering the pope as that decisive figure. The implication of Anselm's rubric is that one ought to have nothing whatsoever to do with him who is an enemy of the pope, as opposed to the Ps.Clement's stipulation that one should avoid him who is an enemy of Christ.

(3) I: 11 Ps.Pius, c. 2 [Hinschius, 117]
  Ut nemo dissentiat a Romana ecclesia, quae est caput omnium ecclesiarum

incipit/explicit: [p. 12]
  Instruimus vos apostolica auctoritate omnes eadem servare debere, quae et nos servamus nec debetis a capite quoquo modo dissidere. . . . . . . 'Tu es P. et s. h. p. aedificabo ecclesiam meam, et portae inferi non prevalebunt adversus eam' et cetera.

In this text, Anselm demands total obedience to Rome by virtue of its divine foundation and its consequent lordship over all the churches. By omitting references in the Ps.Pius text to the human fallacies of astrology and the like, Anselm implicitly stresses that the *plenitudo potestatis* held corporally by Christ has been transferred to the Roman Church, and consequently to Peter and his successors.

(4) I: 14 Ps.Dionysius, c. 2 [Hinschius, 195]
  Quod per universam ecclesiam quicquid nocivum in ea est debet papa corrigere et emendare

incipit/explicit: [p. 13]
  Olim et ab initio tantam percepimus a beato Petro apostolorum principe fiduciam, ut habeamus auctoritatem universali ecclesiae auxiliante Domino sub-

venire . . . . . . et potiores minoribus dilectionem impenderent una concordiae fieret ex diversitate contextio et recte officiorum gereretur amministratio singulorum.

With his rubric, Anselm attests to the obligation of the Roman pontiff actively to exercise his power for the good. The provision becomes almost a mandate for reform, displayed in a hierarchical sense.

(5) I: 17 Ps.Julius, c. 6 [Hinschius, 459]

Quod Romana ecclesia omnibus est prelata non tantum canonum decretis sed voce ipsius Salvatoris

incipit/explicit: [p. 14 (entire text)]

Romana ecclesia omnibus maior et prelata est ecclesiis, quae non solummodo canonum et sanctorum patrum decretis sed Domini salvatoris nostri voce singularem obtinuit principatum: 'Tu es', inquiens, 'P. e. s. h. p.' et reliqua.

Variants:	*Anselm*	*Ps.Julius* [Hinschius]
	Romana ecclesia omnibus	Ipsa namque omnibus

Anselm subtly transforms the Ps.Julius text by stating that it is not so much the legal statutes of the past that have placed Rome at the head of all the churches, but the divine words of Christ. By so doing, he ignores the sense of the Ps.Julius text which acknowledges that the two features together have combined to place Rome at the top, and effectively concedes a human element in the creation of the ecclesiastical hierarchy. Anselm stresses the divine foundation, and consequently seems to imply that the hierarchy is also a divine creation.

(6) I: 18 Ps.Damasus, c. 8 [Hinschius, 502]

Quod ecclesiae columpnae, qui sunt episcopi, confirmatae sunt super firmamentum Petri, quod est sedes apostolica

incipit/explicit: [pp. 14–15]

Scitis fratres carissimi firmamentum a Deo fixum et immobile atque titulum lucidissimum suorum sacerdotum, i.e. omnium episcoporum apostolicam sedem esse constitutam et verticem ecclesiarum . . . . . . atque ligare et solvere potestatem quae in caelis sunt et quae in terris promulgavi.

In a dramatic shift, echoed in *Collectio canonum* I: 60 with a much corrupted text of Peter Damian, Anselm emphasizes the role of the Apostolic See as the institution through which the episcopate exists. (In the corruption of Damian's text, Anselm goes even further by insisting upon Rome's direct instituition of all ecclesiastical dignities. Here, the sense is almost but not quite as narrow.)

(7) I: 32 Ps.Sother, c. 3 [Hinschius, 124]

Quod pro omni statu ecclesiae papa debet curam habere

incipit/explicit: [p. 20 (entire text)]

Divinis preceptis et apostolicis monitis informamur, ut pro omnium ecclesiarum statu impigro vigilemus affectu, ac si quid usquam reprehensione invenitur obnoxium, celeri sollicitudine ab ignorantiae imperitia aut presumptionis usurpatione revocemus.

The Ps.Sother text continues with a specific problem, namely that women and monks are not to be allowed to carry the *vasa sacra* and the *pallas sacratas* to the altar. Anselm, again emphasizing the pontiff's position at the top of the ecclesiastical hierarchy, provides a universal obligation for papal intervention. It would be hard to imagine a more pressing justification for papally-sponsored and led reform.

(8) I: 34 Ps.Fabianus, c. 1 [Hinschius, 156]
   Item de eodem, et ut omnes qui veri filii volunt esse sciant et sequantur, quae in Romana ecclesia sacro ritu aguntur

incipit/explicit: [p. 20 (entire text)]
   Divinis preceptis et apostolicis monemur institutis, ut pro cunctarum ecclesiarum statu impigro vigilemus affectu. Unde consequens est debere vos scire, quae apud Romanam in sacro ritu aguntur ecclesiam, ut eius sequentes exempla eius veri filii inveniamini quae vestra est mater vocata.

Here Anselm moves away from the Petrine commission and looks to equate the Roman Church with the entire Church. Concordance with Rome, and indeed obedience to Rome's stipulations, even in terms of ritual, is identified with true faith. The implications are significant. For Anselm, the failure to be in strict concordance with Rome in every way almost verges on the heretical.

B. Modification of Ps.Isidore

These refer to Ps.Isidorian texts which have been modified either textually, through omission, via the rubric, or a combination of any or all, towards new ends.
(1) II: 4 Ps.Anacletus, c. 17 [Hinschius, 74]
   Ut difficiliores causae et maiora negocia ad sedem apostolicam, si appellatum fuerit, deferantur

incipit/explicit: [MS Vat. 1363, fo. 30^r / pp. 76–7]
   Si difficiliores ortae fuerint questiones aut episcoporum vel maiorum iudicia aut maiores causae fuerint ad sedem apostolicam . . . . . . quam Christus universam construxit ecclesiam dicente ipso ad beatum principem apostolorum Petrum: 'Tu es' inquit 'P. et s. h. p. ae. ae. m.'.

(There is one minor variant.)

Ps.Anacletus, at the beginning of c. 17 (not part of Anselm's text), noted that difficult *causae* should be brought *ad maiorem sedem*, i.e. to the metropolitan, and if this failed to resolve the problem, a *congregatio summorum* should take place to deal with the issue. In the Ps.Anacletus text, the Apostolic See is the final stage in resolving an issue. For Anselm, however, it is an unequivocal fact that all of the more difficult cases should be brought to Rome.

(2) **II: 7 Ps.Marcellus, c. 2 [Hinschius, 224]**

Quod omnes quibus necesse fuerit ad Romanam debent ecclesiam suffugere absque omni impedimento, et ut nullus episcopus iudicetur vel audiatur nisi in synodo apostolica auctoritate convocata, et cetera

incipit/explicit: [pp. 77–8]

Ad Romanam ecclesiam omnes quasi ad caput iuxta apostolorum eorumque successorum sanctiones episcopi qui voluerint vel quibus necesse fuerit suffugere eamque appellare debent. . . . . . Quod tamen, ut praefatum est, per eius vicarios si libuerit erit retractandum et quicquid iniuste actum est reformandum.

Variants: *Anselm*   *Ps.Marcellus* [Hinschius]
           Ad Romanam ecclesiam omnes   Ad quam omnes

Anselm transforms the Ps.Marcellus text's aim of making the judgement of bishops difficult, by emphasizing in effect that nothing can be done without the authority of the Apostolic See or its delegates.

(3) **II: 9 Ps.Victor, cc. 4–6 [Hinschius, 128]**

Quod absque auctoritate apostolica nulli licet episcoporum causas diffinire quamvis scrutari liceat cum provincialibus episcopis

incipit/explicit: [MS Vat. 1363, fo. 31^r / pp. 79–80]

Ad apostolicam delatum est sedem ea vos iudicare quae praeter nostram vobis definire non licet auctoritatem id est episcoporum causas . . . . . . Nichil aliud est, frater, talis presumptio, nisi apostolorum suorumque successorum terminos transgredi eorumque decreta violari. Culpantur enim, ut scriptum est, fratres qui aliter circa episcopos iudicare praesumant, quam apostolicae sedis papae fieri placuerit.

(There are a number of minor variants between the two texts.)

Anselm transforms the Ps.Victor's aim of protecting a bishop from his co-provincial bishops by emphasizing the difference between the full authority of the Apostolic See and the limited right of scrutiny of the episcopate.

(4) **II: 14 Ps.Gaius, c. 7 [Hinschius, 218]**

De eadem re (from c. 13: Quod dubiae ac maiores causae ab apostolica sede debent terminari)

incipit/explicit: [MS Vat. 1363, fo. 31^v//32^r / p. 82]

Sic a patribus nostris institutum est sic quoque et nos fieri decrevimus . . . ut quaecumque difficiles questiones . . . . . . fuerint semper ad sedem apostolicam referantur.

Variants: *MS Vat. 1363*   *Ps.Gaius* [Hinschius]
           Sic a patribus nostris   De episcoporum vero . . . sanctos
           institutum est, sic quoque et   apostolos et successores eorum
           nos fieri decrevimus, scilicet   . . . sufficienter statuisse
           ut quaecumque difficiles. . . .   cognovimus; et idcirco non est

> necesse nos replicare nisi quod illi
> statuerunt. Illud tamen nos
> statuentes vobis et omnibus servare
> mandamus. . . . . . Et quaecunque
> difficiles. . . .

Anselm neatly transforms the Ps.Gaius text, emphasizing not only that major cases are to be brought to Rome, but also highlighting the legislative powers of the Apostolic See in a succinct fashion.

(5) II: 36 Ps.Eleutherus, c. 2 [Hinschius, 125]

Ut episcoporum tantum finitiva iudicia referantur ad sedem Romanam, et in ecclesiis eorum non alii praeponantur donec negocia eorum iuste ibi terminentur

incipit/explicit: [MS Vat. 1363, fo. 35ʳ / p. 91]

De accusationibus clericorum super quibus consulti sumus quia omnes eorum accusationes difficile est ad sedem apostolicam deferre, finitiva episcoporum tantum iudicia huc deferantur et huius sanctae sedis autoritate finiantur. . . . . . . Nec in eorum aecclesiis alii aut praeponantur aut ordinentur ante quam hic eorum iusta terminentur negocia.

Though the transmission of the Ps.Eleutherus text is without alteration, the sense is adulterated in that Anselm again contrasts the definitive authority of the Apostolic See with the limited right of the episcopate to scrutinize and debate issues.

(6) II: 41 Ps.Melciades, cc. 2, 5 [Hinschius, 243]

Ut nemo suspicionis arbitrio iudicetur, et quod sola sedes apostolica privilegium habet a temporibus apostolorum iudicandi episcopos

incipit/explicit: [p. 93]

Nullum iudicium iudicetis suspicionis arbitrio, sed primum probate et postea caritativam proferte sententiam. . . . . . . Audivimus a quibusdam fratribus quibus infesti eratis nimis, quod iurgia et discordiae sunt inter vos; propterea ista scripsimus vobis mandantes, ut ita teneatis sicut ab apostolica sede tenenda mandantur.

Variants: *Anselm*   *Ps.Melciades* [Hinschius]
             nullum iudicium iudicetis   nullum iudicetis
(There are a number of other minor variants, and Anselm also omits part of the text.)

With a historical consciousness, Anselm transforms the Ps.Melciades text into a ringing statement of the papacy's prerogative of judging the episcopate. The large section omitted reveals the Ps.Isidore's concern with noxious local elements who wish to do harm to their bishop, and who are in no way to be allowed to make accusations.

(7) II: 42 Ps.Julius, c. 6 [Hinschius, 459]
Quod ab apostolis eorumque successoribus statutum est, ut absque Romani pontificis sententia nec concilia celebrentur nec episcopi damnentur, et sicut beatus Petrus primus erat apostolorum sic Romana ecclesia primatum habet omnium ecclesiarum

incipit/explicit: [MS Vat. 1363, fo. 36ʳ//36ᵛ / pp. 93–4]
Porro dudum a sanctis apostolis et successoribus eorum in praefatis antiquis decretum fuerat statutis, quae hactenus sancta et universalis apostolica tenet aecclesia non oportere praeter sententiam Romani pontificis concilia celebrari nec episcopum damnari . . . . . . unanimiterque recte sentiant; et ea quae senserint nobis sibimet non discrepando sed Deo placendo perficiatur.

(There are a number of minor variants.)

Anselm explicitly transforms the 'safeguard' of the episcopate into an overt papal power. He makes it all the more resonant by linking the papal power of convoking synods and judgement with the primacy of the Roman Church.

(8) II: 44 Ps.Julius, c. 9 [Hinschius, 461]
Ut omnes observent quod apostolica sedes observat

incipit/explicit: [p. 95 (entire text)]
Satis indignum est vel pontificum vel ordinum quemquam subsequentium hanc regulare refutare, quam beati Petri sedem et sequi videat et docere.

Here Anselm uses an excerpt of a Ps.Julius text which appeared in I: 8 (with the rubric: *Quod ad formam apostolorum facta est quaedam distinctio episcoporum, quibus tamen omnibus beati Petri sedes preminet*) with a different purpose and a different rubric. The text seems curiously out of place in Book II. It is, however, hard to imagine a more unequivocal statement of apostolic supremacy in terms of the obligation to be in complete concordance with Rome.

(9) II: 47 Ps.Julius, c. 13 [Hinschius, 471]
Quod irritum sit concilium nisi fuerit apostolica auctoritate firmatum

incipit/explicit: [MS Vat. 1363, fo. 37ᵛ//38ʳ / p. 92]
Regula vestra nullas habet vires nec habere poterit. . . . . . . Nec ullum ratum est aut erit umquam concilium quod eius non fuerit fultum autoritate. Et post pauca.

Variants: *MS Vat. 1363*	*Ps.Julius* [Hinschius]
Regula vestra nullas habet. . . .	. . . hanc regulam protulistis quae nullas habet. . . .

(There are a number of other minor variants.)

Anselm tightens up the sense of the Ps.Julius text regarding the illegal deposition of Athanasius—a deposition which had been according to Arian rules, and not those of the orthodox Church. Anselm thus transforms an 'episcopal' protection into the customary assertion of papal supremacy that we have come to expect from him, by establishing that all councils not sanctioned by the Apostolic See are *irritae*. By removing the historical details of the Arians, Anselm also updates the text. (The 'et post pauca', found here at the end of the canon, and at the end of each canon in MS Vat. 1363 in II: 45–8, refers to a series of Ps.Julius texts—all of which came from the same decretal.)

(10) II: 48 Ps.Julius, c. 15 [Hinschius, 471–2]

Quod apostolicae sedi privilegia specialiter sunt concessa de congregandis conciliis et iudiciis ac restitutionibus episcoporum et de omnibus negociis summis aecclesiarum

incipit/explicit: [MS Vat. 1363, fo. 38ʳ / pp. 97–8]

Michi cui vice principis apostolorum universalis ecclesiae cura commissa est, summopere providendum est, ne talia deinceps fiant. . . . . . . ut ab ea omnes oppressi auxilium et iniuste damnati restitutionem sumant, et talia ab improbis nec praesumantur absque ultione nec exerceantur absque sua damnatione. Et post pauca.

Variants:	*MS Vat. 1363*	*Ps.Julius* [Hinschius]
	summopere providendum est,	providendum est, auxiliante ipso
	ne talia. . . .	summo apostolo, ne talia. . . .
	Et post pauca	—

Again by ignoring the references of the Ps.Julius text to the reprehension of the Arian bishops, Anselm updates and makes manifest the special apostolic privileges of convoking synods, and judging and restoring the episcopate, as well as dealing with the important cases of all churches. Somewhat curiously Anselm dispenses with the Petrine aid with his omission of the phrase 'auxiliante ipso summo apostolo'.

(11) II: 51 Ps.Athanasius, c. 4 [Hinschius, 480]

Ut apostolicam sedem appellet qui metropolitanum suum vel ceteros episcopos habet suspectos et quod ipsa potestatem habet iniuste dampnatos et excommunicatos restituere et sua eis reddere quia caput omnium est

incipit/explicit: [p. 99]

Similiter et a supradictis patribus est definitum consonanter, ut si quisquam episcoporum aut metropolitanum aut comprovinciales aut iudices suspectos habuerit, vestram sanctam Romanam interpellet sedem. . . . . . . Nam fuit semper vestrae sanctae et apostolicae sedi licentia iniuste dampnatos vel excommunicatos potestative sua auctoritate restituere et sua eis omnia reddere, et illos qui eos condempnaverunt apostolico punire privilegio sicut etiam nostris et anterioribus cognovimus actum temporibus.

While the two texts are the same, Anselm transforms the Ps.Athanasius text, which was a gloss on what had been defined at the Council of Nicaea, into a clear expression of Roman primacy, by emphasizing the differences between the pontiff and even the highest metropolitan. The Apostolic See, as the head of all, has the power to restore those unjustly condemned or excommunicated.

(12) II: 79 Ps.Damasus, c. 18 [Hinschius, 505]

Quod accusati episcopi aut condempnandi sunt apostolica auctoritate aut eius auxilio fulciendi

incipit/explicit: [pp. 112–13]

Monentes instruere debetis vicinos vestros ut a talibus se subtrahant, et quae illicite circa fratres egerunt cito corrigant, et quos nobis inconsultis laesurunt nobis consultis plena satisfactione sanent, et cito sibi eos reconcilient, si noluerint apostolicae sedis suscipere censuram. . . . . . . A talibus deinceps omnes se abstineant sacerdotes, qui noluerunt ab apostolicae petrae super quam Christu, ut predictum est, universalem construxit ecclesiam, cui episcoporum summa iudicia atque maiorum causae . . . reservatae sunt, soliditate atque sacerdotale honore secludi.

(There are a number of minor variants.)

The Ps.Damasus text, warning against those who accuse their bishops hastily and without good cause, notes the distant pontiff as the only figure who can proffer judgement. Anselm transforms the implicit acknowledgement into a universally binding power.

(13) III: 4 Ps.Pius, c. 4 [Hinschius, 117]

Qui a proposito suo ceciderit et apostolicis iussis non obedierit, infamis est

incipit/explicit: [p. 120 (entire text)]

Si quis vero a proposito suo exorbitaverit et iussa apostolicae sedis libenter transgressus fuerit, infamis efficitur.

(There are a few minor variants.)

Anselm's text comes at the end of a chapter stipulating that *pastores* should not be reprimanded or accused by their flocks, as bishops are to be judged by God alone. What this final clause, which is Anselm's text, has to do with the preceding part is a good question. It is clear that the Ps.Isidore wanted to set the pope at the end to protect those pastors accused or judged by their inferiors. Anselm wholly removes this clause from its context, making it a canon of obedience to all the orders of the apostolic See.

(14) III: 80 Ps.Anacletus, c. 15 [Hinschius, 73]

Ut provinciae suos habeant iudices, nisi papa aliter voluerit

incipit/explicit: [MS Vat. 1363, fo. 61ʳ / p. 155]

Una quaeque provincia tam iuxta ecclesiasticas quam iuxta saeculi leges suos debet iustos et non iniquos habere iudices . . . nisi apostolicae huius sedis decreverit auctoritas.

(There are one or two minor variants.)

Anselm transforms the Ps.Anacletus text, which sought to condition the local quality of judging by providing for those instances where external intervention might be desired, by removing that conditionality and making the canon more universal. The impression is that should the pope wish to intervene in a judgement for whatever reason, he is fully entitled to do so.

C. Adherence to Ps.Isidore

These refer to those Ps.Isidorian texts in Anselm which are very close, if not identical, both in textual and especially in ideological terms to the given Ps.Isidorian text.

(1) III: 28 Ps.Eleutherus, cc. 4, 5 [Hinschius, 126]

Ut clericus criminatus sua in provincia audiatur, et ut sententia iudicis, quae absente accusato datur, irrita sit, et proditoris calumnia non audiatur

incipit/explicit: [pp. 130–1]

De accusationibus comprovincialium ita legitur esse statutum. . . . . . . Haec omnia summopere sunt attendenda, nec criminatio minorum, quanto magis episcoporum, facile est recipienda dicente Domino: 'Non sequeris turbas ad faciendum malum.'

(There are a number of minor variants.)

Anselm here follows the tone of the Ps.Eleutherus text, stipulating that judgement cannot be made when the accused is absent. In *Collectio canonum* III: 92, however, Anselm does seem to follow clause 5 of the *Dictatus papae* of Gregory VII, which states that the pope can depose the absent, with a text from the third action of the Council of Chalcedon, though he recognizes that this was a special case. Anselm's insistence (in the omitted text, which is not part of the Ps.Eleutherus text) upon the synodal processes may implicitly reflect the fact that such synods were licit only with the pontiff's knowledge or sanction.

(2) III: 34 Ps.Eusebius, cc. 8–11 [Hinschius, 234, 237]

Quod pravae vitae hominibus non licet episcopos et servos Dei accusare

incipit/explicit: [p. 133]

Errorem vestrum corrigite fratres, et ab omni erroris macula vos custodite, ut purum Deo munus offerre valeatis. . . . . . . Oves ergo . . . debent nec ullatenus accusare possunt, quia facta pastorum oris gladio ferienda non sunt, quamquam recte reprehendenda videantur.

(There are a few minor variants.)

The Ps.Eusebius text, by means of a brief discourse on the Cleansing of the Temple, insists that God alone reserves to himself the judgement of bishops, priests, etc. No grounds exist for judgement save those instances where the figure in question is known to have deviated from the faith. In a lengthy section omitted by Anselm, however, this *nisi a fide* clause is tempered by comments that discretion is to be used in such instances, and that clergy must guard against false witnesses and judges. The text, however, is one with which Anselm most emphatically concurs.

(3) III: 44 Ps.Iohannes [Hinschius, 694]

Quod oves pastorem reprehendere non possunt, nisi in fide erraverit, et quod expoliati non debeant ad synodum vocari nisi prius eis bona sua fuerint restituta

incipit/explicit: [pp. 136–7]

Oves quae pastori suo commissae fuerint eum nec reprehendere, nisi a recta fide exorbitaverit . . . . . . Redintegranda sunt omnia expoliatis vel eiectis epis-copis . . . ante accusationem aut regularem ad synodum vocationem eorum.

(There are a few minor variants.)

Anselm wholly follows the Ps.Iohannes text regarding the despoliation of bish-ops. Of particular significance to Anselm are the appeals found in the omitted text to *in synodalibus patrum decretis* and *antiquitus decretum*, as Anselm, like the Ps.Isidore, was often at pains to demonstrate the weightiest legal precedence possible.

IB. ANSELM'S TRANSMISSION OF PS.ISIDORIAN TEXTS FROM THE 74T

The following examples are intended to demonstrate in greater detail the mod-ifications that Anselm made to his Ps.Isidorian texts via the 74T, as well as to indicate the types of issues to which these texts were addressed.

Each example notes: the location in the *Collectio canonum*; the corresponding location in the 74T, the Ps.Isidorian source in question [with reference to P. Hinschius, ed. *Decretales Pseudo-Isidorianae*]; Anselm's rubric title; the *incipit/explicit* of Anselm's text [identified from MS Vat. lat. 1363 by folio or Thaner's edition by page: Vat. lat. 1363 is used here in those instances where discrepancies were found in the text in Thaner's edition, and especially when noteworthy variations were found between Anselm, the Ps.Isidore, and the 74T; in such cases reference to Thaner is also provided]; the title under which the Ps.Isidorian text was placed by the 74T; the *incipit/explicit* of the 74T text [identified from J. T. Gilchrist, ed. *Diversorum patrum sententie*] *only* when it dif-fers substantially from that in Anselm; the variations between Anselm's text and that of the 74T (*only* where substantial); and finally a brief commentary on Anselm's transmission.

A. *'Seemingly Faithful' Transmission of Ps.Isidorian Texts from the 74T*

These refer to texts in Anselm's collection which, though they are very close in a textual sense to those in the 74T, have been redirected towards different ends.

(1) I: 2 (= 74T c. 2) Ps.Anacletus, c. 30 [Hinschius, 83]

Quod Romana ecclesia caput est omnium aecclesiarum, et ab ipso Domino non ab alio primatum obtinuit[1]

incipit/explicit: [MS Vat. 1363, fo. 3ᵛ / pp. 7–8]

Sacrosancta Romana et apostolica ecclesia non ab apostolis sed ab ipso Domino salvatore nostro primatum obtinuit . . . . . . et sicut cardine hostium regitur, sic huius sanctae sedis auctoritate omnes ecclesiae Domino disponente reguntur.

74T title I. De primatu Romanae ecclesiae

incipit/explicit: [Gilchrist, p. 20]

Sacrosancta Romana et apostolica ecclesia non ab apostolis sed ab ipso Domino salvatore nostro primatum obtinuit . . . . . . disponente reguntur. Igitur si quae causae difficiliores inter vos ortae fuerint, ad huius sanctae sedis apicem eas quasi ad caput referte, ut apostolico terminentur iudicio.

Anselm omits the final line of the 74T text, that cases should be brought to the judgement of the Apostolic See. This is a line which is not found in this specific Ps.Anacletus text; in fact, the Ps.Anacletus text is dramatically different than that of the 74T, and breaks off following the Petrine quotation. While the 74T emphasizes the judicial primacy of Rome as the consequence of the Petrine commission, Anselm does not conditionalize Rome's primacy but stresses it in more encompassing terms.

[1] In his edition, Thaner did not include a rubric. While he did note some of the variant rubrics in his apparatus, he failed to note the rubric of one of his main recensions (V1), that of MS Vat. lat. 1363.

(2) I: 12 (= 74T c. 4) Ps.Calixtus, c. 2 [Hinschius, 136]

Quod a regulis Romanae ecclesiae nullatenus convenit deviare

incipit/explicit: [p. 12]

Non decet a capite membra dissidere, sed iuxta sacrae scripturae testimonium omnia membra caput sequantur. . . . . . . Quicquid ergo sine discretione iustitiae contra huius disciplinam actum fuerit, ratum habere ratio nulla permittit.

74T tit I. De primatu Romanae ecclesiae

Though the two texts are the same apart from one minor word-order reversal, Anselm explicitly makes manifest with his rubric the more judicial aspect of Rome's primacy that the actual text addresses.

(3) II: 6 (= 74T c. 3) Ps.Zepherinus, c. 6 [Hinschius, 132]

Quod ad Romanam ecclesiam ab omnibus oppressis appellandum est, ubi etiam omnes ecclesiasticae causae maiores sunt terminandae

incipit/explicit: [p. 77]

Ad Romanam ecclesiam ab omnibus maxime tamen ab oppressis appellandum est et concurrendum quasi ad matrem. . . . . . . Petro apostolo dictum est:

'Quaecumque ligaveris super terram erunt ligata et in caelis, et quaecumque solveris super terram erunt soluta et in caelis.'

74T tit I. De primatu Romanae ecclesiae

While the two texts are the same, Anselm again, by means of his rubric, stresses the particular topic with which the text is concerned. It is significant that Anselm placed the text in Book II on the liberty of appeal, and not as the 74T specifically supporting primacy.

(4) II: 8 (= 74T c. 7) Ps.Sixtus, cc. 5, 6 [Hinschius, 108, 109]

Ut pulsatus in adversitate episcopus licenter sedem appellet apostolicam, aut si vocatus fuerit veniat non autem revertatur, nisi formatis instructus

incipit/explicit: [pp. 78–9]

Si quis vestrum pulsatus fuerit in aliqua adversitate licenter hanc sanctam et apostolicam appellet sedem et ad eam quasi ad caput suffugium habeat. . . . . . Si quis autem aliter agere presumpserit, sciat censuram huius sedis cum omnibus membris suis sibi non deesse venturam, et sicut egerit ita recipiet: Si bene, bene; si grave, grave; si pessime, pessime, quoniam dignus est mercenarius [operarius] mercede sua.

74T tit I. De primatu Romanae ecclesiae

Despite a few minor variants, the two texts are the same. Yet again, Anselm, by means of his rubric, specifies the issue. Certainly, as was seen in his independent Ps.Isidorian texts, Anselm continued to emphasize Roman primacy outside of Book I. It is clear, however, that by placing this text in Book II, he correctly read his 74T exemplar's assertion of primacy in terms of Rome's judicial privileges.

(5) II: 10 (= 74T cc. 5, 6) Ps.Fabianus, cc. 15, 17 [Hinschius, 162, 167]

Ut ei qui iudicem sibi senserit adversum, liceat appellationis remedio viciatam causam relevare et nulla detentionis iniuria affligatur; etiam his qui in supplicia sunt destinati fas sit appellare

incipit/explicit: [p. 80]

Si in rebus saecularibus suum cuiusque ius et proprius ordo servandus est, quanto magis in ecclesiasticis dispositionibus nulla debet induci confusio. . . . . Pulsatus ante suum iudicem causam dicat et non ante suum iudicem pulsatus si voluerit taceat, et pulsatis quotiens appellaverint induciae dentur nec quemquam sententia non a suo iudice dicta constringat.

74T tit I. De primatu Romanae ecclesiae

Here, Anselm combines two Ps.Fabianus texts from the 74T into one chapter. The texts are the same, save a few minor variants. This text is one of the clearest expressions of the 74T's judicial preoccupation; it has nothing whatsoever to do with an assertion of Rome's supremacy. In fact, the text does not even mention the Apostolic See. Anselm correctly 'reads' the text, and accordingly places it in Book II: it is strictly a question of appeal.

(6) II: 21 (= 74T c. 191) Ps.Annicius, c. 4 [Hinschius, 121]

Ut nullus metropolitanorum causas episcoporum sive aliorum agere presumat nisi quae ad propriam pertinent parrochiam

incipit/explicit: [p. 85 (entire text)]

Si quis metropolitanorum inflatus fuerit et sine omnium comprovincialium presentia vel consilio episcoporum aut eorum aut alias causas nisi eas tantum quae ad propriam suam pertinent parrochiam agere aut eos gravare voluerit, ab omnibus districte corrigatur, ne talia deinceps presumere audeat.

74T tit XXVI. Ut unusquisque suis contentus sit terminis

incipit/explicit: [p. 119]

Si aliquis metropolitanorum inflatus fuerit. . . . audeat. . . . . . Si vero incorrigibilis eisque inobediens apparuerit, ad hanc apostolicam sedem, cui omnia episcoporum iudicia terminare iussa sunt, eius contumacia referatur ut vindicta de eo fiat et ceteri timorem habeant.

Anselm curtails the 74T text, omitting the discussion that the contumacy and disobedience of him who disregards diocesan lines and fails to co-operate with his comprovincials, is to be referred to the Apostolic See. It is puzzling that he did so. Perhaps Anselm did not want to make the point that it was only under such circumstances that the Apostolic See should be called upon. After all, in Anselm's thought, the Apostolic See was to be consulted in all more difficult *causae*, especially those concerning the episcopate.

(7) II: 60 (= 74T c. 90) Ps.Damasus, cc. 8, 9 [Hinschius, 502]

Quod metropolitano cum omnibus comprovincialibus episcopis summas ecclesiasticas causas licet discutere sed non diffinire, nec episcopum dampnare nec synodum congregare absque apostolicae sedis auctoritate

incipit/explicit: [p.103]

Discutere episcopos et summas ecclesiasticorum causas negotiorum metropolitanis. . . . . . Nam, ut nostis, synodum sine eius auctoritate fieri non est catholicum, nec episcopus nisi in legitima synodo et suo tempore apostolica vocatione congregata diffinite dampnari potest, neque ulla concilia umquam rata leguntur, quae apostolica non sunt fulta auctoritate.

74T tit X. De iudicio et examinatione episcoporum

incipit/explicit: [pp. 65–6]

Discutere episcopos et summas ecclesiasticorum causas negotiorum metropolitanos una cum omnibus suis comprovincialibus . . . fulta auctoritate. Accusatores autem episcoporum et testes absque ulla infamia aut suspicione vel manifesta macula et vere fidei pleniter instructi esse debeant et tales, quales ad sacerdotium eligere divina iubet auctoritas.

The two texts are the same until the end, where Anselm omits the final part regarding witnesses. By omitting this section, he places the emphasis on the definitive role of apostolic authority, a point made manifest in the rubric.

(8) III: 37 (= 74T c. 74) Ps.Anacletus, c. 38 [Hinschius, 85]

Quod hi qui culpam suorum produnt prepositorum sententia Cham, qui patris pudenda non operuit, dampnandi sunt

incipit/explicit: [p. 134 (entire text)]

Sententia Cham filii Noe dampnantur, qui suorum doctorum vel prepositorum culpam produnt, ceu Cham qui patris pudenda non operuit, sed deridenda monstravit.

74T tit IX. Quod non possunt oves accusare pastores

incipit/explicit: [pp. 58–9]

Sententia Cham filii Noe damnantur qui suorum doctorum vel prepositorum culpam produnt ceu Cham, qui patris pudenda non operuit sed deridenda monstravit. . . . . . . Unde oportet unumquemque fidelem, si viderit aut cognoverit plebes suas adversus pastorem suum tumescere aut clerum detractionibus vacare, hoc vitium pro viribus extirpare; prudenterque corrigere satagat nec eis in quibuscumque negotiis misceri, si incorrigibiles apparuerint, antequam suo reconcilientur doctori, presumat.

Initially the two texts are the same, though Anselm omits the final part. In so doing, he omits the commentary upon the judgement of Cham regarding those who act against their pastor. It is somewhat interesting that Anselm omitted references to what was essentially a call for the people to assume a role in the reproach of the clergy. Although the text in the 74T was quite specific—if a pastor deviated from the faith, he was to be corrected by the faithful, although for moral indiscretions he was to be tolerated—it did stipulate that the faithful are to warn their pastor if they hear that the people are presuming to go against him. This, albeit implicitly, grants to the people a role in correcting, or at the least, in advising, their pastor. While Gregory VII had called upon the people to refuse and even 'boycott' the ministrations of sinful or unworthy clergy, this text (or rather Anselm's version of it) demonstrates that Anselm may have had misgivings with this, and preferred to insist upon the inviolability of ecclesiastical status with respect to the flock. [Cf. Appendix Ia, B, no. 13]

(9) III: 87 (= 74T c. 107) Ps.Marcellinus, c. 4 [Hinschius, 223]

Quod non licet imperatori quicquam agere, quod apostolicis regulis contrarium sit

incipit/explicit: [p. 157]

Omne quod inreprehensible est, catholica defendit ecclesia. . . . . . . Iniustum iudicium et diffinitio iniusta regio meto vel iussu a iudicibus ordinata non valeat.

74T tit XIII. Ut nemo absens iudicetur et de iniustis iudiciis

Though the two texts are the same, there is a striking difference between Anselm's rubric and the title of the 74T. Anselm's rubric makes the text a strong advocation of the superiority of the Apostolic See, emphasizing that even a christian emperor is far below the head of the Church.

B. *Strict Adherence to the 74T's Transmission*

These refer to texts in Anselm which are very close, if not identical, both in textual and in ideological terms to those in the 74T.

(1) II: 59 (= 74T c. 88) Ps.Felix II, c. 12, no. 20 [Hinschius, 488]

Ut pregravati a comprovincialibus episcopis vel metropolitano sedem appellent apostolicam et nullam interim molestiam patiantur donec ibi res finiatur

incipit/explicit: [pp. 102–3]

Quotiens episcopi se a suis comprovincialibus vel a metropolitano putaverint pregravari vel eos suspectos habuerint, mox Romanam appellent sedem . . . . . . Quod si aliter a quoquam presumptum fuerit, nichil erit, sed viribus carebit.

74T tit X. De iudicio et examinatione episcoporum

Anselm completely adheres to the text of the 74T, though with his rubric, he emphasizes a bit more the right of appeal to Rome, as well as the right of the bishop to maintain his office while that appeal goes forward.

(2) II: 81 (= 74T c. 83) Ps.Victor, c. 5 [Hinschius, 128]

Ut accusatus vel iudicatus a comprovincialibus episcopis licenter papam appellet, qui eius causam retractet, et in loco eius interim alius non ordinetur

incipit/explicit: [pp. 113–14]

Placuit, ut accusatus vel iudicatus a comprovincialibus in aliqua causa episcopus licenter appellet et adeat apostolicae sedis pontificem . . . . . . quoniam quamquam comprovincialibus episcopis accusati causam pontificis scrutari liceat, non tamen diffinire inconsulto Romano pontifice permissum est.

74T tit X. De iudicio et examinatione episcoporum

As previously, Anselm adheres to the text of the 74T, again being a bit more specific with his rubric.

(3) III: 7 (= 74T c. 55) Ps.Felix I, c. 13 [Hinschius, 202]

Quod infamis procurator esse non debet, et qualiter quis accusare vel iudicare debet; et cetera

incipit/explicit: [p.122]

Infamis persona nec procurator potest esse nec cognitor. . . . . . . Si quis autem iudicem adversum sibi senserit, vocem appellationis exhibeat, quam nulli oportet negari.

74T tit V. De ordine accusationis deque accusatorum personis

Anselm adheres to the text of the 74T.

(4) III: 10 (= 74T c. 44) Ps.Anacletus, cc. 3, 4 [Hinschius, 68]

Ut qui suae legis vel religionis normam reliquerit aut recte prohibita neglexerit ad accusationem non admittatur

incipit/explicit: [p. 123]

Accusandi vel testificandi licentia denegatur his qui christianae religionis et nominis dignitatem et suae legis vel propositi normam aut regulariter prohibita neglexerint. . . . . . Omnis autem apostata refutandus est non in accusatione recte agentium suscipiendus.

74T tit V. De ordine accusationis deque accusatorum personis

Apart from one minor variant, Anselm follows the text of the 74T, again being a bit more specific with his rubric.

(5) III: 14 (= 74T c. 45) Ps.Anacletus, c. 35 [Hinschius, 84]

Qui hi qui hodie aut nudius tercius inimici fuerunt accusare vel testificari non possunt

incipit/explicit: [p. 125 (entire text)]

Accusatores esse et testes non possunt, qui ante hesternum diem aut nudiustertius inimici fuerant, ne irati nocere cupiant, ne laesi ulcisci velint. Inoffensus igitur accusatorum et testium affectus quarendus est, et non suspectus.

74T tit V. De ordine accusationis deque accusatorum personis

Apart from one variant, Anselm follows the text of the 74T.

(6) III: 23 (= 74T c. 60) Ps.Silvestri [Hinschius, 449]

Ut nemo clericum trahat ad saeculare iudicium sine consensu episcopi sui

incipit/explicit: [p.128 (entire text)]

Nullus laicus crimen audeat clerico inferre. Testimonium autem clerici adversus laicum nemo suscipiat. Clericum vero quemlibet nemo in publico examinare praesumat nisi in ecclesia.

74T tit V. De ordine accusationis deque accusatorum personis

Anselm follows the text of the 74T, although he places more emphasis on the inviolability of ecclesiastical status with his rubric.

(7) III: 24 (= 74T c. 59) Ps.Marcellinus, c. 3 [Hinschius, 221]

De eadem re

incipit/explicit: [p. 128 (entire text)]

Clericum cuiuslibet ordinis absque pontificis sui permissu nullus presumat ad saeculare iudicium adtrahere, nec laico quemlibet clericum liceat accusare.

74T tit V. De ordine accusationis deque accusatorum personis

Apart from a few minor variants, Anselm adheres to the text of the 74T.

(8) III: 27 (= 74T c. 53) Ps.Stephanus, c. 7 [Hinschius, 184]

Ut etiam habitantes cum inimicis et omnes laici ab accusatione clericorum
ammoveantur

incipit/explicit: [p. 130 (entire text)]

Repellantur cohabitantes inimicis et omnes laici, quia infestationem blasphemiae affectio amicitiae incitare solet. Nec illi, videlicet laici, in vestra sunt
recipiendi accusatione qui vos in sua nolunt recipere infamatione.

74T tit V. De ordine accusationis deque accusatorum personis

Anselm follows the text of the 74T, though he does place more emphasis upon
the inviolability of ecclesiastical status by means of his rubric.

(9) III: 29 (= 74T c. 46) Ps.Telesphorus, c. 1 [Hinschius, 110]

Quod nec clerici laicos nec laici clericos in sua accusatione debent recipere

incipit/explicit: [p. 131 (entire text)]

Sicut laici et saeculares homines nolunt clericos recipere in accusationibus et
infamationibus suis, ita nec clerici debent eos recipere in infamationibus suis,
quoniam in omnibus discreta debet semper esse et segregata vita et conversatio
clericorum ac saecularium laicorum.

74T tit V. De ordine accusationis deque accusatorum personis

Anselm adheres to the text of the 74T, apart from a variant in the inscription.
Anselm, however, places more emphasis with his rubric, underscoring the sep-
arateness of the lay and clerical orders.

(10) III: 48 (= 74T c. 91) Ps.Fabianus, cc. 19, 20 [Hinschius, 165]

De episcopis sine Romana auctoritate expulsis, ut sua eis redintegrentur et
tunc respondeant, si necesse fuerit

incipit/explicit: [p. 140]

Statuimus, ne episcopi a propriis sedibus aut ecclesiis sine auctoritate Romani
pontificis eiciantur. . . . . . . Nulla enim permittit ratio, dum ad tempus eorum
bona vel ecclesiae atque res ab aemulis aut quibuscumque detinentur, ut aliquid
illis obici debeat, nec quisquam potest eis quilibet maiorum vel minorum
obicere, dum ecclesiis vel rebus aut potestatibus carent suis.

74T tit XI. De episcopis sine Romana auctoritate depositis

While there are a number of minor variants between Anselm's text and that of
the 74T, along with different inscriptions, it is clear that the 74T was Anselm's
source. The issue of the expulsion of bishops, and especially their despoliation,
was one which the two compilers viewed identically.

C. *Independent vs. 74T Transmission?*

These refer to texts in Anselm which, though present at least in part in the 74T, seem to have been taken from an 'independent' copy of the Ps.Isidorian Decretals.

(1) I: 9 (cf. 74T c. 12) Ps.Vigilius, c. 7 [Hinschius, 712]

Quod ecclesia Romana omnibus preest ecclesiis, sicut beato Petro datum est preminere ceteris apostolis

incipit/explicit: [MS Vat. 1363 fo. 4ᵛ / p. 10]

Nulli vel tenuiter scienti vel pleniter sapienti dubium est quod aecclesia Romana fundamentum et forma sit aecclesiarum. . . . . . . Quamobrem sancta Romana aecclesia eius merito Domini voce consecrata et sanctorum patrum auctoritate roborata primatum tenet omnium aecclesiarum.

74T tit I. De primatu Romanae ecclesiae

incipit/explicit: [p. 25]

Nulli vel tenuiter scienti vel pleniter sapienti dubium est quod ecclesia Romana fundamentum et forma sit ecclesiarum. . . . . . . Unde omnium appellantium apostolicam sedem episcoporum iudicia et cunctarum maiorum negotia causarum eidem sancte sedi reservata esse liquet; presertim cum in his omnibus eius semper sit expectandum consultum; cuius tramiti si quis obviare temptaverit sacerdotum, causas se non sine honoris sui periculo apud eandem sanctam sedem noverit redditurum.

Variants: MS *Vat. 1363*   74T [Gilchrist]
. . . voce consecrata et   . . . voce consecrata primatum
sanctorum patrum roboratum   tenet omnium ecclesiarum, ad quam
primatum tenet omnium   tam summa episcoporum negotia
ecclesiarum.   et iudicia atque quereles quam et
                                maiores ecclesiarum questiones
                                quasi ad caput semper referandae
                                sunt . . . . . . sedem noverit
                                redditurum.

Anselm omits about one half of the 74T text. This portion, with a few variants, is found at II: 18 under the rubric: *Quod omnium appellationum et episcoporum et cunctorum maiorum negotia apostolica sedi debent reservari*, though, there as well, the text may have been an independent Ps.Isidore. (Thaner did not identify II: 18 as being a 74T text in his apparatus, though Gilchrist noted the connection.) By making Roman primacy contingent upon its role as supreme judiciary, however, the 74T limits the text in a way that Anselm does not. Gilchrist believed that this text had served as Anselm's source. While the text in Ps.Vigilius continues as does that of the 74T, it seems quite probable, as Fuhrmann believed, that Anselm's source was not the 74T. The emphasis of Anselm's rubric would suggest that no such limited primacy, or rather a primacy contingent upon Rome being the appropriate forum for issues of the episcopate as that offered by the 74T, was intended.

(2) II: 43 (cf. 74T c. 96) Ps.Julius, c. 8 [Hinschius, 480]

Quod Romanae sedi a tempore apostolorum concessum est et in Nicena synodo confirmatum est, ut absque eius sententia nullus episcopus dampnetur aut depellatur

incipit/explicit: [pp. 94–5]

Si quis ab hodierna die et deinceps episcopum preter huius sanctae sedis sententiam dampnare aut propria pellere sua presumpserit, sciat se inrecuperabiliter esse dampnatum et proprio carere perpetim honore. . . . . . . Quam in culpam nullo modo potuissetis incidere, si unde consecrationem honoris accipitis, inde legem totius observantiae sumeretis, et beati apostoli Petri sedes, quae vobis sacerdotalis mater est dignitatis, esset et ecclesiasticae magistra rationis.

74T tit XI. De episcopis sine Romana auctoritate depositis

incipit/explicit: [p. 69]

Si quis ab hodierna die et deinceps episcopum preter huius sanctae sedis sententiam damnare ut propria sede pellere presumpserit. . . . . . . Nullus enim debet presumere quae sibi non videntur concessa.

The two texts are basically the same in the beginning. Yet whereas Anselm's text continues as does the Ps.Julius, the 74T follows with redacted text: 'Nullus enim debet presumare quae sibi non videntur concessa'—a phrase which occurs later in Anselm's text. It is obvious that an independent source was used. This seems to be corroborated and even justified by the difference in the purpose of each compiler. The 74T once again is stressing an episcopal safeguard in terms of Rome's judicial supremacy, whereas Anselm makes manifest the all-encompassing power of the Apostolic See, without whom nothing, effectively, can be done.

(3) III: 25 (cf. 74T c. 57) Ps.Euticianus, cc. 8, 9 [Hinschius, 212]

Quod infami et sacrilego adversus christianum non licet dicere testimonium, et ut ecclesiastici iudices causam non audiant quae legibus non continentur

incipit/explicit: [MS Vat. 1363, fo. 51ʳ / pp.128–9]

Nulli umquam infami atque sacrilego de quo cumque negotio liceat adversus religiosum christianum, quamvis humilis servilisque persona sit testimonium dicere . . . . . . quia omnes qui pie volunt vivere in Christo persecutionem patiuntur.

74T tit V. De ordine accusationis deque accusatorum personis

incipit/explicit: [p. 50 (entire text)]

Nulli umquam infami atque sacrilego de quocumque negotio liceat adversus religiosum christianum, quamvis humilis servilisque persona sit, testimonium dicere nec de qualibet re actione vel inscriptione christianum impetere.

The two texts are identical up until 'christianum impetere', after which Anselm continues, excerpting from the Ps.Euticianus text. Although it is clear that Anselm did not use the 74T's transmission of this text, it is impossible to determine why he did not. Unlike previous examples, there is no equally pointed substantive reason.

(4) III: 36 (cf. 74T c. 70) Ps.Anacletus, c. 20 [Hinschius, 77]

Ut qui causas habet contra pastores vel ecclesias eorum primo caritative expectet emendationem, quodsi ante infestare presumpserit, excommunicetur

incipit/explicit: [p. 134]

Si quis adversus pastores vel ecclesias eorum commotus fuerit aut causas habuerit, prius ad eos recurrat caritatis studio . . . . . . antequam per satisfactionem condignam egerint poenitentiam, quoniam iniuria eorum ad Christum pertinet, cuius legatione funguntur.

74T tit VIII. Quod ecclesiarum pastores prius sint admonendi quam accusandi

The two texts are basically the same, though there are a number of variations in word order. These variants, however, are not found between Anselm and the Ps.Anacletus text as represented in Hinschius. It is difficult to say conclusively one way or the other, but it is possible that Anselm used an independent text, though Gilchrist believed that the 74T was the source. Again, however, there is no substantive justification in terms of content. Anselm clearly agreed with the *magis est tolerandus* position of the 74T with regard to the episcopate found in this text. Cf. Appendix Ib, A, no. 8.

(5) III: 45 (cf. 74T c. 58) Ps.Gaius, cc. 2–4 [Hinschius, 214]

Ut nemo episcopum vel quemquam clericorum apud saeculares iudices accuset, et cetera

incipit/explicit: [MS Vat. 1363, fo. 54$^{r/v}$ / pp. 137–8]

Pagani vel heretici sive Iudei non possunt christianos accusare aut vocem infamationis inferre. . . . . . . et suorum amicorum aecclesiasticorum et patrum consiliis uti debeant, sufficienter ab apostolis suorumque decessoribus ac nostris praedecessoribus statutum esse putamus.

74T tit V. De ordine accusationis deque accusatorum personis

incipit/explicit: [p. 51 (entire text)]

Pagani vel heretici sive Iudei non possunt christianos accusare aut vocem infamationis inferre.

The 74T text has only the first line of the Ps.Gaius text, and an incomplete inscription (*Gaius papa Felici episcopo*). Anselm, with the correct inscription (*Dilectissimo fratri Felici episcopo Gaius*) and a much fuller text, clearly used an independent source.

(6) III: 61 (cf. 74T c.79) Ps.Dionysius, c. 4 [Hinschius, 196]

Ut hi qui episcopis crimina impingunt per se ipsos faciant, si tamen repraehensibiles ipsi non sunt [1]

incipit/explicit: [MS Vat. 1363, fo. 57ᵛ / Thaner, pp. 145–6]

Crimina quae episcopis impingere dicis, per alios non sinas ullomodo fieri, nisi per ipsos qui crimina intendunt . . . . . . quia infames omnes esse censemus, qui suam aut christianum praevaricant legem aut apostolicam vel regularem libenter postponunt auctoritatem.

74T tit IX. Quod non possunt oves accusare pastores

incipit/explicit: [p. 60]

Crimina quae episcopis impingi dicis. . . . . . . Nemini enim de se confesso credi potest super crimen alienum quoniam rei professio periculosa est et admitti non debet.

The two texts are initially the same, save a number of word variants. Anselm's text, however, continues with the Ps.Dionysius beyond that of the 74T. Anselm also has the correct inscription. There is, however, no overt substantive reason for the independent transmission, save perhaps Anselm's emphasis upon apostolic authority at the end of his text.

---

[1] Thaner uses a slightly different rubric: . . . *si tamen inreprehensibiles ipsi sunt.*

(7) III: 89 (cf. 74T cc. 290–307) Capitula Angilrammi [Hinschius, 763 ff.]

De accusandi testificandique licentia, quando et ubi vel quomodo

incipit/explicit: [pp. 163–8]

[Capit.28] Placuit eorum accusandi sacerdotes et testificandi in eos vocem obstruere, quos non humanis sed divinis vocibus mortuos esse scimus, quia vocem funestam potius intercidi quam audiri oportet. . . . . . . [Capit.20] Item generali decreto constituimus ut execrandum anathema fiat et velut praevaricator catholicae fidei semper apud Deum reus existat, quicumque regum vel potentum deinceps canonum censuram in quocumque crediderit vel permiserit violandam.

74T tit LXVI. Hec capitula sparsim collecta sunt et Angilranno Mediomatrice urbis episcopo Rome a beato papa Adriano tradita quando pro sui negotii causa inibi agebatur

incipit/explicit: [pp. 172 ff.]

[Capit.35] In criminalibus causis nec accusator nisi per se aliquem accusare potest, nec accusatus per aliam personam se defensare permittitur. . . . . . . [Capit. 20] Generali decreto constituimus ut execrandum anathema fiat . . . deinceps Romanorum pontificum decretorum censuram in quocumque crediderit vel permiserit violandum.

The ongoing popularity of these spurious Carolingian canons, and their use both by Anselm and the compiler of the 74T, was due to their inclusion in the

Ps.Isidorian Decretals. In the preceding chapter [III: 88], Anselm used texts from the *Capitula Angilrammi*, which were undeniably from a Ps.Isidorian source independent of the 74T. Anselm had identified these as: 'et cetera quaedam collecta capitula'. In this chapter, however, he identified the texts as 'ex decretis Adriani papae'—an inscription which leans more closely to the actual heading of the *Capitula Angilrammi*, which also formed the title for the 74T. While certain *capitula* are found both in Anselm and the 74T (though there are a number of internal variations), the order of the *capitula* in the 74T differs radically from that found both in the text represented in the Hinschius edition, and in Anselm's text.

Order of *Collectio canonum* III: 89
Capitula Angilrammi, cc. 28, 29, 30, 31, 32, 33, 34, 35, 36, 37, 38, 39, 40, 41, 42, 43, 44, 45, 46, 47, 48, 49, 50, 51, [second series, Hinschius, 766 ff.]: 1, 2, 3, 4, 5, 6, 7, 8, 9, 10 (cf. III: 19), 11, 12, 13, 14, 15, 16, 17, 18, 19, 20.

Order of 74T (tit LXVI, cc. 290–307)
Capitula Angilrammi, cc. 35, 36, 38, 32, 44, 44, 45, 50, [second series, Hinschius, 766 ff.]: 1, 5, 6, 7, 8, 9, 10, 4, [c. 306: Council of Chalcedon (451), Act.1], 20.

Though Anselm was probably aware of, and may on occasion have used, the 74T's transmission of these texts, it is clear that he had another independent text, as much that is in Anselm is not in the 74T. The final part of the text was repeated by Anselm at XII: 2 (cf. Appendix II).

IC. ANSELM'S TRANSMISSION OF GELASIAN TEXTS FROM THE 74T

The following examples are intended to demonstrate in greater detail the modifications that Anselm made to his Gelasian texts provided by the 74T, as well as to indicate the types of issues to which these particular texts were addressed.

Each example notes: the location in the *Collectio canonum*; the corresponding location in the 74T; the Gelasian source in question [with reference to A. Thiel, ed. *Epistolae Romanorum Pontificum*, and Ps.Isidore (ed. Hinschius), if appropriate]; Anselm's rubric title, the *incipit/explicit* of Anselm's text [identified from MS Vat. lat. 1363 by folio or from Thaner's edition by page: Vat. lat. 1363 is used here in those instances where discrepancies were found in the text in Thaner's edition, and especially when noteworthy variations were found between Anselm and the 74T; in such cases reference to Thaner is also provided]; the title under which the given Gelasian text was placed by the 74T; the *incipit/explicit* of the 74T text [identified from J. T. Gilchrist, ed. *Diversorum patrum sententie*] only when it differs substantially from that of Anselm; the variations between Anselm's text and that of the 74T (*only* where substantial); and finally a brief commentary on Anselm's transmission.

A. Modification and 'Independent' Transmission

These refer to Gelasian texts found in the 74T which have been modified by Anselm, as well as to those which, though found at least in part in the 74T, seem to have been taken from another 'independent' source.

(1) I: 67 (= 74T c. 22) Gelasius, epist. 42 [Thiel, 455; ex Ps.Isidore?, 635]

Quod evangelica auctoritate prima omnium est Romana ecclesia, ubi Petrus et Paulus una die mortui sunt

incipit/explicit: [p. 35]

Quamvis universae per orbem catholicae ecclesiae unus thalamus Christi sit, sancta tamen Romana catholica et apostolica ecclesia nullis synodicis constitutis ceteris ecclesiis prelata est, sed evangelica voce Domini et salvatoris nostri primatum obtinuit. . . . . . . Est ergo prima Petri apostoli sedes Romana ecclesia non habens maculam neque rugam nec aliquid huius modi.

74T tit II. Item de eadem re et quod Petrus et Paulus passi sunt una die

Variants:
Anselm	74T
coronatus est, et pariter	coronatus est, et ambo sanctam
supradictam Romanam	Romanam ecclesiam Christo Domino
ecclesiam Christo Domino	consecrarunt. . . .
consecrarunt. . . .	

Apart from this one variation, which occurs in the ellipsis, the two texts are the same. Yet there is some significant re-direction in Anselm's rubric, with his emphasis upon the evangelical authority by which Rome is pre-eminent. Anselm seems more aware of the wider significance of the Gelasian text, the so-called *Gelasianum* on receiving and not receiving books, than the compiler of the 74T. It is a text which Anselm 'independently' uses elsewhere. See below, no. 2.

(2) I: 68 (cf. 74T c. 22) Gelasius, epist. 42 [Thiel, 454; ex Ps.Isidore?, 635]

Quod Romana ecclesia non synodicis sed evangelicis institutis primatum obtinuit, et quod sanctus Petrus et Paulus una die in urbe Roma coronati sunt

incipit/explicit: [pp. 35–6 (entire text)]

Post propheticas et evangelicas atque apostolicas scripturas quibus ecclesia catholica per gratiam Dei fundata est, etiam illud intimandum putavimus, quod quamvis universae per orbem catholicae ecclesiae unus thalamus Christi sit, sancta tamen Romana et apostolica ecclesia nullis synodicis constitutis, ut supra.

74T tit II. Item de eadem re et quod Petrus et Paulus passi sunt una die

Anselm's text may have been prompted by 74T c. 22 (source of I: 67), a part of which concludes this present text (also indicated internally by the 'ut supra'). It is clear that Anselm used an independent source at least for the initial part of his text, as this is not in the 74T.

(3) I: 71 (cf. 74T cc. 227, 228) Gelasius, epist. 12 [Thiel, 351; ex Ps.Isidore?, 639]

Quod auctoritate pontificum et potestate regum mundus regitur, et regalis tamen potestas subiecta esse debet pontificibus

incipit/explicit [pp. 38–9]

Famuli vestrae pietatis et cetera: Duo sunt, imperator auguste, quibus principaliter mundus hic regitur: auctoritas sacra pontificum et regalis potestas. . . . . . . Quapropter sub conspectu Dei pure sincere pietatem tuam deprecor, obtestor, exhortor, ut petitionem meam non indignanter accipias. Rogo, inquam, ut me in hac vita potius audias deprecantem, quam, quod absit, in divino iudicio sentias accusantem.

74T tit XLI. De auctoritate sacerdotali et postestate regali

incipit/explicit: [p. 142]

Duo sunt, imperator auguste, quibus principaliter hic mundus regitur: auctoritas sacrata pontificum et regalis potestas . . . . . . [c. 228] Si cunctis generaliter sacerdotibus recte divina tractantibus fidelium convenit corda summitti, quanto potius sedis illius presuli consensus est adhibendus, quem cunctis sacerdotibus et divina summa voluit preminere et subsequens ecclesiae generalis iugiter pietas celebravit?

The 74T version of the famous 'Duo sunt' letter to the Emperor Anastasius was not Anselm's source. The text is an excerpted one in the 74T. It seems likely that Anselm used the Ps.Isidorian version, which accounted for the widespread transmission and popularity of the text. Anselm's use of an independent and much fuller text is significant in a number of ways. Most noteworthy is the difference in headings. While Anselm stresses the *auctoritas pontificis*, the 74T adheres to the more conservative reading with *auctoritas sacerdotalis*. Equally striking is the different adjective. In Anselm's version, papal authority is *sacra*—holy in itself. In the 74T, however, this authority is *sacrata*—which indicates that it has been made holy by some external force. With such modifications, Anselm truly transforms the 'Gelasian ideal' into a concrete manifesto for his time.

(4) II: 16 (= 74T c. 10) Gelasius, epist. 26, c. 5 [Thiel, 399, 416; ex Ps.Isidore, 643]

Quod sancta Romana ecclesia fas habet iudicandi de omnibus, de illa vero nullus, et potestatem habet solvendi iniuste damnatos et damnandi quos oportuerit absque synodo

incipit/explicit: [MS Vat. 1363, fo. 32ʳ / pp. 82–3]

Cuncta per mundum novit aecclesia quod sacrosancta Romana aecclesia fas de omnibus habeat iudicandi, neque cuiquam de eius liceat iudicare iudicio . . . . . . et hoc nimirum pro suo principatu quem beatus Petrus apostolus Domini voce et tenuit semper et retinebit.

74T tit I. De primatu Romanae ecclesiae

Variant: *MS Vat. 1363*   *74T*
            fas de omnibus habeat iudicandi   de omni ecclesia fas habeat iudi-
                                               candi

The texts are the same apart from these variants. The initial one, however, is quite striking. On the one hand, in Anselm's version, Rome is given the right of judging everything, as opposed to judging the affairs of all churches, as in the 74T. Even beyond this, Anselm infuses this text with a strident and unique interpretation beyond that actually apparent in the Gelasian text itself, and certainly not made by the 74T. In the rubric, Anselm notes that the Roman Church cannot be judged ('de illa vero nullus'), whereas the actual text stipulates that no one can judge the *judgement* of Rome. The 74T's text is almost certainly from the Ps.Isidore. (Both texts differ from both the long form and the *forma brevior* of Gelasius' text. Gilchrist believed that the 74T text came via the *Collectio Avellana*.) If Anselm used the 74T text, as seems probable, his modifications are substantial.

(5) V: 4 (cf. 74T c. 209) Gelasius, epist. 14, cc. 4, 8, 9 [Thiel, 364, 366; ex Ps.Isidore, 651–2]

Ut novae basilicae non consecrentur absque auctoritate sedis apostolicae

incipit/explicit: [pp. 232–3]

Basilicas noviter institutas non petitis ex more preceptionibus dedicare nemo audeat . . . . . . et cum sedes apostolica superior sit his omnibus favente Domino, quae paternis canonibus sunt prefixa pio devotoque studeat tenere proposito, satis indignum est quemquam vel pontificum vel ordinum subsequentium hanc observantiam refutare quam beati Petri sedem et sequi videat et docere; satisque conveniens sit, ut totum corpus ecclesiae in hac sibimet observatione concordat quam illic vigere conspiciat, ubi Dominus ecclesiae totius posuit principatum.

74T tit XXXI. De ecclesiarum consecrationibus

incipit/explicit: [p. 133 (entire text)]

Basilicas noviter institutas non petitis ex more sedis apostolicae preceptionibus dedicare nemo audeat nec ambiant sibimet episcopi vendicare clericos potestatis aliene.

The 74T text has only the first line of Anselm's; it is, therefore, clear that Anselm had another source for this Gelasian text. Anselm continues with the discussion of how reverence and respect is to be shown to all of the *regulae* of the Apostolic See. The text is a clear indication of the absolute sway that Rome maintained over every aspect of ecclesiastical life in Anselm's thought.

(6) VII: 38 (cf. 74T c. 166) Gelasius, epist. 14, c. 11 [Thiel, 368; ex Ps.Isidore?, 652]

De presbyterorum et diaconorum ordinationibus certis celebrandis temporibus *incipit/explicit*: [p. 379]

Ordinationes presbyterorum et diaconorum nisi certis temporibus et diebus exerceri non debent, id est quarti mensis ieiunio . . . . . . nec cuiuslibet utilitatis seu presbyterum seu diaconum his preferre qui ante ipsos fuerint ordinati.

74T tit XIX. De ordinatione presbyterorum diaconorum et ceterorum

incipit/explicit: [p. 106 (entire text)]

Ordinationes presbyterorum et diaconorum nisi certis temporibus et diebus exercere nemo episcoporum audeat. Itaque primi mensis, quarti, septimi et decimi ieiunio, die sabbati ieiunii circa vesperam ipsas ordinationes noverint celebrandas.

Though the two texts are quite different in strictly textual terms, the meaning remains unaffected. It is clear, however, that the 74T was not Anselm's source.

B. *Strict Adherence*

These refer to Gelasian texts in Anselm which are very close both in textual and in ideological terms to those in the 74T.

(1) VII: 15 (= 74T c. 155) Gelasius, epist. 14, c. 3 [Thiel, 364; ex Ps.Isidore?, 651]

De his qui ad sacros ordines non possunt promoveri

incipit/explicit: [p.370]

Non confidat quisque pontificum fas esse bigamos aut coniugia sortientes ab aliis derelicta . . . . . passim nulla temporis congruentis exspectatione discussos divinis servituros applicare ministeriis.

74T tit XVI. Quibus sacri ordines sint tribuendi quibusve denegandi

Apart from one minor variant, Anselm follows both the text and intention of the 74T.

(2) VII: 145 (= 74T c. 182) Gelasius, epist. 14, c. 28 [Thiel, 378; ex Ps.Isidore?, 654]

Quod clerici si viderint episcopum vel presbyterum vel diaconum excedere statuta Romani pontificis, ipsi debent indicare.

incipit/explicit: [pp. 422–3]

Non confidat quisquam se apostolicae offensae futurum immunem. . . . . . . Sin vero modis omnibus erit unusquisque pontificum ordinis et honoris elisor, si cuiquam clericorum vel aecclesiae totius auditui haec putaverit supprimenda.

74T tit XXIII. De observatione decretorum pontificum Romanorum

Apart from a few minor variants, Anselm adheres to the text of the 74T. He does, however, specify the duty of clerical reproach with the rubric.

(3) VII: 170 (= 74T c. 231) Gelasius, epist. 14, c. 14 [Thiel, 371]

Ut serviles personae in monasteriis non teneantur extra voluntatem dominorum suorum

incipit/explicit: [p. 432]

Quisquis episcopus presbyter diaconus vel eorum qui monasteriis preesse noscuntur serviles personas apud se tenentes . . . . . . non ambigat subiturum, si super hac re cuiusquam verax nos querela pulsaverit.

74T tit XLI. Ne presumat quis clericum servum retinere alienum

Apart from a few minor variants, Anselm adheres to the text of the 74T, noting, however, the monastic interest of the text in his rubric. This is probably not from Ps.Isidore, which only has bits of this text (see Hinschius, p. 652).

(4) IX: 11 (= 74T c. 219) Gelasius, epist. 14, c. 10 [Thiel, 368; ex Ps.Isidore?, 652]

Ut baptisma non fiat preter pascha aut pentecosten nisi cogente necessitate

incipit/explicit: [p. 462]

Baptizandi sibi quispiam passim quocumque tempore nullum credat in esse fiduciam . . . . . . ne morbi crescente periculo sine remedio salutari fortassis aegrotans excidio preventus abscedat.

74T tit XXXVI. De sacramento manus impositionis et baptismatis

Anselm completely follows the text of the 74T, though he does more specifically encapsulate the given text with the rubric.

(5) XI: 80 (= 74T c. 254) Gelasius, epist. 14, c. 20 [Thiel, 373–4; ex Ps.Isidore?, 653]

De eadem re[1]

incipit/explicit: [MS Vat. 1363, fo. 196ʳ]

Virginibus sacris temere se quosdam sociare cognovimus et post dicatum Deo propositum incesta foedera sacrilegia que miscere . . . . . . si tamen poenituerint, non negari.

74T tit LVI. Qualis debeat esse modus penitentiae

Despite a few variants, Anselm's text is almost identical to that found in the 74T. Anselm, however, once again is more specific about the issue in the rubric.

---

[1] c. 79: De his qui violaverint puellas domino sacratas.

(6) XII: 20 (= 74T c. 256) Gelasius, epist. 12, cc. 7, 8 [Thiel, 354; ex Ps.Isidore?, 640]

Quod excommunicatus et communicator eius aeque debent refutari et puniri

incipit/explicit: [MS Vat. 1363, fo. 210ᵛ (entire text)]

Sicut non potest quilibet perversitatis communicatore suscepto non pariter perversus approbari sic non potest refutari perversitas complice perversitatis admisso. Legibus certe vestris criminum conscii susceptoresque latrocinantium pari iudiciorum poena constringuntur, nec expers facinoris estimatur quamlibet ipse non fecerit, facientis tamen familiaritatem fedusque receperit.

74T tit LVII. De illatione criminis

Apart from a few minor variants, Anselm adheres to the text of the 74T, although he does more specifically address the given text with his rubric.

APPENDIX ID. ANSELM AND THE SWABIAN APPENDIX

While the 74T did serve as a formal source for Anselm, it is certain that the Swabian Appendix was not a similar source. The Swabian Appendix, 15 additional titles concerning excommunication added to the Swabian recension of the 74T, may have been the work of Bernold of Constance. This recension is generally thought not to have been completed before 1086, thus effectively nullifying the possibility that it was Anselm's source. Anselm apparently used what is known as the earlier Montecassino recension of the 74T. At the same time, however, it seems likely that Anselm was not the source of the Swabian Appendix texts. Though Book XII of the *Collectio canonum* and the Swabian Appendix have a number of texts in common, these are probably the product of a similar source used by the two compilers. The textual similarities, therefore, reflect more of a shared concern over the contemporary situation of schism and the resulting problems of excommunicates, rather than a specific textual dependency.

The following are texts which are found both in the *Collectio canonum*, Books XI–XII, and in the Swabian Appendix. The references to Anselm are from MS Vat. lat. 1363, as Thaner's edition ends at the early chapters of Book XI, and to the Swabian Appendix from J. T. Gilchrist, ed. *Diversorum patrum sententie.*

(1) XI: 5 (cf. Swabian App., c. 320) Gelasius, epist. 10, c. 3 [Thiel, 342; ex Ps.Isidore?, 637]
No rubric

incipit/explicit: [MS Vat. 1363, fo. 188ᵛ (entire text) / p. 513]
Legatur ex quo est religio christiana vel certe detur exemplum in ecclesia Dei a quibuslibet pontificibus aut ab ipsis apostolis ab ipso denique salvatore veniam nisi corrigentibus fuisse concessam. Auditum autem sub isto caelo non legitur omnino nec dicitur quod eorum voce depromitur: Date nobis veniam, ut tamen nos in errore maneamus.

Swabian Appendix, tit LXXIX. Quod excommunicati nequeant absolvi nisi correcti

incipit/explicit: [p. 182]
Legatur ex quo est religio christiana . . . nec dicitur quod eorum voce depromitur: Date nobis veniam ut tamen nos in errore duremus. . . . . . . scientes in divino iudicio non posse penitus excusari.

Anselm's text is much abbreviated, and contains only the first two lines of that found in the Swabian Appendix. The omission of part of a phrase along with Anselm's use of 'maneamus' instead of 'duremus' clearly indicates that the Swabian Appendix was not Anselm's source of this Gelasian text, and vice versa.

(2) XII: 10 (cf. Swabian App., c. 326) Felix III, ep. 6, cc. 1–2 [JK no. 599; Thiel, 243; ex Ps.Isidore?, 654]

Excommunicatio Felicis papae in Acacium presu[m]ptorem

incipit/explicit: [fo. 209ᵛ]

Multarum transgressionum reperiris obnoxius, et in venerabilis concilii Niceni contumelia sepe versatus. . . . . . . Habe ergo cum his, quos libenter amplecteris, portionem et sententia praesenti, quam pro tuae tibi direximus ecclesiae defensorem: sacerdotali honore et communione catholica, nec non etiam a fidelium numero segregatus, sublatum tibi nomen et munus ministerii sacerdotalis agnosce, sancti spiritus iudicio et apostolica per nos autoritate damnatus, nec iam anathematis vinculis exuendos [us].

Swabian Appendix, tit LXXXV. De excommunicatione Acatii

incipit/explicit: [p. 185]

Habe ergo cum his, quos libenter amplecteris, portionem . . . . . . numquamque anathematis vinculo exuendus. Celius Felix episcopus ecclesiae catholicae in urbe Roma subscripsi cum lxxvii. episcopis. Data V. kalendas augusti, Venantio viro clarissimo consule.

The Swabian Appendix has only the final section of Anselm's text. There are, however, a number of internal variations.

(3) XII: 13 (cf. Swabian App., c. 321) Ps.Calixtus, ep. 2, c. 10 [Hinschius, 138]

Ut excommunicatis nemo communicet in oratione, cibo, potu, osculo, nec ave eis dicat alioquin similiter excommunicatus est

incipit/explicit: [fo. 210ʳ]

Excommunicatos quoque a sacerdotibus nullus recipiat ante utriusque partis examinationem. . . . . . . Quia quicunque in his vel aliis prohibitis scienter excommunicatis communicaverit, iuxta apostolorum institutionem et ipse simili excommunicationi subiaceat.

Swabian Appendix, tit LXXX. Quod excommunicandus sit quicumque excommunicato scienter communicaverit

The two are the same save one variant.

(4) XII: 25 (cf. Swabian App., c. 316) Council of Antioch c.330¹, c. 4 [Mansi,² II, 1310; cf. Hinschius, 270]

Quod si excommunicatus sacrum ministerium contigerit spem restitutionis ultra non habet *incipit/explicit*: [fo. 211ʳ]

Si quis episcopus damnatus a synodo vel presbyter aut diaconus a suo episcopo ausi fuerint aliquid de ministerio sacro contigere . . . . . . omnes abici de ecclesia, et maxime si postquam didicerint adversum memoratos prolatam fuisse sententiam, eisdem communicare temptaverint.

Swabian Appendix, tit LXXV. Ut excommunicentur qui scienter communicaverint sacerdotibus interdictum sibi officium usurpantibus

The two texts are basically the same.

¹ Conventionally, but mistakenly dated 341; its canons were mistakenly attached to those of a synod of that year.

² *Sacrorum conciliorum nova et amplissima collectio*, ed. G. D. Mansi, 53 vols. in 60 parts (Paris–Arnhem, 1901–27).

(5) XII: 26 [cf. Swabian App., c. 317] Council of Carthage a.419, c. 29 [via Dionysius Exiguus: *PL* 67, 192]

De eadem re

incipit/explicit: [fo. 211ʳ]

Placuit universo concilio ut qui excommunicatus fuerit pro suo neglectu, sive episcopus, quilibet sive clericus . . . . . . ipse in se damnationis iudicetur protulisse sententiam.

Swabian Appendix, tit LXXVI. De excommunicatis ante audientiam communicare presumentibus

Apart from a few minor variants, the two are the same.

(6) XII: 28 (cf. Swabian App., cc. 323–4) Gelasius I, frag. 37 [Thiel, 502]

Quod audientia denegatur excommunicatis post annum, et de eadem ut supra

incipit/explicit: [fos. 211ʳ/ᵛ]

Quicumque intra anni spacium causam suam coram suis excommunicatoribus non peregerint, ipsi sibi audientiae claudere auditum videntur. . . . . . . donec ab excommunicatore poenitentiam accipiat, corporis et sanguinis Domini communione privatum se esse cognoscat, et secundum canones poeniteat.

Swabian Appendix, tit LXXXII. (c. 323) Ut excommunicatus deinceps non audiatur si infra annum causam suam peragere neglexerit

Swabian Appendix, tit LXXXIII. (c. 324) De eo qui ante audientiam communicare presumpserit vel qui excommunicato communicaverit

Anselm omits first line as found in Swabian App. c. 324. While the texts are close, there are a number of variants between the two which are not found between Anselm and the text as represented in Thiel.

(7) XII: 31 (cf. Swabian App., c. 325) John VIII, a.877, c. 10 [via Burchard, XI: 49; cf. Mansi, XVIII, 337; JE post 3109]

Ut nomina excommunicatorum publicentur

incipit/explicit: [fo. 211ᵛ]

Curae sit omnibus episcopis excommunicatorum omnino nomina tam vicinis episcopis quam parrochianis pariter indicare . . . . . . quatenus in utraque diligentia et excommunicatis ubique ecclesiasticus auditus excludatur, et excusationis causa ab omnibus auferatur.

Swabian Appendix, tit LXXXIV. Ut excommunicatorum nomina pre foribus ecclesiarum denotentur

This is a clear example of both compilers sharing the same source, Burchard (*Decretum* XI: 49), who was responsible for the erroneous attribution of both Anselm and the Swabian Appendix to 'Honorius papa'.

The Swabian Appendix, tit LXXXVI (c. 327), '*Apologeticae sub XV. capitulis de predicto anathemate*', has a number of substantial excerpts from Gelasius' *epistola* 26, almost the entire text of which is found in Anselm at XII: 67. It is clear again, however, that both compilations used independent (though perhaps on occasion the same) sources. The Swabian Appendix text begins with an excerpt from Gelasius' *Tomus*, then continues with excerpts from epist. 10, epist. 12, epist. 26 for a bit, and then epist. 27 (cf. Appendix II, at XII: 21).

APPENDIX II

Abridged Edition of Books XII and XIII of the Collectio canonum *from Biblioteca Apostolica Vaticana, MS Vat. lat. 1363*

The following is a provisional and much abridged working edition of Books XII and XIII of the *Collectio canonum* of Anselm of Lucca. The base text is taken from Biblioteca Apostolica Vaticana, MS Vat. lat. 1363, though variants from the other 'A' manuscripts as well as from other recensions are noted. Due to space constraints, only variants in the rubrics and the inscriptions are indicated. (It must be emphasized, though, that there are a number of other variants among the different recensions, many of which are minor.) Each entry contains: the rubric, the inscription, reference to the text in a relevant modern edition, a brief *incipit/explicit*, and the foliation of Vat. lat. 1363. Also noted, for Book XIII, are the rubrics given by Edith Pasztor (see above, Introduction, pp. 7–8).

Manuscript Index
Biblioteca Apostolica Vaticana, Vat. lat. 1363 (base text)
A1: Cambridge, Corpus Christi College, 269
A2: Paris, Bibliothèque Nationale, lat. 12519
B1: Vat. lat. 1364
B2: Vat. lat. 6381
C: Vat. lat. 4983
X: Ottob. lat. 224

BOOK XII

[fo. 208ᵛ] *Incipit liber duodecimus de excommunicatione*
1. **Quod excommunicati sunt omnes qui contra sanctam Romanam ecclesiam superbiendo se erigunt**
   Bonifacius*ᵃ* episcopus Eulalio Alexandrinae ecclesiae episcopo salutem*
   Olim et ab inicio tantam percepimus a beato Petro apostolorum principe

fiduciam . . . . . . et omnes qui sanctae Romanae et apostolicae ecclesiae privilegia cessare nituntur.

  * Ps.Boniface II [Hinschius, 703, 704]

  a A1 = Bonifatius

**2. Quod omnes violatores decretorum Romanorum pontificum sint
anathema**
  Adrianus papa*
Generali decreto constituimus, ut execrandum anathema fiat . . . . . . deinceps
Romanorum pontificum decretorum censuram in quocumque crediderit vel per-
miserit violandarum [violandum].

  * Capitula Angilrammi, cor. 20 [Hinschius, 769]

3. Ut anathema sit quicunque praecepta sedis apostolicae contempserit
  Nicholaus papa universali synodo praesidens dixit*
Si quis dogmata interdicta sanctiones vel decreta pro catholica fide . . . con-
tempserit, anathema sit.

  * Nicholas I, Council of Rome a.863 [JE post no. 2747; Mansi, XV, 652]

**4. Quod raptores et alienatores rei ecclesiasticae excommunicati sunt et
qui illis consentiunt |**
  Lucius episcopus episcopis omnibus*
Omnes ecclesiae raptores atque suarum facultatum alienatores . . . sacrilegos esse
iudicamus . . . . . . Par enim poena et agentes et consentientes compraehendit.

  * Ps.Lucius I, ep. 1, 7 [Hinschius, 179]
  [= 74T c. 265]
fo. 209ʳ

5. Qui consentit peccanti aut defendit maledictus erit
  Basilius*
Qui consenserit peccantibus et defendit alium delinquentem, maledictus erit
apud Deum et homines et corripietur correptione severissima.

  * Burchard was responsible for 'Basilius', but the sense of the text is found in *Regulis
  brevioribus beati Basilii*, reg. 7; Isidore's text, up to 'severissima' (where this text ends) is
  found in *Regula beati Pachomii Romae*. Entire text (as in Gratian, C. XI, qu. III, c. 100)
  is found in Smargadus, *Commentaria in regulam s. Benedicti*, c. 69.

**6. Quibus ecclesia ab episcopis interdicitur his et ianua caelestis clau-
ditur**
  No inscription* *a*
Quibus regnum Dei excluditur, proculdubio et ecclesia denegatur . . . . . . ipsis
et ianua regni caelestis clausa erit.

  * Ps.Euticianus, ep. 2, c. 5 [Hinschius, 211]

  a as in A1, A2

**7. Quod qui ab ecclesia excommunicatur in caelo ligatur et qui ab eccle-
sia reconciliatur in caelo solvitur**
  Augustinus super Iohannem*

Quodcumque ligaveris super terram, ligatum erit in caelo. . . . . . . Si in Petri persona significati sunt in ecclesia boni, [in] Iudae persona significati sunt in ecclesia mali.

> * Augustine, *In Iohannis Evangelium*, Tract. L, c. 12 [*PL* 25, 1763]

8. Quod Silverius eos qui ipsum insontem damnaverunt*a* **atque in exilium miserunt anathematizavit**
  Silverius papa*
Vilisarius patricius noster mandavit me ad se venire pacifice . . . | . . . anathema maranatha fieret in conspectu Dei et sanctorum angelorum.

> * Ps.Silverius [Hinschius, 709]

> *a* A1, A2 = dampnaverunt

fo. 209*v*

9. Modus excommunicationis Silverii in Vigilium
  Idem*
Habeto itaque cum his qui tibi consentiunt poenae damnationis sententiam . . .
. . . qui improbabili temeritate quod non acceperit assumpserit.

> * Ps.Silverius [Hinschius, 629]

10. Excommunicatio Felicis papae in Acacium*a* **praesu[m]ptorem***b*
  Felix episcopus sanctae ecclesiae catholicae urbis Romae Acacio*c
Multarum transgressionum reperiris obnoxius . . . . . . sancti spiritus iudicio et apostolica per nos auctoritate damnatus, nec iam anathematis vinculis exuendos [exuendus].

> * Felix III, ep. 6, cc. 1, 2 [JK no. 599; Thiel, 243; also Ps.Isidorian version, 654]
> [cf. 74T c. 326* (Swabian Appendix)]

> *a* A1 = Acatium   *b* A1, A2 = praesumptorem   *c* A1 = Acatio

11. Quod non debet quis ei communicare quem sedes apostolica repellit nisi ab illatis se mundaverit
  Gregorius papa*
Miratus valde sum . . . | . . . et tunc ei vestram dilectio communicaret ne particeps obligationis eius existeret.

> * Gregory I, *Reg.* VI: 26, p. 405

fo. 210*r*

12. No Rubric*a*
  Gregorius papa*
Pervenit ad me quosdam vestrorum ignorantia . . . . . . Ne inde reus ante conspectum eterni iudicis unde poterat salvari consistat.

> * Gregory I, *Reg.* VI: 46, p. 421

> *a* A1, A2 = Item de eadem re

13. Ut excommunicatis nemo communicet in oratione, cibo, potu, osculo, nec ave eis dicat alioquin similiter excommunicatus est
  Calixtus papa*

Excommunicatos quoque a sacerdotibus nullus recipiat . . . . . . iuxta apostolorum institutionem et ipse simili excommunicationi subiaceat.

> * Ps.Calixtus I, ep. 2, c. 10 [Hinschius, 138]
> [= /cf. 74T c. 321* (Swabian Appendix)]

14. Quod hi separati a nobis debent esse, cum quibus nec cibum sumere licet
  Idem*
Manifestum est quod hi extra nos sunt et a nobis discreti esse debent . . . . . . infames efficiuntur.

> * Ps.Fabianus, ep. 2, c. 18 [Hinschius, 164]

15. Quod cum excommunicato non licet orare nec vesci nec loqui nisi de conversione ipsius
  Isidorus*[a]
Cum excommunicato neque orare neque loqui . . . . . . communem statim cum eo excommunicationis contrahet poenam.

> * Isidore of Seville, *Regula monachorum*, c. 18, in *Collectio Hispania*, c. 16, although lacks final clause. Anselm's text comes from Smardagus, *Commentaria in regulam s. Benedicti*, c. 26 [*PL* 102, 851–2], via Regino and Burchard; the major variants between the Smardagus and the Anselm text are due to Burchard's transmission.

---

  [a] A1 = Ysidorus

16. Qui[a] cum excommunicato oraverit communione privetur
  Ex canone apostolorum*
Si quis cum excommunicato saltem in domo simul oraverit, iste communione privetur.

> * *Canones apostolorum*, c.11, via Dionysius Exiguus, *Codex canonum ecclesiasticorum* [*PL* 67, col. 142]

---

  [a] A1 = quod

17. De eadem re
  Ex concilio Cartagenensi*
Qui communicaverit vel oraverit cum excommunicato, si laicus est excommunicetur, si clerus deponatur. |

> * Council of Carthage (IV), c. 73 [Mansi, III, 957; cf. Hinschius, 305]

fo. 210[v]

18. Quod cum excommunicatis non sit communicandum et qui fecerit excommunicetur
  Fabianus episcopus omnibus christianis*
Cum excommunicatis non est communicandum . . . . . . saltem in domo simul locutus fuerit vel oraverit, ille communione privetur.

> * Ps.Fabianus, ep. 1, c. 6 [Hinschius, 159]
> [= 74T c. 309]

19. Ut simili excommunicationi subiaceat qui excommunicato communicat et infidelis iudicatur

No inscription*[a]
Quicumque scienter excommunicatis communicaverit . . . . . . nec cum eis ullam
participationem habere.

* Ps.Calixtus, ep. 2, cc. 10, 11 [Hinschius, 138]

[a] as in A1, A2

20. Quod excommunicatus et communicator eius aeque debent refutari et puniri

Gelasius Anastasio imperatori*
Sicut non potest quilibet perversitatis communicatore suscepto non pariter perversus approbari . . . . . . facientis tamen familiaritatem foedusque receperit.

* Gelasius I, ep. 12, cc. 7, 8 [Thiel, 354; via Ps.Isidore?, 640]
[= 74T c. 256]

21. Quod par culpa est communicare heretico vel ei qui coniunctus[a] est illi

Gelasius papa*
Nec praetendat quisquam . . . . . . si illi non communicet et his tamen communione iungatur, qui ab illius non sunt communione diversi?

* Gelasius I, epist. 27, c. 11 [Thiel, 434; via Ps.Isidore?, 649]
[= /cf. 74T c. 327*, no. 12 (Swabian Appendix)]

[a] A1 = iunctus

22. Ut propter[a] propriam iniuriam nullus excommunicare quemquam praesumat

Gregorius Ianuario Karlitano[b] episcopo*
Inter querelas multiplices. . . . . . . Nam si tale aliquid feceris, in te scias post
modum vindicandum.

* Gregory I, *Reg.* II: 47, pp. 148–9
[= 74T c.314]

[a] A2: 'praeter' corrected to 'propter'   [b] A2 = Karalitano

23. Quod pastores dum pro suis voluntatibus iniuste solvunt vel ligant, ipsa se potestate[a] privant

Gregorius in evangelicorum[b] tractatibus*
Saepe pastores ecclesiae in solvendis ac | ligandis subditis suae voluntatis motus
. . . . Causae ergo pensandae sunt, et tunc ligandi atque solvendi potestas
exercenda.

* Gregory I, *Homilies*, 2, 26, 5 [*PL* 76, 1200]
[= 74T c. 315]

[a] A2: 'ipsam potestate' corrected later to 'ipsa se potestate'   [b] A2 = evangeliorum
fo. 211[r]

24. Item de eadem re[a]

Urbanus*
Quibus episcopi non communicant non communicetis, et quos eiecerunt non
recipiatis. Valde enim timenda est sententia episcopi, licet iniuste liget.

* Ps.Urbanus, ep. 1, cc. 7, 8 [Hinschius, 145]

a A2 = De eadem re

25. Quod si excommunicatus sacrum ministerium contigerit spem restitutionis ultra non habet*a*

Ex concilio Antioceno*

Si quis episcopus damnatus a synodo . . . . . . adversum memoratos prolatam fuisse sententiam, eisdem communicare temptaverint.

* Council of Antioch *c*.330 (conventionally but mistakenly dated to 341, because its canons were mistakenly attached to those of a synod of that year), c. 4 [Mansi, II, 1310; cf. Hinschius, 270]
[= /cf. 74T c. 316* (Swabian Appendix)]

a A1 = habeat

26. De eadem re

Ex concilio africano**a*

Placuit universo concilio ut qui excommunicatus fuerit pro suo neglectu . . . . . . ipse in se damnationis iudicetur protulisse sententiam.

* Council of Carthage a.419, c. 29 (via Dionysius Exiguus) [*PL* 67, 192]
[= /cf. 74T c. 317* (Swabian Appendix)]

a A2 = affricano

27. De clericis qui infra annum causam suam agere non procuraverint

Ex concilio Africano*a* cap. XLVI*

Si forte clerici causae suae . . . . . . contempserint, nulla eorum vox postea penitus audiatur.

* Council of Carthage a.419, c. 79 (via Dionysius Exiguus) [*PL* 67, 206]

a A1 = Affricano

28. Quod audientia*a* denegetur excommunicatis post annum, et de eadem ut supra

Gelasius papa*

Quicumque intra anni spacium causam suam coram suis excommunicatoribus non peregerint . . . | . . . donec ab excommunicatore poenitentiam accipiat, corporis et sanguinis Domini communione privatum se esse cognoscat, et secundum canones poeniteat.

* Gelasius I, frag. 37 [Thiel, 502]
[cf. 74T cc. 323–4* (Swabian Appendix)]

a A1 = audientiam
fo. 211ᵛ

29. Quod absolutionem quam superstes non quaesivit mortuus impetrare non potuit

Gelasius universis episcopis per Dardaniam sive per Illiricum constitutis*

Nec quisquam vobis omnino persuadeat, Acacio praevaricationis suae crimen fuisse laxatum . . . . . . quam maiores nostri semper ab heretica magnopere servaverunt pollutione discretam.

* Gelasius I, epist. 18 [Thiel, 385; JE no. 638]

30. Quod nomina scismaticorum inter divina misteria non sunt recitanda

Sacratissimo ac beatissimo archiepiscopo almae urbis Romae et patriarchae Hormisdae Justinus imperator*
Scias effectum nobis, pater religiosissime, quod diu summis studiis occultabatur patefactum . . . . . . et nulla usque ad ultimum diem sunt poenitentia correcti.

* Justinian to Hormisdas [via *Collectio Avellana*, no. 160 [*CSEL* 35, 610–11], although with an imprecise inscription; epist. 66, Thiel, 861; and via Ps.Isidore (with the same inscription as Anselm's), 687]

31. Ut nomina excommunicatorum publicentur*ᵃ*

Honorius papa cap XI*
Curae sit omnibus episcopis excommunicatorum omnino nomina tam vicinis episcopis quam parrochianis pariter indicare . . . . . . et excusationis causa ab omnibus auferatur.

* John VIII, Council of Ravenna a.877, c. 10 [via Burchard, XI: 49; Mansi, XVII, 337; JE post no. 3109]
[= /cf. 74T c. 325* (Swabian Appendix)]

ᵃ Anselm's rubric is a variant on the Council of Ravenna chapter heading.

32. Si quis presbyter contra episcopum(a) suum inflatus scisma fecerit anathema sit |

Ex concilio Cartagenensis*
Si quis presbyter ab episcopo suo correptus fuerit . . . . . . At si quaerimoniam iustam adversus episcopum habuerit inquirendum est.

* Council of Carthage (II), c. 8 [Mansi, III, 871; cf. Hinschius, 295]

ᵃ A1 = coepiscopum
fo. 212ʳ

33. Quod ecclesiasticae leges praeponendae sunt legibus imperatorum

Nicholaus servus servorum Dei reverentissimis et sanctissimis episcopis qui in convicinum villam publicam secus civitatem Silvanectis concilio convenistis*
Lege imperatorum non in omnibus ecclesiasticis controversiis utendum esse praesertim cum conveniat evangelicae ac canonicae sanctioni aliquotiens obviare.*ᵃ* . . . . . . efficietur una cum omnibus fautoribus et communicatoribus suis penitus alienus.

* *Nicholas* I [JE no. 2723; Mansi XV, 300]

ᵃ A2 has been 'doctored' to convey the opposite of the rubric's intention: i.e. that imperial laws are wholly sufficient for all ecclesiastical controversies, whereas ecclesiastical sanctions are not.

34. | Quod manifesta opera*ᵃ* accusatione non indigent

Idem ad Karolum*ᵇ* imperatorem*
Accusatorem autem habere Lotharium . . . . . . quae sunt fornicatio immundicia et cetera.

* Nicholas I to Louis the German a.867 [JE no. 2183; *PL* 119, 1178]

ª A2 = operatio   *ᵇ* A1 = Carolum
fo. 212ᵛ

35. Ut Lotharius rex a sua pelice abstineat si excommunicari nolit
Eiusdem ad Lotharium regem*

Precipue Waldradae pelicis tuae et dudum a te repudiatae communionem dec-
lina[ns]. . . . . . . secundum Domini praeceptum, duos aut tres testes adhibea-
mus, immo vero, hoc ecclesiae sanctae dicamus, et quod non optamus, de cetero
fias cunctis sicut ethnicus et publicanus.

> * Nicholas I [JE no. 2873; *PL* 119, 1149–50]

36. Quod Innocentius papa imperatorem*ª* cum imperatrice adversar-
ium sancti Iohannis Chrisostomi accerrime excommunicavit
No inscription**ᵇ*

Beatissimus Innocentius papa Romanus audiens beatum Iohannem Crisostomum
tanta ac talia mala pertulisse ab inimicis suis valde contristatus est . . . . . . mandavit atque ad eandem sedem satis reverendum corpus eius cum timore magno
et honore multo revocari praecepit.

> * Innocent I [cf. JK no. 290; interpolated text]

ª A1 = imperatore   *ᵇ* as in A1 and A2

37. Si quis audet transmutare quod sancti patres et universales synodi
statuerunt condemnatus*ª* est |
Gelasius papa*

Si quis secundum sceleratos hereticos quocumque modo aut verbo vel tempore
aut loco terminos transmutans. . . . . . . Haec impie agens huiusmodi in scelera
sceleratorum sit condemnatus, et dicet omnis populus fiat fiat.

> * apocryphal Gelasius [cf. Thiel, 612, no.7]

ª A1 = condempnatus
fo. 213ʳ

38. No Rubric*ª*
Leo episcopus urbis Romae Ianuario episcopo Aquileiensi*

Dilectionem tuam duximus commonendam insinuantes ad animae periculum
pertinere. . . . . . . ut in magno habeant beneficio, si adepta sibi omni spe pro-
motionis, in quo inveniuntur ordine stabilitate perpetua maneant, si tamen iter-
ata tinctione non fuerint maculati.

> * Leo I, ep. 18 [*PL* 54, 707–8]

ª A1, A2 = Si quis in sectam [A1 = septam] hereticorum atque scismaticorum labitur,
ad ecclesiam reversus in eo gradu quo erat sine promotione permaneat

39. Quod Cornelius papa in synodo*ª* LXta*ᵇ* episcoporum damnavit*ᶜ*
Novatum
Ex hystoria Anastasii*

Mundi anno quinquies millesimo DCCXLIIII divinae incarnationis anno
CCXLIIII . . . | . . . convenerunt in urbe Roma cum pluribus presbiteris et
diaconibus praesidente Cornelio episcopo urbis.

* Anastasius Bibliothecarius, 'Ex Syncello', *Historia ecclesiastica sive Chronographia tripertita*, ed. I. Bekker [*Corpus scriptorum historiae Byzantinae*, 47, 35]

a A1 = sinodo   *b* A1 = septuaginta   *c* A1, A2 = dampnavit
fo. 213^v

40. Quod heretici in aecclesia nichil habeant^a potestatis et iuris
Cyprianus Magno filio salutem*
Dicimus omnes omnino hereticos et scismaticos nichil habere potestatis ac iuris
. . . . . . manifestum est nec remissionem peccatorum pro eos dari posse, quos constat Spiritum sanctum non habere.

* Cyprian, epist. 69 [*CSEL* 3/2, 749 ff.]

a A1 = habeat; A2 = habent

41. Quod non est consecratio sed execratio^a quae extra aecclesiam sit
*Pelagius papa
Pudenda ut ita dicam, rapina indivisione | est non consecratus sed execratus episcopus. . . . . . . et excludi non possit, sed pro temporum ratione toleranda iudicetur ullo modo valeat extinguere.

* Pelagius I [JK no. 983; *PL* 69, 411]
  [cf. British Library, MS Addit. 8873, Collectio Brittanica, Pelagii epist., no. 11]

a A1 = exsecratio
fo. 214^r

42. Quod papa Aquileiensem^a et Mediolanensem episcopum ad principem sub custodia dirigi praecipit, et quotiens de universali synodo dubitatur, ab apostolica sede veritas requiratur
Pelagius papa*
Istud est quod a vobis poposcimus, et nunc iterum postulamus . . . | . . . aut attrahi ad salutem quomodo necesse est aut ne aliorum perditio esse possint, secundum canones per saeculares opprimi potestates.

* Pelagius I [JK no. 1018; *PL* 69, 397 (413)]
  [cf. Collectio Brittanica, Pelagii epist., no. 46]

a A1 = Aquilegensem
fo. 214^v

43. Quod scismaticus non conficit corpus Christi cui catholici non debent sociari
Pelagius papa*
Scisma siquidem ipsum quod graecum nomen est scissuram sonat, sed in unitate scissura esse non potest. . . . | . . . constat esse aecclesiam in duo vel in plura dividi non potest. Simul enim cum ab ea quisque discesserit esse desistit aecclesia.

* Pelagius I [JK no. 994; *PL* 69, 412]
  [cf. Coll. Britt., Pelagii epist., no. 22]
fo. 215^r

44. Quod aecclesia non persequitur sed diligit cum punit vel prohibet malum, et divisi a sede apostolica scismatici sunt, et quod comprimendi sunt a saecularibus iniusti episcopi

Pelagius papa*

Non vos hominum vaniloquia retardent dicentium, quia persecutionem ecclesia faciat . . . | . . . et is qui ordinabatur et is qui ordinaturus erat providentia culminis vestri deducti sunt.

> * Pelagius I [JK no. 1018; *PL* 69, 394]
> [cf. Coll. Britt., Pelagii epist., no. 46]
> fo. 215^v

45. Quod nullis [nullum]^a sacrificium Deo a potestatibus gratius est quam ut scismatici episcopi ab^b [ad] obediendum coerceantur^c

Item idem*

Quali nos de gloriae vestrae studiis iudicio gratulemur . . . . . . Nec quicquam maius est unde Deo possitis sacrificium offerre, quam si id ordinetis, ut hi qui in suam et aliorum perniciem debachantur cum potenti debeant vigore compesci.

> * Pelagius I [JK no. 1024; *PL* 69, 393]
> [cf. Coll. Britt., Pelagii epist., no. 52]

---

^{a} A2 = nullum ^{b} A1, A2 = ad ^{c} A1 = coherceantur; A2 = episcopi coerceantur ad obediendum

46. De scismaticis coercendis a secularibus

Pelagius papa Iohanni patricio*

Relegentes litteras excellentiae vestrae | de iniuria quidem quam vobis iniquorum hominum praesumptio ingessit . . . . . . qui et in scismate et a scismatico maledictus, nec honorem episcopi potest obtinere nec meritum.

> * Pelagius I [JK no. 1012; *PL* 69, 396]
> [cf. Coll. Britt., Pelagii epist., no. 40]
> fo. 216^r

47. Non esse veram fidem quae cum Romana ecclesia non convenit

Ambrosius episcopus*

Advocavit ad se episcopum Satyrus nec ullam putavit veram nisi verae fidei gratiam percontatusque ex eo est, utrumnam cum episcopis catholicis . . . | . . . Quam quidem statim, ubi primum copia liberior ecclesiae fuit, implere non distulit Dei gratiam et accepit desideratam et servavit acceptam.

> * Ambrose, *De excessu fratris*, I, no. 47 [*CSEL* 73, 235]
> fo. 216^v

48. Quod heresis perversum dogma habeat, scisma vero dissensionem^a

Ieronimus*^{b}

Inter heresim et scisma hoc esse arbitramur . . . . . . Ceterum nullum scisma non sibi aliquam confingit heresim, ut recte ab ecclesia recessisse videatur.

> * Jerome, *Comm. in epist. ad Titum*, c. 3 [*PL* 26, 633]

---

^{a} A2 = disscessionem ^{b} A2 adds 'In epistola ad Galathas'

49. Quod heresis graece ab electione dicitur

Ieronimus in epistola ad Galathas*

Heresis graece, ab electione dicitur . . . . . . tamen hereticus appellari potest, et de carnis operibus est, eligens quae peiora sunt.

* Jerome, *Comm. in epist. ad Galathas*, c. 5 [*PL* 26, 445]

50. Qualiter fiat quisque hereticus
Augustinus*
Qui in ecclesia Christi morbidum aliquid pravumque sapiunt, si correcti, ut sanum rectumque sapiant, resistunt contumaciter suaque pestifera et mortifera dogmata emendare nolunt, sed defensare persistunt, heretici fiunt.

* Augustine, *De civitate Dei*, Bk. XVIII, c. 51 [*CSEL* 40, 351–2]

51. Quod hereticus amittat Spiritum Sanctum
Innocentius*
Heretici cum a fide catholica desisterent perfectionem Spiritus quam acceperant amiserunt.

* Innocent I, epist. 45 [JK no. 305; Coustant, p. 843; via Ps.Isidore?, p. 547]

52. Quod*a* sit hereticus. Augustinus ex libro de utilitate credendi
Augustinus*b
Hereticus est qui alicuius temporalis commodi . . . homo hic est imaginatione quadam veritatis illusus.

* Augustine, *Liber de utilitate credendi*, c. 1 [*CSEL* 25, 1]

a A2 = Quid   *b* A2 = Augustinus de utilitate credendi

53. De hereticis per saeculares potestates coercendis*a*
Augustinus super Iohannem*
Quando vult Deus concitare potestates adversus hereticos, adversus scismaticos, adversus dissipatores. | . . . Sempiternas mortes faciunt, et temporales se perpeti conqueruntur.

* Augustine, *In Iohan. evang.*, Tract. XI, 13 ff. (excerpts) [*PL* 35, 1482]

a A1 = cohercendis
fo. 217ʳ

54. Ut excommunicati cohibeantur a saecularibus
Augustinus Vincentio*
Donatistae nimium inquieti sunt, quos per ordinatas a Deo potestates cohiberi atque corrigi non videtur inutile. . . . | . . . sed propter bonos mali tolerandi, sicut toleraverunt prophetae, contra quos tanta dicebant, nec communionem sacramentorum illius populi relinquebant.

* Augustine, epist. 93 (excerpts) [*CSEL* 34/2, 445 ff.]
fo. 217ᵛ

55. De malis cogendis ad bonum
Augustinus Donato presbytero*
Displicet tibi quod traheris ad salutem, cum tam multos nostros ad perniciem traxeritis. . . . | . . . Nam sicut dictum est 'compelle', ita significata sunt aecclesiae primordia adhuc crescentis, ut essent vires etiam compellendi.

* Augustine, epist. 173, c. 1 ff. [*CSEL* 44, 640 ff.]
fo. 218ᵛ

56. Quod scismatici*a* nec divino iure nec humano res ecclesiarum debent possidere

Augustinus super Iohannem*

Ecce sunt villae, quo iure defendis villas? Divino an humano? . . . | . . . Ergo fratres mei, si ubique non habent quod dicant, ego dicam quod faciant, veniant ad catholicam fidem, et nobiscum habebunt non solum terram, sed etiam illum qui fecit caelum et terrarum [terram].

* Augustine, *In Iohannis evang.*, Tract. VI, 25–6 [*PL* 35, 1436–7]

a A2: 'scismaci' corrected later to 'scismatici'

fo. 219*r*

57. Ut catholici res possideant*a* excommunicatorum usque ad conversionem*b* illorum

Augustinus*

Quod autem nobis obiciunt, quod res eorum concupiscamus et auferamus . . . | . . . Scriptum est enim: Omnia vestra, vos autem Christi, Christi autem Dei.

* Augustine, epist. 185, cc. 35–6 [*CSEL* 57, 31 ff.]

a A1 = posideant   *b* A1 = conversationem

fo. 219*v*

58. Quod qui extra ecclesiam sunt nullo iure possidere*a* possunt bona aecclesiae

Augustinus*

Quamvis res quaeque terrena non recte a quoquam possideri possit . . . . . . neque propter edos in fine segregandos deserimus gregem Domini nec propter vasa facta in contumeliam migramus de Domini domo.

* Augustine, epist. 93, c. 50 [*CSEL* 34, 493]

a A1 = posidere

59. Quod separatus ab ecclesia quantumcumque laudabiliter vivat non tamen habebit vitam aeternam |

Augustinus*

Quisquis a catholica ecclesia fuerit separatus . . . . . . non habebit vitam, sed ira Dei manet super eum.

* Augustine, epist. 141, c. 5 [*CSEL* 44, 238]

fo. 220*r*

60. De scismaticis ad correctionem cogendis

Augustinus Bonifacio**a*

Ipsa pietas, veritas, caritas non permittit . . . | . . . Non invidemus, immo amplectimur, optamus, hortamur, et quos in viis aut in sepibus invenimus, intrare cogimus, et sic nondum quibusdam persuademus, quia iam non res eorum, sed ipsos querimus.

* Augustine, epist. 185, c. 6 ff. (excerpts) [*CSEL* 57, 5 ff.]

a A2 =Bonifatio

fo. 220*v*

61. Qui non sunt inter hereticos habendi
Augustinus*

Dixit Apostolus: Hereticum hominem post primam et secondam correctionem de vita sciens . . . . . . quaerunt autem cauta sollicitudine veritatem corrigi parati, cum invenerint, nequaquam | sunt inter hereticos deputandi.

* Augustine, epist. 43, c. 1 [*CSEL* 34, 85]
fo. 221ʳ

62. Quod mali bonos non contaminent
Augustinus Emerito*

Illud attendat vigilantia mentis tuae, neminem contaminari posse . . . . . . si eos a communione prohibendi aut potestas desit, aut aliqua ratio conservandae pacis impediat.

* Augustine, epist. 87, c. 2 [*CSEL* 34, 398]

63. Quando mali tolerandi sunt et quando separandi a nobis
Augustinus*

Quidam cum bonorum malorumque commixtionem in aecclesia demonstratam vel praedicatam esse perspexerint . . . | . . . nec patientiae nomine torpescamus, nec obtentu diligentiae serviamus [seviamus].

* Augustine, *De fide et operibus*, 6 ff. [*CSEL* 41, 41 ff.]
fo. 221ᵛ

64. Quomodo recedere debeamus a malis
Augustinus*

'Ecce inquiunt', dicit propheta, 'recidite, exite inde et immundum ne tetigeretis [Isa. 52: 11].' . . . . . . nobis, quantum potestis improbate, ut corde recedatis, et redarguite ut exeatis inde, et nolite consentire, ut immundum non tangatis.

* Augustine, *Sermo* 88, no. 23, 25 [*PL* 38, 551 ff.]

65. Eiusdem. De eadem re
Augustinus *

Quid sibi vult tantus furor separationis istorum ab unitate corporis Christi . . . | . . . Sic nec cum malis unum fiunt, nec ab ecclesiae unitate discedunt.

* Augustine ? [unknown]
fo. 222ʳ

66. Quod excommunicatio iniusta ei potius oberit qui facit quam qui patitur
Augustinus*ᵃ

Illud plane non temere dixerim . . . . . . Spiritus enim sanctus habitat in sanctis per quem quisque ligatur aut solvitur, immeritam nulli ingerit poenam.

* Augustine, epist. 250A [*CSEL* 57, 598–9]

ᵃ A2 adds 'ad Cassianum'

67. Quod Acaciusᵃ iuste et canonice sit damnatusᵇ
Gelasius episcopis Dardaniae*

Valde mirati sumus, quod vestra dilectio quasi novam et veluti difficilem

quaestionem, et adhuc tamquam inauditam qui propriam [quippiam] nosse
desiderat . . . . | . . . quibus insolubilis lata sit sententia, sed a talibus recedentes,
ab eadem sententia non teneri: quae sicut in errore durantibus numquam sol-
venda praefixa est, sic ab his erit aliena, qui extiterint puniendae pravitatis
immunes.

* Gelasius, epist. 26 [JK no. 664; Thiel, 392 ff.; via Ps.Isidore ?, 641 ff.]

―――――
a A1 = Acatius   *b* A1, A2 = dampnatus
This text, the longest in the *Collectio canonum*, not surprisingly has a great number of
variants (most of which, however, are minor).
fo. 229ᵛ

68. Edictum imperatorum in damnatione*a* hereticorum. Capitula ex codice*b*

Imperatores Theodosius et Valentinus Augusti Florentio praefecto [praefept-
ori—crossed out] praetorii*

Arriani et Macedoniani, Preneumatomachi, et Apollinariani, et Novatiani sive
Sabatiani, Eunominiani, Tetraditae . . . | . . . Illis etiam in sua omnibus per-
manentibus firmitate, quae de militia poenisque variis diversisque sunt hereticis
promulgata, ut nec speciale quidem beneficium adversus legem valeat impetrari.

* Codex Iustinianus, I, 5, 5 [*Corpus Iuris Civilis*, II, 51]

―――――
a A1, A2 = dampnatione   *b* A1 omits 'Capitula ex codice'
fo. 230ʳ

69. Ut omnes hereses et earum ministri conquiescant

Imperatores Valentinus et Gratianus et Theodosius Augusti ad Hesperium*a*
praefectum praetorii*

Omnes vetitae legibus et divinis et imperialibus constitutionibus hereses per-
petuum conquiescant . . . . . . et latis adversus eos sanctionibus debet succum-
bere, qui vel levi argumento, iudicio catholicae religionis, et tramite decreti
fuerint obviare.

* Cod. Iust. I, 5, 2, [*CIC* II, 50 ff.]

―――――
a A1 = Esperium

70. Ut adimantur hereticis omnia suarum celebrationum loca

Imperatores Archadius et Honorius Augusti Clearchorio*

Cuncti heretici proculdubio noverint omnia sibi loca adimenda esse . . . . . . si
quid huiusmodi fieri vel publico, vel in privatis edibus concedatur.

* Cod. Iust., I, 5, 3 [*CIC* II, 51]

71. Ut heretici nichil habeant cum ceteris commune

Imperatores Archadius et Honorius Augusti Senatori*

Manicheos seu Manicheas vel Donatistas meritissima severitate persequimur.
. . . | . . . Preterea non donandi, non vendendi, non emendi, non postremo con-
trahendi cuiquam convicto tribuimus facultatem in mortem quoque inquisitio
tradatur.

* Cod. Iust., I, 5, 4 [*CIC* II, 51]

fo. 230ᵛ

72. Ut nullus hereticis[a] ministeriorum locus pateat

Imperatores Martianus, Valentinus et Theodosius Eutropio pp.*

Nullus hereticis ministeriorum locus . . . . . . Qui vero isdem non inserviunt, desinant affectatis dolis alienum religionis nomen assumere et suis apertis criminibus denotentur, et ab omnium summoti ecclesiarum limine penitus arceantur.

* Codex Iust., I, 1, 2 [*CIC* II, 5 (text actually from Gratianus, Valentinianus et Theodosius ad Eutropio)]

---

[a] A1 = hereticus

[Roman capitals LXXIII for c. 73 follow 'arceantur'. There is no text; and in the capitulationes for Book XII [fos. 207ᵛ–208ʳ], there is no c.73. This is also the case in A2.]

BOOK XIII

[fo. 231ᵛ] *Incipit tercius decimus liber de iusta vindicta*

1. Quod Moyses nichil crudele fecit quando praecepto Domini quosdam trucidavit

Augustinus contra Faustum*[a]

Quid crudele Moyses aut mandavit aut fecit, cum commissum sibi populum sanctae zelans et univer[s]o Deo subditum cupiens . . . . . . Tradidit et alios, ut discerent non blasphemare.

* Augustine, *Contra Faustum*, Lib. XXII, c. 79 [*CSEL* 25/1, 680, 681]

---

[a] A1, B1 have no inscription

2. De vindicta non odio sed amore[a] facienda

Idem in sermone Dei in monte*[b]

Magni et sancti viri qui iam optime scirent mortem istam quae animam dissolvit a corpore, non esse formidandam . . . | . . . . Quod non cum odio sed amore fecisse manifestat illud adiectum, 'ut anima salva sit [1 Cor. 5: 5]'. [in sermone de puero centurionis ex verbis evangelii][c]

* Augustine, *De sermone Domini in monte*, I, cc. 64–5 [*PL* 34, 1262 ff.]

---

[a] A2: 'amare' corr. to 'amore'   [b] A1, B1: no inscription   [c] Not part of the Augustinian text; probably an erroneous inscription from original exemplar. The tale of the centurion, widely used by Augustine, is found in the text of XIII: 4.

fo. 232ʳ

3. Quod bella cum benivolentia sunt gerenda

Idem Marcellino*[a]

Paratus debet esse homo iustus et pius patienter eorum maliciam sustinere . . . | . . . Dictum est autem eis: 'Neminem concusseritis, neque calumniam feceritis, sufficiat vobis stipendium vestrum [Luke 3: 14].' Quibus proprium stipendium sufficere debere praecipit, militare utique non prohibuit.

* Augustine, epist. 138, cc. 12 ff. (excerpts) [*CSEL* 44, 138 ff.]

ᵃ B1: no inscription

fo. 232ᵛ

4. Quod militantes etiam possunt esse iusti*ᵃ*

Augustinus Bonifacio illustri viro*ᵇ

Noli existimare neminem Deo placere posse, qui armis bellicis ministrat . . . . . .
Sicut rebellanti et resistenti violentia redditur, | ita victo vel capto misericordia
iam debetur, maxime in quo pacis perturbatio non tenetur.

* Augustine, epist. 189, cc. 4, 6 [*CSEL* 57, 133, 135]

ᵃ B1, C, X continue: et hostem deprimere necessitas non voluntas debet [as does
Pasztor]   *ᵇ* B1: no inscription

fo. 233ʳ

5. De eadem re. Idem ad eundem*ᵃ*

Augustinus*ᵇ

Gravi de pugna conquaereris . . . . . . Quia quando pugnatur, Deus apertis caelis
spectat, et partem quam inspicit iustam defendit.

* Ps.Augustine, epist. 13 [*PL* 33, 1098]

ᵃ A1 = Idem de eadem re; B1, C, X = Quod pugnaturo orandus est [as Pasztor]
ᵇ B1: no inscription

6. De persequendo hostes*ᵃ*

Gregorius Veloci magistro*ᵇ

Et pridem gloriae vestrae, quia milites illic erant parati venire. . . . . . . sine aliqua mora vel excusatione relaxes, quatenus venientes illic homines praedicti viri,
cum eis sine aliquo impedimento debeant ambulare. Data die V. Kal.
Octobriarum., Indictione X.

* Gregory I, *Reg.* II: 7, p. 106

ᵃ A1 = Gregorius Veloci magistro de persequendo hostes; X = De prosequendo hostes
ᵇ B1: no inscription

7. Item de eadem re*ᵃ*

Gregorius ad Mauritium et Vitalianum magistros militum*

Gloriae vestrae suscipientes epistolas, Deo gratias egimus. . . . . . . Speramus in
omnipotentis Dei virtute[m], et in ipsius beati Petri principis apostolorum, in
cuius natale sanguinem effundi desiderat, quia ipsum sibi contrarium sine mora
inveniet.

* Gregory I, *Reg.* II: 32, pp. 128 ff.

ᵃ A1 = De persequendo hostes; C, X = De eadem re [as Pasztor]

8. De predando hostes*ᵃ*

Gregorius Mauritio et Vitaliano magistris militum*

Suppliciter gloriae vestrae per filium nostrum Vitalianum . . . | . . . ut [et] si
hic excursum Deo sibi iratum mittere voluerit, vos loca ipsius, quantum vos
Dominus adiuvaverit, depraedate, aut certe culpas [copias?] quos mittetis sol-
licite requirant, ne dolens factum ad vos discurrat.

* Gregory I, *Reg.* II: 33, pp. 129 ff.

^a B1, C, X continue: ecclesiae [as does Pasztor]
fo. 233^v

9. De habenda oboedientia^a

Gregorius universis militibus in Neapoli*

Summa militiae laus inter alia bona merita, hoc est obedientiam rei publicae util-
itatibus exhibere . . . . . . quatenus quicquid a vobis hactenus bene gestum
agnoscitur, per praesentem temporis vigilantiam ac sollicitudinem augumentetis.

* Gregory I, *Reg.* II: 34, p. 130

^a B1, X continue: rei publicae utilitatibus; C continues: reipublicae [as Pasztor]

10. Ut temperetur^a vindicta

Augustinus*^b [glossed: ad Marcellinum]

Circumcelliones illos, et clericos partis Donati, quos de Ipponiensi ad iudicium
pro factis eorum publicae disciplinae cura deduxerat . . . | . . . . Inquirendi quam
puniendi necessitas maior est; ad hoc enim et mitissimi homines facinus occul-
tandum diligenter atque instanter examinant, ut inveniant, quibus parcant.

* Augustine, epist. 138, cc. 1 ff. [*CSEL* 44, 80 ff.]

^a A2: 'teperetur' corr. to 'temperetur'   ^b A2 continues: ad Marcellinum
fo. 234^r

11. Sacerdotalis intercessio pro reis^a

Augustinus Marcellino*^b

Poena illorum quamvis de tantis sceleribus confessorum . . . . . . et quasi disso-
lutionis et neglegentiae simile, transactis tamen motibus animorum, qui recen-
tioribus factis solent turbulentius excitari, egregie luculenta bonitas apparebit.

* Augustine, epist. 139, c. 2 [*CSEL* 44, 150]

^a B1, C, X = De sacerdotali intercessione pro reis [as Pasztor]   ^b B1: no inscription

12. Ut mali non occidantur sed corrigantur^a

Augustinus Donato*

Unum solum est, quod in tua iusticia pertimescimus, ne forte, quoniam quic-
quid mali contra christianam societatem ab hominibus impiis | ingratisque com-
mittitur . . . . . . necessitate nobis impacta, ut etiam occidi ab eis eligamus, quam
eos occidendos vestris iudiciis ingeramus.

* Augustine, epist. 100, cc. 1 ff. (excerpts) [*CSEL* 34, 536 ff.]

^a Pasztor = Ut mali non occidenter . . . [B1, C, X = occidantur]
fo. 234^v

13. Quod inoboedientes severius sint^a corrigendi

Calixtus papa*

Iustum est, ut qui divina contempnunt mandata, et inoboedientes patris
[patrum] existunt iussionibus, severioribus corrigantur vindictis.

* Ps.Calixtus [Hinschius, 138]

^a A2: 'sunt' corrected later to 'sint'; B1 = . . . servi sint corrigendi

[B1, c. 14 (though not numbered) has a text from Innocent I which does not corre-spond to any text in the A recensions; there is no rubric or inscription. The subsequent numeration in B1 is thus at odds with A.]

14. Quod aecclesia persecutionem possit facere
Augustinus*

Si aecclesia vera ipsa est, quae persecutionem patitur, non quae facit, quaerant ab apostolo, quam aecclesiam significabat Saraa . . . . . . Proinde ista diligendo; illi seviendo. Ista ut corrigat; illi ut illam evertant. Ista ut revocet ab errore; illi ut praecipitent in errorem.

  * Augustine, epist. 185, c. 11 [*CSEL* 57, 9 ff.]

15. De eadem re
Augustinus*

Quod autem dicunt qui contra suas impietates leges iniustas institui nolunt . . . | . . . Aliter enim servit, quia homo est, aliter, quia etiam rex est; quia homo est, ei servit vivendo fideliter, quia vero etiam rex est, servit leges iusta prae-cipientes, et contraria prohibentes convenienti vigore sanciendo.

  * Augustine, epist. 185, c. 19 [*CSEL* 57, 17]

fo. 235^r

16. Item ad eundem de eadem re^a
Augustinus*

Quis nos potest amplius amare quam Christus, qui animam suam posuit pro ovibus suis? . . . . . . plus illis omnibus, qui solo verbo vocati sunt, in evangelio laboravit et, quem maior timor compulit ad caritatem, eius 'perfecta caritas foras mittit timorem [John 4: 18].' Cur ergo non cogeret aecclesia perditos filos ut redirent.

  * Augustine, epist. 185, cc. 22 ff. [*CSEL* 57, 20 ff.]

-----

  ^{a} B1, C, X = De eadem re [as Pasztor]

17. De eadem re
Augustinus*

Quicquid ergo nomine aecclesiarum a parte Donati possidebatur, Christiani imperatores legibus religiosis cum ipsis aecclesiis ad catholicam transferre iusserunt . . . | . . . ab huius cupiditatis sordibus quolibet inimico iudicante pur-gavimus, quando eos ipsos, quorum labores dicuntur, ut nobiscum et illis et nos-tris in societate catholica utantur, quantum valemus, inquirimus.

  * Augustine, epist. 185, cc. 36 ff. (excerpts) [*CSEL* 57, 32 ff.]

fo. 235^v

18. Non imputetur siquid mali acciderit per ea quae propter bonum facimus^a
Augustinus*^{b} [glossed: epistola ad Publicolam]

De occidendis hominibus, ne ab eis quisque occidatur, non mihi placet consil-ium, nisi forte sit miles, aut publica functione teneatur, ut non pro se hoc faciat, sed pro aliis . . . . . . Et quid plura commemorem cum ea commemorando finire non possim? Quid est in usu hominum bono ac licito, unde non possit etiam pernicies irrogari ?

  * Augustine, epist. 47, c. 5 [*CSEL* 34, 135 ff.]

  a A1 = faciamus; B1, C = Ut non nobis imputetur . . . ; X = Ut non imputetur . . . [Pasztor = Quod nobis non imputetur . . .]   *b* A2 = Augustinus in epistola ad Publicolam

19. Qui potest perturbare perversos et non facit eorum impietati*a* consentit

  Anastasius et Damasus*b

Qui potest obviare et perturbare perversos et non facit, nichil est aliud quam favere eorum impietati. Nec caret scrupulo societatis occultae, qui manifesto facinori desinit obviare.

  * Ps.Damasus [Hinschius, 508]

  a A1: 'impietate' corrected to 'impietati'; X = Quod qui . . . [as Pasztor]   *b* B1: no inscription

20. Quando mali sunt tolerandi vel quando deserendi

  Gregorius in libro dyalogorum*a

Ibi aequanimiter portandi sunt mali ubi inveniuntur aliqui qui adiuventur boni . . . | . . . Unde ipse venerabilis Beda [Benedictus], si libenter audis, citius agnoscis, quia vivos ipse indocibiles deserit, quam multos in locis aliis ab animae morte suscitavit.

  * Gregory I, *Vita s. Benedicti*, II, c. 3 (*Ex libro II dialogorum S. Gregorii Magni*) [*PL* 66, 138 ff.]

  a A1, A2 = dialogorum; B1: no inscription
fo. 236^r

21. Quod homini misericordia peccatis persecutio debeatur*a*

  Augustinus*

Duo ista nomina cum dicimus, homo, peccator, non utique frustra dicuntur, quia peccator est, corripe, et quia homo est, misere. . . . . . . Persequamur in eis propriam iniquitatem, misereamur communem conditionem, et sic infatigabiles cum tempus habemus operemur bonum ad omnes, maxime autem ad domesticos fidei.

  * Bede, *Super Epist. ad Galatians*, c. 6? [Alfons Stickler was unable to identify this text; it went into Gratian C. 23, qu. 4, c. 35 under the same inscription—not noted by Stickler. Friedberg identified the text as Bede. Unfortunately, it is not found as cited.]

  a A2 = deberatur

22. Quod non putetur fallax qui quod promisit superna dispositione*a* praeventus adimplere praetermisit

  Gelasius*

Si vero sicut potius optamus fuerint ad meliora conversi . . . | . . . Quos ergo non esse iam constat super terram, non humano, sed suo reservavit iudicio, nec audet aecclesia vendicare, quod ipsis beatis apostolis conspiciat non fuisse concessum.

* Gelasius I, epist. 30, cc. 11 ff. [Thiel, 444 ff.; not via Ps.Isidore]

a A2 = dispositionem; X = Quod non imputetur fallax . . . [as Pasztor]
fo. 236ᵛ
[In C, there is no number 23; subsequent numeration is off by one in C]

23. No Rubric*a* [although space left for rubrics from here through the end of the text in Vat. lat. 1363]

Gregorius Brunichildae*b* reginae francorum inter cetera*
Si quos igitur violentos, si quos adulteros, si quos fures vel aliis pravis actibus studere cognoscitis, Deum de eorum correctione placare festinate, ut per vos flagellum | perfidarum gentium . . . excitatum est . . . . . . ne, si, quod non credimus, divinae ultionis iracundia sceleratorum fuerit actione commota, bellipetis [belli pestis] interimat, quos delinquentes ad rectitudinis viam Dei praecepta non revocant.

* Gregory I, *Reg.* VIII: 4, vol. 2, p. 7

a A1, A2 = Quod reginae corrigendi malefactores potestas datur; B1, C = Quod saeculi potestates a pravis actibus malos revoca[re studeant (as in X)] [as Pasztor]; B2 = Quod Dominus pacatur de vindicta malorum   *b* A2 = Brunicheldae
fo. 237ʳ

24. No Rubric*a*

Augustinus Honorato episcopo inter cetera*
'Cum persequentur vos in civitate ista, fugite in aliam [Matt. 10: 23].' Quis autem credat ita hoc Dominum fieri voluisse, ut necessario ministerio, sine quo vivere nequeunt, desererentur greges, quos suo sanguine comparavit? . . . | . . . Melius tamen, quod in his periculis faciamus, invenire non possumus quam orationes ad Dominum Deum nostrum, ut misereatur nostri. Quod ipsum scilicet ut ecclesias non desererent, Dei dono nonnulli prudentes et sancti viri et velle et facere meruerunt et inter dentes obtrectantium a sui proposito intentione minime defecerunt.

* Augustine, epist. 228, cc. 2, 3, 6, 7, 8, 10, 11, 12, 14 (excerpts) [*CSEL* 57, 485 ff.]

a A1, A2 = Quando fugiendum sit propter persecutionem quando minime; B1 = De eo quod scriptum est, si vos persecuti fuerint, de una civitate fugite in alia; B2 = Quod persecutio fugienda est de civitate in civitatem; C = De eo quod scriptum est, si vos persecuti fuerint in unam civitatem, fugite in aliam; X = De eo quod scriptum est, si vos persecuti fuerint in vestram civitatem, fugiti [sic] in aliam; [Pasztor = Augustinus Honorato episcopo inter cetera]
fo. 238ʳ

25. No Rubric*a*

Gregorius*
Summopere praecavere debent rectores aecclesiae . . . . . . et iuxta quod Dominus imperabat, iudicia proponebat | nimirum nos instituens ut non ex corde nostro, sed praecepto divino condemnationis vel iustificationis sententiam proferamus.

* Gregory I, *Moralia in Job*, Lib. 19, c. 23? [Alfons Stickler was also unable to identify this text; it went into Gratian C. 11, qu. 3, c. 70 under the same inscription—not noted by Stickler. Friedberg identified the text as *Moralia in Job*. Unfortunately it is not found as cited.]

a A1, A2 = Ut rectores ecclesiae et iudices saeculares non temere proferant sententiam; B1, C, X = Quod secundum divinam et humanam legem sine personarum acceptione rectorum sententia proferatur [X = proferanda est; Pasztor =preferatur]; B2 = Quod rectores ecclesiarum non sint praecipites in dandis sententiis
fo. 238ᵛ

26. No Rubric*a*
Ieronimus in epistola ad Ephesios***b**
Si Dominus ea iubet quae non sunt adversa scripturis sanctis, subiciatur Domino servus. . . . . . Si bonum est quod praecipit imperator iubentis exequere voluntatem. Si malum, responde: 'Obedire oportet Deo magis quam hominibus [Acts 5: 29]'.

* Jerome, *Commentarium in epist. ad Titum*, II: 9; III: 1 [*PL* 26, 619, 626]

a A1, A2 = Quod magis sit obediendum Deo quam hominibus; B1, C, X = Quod magis obediendum est spiritus quam corporis Domini [Pasztor omits 'est']; B2 = Quod servi non debent obedire Domino praecipienti contra Deum   *b* B1: no inscription

27. No Rubric*a*
Ambrosius in libro de officiis***b**
Non satis est bene velle, sed etiam bene facere. Nec satis est iterum bene facere, nisi id ex bono fonte, hoc est, bona voluntate proficiscatur. . . . | . . . Aurum sacramenta quaerunt, neque auro placent, quae auro non emuntur ornatus sacramentorum redemptio captivorum est. *Et infra.* Pasce fame morientem est. Quisquis enim pascendo hominem, servare poteris, si non paveris occidisti.

* Ambrose, *Libri de officiis*, I, 30 ff; II: 15, 21, 28 [*PL* 16, 70 ff.]

a A1, A2 = De operibus misericordiae; B1, C, X = Quod bene velle non sufficit, nec iterum bene facere, nisi ex bono fonte processerit [X = processit], et de liberalitate probabili [as Pasztor]; B2 = De diversitate elemosinarum   *b* A2 = offitium; B1: no inscription
fo. 239ᵛ

28. No Rubric*a*
Gregorius Genandio patricio et exarcho Africae***b**
Sicut excellentiam vestram hostilibus bellis in hac vita Dominus victoriarum fecit in hac luce fulgere, ita oportet esse inimicis aecclesiae eius, omni vivacitate mentis et corporis obviare . . . | . . . Persolventes preterea paternae caritatis affectum Dominum petimus, quo [qui] brachium vestrum ad comprimendos hostes forte efficiat, et mentem eius fidei zelo velut mucronem gladii vibrantis exacuat.

* Gregory I, *Reg.* I: 72, pp. 92 ff.

a A1, A2 = Quod christianus princeps sicut terrenum peragit bellum sic contra hereticos [A2 adds 'ad'] aecclesiasticum peragat praelium; B1, B2, C, X = Quod aecclesiae inimicis omni vivacitate mentis et corporis sit obviandum [as Pasztor]   *b* A1 = exarco Affricae
fo. 240ʳ

29. No Rubric[a]

Gregorius ad eundem*[b]

Si non ex fidei merito et christianae religionis gratia tanta excellentiae vestrae
bellicorum actuum prosperitas eveniret . . . . . . Quaeque hic illi christianissima
mente confertis, horum retributionem per spem futuro iudicio sustinetis.

* Gregory I, *Reg.* I: 73, p. 93

---

[a] A1, A2 = Quod victoria religiosi principis non ex opinione humana sed ex Deo disponente proveniat; B1, C = De victoria orationibus praevenienda et bello non appetendo
desiderio fundendi sanguinis [as Pasztor]; B2, X = De victoria orationibus praevenienda
et bello desiderio sanguinis fundendi non appetendo   [b] B1: no inscription

Tables

TABLE I
Breakdown of Anselm's Material Sources

This table is based is based on Thaner's edition together with MS Vat. Lat. 1363. With the large number of *capitula* in the collection, it seems advisable to present the breakdown of Anselm's material sources in genre classification, rather than in specific number of each author, work, council, etc. This is a somewhat artificial system as the canonical texts in the collection were not ordered by genre, though on occasion there are series of decretals or conciliar canons, as well as series from a particular text.

Book I. De potestate et auctoritate [primatu] apostolicae sedis

Papal Decretals
(*a*) False	33	Ps.Isidorian
	1	spurious Gregory IV
(*b*) Genuine	33	Gelasius: 8; Leo I: 8; Gregory I: 2; Hilary: 2; Symmachus: 1; etc.
Conciliar:	1	spurious letter from Nicaea
Secular:	4	Codex Iustinianus: 1; Novellae: 2; Promissio Ottonis (a. 962): 1
Patristic:	7	Cyprian: 1; Ambrose: 3; Jerome: 1; Leo I: 1; Gregory I: 1
*Misc.:	$\underline{10}$	
	89	

*Ps.Constitutum Silvestri: 1; Ennodius, *Libellus pro synodo*: 1; Peter Damian, *De rebus Mediolan. ad Hildebrandum*: 1; *Liber pontificalis*: 4; Anastasius, *Historia*: 3

Book II. De libertate appellationis

Papal Decretals
(*a*) False	48	Ps.Isidorian
	3	spurious Gregory IV
(*b*) Genuine	21	Leo I: 6; Nicholas I: 6; Gelasius: 4; Innocent I: 3; Gregory I: 1; John VIII: 1
Conciliar:	3	Council of Constantinople VIII (via Anastasius): 1; Council of Sardis: 1; Council of Ephesus: 1

Secular:	2	Codex Iustinianus
Patristic:	0	
*Misc.:	5	
	82	

*Ennodius, *Libellus pro synodo*: 2; *Liber pontificalis*: 1; Biblical: 2

Book III. De ordine accusandi, testificandi et iudicandi

Papal Decretals
(*a*) False	82	Ps.Isidorian
(*b*) Genuine	8	Gregory I: 7; Innocent I: 1
Conciliar:	14	Council of Chalcedon (451): 4; Council of Ephesus: 2; Council of Constantinople (VI): 2; etc.
Secular:	2	Codex Iustinianus: 1; Cod. Theodosii: 1
Patristic:	1	Augustine
*Misc.:	7	
	114	

*Benedictus Levita: 1; *Gesta Liberii* : 1; *Liber pontificalis*: 1; Anastasius, *Historia*: 3; c. 78: unknown (cited as Augustine, via Burchard XVI: 23)

Book IV. De privilegiorum auctoritate

Papal Decretals
(*a*) False	5	Ps.Isidorian
(*b*) Genuine	22	Gregory I: 6; Leo I: 3; Gelasius: 2; John VIII: 4; Symmachus: 2; Nicholas I: 1, etc.
Conciliar:	2	Council of Constantinople (VIII): 1; Council of Nicaea: 1
Secular:		
(*a*) Justinian Code	12	
(*b*) Theodosian Code	6	
(*c*) other	5	Privilegium Ludovici: 1; Priv. Ottonis I: 1; Priv. Heinrici II: 1; Capit. Karoli: 2
Patristic:	0	
*Misc.:	3	
	55	

Vita s. Silvestri: 1; Ps.Constitutum Silvestri: 1; Flavianus, Bishop of Constantinople to Leo I: 1

Book V. De ordinationibus ecclesiarum et de omni iure ac statu illarum

Papal Decretals

(a) False	10	Ps.Isidorian
(b) Genuine	35	Gregory I: 16; Gelasius: 8; Gregory VII: 2; Symmachus: 4; John VIII: 1; etc.
Conciliar:	6	Council of Chalcedon (451): 2; Council of Carthage (419): 1; Council of Aurelia (549): 1; etc.
Secular:	1	Institutionum Iustiniani
Patristic:	6	Cyprian: 2; Augustine: 2; Gregory I: 1; Ambrose: 1
*Misc.:	$\dfrac{6}{64}$	

*Anastasius, *Historia*: 1; Theodorii Poenit.: 1; spurious additions to Augustine's *Sermo* 277: 1 (c. 31); unknown: 3 (cc. 13, 16, 18 via Burchard)

Book VI. De electione et ordinatione ac de omni potestate sive statu episcoporum

Papal Decretals:

(a) False	27	Ps.Isidorian
(b) Genuine	106	Gregory I: 44; Leo I: 13; Gelasius: 8; Pelagius: 8; Innocent: 5; Nicholas II: 2; Gregory VII: 2; etc.
Conciliar:	27	Council of Nicaea: 5; Council of Sardis: 2; Council of Constantinople (VIII): 2; Council of Chalcedon (451): 3; Council of Carthage (407, 419): 3; Council of Antioch: 3; Council of Nicaea (II): 4; etc.
Secular:	4	Codex Iustinianus: 1; Novellae: 1; Privil. Ottonis I: 1; Capit. Lotharii: 1
Patristic:	8	Augustine: 4; Cyprian: 2; Gregory I: 1; Origen: 1
*Misc.	$\dfrac{18}{190}$	

Ordo Romanus: 4; *Liber pontificalis*: 3; Canones apostolorum: 3; Ennodius, *Libellus pro synodo*: 1; *Vita Gregorii magni*: 1; Eusebius, *Historia*: 1; Capitula Martini Bracensis: 1; Statuta ecclesiae antiquae: 1; Emperor Anastasius to Pope Hadrian: 1; Regula formatarum: 1; Epist. a clericis Noviomensibus (cited as Jerome): 1

Book VII. De communi vita

Papal Decretals

(*a*) False	28	Ps.Isidorian
	1	spurious Hormisdas
(*b*) Genuine	80	Gregory I: 26; Gelasius: 13; Innocent I: 9; Leo I: 8; Pelagius I: 7; Siricius: 4; etc.
Conciliar:	32	Council of Toledo (IV): 6; Council of Carthage (397): 3, (419): 5; Council of Chalcedon (451): 4; Council of Nicaea: 4; etc.
Secular:	0	
Patristic:	12	Jerome: 7; Augustine: 3; Ambrose: 2
**Misc.*	$\frac{21}{174}$	

*Statuta ecclesiae antiquae: 10; Ordo Romanus: 2; Ps.Jerome, *De septimis ordinibus ecclesiae*; 2; Gennadius (cited as Augustine): 1; Canones apostolorum: 1; Ps.Constitutum Silvestri: 1; Poenit. Theodorii: 1; *Vita Gregorii magni*: 1; St Paul, I Timothy: 1; Capitula ecclesiastica Haitonis episcopi: 1 (cited as Augustine, via Burchard II: 2)

Book VIII. De lapsis

Papal Decretals

(*a*) False	2	Ps.Isidorian
(*b*) Genuine	17	Gregory I: 9; Innocent I: 3; Siricius: 2; Leo I: 2; Eugenius II: 1
Conciliar:	6	Council of Chalcedon (451): 2; Council of Nicaea: 1; Council of Ancrya: 1; Council of Toledo (IV): 1; etc.
Secular:	0	
Patristic:	7	Cyprian: 4; Augustine: 1; Gregory I: 1; Isidore: 1
**Misc.*:	$\frac{2}{34}$	

*Ps.Constitutum Silvestri: 1; Julianus Pomerius, *De vita contemplatione*: 1 (attributed to Prosper of Aquitaine)

Book IX. De sacramentis

Papal Decretals:

(*a*) False	7	Ps.Isidorian
(*b*) Genuine	9	Leo I: 5; Innocent I: 2; Gregory I: 1; Gelasius: 1

Conciliar:	2	Council of Carthage (397): 1; Council of Laodicea: 1
Secular:	0	
Patristic:	28	Augustine: 23; Ambrose: 3; Cyprian: 2
*Misc.:	3	
	49	

* Poenit. Theodorii: 1; Council of Coblenz (922): 1 (cited as Leo I via Burchard IV: 25); unknown: 1 (c. 25)

Book X. De coniugiis

Papal Decretals

(*a*) False	1	Ps.Isidorian
(*b*) Genuine	12	Gregory I: 4; Gelasius: 1; Innocent I: 1; Zacharias: 1; Leo I: 1; Gregory II: 1; etc.
Conciliar:	5	Council of Ancyra: 1; Council of Carthage (407, 419): 1; Council of Toledo (II): 1; etc.
Secular:	0	
Patristic:	14	Augustine: 11; Jerome: 1; Ambrose: 2
*Misc.:	13	
	45	

**Vita Gregorii magni*: 1; unknown: 2 (cc. 3 (via Burchard IX: 2), 28); apocryphal canon: 1; Regula S. Basilii: 1; erroneous citations via Burchard: 8—

    c. 4 cited as Hormisdas, but Benedictus Levita, *error* via Burchard [IX: 23]

    c. 6 cited as Eusebius, but Poenit.Theodorii, *error* via Burchard [VIII: 19]

    c. 23 cited as Gregory I, but apocryphal, *error* via Burchard [IX: 44]

    c. 24 cited as Gregory I, but Rhabanus Maurus, *error* via Burchard [IX: 40]

    c. 25 cited as Nicholas I, but Interpret. Sent.Paulii (Lex romana visigoth), *error* via Burchard [IX: 28]

    c. 26 cited as Fabianus, but Interpret. Sent.Paulii, *error* via Burchard [IX: 30]

    c. 29 cited as Deusdedit, but apocryphal, *error* via Burchard [XVII: 44]

    c. 38 cited as Pius, but capitulary text from council of Worms in 829, *error* via Burchard [V: 37]

Book XI. De poenitentia

Papal Decretals

(*a*) False	7	Ps.Isidorian
(*b*) Genuine	36	Leo I: 9; Gregory I: 7; Innocent I: 3; Gelasius: 3; Pelagius: 2; Siricius: 1, etc.

Conciliar:	31	Council of Ancyra: 6; Council of Carthage (419): 4; Council of Nicaea: 3; Council of Agathyra (506): 2; Council of Toledo (X): 1 (attributed to Augustine); etc.
Secular:	0	
Penitential:		
(*a*) Poenit. Theodori	15	
(*b*) Poenit. Romano	6	
(*c*) 'Iudicum canonicum'	8	Capitula Iudiciorum
Patristic:	41	Augustine: 26; Gregory I: 9 (one of which, c. 139, attributed to Augustine); Jerome: 4 (one of which, c. 138, attributed to Augustine); Isidore: 1; Ambrose: 1
*Misc.	$\dfrac{7}{151}$	152 normally given, but c. 102 has no canon in 'A'; only number

*Canones apostolorum: 1; Statuta patruorum (sic): 1; Ex poenit. (unknown): 1; unknown: 4 (cc. 99, 103, 106–7)

Book XII. De excommunicatione

Papal Decretals

(*a*) False	11	Ps.Isidorian
	1	spurious Gelasius
(*b*) Genuine	23	Pelagius: 6; Gelasius: 5; Nicholas I: 4; Gregory I: 3; Innocent I: 2; Leo I: 1; Felix III: 1; John VIII: 1
Conciliar:	5	Council of Carthage (IV): 3; Council of Carthage (II): 1; Council of Antioch: 1
Secular:	6	Codex Iustinianus: 5; Justinian to Hormisdas, via *Collectio Avellana*: 1
Patristic:	23	Augustine: 16; Isidore: 2; Jerome: 2; Cyprian: 1; Ambrose: 1; Gregory I: 1
*Misc.:	$\dfrac{3}{72}$	

*Anastasius, *Historia*: 1; Canones apostolorum: 1; unknown: 1 (cited as Augustine)

Book XIII. De iusta vindicta

Papal Decretals

(*a*) False	2	Ps.Isidorian
(*b*) Genuine	8	Gregory I: 7; Gelasius: 1
Conciliar:	0	
Secular:	0	
Patristic:	17	Augustine: 13; Gregory I: 2; Jerome: 1; Ambrose: 1
*Misc.:	2	
	29	

* Ps.Augustine: 1; unknown: 1 (cited as Bede)

TABLE II

Dispersion and Disposition of Pseudo-Isidorian Texts in the Collectio canonum

This table is based is based on Thaner's edition together with MS Vat. Lat. 1363 and with reference to Fuhrmann's table, III, 1031–5. The texts in bold type are ones which, though at least partially found in the 74T, were probably not taken from the 74T, but from an independent Ps.Isidore. Cf. Appendix Ib.

A Note on Terminology: 'independent' refers to texts which seem to have been taken directly from a copy of the Decretals, and not through the medium of another collection such as Burchard of the 74T. Chapter numbers in [ ] refer to Anselm.

Book I. De potestate et auctoritate [primatu] apostolicae sedis

Total Ps.Isidorian texts: 33
28 independent [cc. 3–8, 11, 13–18, 22, 23, 32–6, 38, 39, 53–5, 59, 60, 66]
 3 via 74T [cc. 2, **9**, 12]
 2 via Burchard [c. 1 [= *Decretum* I: 1]; c. 52 [= *Decretum* I: 42]]

Book II. De libertate appellationis

Total Ps.Isidorian texts: 48
40 independent [cc. 4, 5, 7, 9, 11–15, 18, 23, 26, 27, 33–42, 44–52, 58, 61–3, 77, 79, 80, 82]
 8 via 74T [cc. 6, 8, 10, 21, **43**, 59, 60, 81]

Book III. De ordine accusandi, testificandi et iudicandi

Total Ps.Isidorian texts: 82 (84 according to Fuhrmann; cc. 34 and 46 have 2 texts each)
38 independent [cc. 1–4, 6, 9, 11–13, 15–22, 26, 28, 31–5, 44, 46, 47, 55, 59, 60, 62, 63, 65, 73, 80, 88, 89, 109]
42 via 74T [cc. 5, 7, 8, 10, 14, 23, 24, **25**, 27, 29, **36**, 37–41, 43, **45**, 48–54, 56–8, **61**, 64, 66, 70–2, 74, 76, 79, 82–4, 86, 87]
 2 via Burchard [c. 77 [= *Decretum* XVI: 6]; c. 81 [= *Decretum* I: 132]]

Book IV. De privilegiorum auctoritate

Total Ps.Isidorian texts: 5

3   independent [cc. 33, 41, 48]
2   via 74T [cc. 1, 47]

Book V. De ordinationibus ecclesiarum . . .

Total Ps.Isidorian texts: 10
5   independent [cc. 21, 27, 40, 59, 63]
4   via 74T [cc. 10, 23, 32, 33]
1   via Burchard [c. 37 [= *Decretum* XI: 27]]

Book VI. De electione . . . episcoporum

Total Ps.Isidorian texts: 27
8   independent [cc. 93, 101, 102, 104, 105, 121, 152, 178]
19   via 74T [cc. 33, 45, 90, 91, 98, 99, 103, 113, 114, 115, 117, 122, 123, 126,
     127, 138, 139, 140, 149]

Book VII. De communi vita

Total Ps.Isidorian texts: 28 (31 according to Fuhrmann; c. 58 has 3 texts)
14   independent [cc. 4, 58, 71, 72, 73, 74, 84, 95, 105, 110, 117, 120, 130,
     161]
14   via 74T [cc. 19, 20, 36, 40, 59, 89, 107, 108, 118, 119, 147, 149, 150, 156]

Book VIII. De lapsis

Total Ps.Isidorian texts: 2
2   independent [cc. 2, 16]
0   via 74T

Book IX. De sacramentis

Total Ps.Isidorian texts: 7
1   independent [c. 19]
6   via 74T [cc. 1, 2, 20, 21, 23, 27]

Book X. De coniugiis

Total Ps.Isidorian texts: 1
0   independent
1   via 74T [c. 2]

Book XI. De poenitentia

Total Ps.Isidorian texts: 7
7   independent [cc. 6, 7, 29, 36, 37, 69, 77]
0   via 74T

Book XII. De excommunicatione

Total Ps.Isidorian texts: 11
9   independent [cc. 1, 2, 6, 8, 9, 13 (cf. Swabian Appendix, c. 321*), 14, 19,
     24]
2   via 74T [cc. 4, 18]

Book XIII. De iusta vindicta

Total Ps.Isidorian texts: 2

2   independent [cc. 13, 19]

0   via 74T

TABLE III

Dispersion and Disposition of 74T Texts in the Collectio canonum

This Table is based on Gilchrist's edition of the 74T together with Thaner's edition and Vat. Lat. 1363, and with reference to Fuhrmann. Texts in bold type are ones which, though in the 74T, none the less seem to have been taken from an independent Ps.Isidore, or another source. See Appendices Ib, C; and Ic.

A Note on Terminology: 'Ps.Isidore' refers to false texts; 'genuine' (as before) is a somewhat loose term, covering all of the 74T texts except those which are false Ps.Isidorian. As indicated above, the compiler of the 74T used the Ps.Isidore for genuine documents.

Book I. De potestate et auctoritate [primatu] apostolicae sedis

Total 74T texts: 12
- 3   Ps.Isidorian [cc. 2, **9**, 12]
- 9   genuine [cc. 10, 19–21, 24, 67, **68***, **69***, 71] (*via Ps.Isidore?)

Book II. De libertate appellationis

Total 74T texts: 14
- 8   Ps.Isidorian [cc. 6, 8, 10, 21, **43**, 59, 60, 81]
- 6   genuine [cc. 1, **16**, 17, 19, 20, 76]

Book III. De ordine accusandi, testificandi et iudicandi

Total 74T texts: 44
- 42   Ps.Isidorian [cc. 5, 7, 8, 10, 14, 23, 24, **25**, 27, 29, **36**, 37–41, 43, **45**, 48–54, 56–8, **61**, 64, 66, 70–2, 74, 76, 81–4, 86, 87]
- 2   genuine [cc. 75, 85]

Book IV. De privilegiorum auctoritate

Total 74T texts: 18
- 2   Ps.Isidorian [cc. 1, 47]
- 16   genuine [cc. 2–9, 13–18, 28, 29]

Book V. De ordinationibus ecclesiarum . . .

Total 74T texts: 13
 4 Ps.Isidorian [cc. 10, 23, 32, 33]
 9 genuine [cc. 1, 2, 4, 28, 34, 35, 54–6]

Book VI. De electione . . . episcoporum

Total 74T texts: 54
 19 Ps.Isidorian [cc. 33, 45, 90, 91, 98, 99, 103, 113–15, 117, 122, 123, 126,
    127, 138–40, 149]
 35 genuine [cc. 1, 15–19, 21, 28, 29, 48, 61, 65–74, 78, 79, 85, 92, 116, 118,
    125, 128, 131–3, 141, 143, 184]

Book VII. De communi vita

Total 74T texts: 48
 14 Ps.Isidorian [cc. 19, 20, 36, 40, 59, 89, 107, 108, 118, 119, 147, 149, 150,
    156]
 34 genuine [cc. 7–16, 21, 23, 28–30, 33, 34, 37, 38, 60, 94, 101, 102, 122,
    136, 140, 141, 145, 152, 163–5, 169, 170]

Book VIII. De lapsis

Total 74T texts: 6
 0 Ps.Isidorian
 6 genuine [cc. 4, 5, 10, 14, 18, 34]

Book IX. De sacramentis

Total 74T texts: 13
 6 Ps.Isidorian [cc. 1, 2, 20, 21, 23, 27]
 7 genuine [cc. 4, 5, 11, 12, 15, 22, 28]

Book X. De coniugiis

Total 74T texts: 6
 1 Ps.Isidorian [c. 2]
 5 genuine [cc. 18, 19, 22, 34, 36]

Book XI. De poenitentia

Total 74T texts: 4*
 0 Ps.Isidorian
 4 genuine [cc. 11, 25, 79, 80]
*3 additional texts [cc. 5, 11, 12] are also found in the Swabian Appendix.

Book XII. De excommunicatione

Total 74T texts: 5*
 2 Ps.Isidorian [cc. 4, 18]
 3 genuine [cc. 20, 22, 23]

*7 additional texts [cc. 11, 13, 25, 26, 28 (2 texts), 31] are found in the Swabian Appendix. c. 11 is Ps.Isidorian; c. 31 may possibly be from Burchard.

Book XIII. De iusta vindicta

No 74T texts!

TABLE IV
Anselm's 'Dictatus papae' *Texts*

Dictatus papae [*Reg.* II: 55a]	Anselm, *Collectio canonum*
1. Quod Romana ecclesia a solo Domino sit fundata	I: 2 (Vat. lat. 1364) Quod sacrosancta Romana ecclesia caput est omnium ecclesiarum a Domino constituta [Ps.Anacletus, c. 30, p. 83 (= 74T c. 2); I: 17 Quod Romana ecclesia omnibus est prelata non tantum canonum decretis sed voce ipsius Salvatoris [Ps.Julius, c. 6, p. 459]; I: 63 Quod Romana ecclesia omnes instituit dignitates ecclesiasticas, ipsam autem verbum illud fundavit per quod creata sunt omnia [Peter Damian, Reindel II, no. 65, p. 232]
2. Quod solus Romanus pontifex iure dicatur universalis	Anselm argues the opposite. VI: 117 Ne universalis quisquam vocetur [Ps.Pelagius II, p. 721 (= 74T c. 184)]; VI: 118 De eadem re [Gregory I, *Reg.* VIII: 29 (= 74T c. 185)]
3. Quod ille solus possit deponere episcopos vel reconciliare	II: 16 Quod sancta Romana ecclesia fas habet iudicandi de omnibus, de illa vero nullus, et potestatem habet solvendi iniuste damnatos et damnandi quos oportuerit absque synodo [Gelasius, ep. 26 (= 74T c. 10)]; II: 25 Quod papa renovare possit iudicia dampnatorum [Ennodius, *Libellus pro synodo*]; VI: 119 Quod papa episcopum dampnatum possit restituere [Gregory I, *Reg.* III: 7]

Dictatus papae [*Reg.* II: 55a]	Anselm, *Collectio canonum*
4. Quod legatus eius omnibus episcopis presit in concilio etiam inferioris gradus et adversus eos sententiam depositionis possit dare	I: 25 Ut papa vices suas alteri committat, ubi presens ipse non potest esse, quod etiam subdiacono potest [Gregory I, *Reg.* I: 1]; V: 12 Quod papa cui cura debet esse omnium ecclesiarum visitationis vicem in Capuana ecclesia alteri cuidam episcopo committit [Gregory I, *Reg.* V: 13]
5. Quod absentes papa possit deponere	III: 92 De dampnatione Dioscori episcopi, qui vocatus ad synodum noluit venire [Council of Chalcedon (451), 3rd action]; cf. III: 91, 93. Elsewhere, Anselm opposes the judgement of the absent, see *Dp* 24.
6. Quod cum excommunicatis ab illo inter caetera nec in eadem domo debemus manere	I: 6 Quod nec loqui debemus cui papa non loquitur [Ps.Clement, c. 17, p. 36]; XII: 11 Quod non debet quis ei communicare quem sedes apostolica repellit nisi ab illatis se mundaverit [Gregory I, *Reg.* VI: 26]; XII: 13 Ut excommunicatis nemo communicet in oratione, cibo, potu, osculo, nec ave eis dicat alioquin similiter excommunicatus est [Ps.Calixtus, c. 10, p. 138]; cf. XII: 14–19.
7. Quod illi soli licet pro temporis necessitate novas leges condere, novas plebes congregare, de canonica abbatiam facere, et e contra, divitem episcopatum dividere et inopes unire	II: 33 Quod papa canonum decreta ita librare debet, ut quae necessitas temporum relaxanda exposcit temperet, quantum fieri potest [Ps.Symmachus VI, p. 679]; VIII: 27 Quod vigor antiquitatis servetur in lapsis usque ad auctoritatem et consilium papae [Cyprian, ep. 30]; V: 24 Quod papa duas dioceses uni episcopo committit [Gregory I, *Reg.* II: 48]; VI: 96 Quod papa episcopatus duos potest redigere in unum [Gregory I, *Reg.* II: 44]

Dictatus papae [*Reg.* II: 55a]	Anselm, *Collectio canonum*
8. Quod solus possit uti imperialibus insigniis	IV: 33 Quod Constantinus imperator papae concessit coronam et omnem regiam dignitatem in urbe Romana et Italia et in partibus occidentalibus [*Vita s. Silvestri*, Ps.*Constitutum Constantini*, p. 252, etc.]
9. Quod solius papae pedes omnes principes deosculentur	—
10. Quod illius solius nomen in ecclesiis recitetur	VII: 80 Ut personae ad sacros ordines promovendae diligenter inquirantur, et presbyteri semper recitent nomina apostolici et ordinatoris sui [Pelagius I, JK no. 1002 (*Collectio Brittanica*, ep. Pelagii no. 30)]
11. Quod hoc unicum est nomen in mundo	—
12. Quod illi liceat imperatores deponere	I: 80 Quod apostolico licet imperatores excommunicare ac deponere, quod etiam aliqui fecerunt episcopi [Gregory VII, *Reg.* VIII: 21]; Anselm also used two texts from Anastasius Bibliotecarius' *Chronographia*: I: 76 Qualiter Gregorius papa regnum a Leone imperatore separavit propter eius impietatem; I: 77 Quod Stephanus papa Pipinum in regem provehit et antecessorem eius regem totondit et in monasterio conscripsit, illum vero sacramento regi commisso absolvit
13. Quod illi liceat de sede ad sedem necessitate cogente episcopos transmutare	VI: 90 Quod mutationes episcoporum communi consilio et utilitate per apostolicam auctoritatem fieri possunt [Ps.Anterus, c. 2, 4, pp. 152, 153]; VI: 93 Quod causa necessitatis aut utilitatis mutationes episcoporum fieri possunt [Ps.Pelagius II, p. 726]; VI: 99 Ut ecclesia non iudicetur nisi a suo episcopo qui si persecutus fuerit in sua, fugiat ad aliam, aut si utilitatis causa fuerit mutandus, non per se hoc agat [Ps.Calixtus, c. 15, p. 139 (= 74T c. 187)]

Dictatus papae [*Reg.* II: 55a]	Anselm, *Collectio canonum*
14. Quod de omni ecclesia quocunque voluerit clericum valeat ordinare	—
15. Quod ab illo ordinatus alii ecclesiae preesse potest, sed non militare; et quod ab aliquo episcopo non debet superiorem gradum accipere	VII: 68 Quod in Romana ecclesia ordinatus inde ulterius egredi non debeat [Gregory I, *Reg.* V: 35]
16. Quod nulla synodus absque praecepto eius debet generalis vocari	I: 52 Quod auctoritas congregandarum synodorum generalium soli apostolicae sedi sit commissa, nec sine eius auctoritate rata esse potest [cited as Gelasius, but Ps.Isidore, *Praefatio*, c. 8, p. 19]; II: 27 Quod ideo Romanae ecclesiae concessa sunt privilegia a congregandorum conciliorum ac restitutionum episcoporum et iudiciorum, ut omnibus oppressis succurrat [Ps.Julius, c. 15, p. 471]; II: 47 Quod irritum sit concilium nisi fuerit apostolica auctoritate firmatum [Ps.Julius, c. 13, p. 471]; cf. II: 26, 42, 45–6, 48, etc.
17. Quod nullum capitulum nullusque liber canonicus habeatur absque illius auctoritate	VI: 186 De falsis et apocryphis libris, ut in usu lectionis non habeantur [Leo I, ep. 15, c. 15]; VI: 187 Qui libri sint legendi [Gelasius, ep. 42, c. 3]; VI: 188 Quod ideo non sunt recipiendi quilibet apocryphi libri, quod aliqua ex eis sancti patres exceperunt [Origen, *In cant. canticorum*, prologue]; VI: 189 Qui libri recipiantur in canone sanctorum patrum scripturaram brevis annexus ostendit [Innocent I, ep. 6]; VI: 190 Ut preter scripturas catholicas vel canonicas nichil in ecclesia legatur sub nomine divinarum scripturarum [Council of Carthage (397, 419), c. 24]; XII: 37 Si quis audet transmutare quod sancti patres et universales synodi statuerunt condemnatus est [apocryphal Gelasius, see Thiel, p. 612]

Dictatus papae [*Reg.* II: 55a]	Anselm, *Collectio canonum*
18. Quod sententia illius a nullo debeat retractari et ipse omnium solus retractare possit	I: 21 Ut nemo presumat iudicium primae sedis retractare aut iudicare [Nicholas I, JE no. 2879]; II: 24 Quod apostolica sedes ab aliis ligatos potest solvere, ab illa vero ligatos nemo, de qua presumptione Acatius dampnatus est [Gelasius, ep. 26]; II: 56 Quod de iudicio sedis apostolicae nullus debeat iudicare, ipsa vero de omnibus [Gelasius, ep. 10]
19. Quod a nemine ipse iudicare debeat	I: 19 Ut prima sedes a nullo iudicetur [*Constitutum Constantini*, c. 20 (= 74T c. 8)]; I: 24 Quod papa a nullo nisi a Deo erit iudicandus [Ennodius, *Lib. pro synodo* (= 74T c. 11)]; I: 53 Quod papa a solo Deo sit iudicandus [Ps.Anterus, c. 5]; II: 67 Quod nemo potest ab his qui inferioris sunt dignitatis vel ordinis iudicari [Nicholas I, JE no. 2796]
20. Quod nullus audeat condemnare apostolicam sedem appellantem	II: 36 Ut episcoporum tantum finitiva iudicia referantur ad sedem Romanam, et in ecclesiis eorum non alii praeponantur donec negotia eorum iuste ibi terminentur [Ps.Eleutherus, c. 2, p. 125]; II: 40 Quod absque auctoritate sedis apostolicae nulla potest synodus regulariter congregari, nec episcopus qui eam appellaverit potest sine illa damnari [Ps.Marcellus, c. 9, p. 228]; II: 81 Ut accusatus vel iudicatus a comprovincialibus episcopis licenter papam appellet, qui eius causam retractet et in loco eius interim alius non ordinetur [Ps.Victor, c. 5, p. 128]; etc.
21. Quod maiores causae cuiuscunque ecclesiae ad eam referri debeant	II: 4 Ut difficiliores causae et maiora negocia ad sedem apostolicam, si appellatum fuerit, deferantur [Ps.Anacletus, c. 17, p. 74]; II: 5 De eadem re [Ps.Anacletus, c. 34, p. 84]; II: 13 Quod dubiae ac maiores causae ab apostolica sede debent terminari

Dictatus papae [*Reg.* II: 55a]	Anselm, *Collectio canonum*
	[Ps.Felix I, c. 17, p. 204]; II: 18 Quod omnium appellationum et episcoporum et cunctorum maiorum negotia apostolicae sedi debent reservari [Ps.Vigilius, c. 7, p. 712 (cf. 74T c. 12)]; etc.
22. Quod Romana ecclesia nunquam erravit nec imperpetum scriptura testante errabit	I: 13 Quod Romana ecclesia nunquam a fide erravit [Ps.Lucius, c. 8, p. 179]; I: 35 Quod ecclesia Romana mater omnium ecclesiarum numquam a fide erravit [Ps.Lucius, c. 7, 8, p. 179]
23. Quod Romanus pontifex, si canonice fuerit ordinatus, meritis beati Petri indubitanter efficitur sanctus, testante sancto Ennodio Papiensi episcopo ei multis sanctis patribus faventibus, sicut in decretis beati Symmachi papae continetur	VI: 2 Ut sanctum esse nemo dubitet, quem apostolicae dignitatis apex iuste attolit [Ennodius, *Libellus pro synodo*]
24. Quod illius precepto et licentia subiectis liceat accusare	Anselm maintains the opposite. II: 67 Quod nemo potest ab his qui inferioris sunt dignitatis vel ordinis iudicari [Nicholas I, JE no. 2796]; III: 43 Ut inferiores gradus superiores non accusent. . . . [Ps.Silvestro, cc. 2–4, p. 449]; III: 58 Ut inferiores ordine non accusent superiores, et in re dubia certa non detur sententia et absens nemo iudicetur [Ps.Zepherinus, c. 3, p. 131 (= 74T c. 66)]; cf. XII: 32 (Appendix II)
25. Quod absque synodali conventu possit episcopos deponere et reconciliare	II: 16 Quod sancta Romana ecclesia fas habet iudicandi de omnibus, de illa vero nullus, et potestatem habet solvendi iniuste damnatos, et damnandi quos oportuerit absque synodo [Gelasius, ep. 26]
26. Quod catholicus non habeatur qui non concordat Romanae ecclesiae	XII: 47 Non esse veram fidem quae cum Romana ecclesia non convenit [Ambrose, *De excessu fratris*, I, no. 47]

Dictatus papae [*Reg.* II: 55a]	Anselm, *Collectio canonum*
27. Quod a fidelitate iniquiorum subiectos possit absolvere	I: 80 Quod apostolico licet imperatores excommunicare ac deponere, quod etiam aliqui fecerunt episcopi [Gregory VII, *Reg.* VIII: 21], which refers to oaths in the text. The absolution of oaths, however, is mentioned in the rubric of I: 77, regarding the deposition of Childebert (see text at *Dp* 12, from Anastasius Bibliotecarius)

TABLE V

The Canonical Sources of the Liber contra Wibertum

The texts marked by * are also found in the *Collectio canonum*. For the shared texts specifically about coercion, see Pasztor, 'Lotta per le investiture e "*Ius belli*"', 394 ff. Pasztor did not, however, note all of the canonical sources in the *Liber*.

Liber contra Wibertum, p. 521

1. Ambrose, epist. 20, c. 7: 'Convenior a comitibus . . .'
2. Ambrose, epist. 20, cc. 16, 23: 'Nec mihi fas est . . .'
3. Cyprian, *Liber de catholicae ecclesiae unitate.*, c. 6: 'Quisquis ab ecclesia . . .'
4. Gelasius, epist. 27, p. 293: 'Ad sacerdotes . . .'
5. Gelasius, epist. 27, [not verbatim]: 'Obsequi solere . . .'
6. Cyprian, epist. 55, c. 8: 'Factus est episcopus . . .'

Liber, p. 522

*7. Cyprian, epist. 69, c. 3: 'Ecclesia una est . . .' [= XII: 40]

Liber, p. 523

*8. Augustine, epist. 185, c. 11: 'Si ecclesia vera . . .' [= XIII: 14]
*9. Ibid., epist. 185, c. 19: 'Quod autem dicunt . . .' [= XIII: 15]
*10. Ibid., epist. 185, c. 22: 'Ubi est quod isti . . .' [= XIII: 16]
*11. Ibid., epist. 47, c. 5: 'Non mihi placet . . .' [= XIII: 18]
*12. Ibid., epist. 138, cc. 12 ff.: 'Si christiana disciplina omnia bella culparet . . .' (pp. 523–4) [= XIII: 3]

Liber, p. 524

*13. Ps.Augustine, epist. 13: 'Gravi de pugna . . .' [= XIII: 5]
*14. Augustine, epist. 189, cc. 4, 6: 'Noli existimare . . .' [= XIII: 4]
*15. Ibid., epist. 173, cc. 1 ff.: 'Displicet tibi . . .' [= XII: 55]
*16. Pelagius I, JK no. 1018: 'Non vos hominum vaniloquia retardent dicentium . . .' [= XII: 44]
*17. Ibid., JK no. 1024: 'Nec putetis alicuius . . .' [= XII: 45]
18. Jerome, *Comment. super Ezechielem*, III, c. 9: 'Qui malos . . .'

19. Ambrose [cited as Augustine], *Exposit. in psalm. 118: 58*: 'Est iniusta . . . '
*20. Augustine, epist. 185, cc. 36 ff.: 'Quicquid a parte Donati . . . ' [= XIII: 17 (with different beginning)]

Liber, p. 525

*21. Gregory I, *Reg.* II: 8: 'Nunc utile visum est . . . ' [= XIII: 6]
*22. Ibid., *Reg.* II: 33 (not II: 30 as in *MGH* edn.): 'Gloriosi filii, estote . . . ' [= XIII: 8]
[pp. 525–6, cf. Augustine, epist. 185, cc. 6 ff.; cf. XII: 60]

Liber, p. 526

23. Ambrose, *Expos. evang. Luc.*, c. 9: 'Si qua est ecclesia . . . '
24. Innocent I ???: 'Error, cui non resistitur . . . '
25. Ps.Eleutherus, p. 127; Ps.Felix II, p. 483 [cited as Innocent]: 'Neglegere quippe . . . '
26. Ps.Pius, p. 117: 'Quid prodest . . . ' (pp. 526–7)

Liber, p. 527

27. Ps.Clement, p. 54: 'Certissimum est . . . '
28. Ps.Fabianus, p. 166: 'Qui omnipotentem Deum . . . '
29. Leo ???: 'Qui alios ab errore . . . ' [cf. XIII: 19]
30. Augustine ???: 'Quisquis metu alicuius . . . ' [cf. XIII: 19]
31. Gregory I ???: 'Consentire videtur erranti . . . ' [cf. XIII: 19]

Selected Bibliography

I. SOURCES

A. Manuscript Sources

Cambridge, Corpus Christi College
  269 (Anselm, *Collectio canonum*, incip. s. XII)
London, British Library
  Additional 8873 (*Collectio Brittanica*, c.1090)
  Harley 3052 (Ans. 1)
Paris, Bibliothèque Nationale
  Par. lat. 12519 (Anselm, *Collectio canonum*, incip. s. XII)
Vatican City, Biblioteca Apostolica Vaticana
  Barb. lat. 535 (Anselm, *Collectio canonum*, [Bks I–VII] incip. s. XII)
  Ottob. lat. 224 (Anselm, *Collectio canonum*, s. XII/XVI)
  Reg. lat. 325 (Anselm, *Collectio canonum*, fragments)
  Vat. lat. 1348 (*Collectio altera V. librorum*, c.1080–85)
  Vat. lat. 1363 (Anselm, *Collectio canonum*, incip. s. XII)
  Vat. lat. 1364 (Anselm, *Collectio canonum*, ex. s. XI)
  Vat. lat. 3531 (Anselm, *Collectio canonum*, [Bks I–VII])
  Vat. lat. 3809 (*'Redactio Gregoriana' Decretum Burchardi*, c.1060)
  Vat. lat. 3830 (anon. *Collectio canonum*, c.1050)
  Vat. lat. 4983 (Anselm, *Collectio canonum*, s. XVI)
  Vat. lat. 6381 (Anselm, *Collectio canonum*, s. XII/XVI)

B. Printed Sources

Annales Romani, in *Le Liber Pontificalis*, 2, ed. L. Duchesne (Bibliothèque des écoles francaises d'Athènes et de Rome, 3 vols.; Paris, 1884–92).
Anselmi Gesta episcoporum Leodiensium (*MGH, SS*, 7), 189–234.
ANSELM OF LUCCA, *Anselmi episcopi Lucensis Collectio canonum una cum collectione minore*, ed. F. Thaner (Innsbruck, 1906, 1915).
—— *Liber contra Wibertum*, ed. E. Bernheim (*MGH, LdL*, 1), 517–28.

ANSELM OF LUCCA, *Sermo Anselmi episcopi de caritate*, ed. E. Pasztor, in 'Motivi dell'ecclesiologia di Anselmo di Lucca in margine a un sermone inedito', *Bull. Ist. Stor. Ital.* 77 (1965), 44–95 (text, 96–104).

—— 'Cinq textes de prière composés par Anselme de Lucques pour la Comtesse Mathilde', ed. A. Wilmart, *Revue d'ascétique et de mystique*, 19 (1938), 23–48 (text, 49–72).

—— *Commentary on Psalm II* (fragments), in Paul of Bernried, *Vita Gregorii VII.*, c. 112, *Pontificum Romanorum Vitae*, ed. J. M. Watterich (Leipzig, 1862), I, 474–546.

—— [misc.] *Vita Anselmi episcopi Lucensis*, ed. R. Wilmans (*MGH, SS*, 12), 1–35.

—— [misc.] *Vita Metrica S. Anselmi Lucensis episcopi Auctore Rangerio Lucensi* (*MGH, SS*, 30), 1152–1307.

Antiquitates Italicae medii aevi, I, ed. L. A. Muratori (Milan, 1738).

ARNULF OF MILAN, *Gesta archiepiscoporum Mediolanensium* (*MGH, SS*, 8), 1–31.

ATTO, *Breviarium*, ed. A. Mai, in *Scriptorum veterum nova collectio e vaticanis codicibus edita*, 10 vols. (Rome, 1825–38), vol. 6, pt. II, 60–102.

BARSOCCHINI, B., ed., *Raccolta di documenti per servire alla storia ecclesiastica lucchese* (Memorie e Documenti per servire all' istoria del principato Lucchese; Lucca, 1844), vol. 5, pt. I.

Benonis aliorumque cardinalium schismaticorum contra Gregorium VII. et Urbanum II. scripta (*MGH, LdL*, 2), 366–422.

BERNOLD OF CONSTANCE, *Chronicon* (*MGH, SS*, 5), 400–67.

—— *Libellus de vitanda excommunicatorum communione* (*MGH, LdL*, 3), 597–601.

Bertholdi Annales (*MGH, SS*, 5), 264–326.

BONIZO OF SUTRI, *Liber de vita christiana*, ed. E. Perels (Texte zur Geschichte des römischen und kanonischen Rechts im Mittelalter, I; Berlin, 1930).

Briefsammlungen der Zeit Heinrichs IV, ed. C. Erdmann and N. Fickermann (*MGH, BdK*, 5; Weimar, 1950).

BURCHARD OF WORMS, *Decretum libri XX*, in *PL* 140, 537–1053.

Codex Udalrici, ed. P. Jaffé (Biblioteca rerum Germanicarum, 5; Berlin, 1869).

Collectio canonum in V. libris, bks I–III, ed. M. Fornasari (Corpus Christianorum, ser. latina: Continuatio Medievalis, 6; Turnhout, 1970).

Constitutiones et Acta publica imperatorum et regum, I (*MGH, Legum, sectio IV*).

Corpus Iuris Civilis, ed. P. Kruger, T. Mommsen, R. Scholl, G. Kroll, 3 vols. (Berlin, 1954).

Der sogennante Traktat 'De ordinando pontifice': Ein Rechtsgutachten in Zusammenhang mit der Synode von Sutri (1046), ed. H. H. Anton (Bonner Historische Forschungen, 48; Bonn, 1982).

De thesauro Canusinae ecclesiae Romanam transmisso, et de compensatione ecclesiae Canusinae facta (RIS, n.s. 5, pt. II) 109–10.

DEUSDEDIT, *Die Kanonessammlung des Kardinals Deusdedit*, ed. V. Wolf von Glanvell (Paderborn, 1905).

Diversorum patrum sententie sive Collectio in LXXIV titulos digesta, ed. J. T. Gilchrist (MIC, Ser. B: Corpus Collectionum, I; Vatican City, 1973).

DONIZO, *Vita Matildis celeberrimae principis Italiae carmine scripta a Donizone presbytero*, ed. L. Simeoni (RIS, n.s. 5, pt. II).

Epistolae Romanorum pontificum s. Clemente usque ad Innocentium III., I, ed. P. Coustant (Paris, 1721).

Epistolae Romanorum Pontificum genuinae et quae ad eos scriptae sunt a s. Hilaro usque ad Pelagium II., ed. A. Thiel (Braunsberg, 1868).

FIORENTINI, F. M. (ed.), *Memorie della Gran Contessa Matilda* (Lucca, 1756).

Gebhardi Salisburgensis archiepiscopi epistola ad Herimannum Mettensem episcopum, ed. K. Francke (*MGH, LdL*, I), 261–79.

GRATIAN, *Concordia discordantium canonum*, ed. E. Friedberg (Leipzig, 1879).

—— [misc.] *Wortkonkordanz zum Decretum Gratiani*, ed. T. Reuter and G. Silagi, 5 vols. (*MGH, Hilfsmittel*, 10/1–5; Munich, 1990).

GREGORY I, *Registrum epistolarum*, ed. P. Ewald and L. M. Hartmann (*MGH, Epp.*, 1–2; Berlin, 1891–9).

GREGORY VII, *Registrum Gregorii VII.*, ed. E. Caspar (*MGH, Ep. sel.* t. 2, 2 vols.; Berlin, 1920–3).

—— *The Epistolae Vagantes of Pope Gregory VII*, ed. H. E. J. Cowdrey (Oxford, 1972).

HENRY IV, *Die Briefe Heinrichs IV.*, ed. C. Erdmann (*MGH, Deutsches Mittelalter*, 1; Leipzig, 1937).

—— [misc.] *Vita Heinrici IV. Imperatoris*, ed. W. Eberhard (*MGH, SRG*, 58; Hanover, 1899).

Historia dedicationis sancti Remigii apud Remos, ed. J. Mabillon (*Acta Sanctorum O.S.B.*; Paris, 1701), 6, I, 711–27.

HUGH OF FLAVIGNY, *Chronicon* (*MGH, SS*, 8), 288–502.

Humberti Cardinalis libri III. adversus simoniacos, ed. F. Thaner (*MGH, LdL*, I), 95–253.

Inventori del vescovato della cattedrale e di altre chiese di Lucca, ed. P. Guidi (Studi e Testi, 34; Rome, 1921).

Italia Sacra sive De episcopis Italiae, ed. F. Ughelli, 9 vols. (Rome 1644–62).

Leonis IX. Vita ab ipsius in ecclesia Tullensi archidiacono Wiberto conscripta, ed. J. M. Watterich, *Pontificum Romanorum Vitae*, I (Leipzig, 1862), 127–70.

Leonis Marsicani et Petri diaconi Chronica monasterii Casinensis (*MGH, SS*, 7), 551–844.

Liber de unitate ecclesiae conservanda (*MGH, LdL*, 2), 173–284.

Papsturkunden 896–1046, ed. H. Zimmermann, 3 vols.(Veröffentlichungen der Historischen Kommission, 3: Denkschriften 174, 177, 178; Vienna, 1984–5, 1989).

PAUL OF BERNRIED, *Vita Gregorii VII.*, in ed. J. M. Watterich, *Pontificum Romanorum Vitae* (Leipzig, 1862), 474–546.

PETER DAMIAN, *Die Briefe des Petrus Damiani*, ed. K. Reindel, 4 vols. (*MGH, BdK*, 5/1–4; Munich, 1983–93).

PSEUDO-ISIDORE, *Decretales Pseudo-Isidorianae et Capitula Angilrammi*, ed. P. Hinschius (Leipzig, 1863).

Quellen und Forschungen zum Urkunden-und Kanzleiwesen Papst Gregors VII., ed. L. Santifaller (Studi e Testi, 190; Vatican City, 1957).

Quellen zur Geschichte Kaiser Heinrichs IV., ed. F.-J. Schmale (Ausgewählte Quellen zur Deutschen Geschichte des Mittelalters, 12; Darmstadt, 1974).

Regesta Pontificum Romanorum, ed. P. Jaffé, 2nd edn. by S. Loewenfeld (JL: an. 882–1198), F. Kaltenbrunner (JK: an. ?–590), P. Ewald (JE: an. 590–882), 2 vols. (Berlin, 1885–89).

Regesto del Capitolo di Lucca, ed. P. Guidi and O. Parenti, 3 vols. (Regesta chartarum Italiae, 6, 9, 18, 18*; Rome, 1910–39).

Sacrorum conciliorum nova et amplissima collectio, ed. G. D. Mansi, 53 vols. in 60 pts. (Paris–Arnhem, 1901–27).

SIGEBERT OF GEMBLOUX, *Chronica* (*MGH, SS*, 6), 300–74.

—— *Catalogus Sigeberti Gemblacensis monachi de viris illustribus*, ed. R. Witte (Lateinische Sprache und Literatur des Mittelalters, 1; Frankfurt, 1974).

Wenrici scolastici Trevirensis epistola sub Theoderici episcopi Virdunensis nomine composita, ed. K. Francke (*MGH, LdL*, I), 282–99.

WIDO OF FERRARA, *De scismate Hildebrandi* (*MGH, LdL*, 1), 529–67.

II. SECONDARY WORKS

ANGELI, C. M., 'L'episcopato lucchese di Anselmo I da Baggio: l'amministrazione delle finanze e del patrimonio della chiesa', *Actum luce: rivista di studi lucchesi*, 15 (1986), 95–117.

ARQUILLIÈRE, H.-X., 'La IIe lettre de Grégoire VII à Herman de Metz (1081): ses sources patristiques', *Recherches de science religieuse*, 40 (1951–2), 231–42.

—— *St. Grégoire VII: essai sur sa conception du pouvoir pontifical* (Paris, 1934).

AUTENRIETH, J., 'Bernold von Konstanz und die erweiterte 74T', *DA* 14 (1958), 206–38.

BACCHINI, B., *Dell'istoria del monastero di san Benedetto di Polirone nello stato di mantova* (Modona [sic], 1696).

BENEDINI, B., *I manoscritti polironiani della biblioteca di Mantova* (Mantua, 1958).

BENSON, R. L., 'The Gelasian Doctrine: Uses and Transformations', in *La Notion d'autorité au moyen age: islam, byzance, occident*, ed. G. Makdisi (Colloques internationaux de la napoule; Paris, 1982), 13–44.

—— *The Bishop-Elect: A Study in Medieval Ecclesiastical Office* (Princeton, 1968).

—— '*Plenitudo potestatis*: Evolution of a Formula from Gregory IV to Gratian', *Studia Gratiana*, 14 (1967), 193–217.

BERMAN, H. J., *Law and Revolution: The Formation of the Western Legal Tradition* (Cambridge, Mass., 1983).

BERTOLINI, M. G., 'Enrico IV e Mathilde di Canossa di fronte alla città di Lucca', in *Sant'Anselmo vescovo di Lucca*, 331–89.

BLUMENTHAL, U.-R., 'History and Tradition in Eleventh-Century Rome', *Catholic Historical Review*, 79 (1993), 185–96.

—— 'Rom in der Kanonistik', in *Rom in hohen Mittelalter*, ed. B. Schimmelpfennig and L. Schmugge (Sigmaringen, 1992), 29–39.

—— 'Papal and Local Councils: The Evidence of the *"pax"* and *"treuga Dei"*', in *La riforma gregoriana e l'Europa* (*SG* 14; Rome, 1991), 137–44.

—— 'Fälschungen bei Kanonisten der Kirchenreform des 11. Jahrhunderts', in *Fälschungen im Mittelalter*, 6 vols. (*MGH, Schriften*, 33/1–6; Hanover, 1988), II, 241–67.

—— *Der Investiturstreit* (Stuttgart, 1982; English as *The Investiture Controversy: Church and Monarchy from the Ninth to the Twelfth Century*, Philadelphia, 1988).

—— 'The Beginnings of the Gregorian Reform: Some New Manuscript Evidence', in *Reform and Authority in the Medieval and Reformation Church*, ed. G. F. Lytle (Washington, DC, 1981), 1–13.

—— 'Ein neuer Text für das Reimser Konzil Leos IX (1049)?', *DA*, 32 (1976), 23–48.

—— 'Paschalian Additions to the MSS. of the *Collectio canonum* of Anselm of Lucca', *Manuscripta*, 20 (1976), 3–4.

BORINO, G. B., 'Il monacato e l'investitura di Anselmo vescovo di Lucca', *SG* 5 (1956), 361–74.

—— 'L'archidiaconato di Ildebrando', *SG* 3 (1948), 463–516.

—— 'Un'ipotesi sul *Dictatus papae* di Gregorio VII', *Archivio della r. deputazione romana di storia patria*, 67 (1944), 237–52.

BROOKE, Z. N., 'English MSS. Containing Collections of Ecclesiastical Law', in id., *The English Church and the Papacy* (Cambridge, 1931), 241 ff.

BRUNDAGE, J. A., *Medieval Canon Law* (London, 1995).

CAPITANI, O., *'Ecclesia romana* e riforma: *utilitas* in Gregorio VII', in *Chiesa, diritto e ordinamento della 'societas christiana' nei secoli XI e XII* (Miscellanea del centro di studi medioevali, 11; Milan, 1986), 89–112.

—— 'L'interpretazione "pubblicistica" dei canoni come momento della definizione di istituti ecclesiastici (secc. XI–XII)', in *Fonti medioevali e problematica storiografica*, 2 vols. (Rome, 1976–7), I, 253–82.

—— 'Storiografia e riforma della chiesa in Italia', *La storiografia altomedioevale*, 2 vols. (Settimane di studio del centro italiano di studi sull'alto medioevo, 17; Spoleto, 1970), II, 557–629.

—— *Immunità vescovili ed ecclesiologia in età 'pregregoriana' e 'gregoriana': l'avvio alla 'restaurazione'* (Biblioteca degli studi medievali, 3; Spoleto, 1966).

—— 'Esiste un'età gregoriana? Considerazione sulle tendenze di una storiografia medievistica', *Rivista di storia e letteratura religiosa*, 1 (1965), 454–81.

—— 'La figura del vescovo in alcune collezioni della seconda metà del secolo XI', in *Vescovi e diocesi in Italia nel medioevo (sec. IX–XIII)* (Italia sacra, 5; Padua, 1964), 161–91.

CASPAR, E. R., 'Gregor VII. in seinen Briefen', *Historische Zeitschrift*, 130 (1924), 1–30.

230   *Bibliography*

Catalogue of Canon and Roman Law Manuscripts in the Vatican Library, ed. S. Kuttner with R. Else, 2 vols. (Studi e Testi, 322, 328; Vatican City, 1986–7).

CONSTABLE, G., 'Past and Present in the Eleventh and Twelfth Centuries: Perceptions of Time and Change', *L'Europa dei secoli XI e XII fra novità e tradizione sviluppi di una cultura* (Miscellanea del centro di studi medioevali, 12; Milan, 1989), 135–70.

—— 'Papal, Imperial and Monastic Propaganda in the 11th and 12th Centuries', in *Prédication et propagande au moyen age: islam, byzance, occident* (Pennsylvania–Paris–Dumbarton Oaks Colloquia, 3; Paris, 1983), 179–99.

CORSI, M. L., 'Nota sulla famiglia da Baggio (secoli IX–XIII)', *Raccolta di studi in memoria di Giovanni Soranzo* (Pubblicazioni dell'università cattolica del sacro cuore, ser. 3, 10; Milan, 1968), 166–204.

COWDREY, H. E. J., 'The Spirituality of Gregory VII', in *The Mystical Tradition and the Carthusians*, vol. 1, ed. J. Hogg (Analecta Cartusiana, 130; Salzburg, 1995), 1–22.

—— 'Pope Gregory VII and the Bishoprics of Central Italy', *Studi medievali*, 34 (1993), 613–48.

—— *The Age of Abbot Desiderius: Montecassino, the Papacy and the Normans in the Eleventh and Early Twelfth Centuries* (Oxford, 1983).

—— 'Anselm of Besate and Some Northern Italian Scholars of the Eleventh Century', *JEH* 23 (1972), 115–24.

—— *The Cluniacs and the Gregorian Reform* (Oxford, 1970).

—— 'The Papacy, the Patarenes and the Church of Milan', *TRHS*, 5th ser. 18 (1968), 25–48.

DE MATTEIS, M. C., 'Tematica della povertà e problema delle *res ecclesiae*: notazione ed esemplificazione sui alcuni collezioni canoniche del periodo della riforma ecclesiastica del sec. XI', *Bull. Ist. Stor. Ital.* 90 (1982–3), 177–226.

DEREINE, C., 'Le Problème de la vie commune chez les canonistes d'Anselme de Lucques à Gratien', *SG* 3 (1948), 287–98.

Dictionnaire du Droit Canonique, 7 vols. (Paris, 1935–65).

ERDMANN, C., *The Origin of the Idea of Crusade*, trans. M. W. Baldwin and W. Goffart (Princeton, 1977).

—— *Studien zur Brieflitteratur Deutschlands im elften Jahrhundert* (Schriften, Reichsinstitut für ältere deutsche Geschichtskunde, 1; Leipzig, 1938).

FABRE, P., *Étude sur le liber censuum de l'église romaine* (Bibliothèque des écoles françaises d'Athènes et de Rome, fasc. 62; Paris, 1892).

FEINE, H., 'Kirchenreform und Wiederkirchenwesen: Rechtsgeschichte Beiträge zur Reformfrage, vornehmlich in Bistum Lucca im 11. Jahrhundert', *SG* 2 (1947), 505–24.

FLECKENSTEIN, J., 'Heinrich IV und der Deutsche Episkopat in den Anfangen des Investiturstreites: Ein Beitrag zur Problematik von Worms, Tribur und Canossa', in *Adel und Kirche: Gerd Tellenbach zum 65. Geburstag*, eds., J. Fleckenstein and K. Schmid (Freiburg–Basle–Vienna, 1965), 221–37.

FLICHE, A., 'La Valeur historique de la collection canonique d'Anselme de Lucques', in *Miscellanea historica in honorem Alberti de Meyer*, 2 vols. (Recueil de travaux d'histoire et de philologie, ser. 3, fasc. 22–23; Brussels, 1946), I, 348–57.

—— *La Réforme grégorienne*, 3 vols. (Spicilegium sacrum Lovaniense, études et documents, fasc. 6, 9, 16; Paris, 1924–37).

FONSECA, C. D., 'Il capitolo di s. Martino e la riforma canonicale nella seconda metà del secolo IX', in *Sant'Anselmo vescovo di Lucca*, 51–64.

FORNASARI, G., 'Verita, tradimento della verita e falsità nell'epistolario di Gregorio VII: un abbozo di ricerca', in *Fälschungen im Mittelalter*, 6 vols. (*MGH, Schriften*, 33/1–6; Hanover, 1988), II, 217–40.

—— 'S. Anselmo e il problema della *caritas*', in *Sant'Anselmo, Mantova*, 301–12.

—— '"*Iuxta patrum decreta et auctoritatem canonum*": alla ricerca delle fonti della dottrina teologica e canonistica di Gregorio VII', in *Chiesa, diritto e ordinamento della 'societas christiana' nei secoli XI e XII* (Miscellanea del centro di studi medioevali, 11; Milan, 1986), 401–60.

—— 'Enrico II e Benedetto VIII ed i canoni del presunto concilio di Ravenna del 1014', *Rivista della storia della chiesa in Italia*, 18 (1964), 46–55.

FOURNIER, P., 'Un tournant de l'histoire du droit (1060–1140)', *Nouvelle revue historique de droit français et étranger*, 41 (1917), 129–80.

—— 'Les Collections canoniques romaines à l'époque de Grégoire VII', *Mémoires de l'academie des inscriptions et belles-lettres*, 41 (1920), 271–395.

—— 'Un Groupe de recueils canoniques italiens des Xe et XIe siècles', *Mémoires de l'academie des inscriptions et belles-lettres*, 40 (1915), 95–213.

—— 'Études sur les fausses décrétales', *Revue d'histoire ecclésiastique*, 7 (1906), 33–51, 301–16, 543–64, 761–84; cont'd in 8 (1907), 19–56.

—— 'Observations sur les diverses récensions de la collection canonique d'Anselme de Lucques', *Annales de l'université de Grenoble*, 13 (1901), 427–58.

—— 'Le premier manuel canonique de la réforme grégorienne au XIe siècle', *Mélanges d'archéologie et d'histoire de l'école française de Rome*, 14 (1894), 147–223.

—— and LE BRAS, G., *Histoire des collections canoniques en occident depuis les fausses décrétales jusqu'au décret de Gratien*, 2 vols. (Societé d'histoire de droit; Paris, 1931–2).

FRANSEN, G., 'Anselme de Lucques, canoniste?', in *Sant'Anselmo vescovo di Lucca*, 143–56.

—— *Les Collections canoniques* (Typologie des sources du moyen âge occidental, 10; Turnhout, 1973).

FUHRMANN, H., 'Widerstande gegen den päpstlichen Primat im Abendland', in *Il primato del vescovo nel primo millenio: ricerche e testimonianze*, ed. M. Maccarrone (Pontificio comitato di scienze storiche, atti e documenti, 4; Vatican City, 1991), 707–36.

—— 'Papst Gregor VII. und das Kirchenrecht: zum Problem des *Dictatus Papae*', *La riforma gregoriana e l'Europa* (*SG* 13; Rome, 1989), 123–49.

FUHRMANN, H., 'Reflections on the Principle of Editing Texts: The Pseudo-Isidorian Decretals as an Example', *BMCL*, n.s. 11 (1981), 1–9.

—— '"Quod catholicus non habeatur qui non concordat Romanae ecclesiae": Randnotizien zum *Dictatus papae*', in *Festschrift für Helmut Beumann*, ed. K. U. Jaschke and R. Wenskus (Sigmaringen, 1977), 263–87.

—— *Einfluss und Verbreitung der pseudoisidorischen Fälschungen*, 3 vols. (*MGH, Schriften*, 24/1–3; Stuttgart, 1972–4).

—— 'Das Reformpapsttum und die Rechtswissenschaft', in *Investiturstreit und Reichsverfassung*, ed. J. Fleckenstein (Konstanzer Arbeitskreis für mittelalterliche Geschichte, Vorträge und Forschungen, 17; Sigmaringen, 1973), 175–204.

—— 'Über den Reformgeist der 74-Titel Sammlung', in *Festschrift für Hermann Heimpel*, 4 vols. (Veröffentlichen des Max-Planck-Institut für Geschichte, 36; Göttingen, 1971–2), II, 1101–20.

—— 'Pseudoisidor in Rom vom Ende der Karolingerzeit bis zum Reformpapsttum: Eine Skizze', *Zeitschrift für Kirchengeschichte*, 78 (1967), 15–66.

FUSCONI, G. M., 'Anselmo II, vescovo di Lucca', *Biblioteca Sanctorum*, II (1962), 26–36.

GAUDEMET, J., 'La Primauté pontificale dans les collections canoniques grégoriennes', in *Cristianità ed Europa: Miscellanea di studi in onore di Luigi Prosdocimi*, ed. C. Alzati (Rome, 1994), 59–90.

—— 'Charisme et droit: le domaine de l'évêque', *ZSSRG*, kan. Abt. 105 (1988), 44–70.

—— 'La Bible dans les collections canoniques', in *Le Moyen âge et la bible*, ed. P. Riché and G. Lobrichon (Bible de tous les temps, 4; Paris, 1984), 327–69.

GHILARDUCCI, G. 'L'edizione dei documenti del secolo XI dell'archivio arcivescovile di Lucca', in *Sant'Anselmo vescovo di Lucca*, 423–6.

GILCHRIST, J. T., 'The *Collectio canonum* of Bishop Anselm II of Lucca (d. 1086): Recension B of Berlin, Staatsbibliothek Preussicher Kulturbesitz Cod. 597', in *Cristianità ed Europa: Miscellanea di studi in onore di Luigi Prosdocimi*, ed. C. Alzati (Rome, 1994), 377–403.

—— *Canon Law in the Age of Reform, 11th–12th Centuries* (Variorum Collected Studies Series, CS406; Ashgate, 1993).

—— 'The Erdmann Thesis and the Canon Law, 1083–1141', in *Crusade and Settlement*, ed. P. W. Edbury (Cardiff, 1985), 37–45.

—— *The Collection in Seventy-four Titles: A Canon Law Manual of The Gregorian Reform* (Pontifical Institute of Medieval Studies, Medieval Sources in Translation, 22; Toronto, 1980).

—— 'The *Epistola Widonis*, Ecclesiastical Reform and Canonistic Enterprise, 1049–1141', in *Authority and Power: Studies on Medieval Law and Government Presented to Walter Ullmann on his 70th Birthday*, ed. B. Tierney and P. Linehan (Cambridge, 1980), 49–58; also in *Canon Law in the Age of Reform*.

—— 'The Reception of Pope Gregory VII into the Canon Law (1073–1141)',

ZSSRG, kan. Abt. 90 (1973), 35–82; cont'd in 97 (1980), 192–229; also in *Canon Law in the Age of Reform.*

—— 'Eleventh and Early Twelfth Century Canonical Collections and the Economic Policy of Gregory VII', *SG* 9 (1972), 377–417; also in *Canon Law in the Age of Reform.*

—— 'Cardinal Humbert of Silva-Candida, the Canon Law and Ecclesiastical Reform in the Eleventh Century', *ZSSRG, kan. Abt.* 89 (1972), 338–49.

—— 'Was There a Gregorian Reform Movement in the Eleventh Century?', *Canadian Catholic Historical Association, Study Sessions,* 37 (1970), 1–10; also in *Canon Law in the Age of Reform.*

—— 'Gregory VII and the Primacy of the Roman Church', *Tijdschrift voor Rechtsgeschiedenis,* 36 (1968), 123–35.

—— 'Gregory VII and the Juristic Sources of his Ideology', *Studia Gratiana,* 12 (1967), 1–37; also in *Canon Law in the Age of Reform.*

—— '*Simoniaca haeresis* and the Problem of Orders from Leo IX to Gratian', *Proceedings of the Second International Congress of Medieval Canon Law,* ed. S. Kuttner and J. J. Ryan (MIC, ser. C: Subsidia, 1; Vatican City, 1965), 209–35; also in *Canon Law in the Age of Reform.*

—— 'Humbert of Silva-Candida and the Political Concept of *Ecclesia* in the Eleventh-Century Reform Movement', *Journal of Religious History,* 2 (1962–3), 13–28; also in *Canon Law in the Age of Reform.*

—— 'Canon Law Aspects of the Eleventh-Century Reform Programme', *Journal of Ecclesiastical History,* 13 (1962), 21–38; also in *Canon Law in the Age of Reform.*

Giusti, M., 'Le canoniche della città e diocesi di Lucca al tempo della riforma gregoriana', *SG* 3 (1948), 321–67.

Goez, W., 'Le diocesi toscane e la riforma gregoriana', in *Sant'Anselmo vescovo di Lucca,* 113–28.

—— 'Papa qui et episcopus: zum Selbstverständnis des Reformpapsttum im 11. Jahrhundert', *Archivum Historiae Pontificae,* 8 (1970), 27–59.

Golinelli, P., 'Prima di Canossa: considerazioni e notazioni sui rapporti di Gregorio VII con Beatrice e Matilde', *La riforma gregoriana e l'Europa* (*SG* 14; Rome, 1991), 195–206.

—— '*Indiscreta sanctitas': Studi sui rapporti tra culti, poteri e società nel pieno medioevo* (Istituto storico italiano per il medio evo, studi storici, fasc. 197–98; Rome, 1988).

—— (ed.), *Sant'Anselmo, Mantova e la lotta per le investiture* (Atti del convegno internazionale di studi, Mantova, 23–25 maggio 1986; Bologna, 1987).

—— 'Culto dei santi e monasteri nella politica dei Canossa nella pianura padana', *Studi Matildici* (Modena 1978), 427–44.

—— and Andreolli, B., *Storia di san Benedetto di Polirone* (Bologna, 1983).

Grégoire, R., 'Liturgia e agiografia a Lucca durante gli episcopati di Giovanni II (1023–56), Anselmo I (1056–73) e Anselmo II (1073–86)', in *Sant'Anselmo vescovo di Lucca,* 273–82.

HALLER, J., *Das Papsttum: Idee und Wirklichkeit*, 5 vols. (Basle, 1951–3).

HEFELE, C. J. and DE CLERCQ, C., *Histoire des conciles d'après les documents originaux*, 11 vols. (Paris, 1907–49).

HEES, H., 'Zur Collectio quinque librorum', *BMCL*, n.s. 4 (1974), 63–4.

HOESCH, H., *Die kanonischen Quellen im Werk Humberts von Moyenmoutier: Ein Beitrag zur Geschichte der vorgregorianischen Reform* (Forschung zur kirchlichen Rechtsgeschichte und zum Kirchenrecht, 10; Vienna–Cologne, 1970).

HOFFMANN, H., *Gottesfriede und Treuga Dei* (*MGH, Schriften*, 20; Stuttgart, 1964).

—— and PORKORNY, R., *Das Dekret des Bischofs Burchard von Worms: Textstufen—frühe Verbreitung—Vorlagen* (*MGH, Hilfsmittel*, 12; Munich, 1991).

HOFFMANN, K., 'Der *Dictatus Papae* Gregors VII. als Index einer Kanonessammlung?', *SG* 1 (1947), 531–7.

HÜBINGER, P. E., *Die letzen Worte Papst Gregors VII* (Rheinisch-Westfälische Akademie der Wissenschaften, Vorträge G185; Oppladen, 1973).

JASPAR, D., *Das Papstwahldekret von 1059: Überlieferung und Textgestalt* (Beiträge zur Geschichte und Quellenkunde des Mittelalters, 12; Sigmaringen, 1986).

KELLER, H., 'Le origini sociali e famigliari del vescovo Anselmo', in *Sant'Anselmo vescovo di Lucca*, 27–50.

—— 'Origini sociali e formazione del clero cattedrale dei secoli XI e XII nella germania e nell'italia settentrionale', in *Le istituzioni ecclesiastiche della 'societas christiana' dei secoli XI–XII: diocesi, pievi e parrocchie* (Miscellanea del centro di studi medioevali, 8; Milan 1977), 136–86.

KITTEL, E., 'Der Kampf um die Reform des Domkapitels in Lucca', in *Festschrift Albert Brackmann*, ed. L. Santifaller (Weimar, 1931), 207–46.

KNOX, R., 'Accusing Higher Up', *ZSSRG, kan. Abt.* 108 (1991), 1–31.

—— 'Finding the Law: Developments in Canon Law During the Gregorian Reform', *SG* 9 (1972), 419–66.

KRAUSE, H. G., *Die Papstwahl Dekret von 1059 und seine Rolle im Investiturstreit* (*SG* 7; Rome, 1961).

KUTTNER, S. G., 'Some Roman Manuscripts of Canonical Collections', *BMCL*, n.s. 1 (1971), 7–29.

—— *Harmony from Dissonance: An Interpretation of Medieval Canon Law* (Latrobe, Penn., 1961).

—— 'Methodological Problems Concerning the History of Canon Law', *Speculum*, 30 (1955), 539–49.

—— '*Liber Canonicus*: A Note on *Dictatus papae*, c. 17', *SG* 2 (1947), 387–401.

—— '*Cardinalis*: The History of a Canonical Concept', *Traditio*, 3 (1945), 129–214.

LADNER, G. B., 'Gregory the Great and Gregory VII: A Comparison of their Concepts of Renewal', *Viator*, 4 (1973), 1–27.

—— 'Two Gregorian Letters on the Sources and Nature of Gregory VII's Reform Ideology', *SG* 5 (1956), 221–42.

LANDAU, P., 'Gefälschtes Recht in den Rechtssammlungen bis Gratian', in *Fälschungen im Mittelalter*, 6 vols., (*MGH, Schriften*, 33/1–6; Hanover, 1988), II, 11–49.

—— 'Erweiterte Fassungen der Kanonessammlung des Anselm von Lucca aus dem 12. Jahrhundert', (also Italian as 'Intorni alle redazioni più ampie del XII secolo della raccolta dei canoni di Anselmo da Lucca'), in *Sant' Anselmo, Mantova*, 323–37 (German), 339–48 (Italian).

—— 'Die Rezension C. der Sammlung des Anselm von Lucca', *BMCL*, n.s. 16 (1986), 17–54.

—— 'Die Anklagemöglichkeit Untergeordneter vom *Dictatus papae* zum Dekret Gratians: ein Beitrag zur Wirkungsgeschichte gregorianischen Rechtsdenkens', in A. Gabriels and H. J. F. Reinhardt, ed., *Ministerium iustitiae: Festschrift für Heribert Heinemann zur Vollendung des 60. Lebensjahres* (Essen, 1995).

—— 'Neue Forschungen zu vorgratianischen Kanonessammlungen und den Quellen des gratianischen Dekrets', *Ius commune*, 11 (1984), 1–29.

LAUDAGE, J., *Priesterbild und Reformpapsttum im 11. Jahrhundert* (Cologne, 1984).

LECLERCQ, J., *St Pierre Damien: Ermite et homme d'église* (Uomini e dottrini, 8; Rome, 1960).

LEFEBVRE, C., *Les Pouvoirs du juge en droit canonique* (Paris, 1938).

LEYSER, C., 'Cities of the Plain: The Rhetoric of Sodomy in Peter Damian's "Book of Gomorrah"', *Romanic Review*, 86 (1995), 191–211.

LEYSER, K. J., *Communications and Power in Medieval Europe: The Carolingian and Ottonian Centuries*, ed. T. Reuter (London–Rio Grande, 1994).

—— *Communications and Power in Medieval Europe: The Gregorian Revolution and Beyond*, ed. T. Reuter (London–Rio Grande, 1994).

—— 'Gregory VII and the Saxons', *La riforma gregoriana e l'Europa*, (*SG* 14; Rome, 1991), 231–8; also in *The Gregorian Revolution and Beyond*, 69–76.

—— Review of H. Zimmermann, *Papsturkunden*, in *JEH* 39 (1988), 246–8.

—— *The Ascent of Latin Europe: An Inaugural Lecture delivered before the University of Oxford, November 1984*, now in *The Carolingian and Ottonian Centuries* (as above), 215–37.

—— 'Early Medieval Canon Law and the Beginnings of Knighthood', *Institutionen, Kultur and Gesellschaft im Mittelalter: Festschrift für Josef Fleckensteim zu seinem 65. Geburtstag*, ed. L. Fenske, W. Rosener, T. Zotz (Sigmaringen, 1984), 549–66; also in *The Carolingian and Ottonian Centuries*, 51–72.

—— 'The Polemics of the Papal Revolution', in id., *Medieval Germany and Its Neighbours* (London, 1982), 138–60.

MÄRTL, C., 'Zur Überlieferung des *Liber Contra Wibertum* Anselms von Lucca', *DA* 41 (1985), 192–202.

MEYER VON KNONAU, L. G., *Jahrbücher des deutschen Reiches unter Heinrich IV. und Heinrich V.*, 7 vols. (Leipzig, 1890–1909).

MILLER, M. C., *The Formation of a Medieval Church: Ecclesiastical Change in Verona, 950–1150* (Ithaca, NY–London, 1993).

MOORE, R. I., 'Postscript: The Peace of God and the Social Revolution', in *The Peace of God: Social Violence and Religious Response in France Around the Year 1000*, ed. T. Head and R. Landes (Ithaca, NY–London, 1992), 308–26.

—— *The Formation of a Persecuting Society: Power and Deviance in Western Europe, 950–1250* (Oxford, 1987).

—— 'Family, Community and Cult on the Eve of the Gregorian Reform', *TRHS*, 5th ser., 30 (1980), 49–69.

MORDEK, H., 'Dalla riforma gregoriana alla *Concordia discordantium* di Graziano: osservazioni marginali di un canonista su un tema non marginale', in *Chiesa, diritto e ordinamento della 'societas christiana' nei secoli XI e XII* (Miscellanea del centro di studi medioevali, 11; Milan, 1986), 89–112.

—— 'Kanonistik und Gregorianische Reform', in *Reich und Kirche vor dem Investiturstreit*, ed. K. Schmid (Sigmaringen, 1985), 65–82.

—— ' *"Dictatus Papae"* e *"Proprie auctoritates apostolicae sedis"*': intorno all'idea del primato pontificio di Gregorio VII', *Rivista di storia della chiesa in Italia*, 28 (1974), 1–22.

—— 'Handschriftenforschung in Italien. I: Zur Überlieferung des Dekrets Bischof Burchards von Worms', *Quellen und Forschungen aus italienischen Archiven und Bibliotheken*, 51 (1972), 626–51.

MORRIS, C., *The Papal Monarchy: The Western Church from 1050–1250* (Oxford, 1989).

MOTTA, G., 'La redazione A "Aucta" della *Collectio Anselmi episcopi Lucensis*', in *Studia in honorem eminentissimi cardinalis A. M. Stickler*, ed. R. I. Card. Castillo Lara (Studia e textus historiae iuris canonici, 7; Rome, 1992), 375–449.

—— 'I codici canonistici di Polirone', *Sant' Anselmo, Mantova*, 349–74.

—— 'I rapporti tra la collezione canonica di s. Maria Novella e quella in cinque libri: Firenze, Bib. Naz. Conventi soppressi MS A. 4. 269 e Bib. Vaticana, Vat. Lat. 1348', *BMCL*, n.s. 7 (1977), 89–96.

MUNIER, C., *Les Sources patristiques du droit de l'église du VIIIe au XIIIe siècles* (Mulhouse, 1957).

MURRAY, A., *Reason and Society in the Middle Ages* (Oxford, 1985).

—— 'Pope Gregory VII and His Letters', *Traditio*, 22 (1966), 149–202.

NITSCHKE, A., 'Das Verständnis für Gregors VII. Reformen im 11. Jahrhundert', *SG* 9 (1972), 143–66.

OSHEIM, D. J., *An Italian Lordship: The Bishopric of Lucca in the Late Middle Ages* (Berkeley, 1977).

OVERMANN, A., *Gräfin Mathilde von Tuscien, ihre Besitzungen, Geschichte ihres Gutes von 1115–1230 und ihre Regesten* (Innsbruck, 1895).

PALAZZINI, A., 'Il diritto strumento di riforma ecclesiastica in San Pier Damiani', *Ephemerides Iuris Canonici*, 11 (1955), 361–408.

PASZTOR, E., 'La "Vita" anonima di Anselmo di Lucca: una rilettura', *Sant'Anselmo vescovo di Lucca*, 207–22.

—— 'Lotta per le investiture e *"Ius belli"*: la posizione di Anselmo di Lucca', *Sant'Anselmo, Mantova*, 375–421.

—— 'Motivi dell'ecclesiologia di Anselmo di Lucca in margine a un sermone inedito', *Bull. Ist. Stor. Ital.*, 77 (1965), 45–104.

—— 'Sacerdozio e regno nella *Vita Anselmi episcopi Lucensis*', *Archivum Historiae Pontificae*, 2 (1964), 91–115.

—— 'Una fonte per la storia dell'età gregoriana: la *Vita Anselmi episcopi Lucensis*', *Bull. Ist. Stor. Ital.*, 72 (1960), 1–33.

PELSTER, F., 'Das Dekret Burchards von Worms in einer Redaktion aus dem Beginn der gregorianischen Reform', *SG* 2 (1947), 321–51.

PICASSO, G., 'La *Collectio canonum* di Anselmo nella storia delle collezioni canoniche', *Sant'Anselmo, Mantova*, 313–21.

—— '*Reformatio ecclesiae* e *disciplina canonica*', in *Chiesa, diritto e ordinamento nella 'societas christiana' nei secoli XI e XII* (Miscellanea del centro di studi medioevali, 11; Milan, 1986), 70–88.

POOLE, R. L., 'Benedict IX and Gregory VI', *Proceedings of the British Academy*, 8 (1917), 199–235.

REINDEL, K., 'Petrus Damiani und seine Korrespondenten', *SG* 10 (1975), 203–20.

REMENSYNDER, A. G. 'Pollution, Purity and Peace: An Aspect of Social Reform between the Late Tenth Century and 1076', in *The Peace of God: Social Violence and Religious Response in France around the Year 1000*, ed. T. Head and R. Landes (Ithaca, NY–London, 1992), 280–307.

RESNICK, I. M., 'Odo of Tournai and Peter Damian: Poverty and Crisis in the Eleventh Century', *Revue Benedictine*, 98 (1988), 114–40.

ROBINSON, E. G., 'Humberti Cardinalis Libri III. Adversus Simoniacos: A Critical Edition with an Introductory Essay and Notes', Ph.D. thesis (Princeton, 1972).

ROBINSON, I. S., *The Papacy 1073–1198: Continuity and Innovation* (Cambridge, 1990).

—— 'The Dissemination of the Letters of Pope Gregory VII during the Investiture Contest', *JEH* 34 (1983), 175–93.

—— 'Pope Gregory VII, The Princes, and the *Pactum*, 1077–1080', *EHR* 94 (1979), 721–56.

—— 'The Friendship Network of Pope Gregory VII', *History*, 63 (1978), 1–23.

—— 'Zur Arbeitsweise Bernolds von Konstanz und seines Kreise', *DA* 34 (1978), 51–122.

—— '*Periculosus Homo*: Pope Gregory VII and Episcopal Authority', *Viator*, 9 (1978), 103–33.

—— *Authority and Resistance in the Investiture Contest: The Polemical Literature of the Late Eleventh Century* (Manchester, 1978).

—— 'Gregory VII and the Soldiers of Christ', *History*, 58 (1973), 169–92.

ROSENWEIN, B., *To Be the Neighbor of Saint Peter: The Social Meaning of Cluny's Property, 909–1049* (Ithaca, NY–London, 1989).

ROUGH, R. H., *The Reformist Illuminations in the Gospels of Matilda, Countess of Tuscany* (The Hague, 1973).

RUGGIERI, C., 'Alcuni usi dell'antico testamento nella controversia gregoriana', *Christianesimo nella storia*, 8 (1987), 51–91.

RUSSELL, F. H., *The Just War in the Middle Ages* (Cambridge, 1975).

RUSSELL, J. B., *Dissent and Order in the Middle Ages: The Search for Legitimate Authority* (New York, 1992).

RYAN, J. J., 'Observations on the pre-Gratian Canonical Collections: Some Recent Work and Present Problems', *Congrès de droit canonique médiévale* (Bibliothèque de la Revue d'histoire ecclésiastique, 33; Louvain, 1959), 88–103.

—— *St. Peter Damiani and His Canonical Sources: A Preliminary Study in the Antecedents of the Gregorian Reform* (Pontifical Institute of Medieval Studies, Studies and Texts, 2; Toronto, 1956).

—— 'Letter of an Anonymous French Reformer to a Byzantine Official in S. Italy *de simoniaca heresis*', *Medieval Studies*, 15 (1953), 233–43.

SCHIEFFER, R., *Die Entstehung des päpstlichen Investiturverbots für den deutschen König* (*MGH, Schriften*, 28; Stuttgart, 1981).

—— '*Spirituales Latrones*: Zu den Hintergrunden der Simonieprozesse in Deutschland zwischen 1069 und 1075', *Historisches Jahrbuch*, 92 (1972), 19–60.

SCHMIDT, T., *Alexander II. (1061–73) und die römische Reformgruppe seiner Zeit* (Päpste und Papsttum, 11; Stuttgart, 1977).

SCHWARTZMAIER, H., *Lucca und das Reich bis zum Ende des 11. Jahrhunderts* (Tübingen, 1972).

SEVERINO, G., 'La "Vita metrica" di Anselmo da Lucca scritta da Rangerio', *Sant'Anselmo vescovo di Lucca*, 223–71.

SOMERVILLE, R., 'The Councils of Gregory VII', *La riforma gregoriana e l'Europa* (*SG* 13; Rome, 1989), 123–49.

—— 'The Letters of Pope Urban II in the *Collectio Brittanica*', *Proceedings of the Seventh International Congress of Medieval Canon Law*. ed. P. Linehan (MIC, Ser. C: Subsidia, 8; Vatican City, 1988), 103–14.

—— 'Note on Paris, Bibl. de l'Arsenal, MS 713', *BMCL*, n.s. 17 (1987), p. xxi.

—— 'Anselm of Lucca and Wibert of Ravenna', *BMCL*, n.s. 10 (1980), 1–13.

SPICCIANI, A. 'L'episcopato lucchese di Anselmo II da Baggio', *Sant'Anselmo vescovo di Lucca*, 65–112.

STICKLER, A. M., 'I presupposti storico-giuridici della riforma gregoriana e dell'azione personale di Gregorio VII', *La riforma gregoriana e l'Europa* (*SG* 13; Rome, 1989), 1–15.

—— *Historia iuris canonici latini*, I: *Historia fontium* (Rome, 1974).

—— 'Il *gladius* nel registro di Gregorio VII', *SG* 3 (1948), 89–103.

—— 'Il potere coattivo materiale della Chiesa nella riforma gregoriana secondo Anselmo di Lucca', *SG* 2 (1947), 235–85.

STOCK, B., *The Implications of Literacy: Written Language and Models of Interpretation in the Eleventh and Twelfth Centuries* (Princeton, 1983).

STOLLER, M. E., 'Schism in the Reform Papacy: The Documents and Councils of the Anti-Popes, 1061–1121', Ph.D thesis (New York, 1985).

—— 'Eight Anti-Gregorian Councils', *Annuarium Historiae Conciliorum*, 17 (1985), 252–321.

TELLENBACH, G., *The Church in Western Europe from the Tenth to the Early Twelfth Century*, trans. T. Reuter (Cambridge, 1993).

—— *Church, State and Christian Society at the Time of the Investiture Contest*, trans. R. Bennett (Oxford, 1939).

THEINER, A., *Disquisitiones criticae in praecipuas canonum et decretalium collectiones* (Rome, 1836).

TOUBERT, P., *Études sur l'Italie médiévale, IX–XIVe siècles* (London, 1976).

ULLMANN, W., 'A Note on Inalienability in Gregory VII', *SG* 9 (1972), 115–40.

—— '"*Romanus pontifex indubitanter efficitur sanctus*": *Dictatus papae* 23 in Retrospect and Prospect', *SG* 6 (1959–61), 229–64.

—— 'Cardinal Humbert and the *Ecclesia Romana*', *SG* 4 (1952), 111–27.

VAUGHN, S. N., 'Lanfranc, Anselm and the School of Bec: In Search of the Students of Bec', in *The Culture of Christendom: Essays in Medieval History in Commemoration of Denis L. T. Bethell*, ed. M. A. Meyer (London, 1993), 155–81.

VILLEY, M., *La Croisade: Essai sur la formation d'une théorie juridique* (Paris, 1942).

VIOLANTE, C., 'Il secolo XI: una svolta? Introduzione ad un problema storico', in *Il secolo XI: una svolta?*, ed. C. Violante and J. Fried (Annali dell'istituto storico italo-germanico, 35; Bologna, 1993), 7–40.

—— (ed.), *Sant'Anselmo vescovo di Lucca (1073–1086) nel quadro delle trasformazioni sociali e della riforma ecclesiastica* (Istituto storico italiano per il medio evo, studi storici, 13; Rome, 1992).

—— 'La riforma ecclesiastica del secolo XI come progressiva sintesi di contrasti idee e strutture', *Sant'Anselmo vescovo di Lucca*, 1–15.

—— 'Pievi e parrochie dalla fine del X secolo all'inizio del XIII secolo', in *Le istituzioni ecclesiastiche della 'societas christiana' dei secoli XI–XII: diocesi, pievi e parrochie* (Miscellanea del centro di studi medioevali, 8; Milan, 1977), 643–799.

—— *La pataria milanese e la riforma ecclesiastica (1048–57)* (Rome, 1955).

—— 'Anselmo da Baggio', *Dizionario biografico degli Italiani*, 3 (1961), 399–407.

VODOLA, E., 'Sovereignty and Tabu: Evolution of the Sanction against Communication with Excommunicates, Part 2. Canonical Collections', in *Studia in honorem eminentissimi cardinalis A. M. Stickler*, ed. R. I. Card. Castillo Lara (Rome, 1992), 581–98.

—— *Excommunication in the Middle Ages* (Berkeley, 1986).

VOOSEN, E., *Papauté et pouvoir civile à l'époque de Grégoire VII* (Gembloux, 1927).

WATTENBACH, W., and HOLTZMANN, R., *Deutschlands Geschichtsquellen im Mittelalter: Die Zeit der Sachsen und Salier*, 3 vols., new edn. by F. J. Schmale (Cologne, 1967).

WHITTON, D. R., 'Papal Policy in Rome, 1012–1124', D.Phil thesis (Oxford, 1980).

WICKHAM, C., 'Economia e società rurale nel territorio lucchese durante la seconda metà del secolo XI: inquadramenti aristocratici e strutture signorili', *Sant'Anselmo vescovo di Lucca*, 391–422.

—— *The Mountains and the City: The Tuscan Apennines in the Early Middle Ages* (Oxford, 1988).

—— 'Vendite di terra e mercato della terra in Toscana nel secolo XI', *Quaderni storici*, 65 (1987), 355–77.

—— 'Settlement Problems in Early Medieval Italy: Lucca Territory', *Archeologia medievale*, 5 (1978), 495–503.

WILLIAMS, S., *Collectionis Isidori Mercatoris codicum manuscriptorum catalogis* (MIC, ser. C, Subsidia, 3; New York, 1971).

WOLF VON GLANVELL, V., 'Die Canonessammlung des Cod. Vaticanus latinus 1348', *Sitzungsberichte der kaiserlichen Akademie der Wissenschaften*, 136 (1897).

WOODY, K. M., '*Sagena piscatoris*: Petrus Damiani and the Papal Election Decree of 1059', *Viator*, 1 (1970), 33–54.

—— 'Damiani and the Radicals', Ph.D. thesis (New York, 1966).

ZAFARANA, Z., 'Sul "conventus" del clero romano nel maggio 1082', *Studi Medievali*, ser. 3, 7 (1966), 399–403.

ZECHIEL-ECKES, K. 'Eine Mailänder Redaktion der Kirchenrechtssammlung Bischof Anselms II. von Lucca (1073–1086)', *ZSSRG, kan. Abt.* 112 (1995), 130–47.

ZEMA, D. B., 'Economic Reorganization of the Roman See during the Gregorian Reform', *SG* 1 (1947), 137–68.

—— 'Reform Legislation in the Eleventh Century and its Economic Import', *Catholic Historical Review*, 27 (1941), 16–38.

ZIMMERMANN, H., 'Anselm II. zwischen Gregor VII., Mathilde von Canossa und Heinrichs IV.', *Sant'Anselmo vescovo di Lucca*, 129–42.

Index

absolution of sworn oaths 38, 107 n., 218, 222

aequitas 25

Alexander II, pope 2, 12, 31–4, 43, 44, 45, 46–8, 49, 50, 57, 59, 89

Anastasius Bibliotecarius 26, 66, 67, 71

Anno, archbishop of Cologne 23 n., 31–2, 33

Anselm I, bishop of Lucca, *see* Alexander II, pope

Anselm II, bishop of Lucca 1–8, 12, 43–63
  at Canossa 56–7
  and *caritas* 114–16, 122, 128, 130, 135
  and cathedral canons 60–3, 109
  and coercion 122–41
  Collectio canonum: canonical sources 65–6, 69–72, 86–95, 105–6, 147–75, 203–24; and Deusdedit 95–102; and *Diversorum patrum sententie* (74T) 78–85, 120–1, 157–75, 210–15; editions 5, 7–8, 179–200; general 5–8, 65, 69–70, 142–3; manuscripts 5–8, 104, 142–3, 179–200; methods 68–9, 71–2, 89–90, 102; polemical quality 102, 104–6, 120–1, 142–3; and Pseudo-Isidore 72–8, 147–69, 210–12; and Swabian Appendix 175–8
  devotion to Gregory VII 1, 49, 60–3, 103–6, 141
  and *Dictatus papae* 106–10, 216–22
  on ecclesiastical property 137–41
  education 44, 45, 46–8
  election to Lucca 48–53
  episcopacy 51–7, 59–63
  on excommunicates, schismatics and heretics 122–41, 179–93
  family 43–4
  investiture crisis 48–54
  Liber contra Wibertum 4, 114, 126, 133–7, 223–4
  and Matilda 2, 51, 52, 53, 55–7, 60–3, 133–4 and n.42, 136 n., 138 and n.61
  monastic retirement 53–5
  reform agenda 11–12, 102, 116–17, 120–1, 124–7, 136–7, 142–3
  and revolution 105, 121
  and Roman primacy 75–8, 80–5, 99–101, 103–21, 147–50, 157–60, 170–3
  Sermo de caritate 4, 113–16, 132
  Vitae Anselmi 1–4, 46–7, 48–9, 53–5, 63

Anselmo Dedicata 67, 73, 86

Apostolic See 26–7, 38, 79, 100–1, 155, 160, 162, 172
  see also papacy

appeals 38, 73, 108, 159, 160, 162
  canonical sources for 203–4, 210, 213, 220

Arnulf of Milan, chronicler 53

Atto, cardinal-priest of San Marco 24, 65, 97, 126

auctoritas (authority) 36, 85, 92
  auctoritas regendi et disponendi 30–1, 137–8
  see also papal privileges

Augsburg, synod (1062) 31–3

Augustine 61 n., 69, 71, 93–5, 115
  as Anselm's canonical source 128–33, 135, 139, 180–1, 189–91, 193–4, 195, 196–7, 198

Baggio 43

baptism 94 and n.117

Beatrice, countess of Tuscany 47, 50, 51, 52, 53, 56

Benedict VIII, pope 15, 16

Benedict IX, pope 15, 16

Benonis aliorumque cardinalium . . . scripta 99 n., 103, 106

Bernard, abbot of Clairvaux 114 n.

Bernold of Constance, chronicler and
    polemicist 1, 24, 57 and n.73, 111,
    138 n., 175
bishops, *see* episcopal power, episcopate
Blumenthal, Uta-Renate 20 n., 21 n., 99,
    100
Bonizo, bishop of Sutri 31 n.
Burchard, bishop of Worms
    Decretum libri XX. 22 n., 65, 67, 127 n.,
        142
    false attributions 68–9 and n.12, 204,
        205, 206, 207
    as formal source 73, 86, 88, 91–2,
        177–8, 210, 211
    hierarchy of sources 91–2

Cadalus, bishop of Parma (anti-pope
    Honorius III) 31–3
canon law 11–12, 64–72
    absolution of sworn oaths 38, 107 n.,
        218, 222
    bringing accusations (by inferiors)
        109–10; (sources) 204, 210, 213
    canonical tradition 11–12, 37–9, 65, 117
    and Gregory VII 34–9
    hierarchy of sources 24, 91–2, 98–9
    inscriptio 67
    'intermediate' collections 66, 71, 93, 95,
        97–8
    inviolability of ecclesiastical status
        109–10, 161, 163, 164, 165
    judgement *in absentia* 38, 108–9, 156,
        217, 221
    and Leo IX 18–22
    papal election decree (1059) 29–31
    papal immunity 107
    and Peter Damian 23–7, 109 n.
    polemical quality 11–12, 65–6, 110–12,
        120–1, 142–3
    rubrics 67–8
    and schism (1080) 124–6
    sources 65–71, 203–24
    see also Anselm of Lucca, Burchard of
        Worms, Deusdedit, *Diversorum
        patrum sententie,* Pseudo-Isidore,
        reform collections
canonical collections 64–9, 96, 143
    see also reform collections and under
        individual titles
canonical reform 60–3, 64–5, 67, 143
    Leo IX, pope 18–22
    Peter Damian (*Liber gomorrhianus*) 23–5
    Rule of Aix 61 n.

see also communal life, cathedral canons
canons, *see* canon law, cathedral canons
Canossa 56–7, 138
Capitula Angilrammi 71, 168–9
cardinals 28–30 (cardinal-bishops) 101
    (cardinal-priests)
caritas 114–16, 122, 128, 130–2, 135, 137,
    140, 193–5
cathedral canons 60–3
    see also canonical reform
chastity 39, 94 and n. 117
Church 11–12, 25–9, 39, 85, 112–15,
    117–18, 121, 125–7, 129, 130–2, 134,
    135, 137, 140–1, 143
    sources for rights and status 205, 211,
        214
    see also Roman Church
civil law 79, 203–9
    see also Roman law
clerical concubinage 19 n., 39
clerical marriage 19 n., 39
coercion 5, 89, 95, 122–41
    exercise of coercive force 89, 131–3,
        187–8, 189
    canonical sources for 193–200, 209,
        212, 215
    see also de iusta vindicta
Collectio altera in V. libris 93 n.
    see also reform collections
Collectio Brittanica 32 n., 66 n., 88, 187–8
    see also reform collections
Collectio canonum, *see* Anselm of Lucca,
    Collectio canonum
Collectio canonum in V. libris 88
    see also reform collections
communal life 61, 83–4
    canonical sources for 206, 211, 214
conciliar canons 24, 66, 70–1, 79, 98,
    203–9
Concordat of Worms (1122) 123
councils:
    Gregory VII's Lenten and November
        synods 37, 39, 90, 138
    Rheims (1049) 19–22
    Rome (1049) 19
    Rome (1059) 15 n., 29 n.
    see also conciliar canons

de iusta vindicta (legitimate coercive force)
    124, 131–2, 193–200
    canonical sources for 193–200, 209,
        212, 215
    see also coercion

De ordinando pontifice 45
decreta sanctorum patrum 35
decretals, *see* papal decretals
deposition of emperors 38, 91, 218, 222
Deusdedit, cardinal-priest and canonist
    12, 24, 65, 68, 78, 104, 111, 143
  Collectio canonum 95–102, 103;
    hierarchy of sources 98–9; idea of
    primacy 99–101; method 96–7;
    polemical quality 101–2; rejection of
    papal election decree (1059) 101;
    sources (tomi) 97–8
Dictatus papae 37–9, 104–10, 121, 156,
    216–22
Dionysio-Hadriana 67, 70, 86
Diversorum patrum sententie (74T) 12,
    64–5, 68, 70, 72–4, 77, 78–85, 86, 88,
    117, 120, 126, 142, 143, 175
  and episcopate 79, 81, 162–3
  idea of primacy 79–80, 158–9, 165–6
  as source for Anselm 78–85, 157–75,
    180, 182, 183, 210–12, 213–15
  sources 78–9

ecclesiastical property 90–1, 125–6,
    137–41, 180, 190
  see also *res ecclesiae*
ecclesiastical reform 2–3, 11–15, 21, 22–3,
    27–9, 31, 33, 34–5, 39, 63, 99, 120–1,
    143
  see also Gregorian reform, Gregorian
    revolution, reform, reform movement
Ekkehard of Aura, chronicler 2
electus 29–31, 48–53
episcopal power 58–60, 74–8, 79, 81
  versus papal authority 118–21, 151,
    152, 153–4, 160–1
episcopate 38, 74–5, 79, 81, 112, 151–2,
    153–4, 155, 156–7, 160, 162–3, 164,
    166, 167, 205, 211, 214
eschatology 92
excommunication 38–9 n., 89, 107 n.,
    122–41, 179–93
  excommunicates and ecclesiastical prop-
    erty 139–41, 175
  canonical sources for 179–93, 208, 211,
    214–5, 217

fideles sancti Petri 55, 127 n., 129, 134 and
    n.42
Fliche, Augustin 12
Fournier, Paul 66 n., 99
Fransen, Gérard 7, 67 n., 68 n.

Fuhrmann, Horst 5 n., 73, 82, 85, 99,
    165, 210, 211

Gebhard, archbishop of Salzburg 107 n.
Gelasius I, pope:
  as canonical source 32–3, 37, 71, 79,
    84–5, 88–9, 169–75, 183, 184, 185,
    186, 191–2, 197–8, 203–209
Gilchrist, John T. 12, 39, 78, 82, 85,
    142–3, 165, 167, 172
Godfrey, duke of Lower Lotharingia 27,
    28–9 n.
Gratian 24, 67, 142
Gregorian reform 12–15, 34–5, 63, 99,
    120–1, 142–3
  see also ecclesiastical reform, Gregorian
    revolution, reform, reform movement
Gregorian revolution 13–15, 39, 63, 64, 121
Gregory I, pope:
  as canonical source 30 n., 71, 79, 83–4,
    86–7, 139, 181, 183, 194–5, 197, 198,
    199, 200, 203–9
Gregory VII, pope 1, 11, 12, 14–15, 34–9,
    47, 48, 49, 50, 51, 52, 53, 55–7,
    60–2, 63, 98–9, 103, 104, 105, 106,
    108–9, 114, 117–19, 121, 122–3, 128,
    129, 133, 138, 141, 156, 161
  canonical sources 35–6 and n. 98
  councils 39, 90
  Dictatus papae 37–9, 106–10, 216–22
  discipulus Hildebrandi 99, 103, 104 n.
  doctrinam Hildebrandi 105
  knowledge of canon law 35–6, 103
  legislation 37–9
  reception in canon law 39
  as source for Anselm 90–1, 106–10,
    216–22
  see also Hildebrand
Henry III, king of Germany, emperor 11
    n., 22 and n.41, 44 and n.11, 45 n.
Henry IV, king of Germany, emperor 3,
    14, 38, 44, 48, 49, 50, 51, 52, 55, 63,
    123, 134, 135, 136, 138
  Canossa 56–7
  minority 31–2
  relations with Gregory VII 14, 55–7
heresy 26–7, 89, 124–25, 187, 188–9, 191,
    192–3
Hermann, bishop of Metz 5, 36, 91, 105,
    122
hierarchy of sources 24, 91–2, 98–9
Hildebrand 2, 12, 25, 26, 27, 28, 31, 33
  see also Gregory VII

homosexuality 23 and n. 45
Hugh, abbot of Cluny 56 n.
Hugh, bishop of Die 51
Hugh of Flavigny, chronicler 5 n., 51
Humbert, cardinal-bishop of Silva-
 Candida 12, 15, 28, 31

investiture 39, 53, 90
 investiture contest 13, 48, 49–51, 53
  and n.52
 see also lay investiture
ius belli 129, 130, 135
 see also war
iustitia (justice) 24–5, 34, 137
Ivo of Chartres, bishop and canonist 24,
 142

John XIX, pope 15, 16
jurisdiction 29–31, 112–13, 131–3

Lanfranc of Pavia, archbishop of
 Canterbury 45, 46–8
Landulf (Senior) of Milan, chronicler 44
 and n.11
lapsed 206, 211, 214
lay investiture 49–51, 53 and n.52
Leo IX, pope 12, 18–22, 23, 37, 61
 Council of Rome (1049) 19
 Council of Rheims (1049) 19–22
 and ecclesiastical law 18–22
Leyser, Karl J. 11, 15, 17, 39
Liber pontificalis 71, 97
Liemar, bishop of Bremen 119 n.
Lucca 48, 49, 52, 53, 55–6, 57, 58
 episcopal patrimony 57–9
 see also Lucchesia
Lucchesia 53, 58–9

marriage 70, 94 and n.118
 canonical sources for 207, 211, 214
Matilda, countess of Tuscany 1, 2, 4, 47,
 50–3, 55, 56–7, 60–2, 133–4, 136 n.,
 138 and n.61
Milan 43, 44, 45
misericordia 25, *see also* papal privileges
monasticism 53–5, 174
 Bec 46–8
 Cluny 16, 54 and n.64
 Polirone 47, 54, 66, 93
 St Etienne, Caen 46–7
 St Gilles 54
Mordek, Hubert 66 n., 106 n., 111 n.
mutation 13–14

Nicholas II, pope 12, 25, 26, 27–31
 see also papal election decree (1059)
nobility 43–4, 58–60

obedience 92, 111, 120–1, 150, 153, 155,
 180, 195, 221
Otto, bishop of Constance 35

papacy 12, 17–18, 25–7, 143, 171
 Gregory VII's conception of papal
  office 34–5, 37
 legislative prerogatives 21–2
 moral duty versus legal rights 116–18,
  143
 papal elections 27–31
 pontiff's mandate for reform 116–17,
  148–50
 pre-reform papacy 15–17
 see also Apostolic See, Church, papal
  immunity, papal privileges, *plenitudo
  potestatis*, Roman Church, Roman
  primacy, and individual popes
papal decretals 66, 70–1, 78–9, 86–9,
  90–1, 97–8, 203–9, 210–15
 see also Pseudo-Isidore (Ps.Isidore)
papal election decree (1059) 29–31, 32–3,
  101
papal immunity 107, 113, 172, 220
papal legates 2, 18, 57, 106, 217
papal *ordus* (769) 101
papal primacy 5, 25–7, 103–21
 see also Roman primacy, *plenitudo potestatis*
papal privileges 17–19, 21–2, 25–7, 34–5,
  37, 39, 107–10, 120–1, 150–6, 160–1,
  168, 172
 auctoritas regendi et disponendi 30–1, 137–8
 Dictatus papae 37–9, 106–10, 216–22
 judgement *in absentia* 38, 108–9
 jurisdiction versus moral obligation
  112–17, 119–21, 123–4
 papal discretion (*misericordia*) 12, 24, 143
 Roman sanction for canons 23–4, 98–9
 sources for 5, 106–10, 111–17 n., 204,
  210–11, 213, 216–22
Pasztor, Edith 3, 7, 179
Pataria (Patarenes) 25, 44 and n. 11
patristic sources 66, 67, 71, 79, 91–5, 98,
  203–9
peace movement 13, 20–1
Pelagius I, pope 87–8, 133, 187–8
penance 70, 94–5 and n. 119
 sources for 207–8, 211, 214

penitentials 23, 70, 203–9
persecutio 125, 131, 187, 196, 193–200
   see also *de iusta vindicta,* coercion
Peter Damian, cardinal-bishop of Ostia 12,
   19 n., 22–7, 37, 45, 64, 89, 104, 149
   and canon law 23–7, 109 n.
   Disceptatio synodalis (Cadalan schism)
     32–4
   Lateran ideology 29
   Liber gomorrhianus 23–5
   and papal election decree (1059) 29 n.
   and Roman primacy (*De privilegio
     Romanae ecclesiae*) 25–7
   reluctance at election of Nicholas 28–9
Petrine powers 35–6, 115–16
   see also papacy
plenitudo potestatis 82, 100 n., 110, 117,
   148
polemic 107 n., 110–12, 113 n., 123–6
Polirone (San Benedetto di Polirone) 47,
   54, 66 and n. 5
pontiff 107–9, 116–18, 210–22
   see also papacy and individual popes
pope, see papacy and individual pontiffs
primacy, see papal primacy, *plenitudo
   potestatis,* Roman primacy
privilegium, see papal privileges
Pseudo-Isidore (Ps.Isidorian Decretals) 5,
   24, 67, 68, 69, 70, 71, 72–8, 86, 88,
   97, 103, 112, 203–9, 210–12
   pro-episcopal quality 74–8, 108, 109, 112
   as source for Anselm (independent)
     72–8, 147–57, 170–3, 174–5, 180,
     181, 182, 183, 184, 195, 197, 210–12;
     (via 74T) 78–85, 157–69, 180, 182,
     213–15
   sources of 72–3

Rangerius, bishop of Lucca
   Vita Metrica Anselmi 3–4, 53–4, 62
reform 2–3, 11–15, 44–5, 63, 64–5, 120–1
   strategies for 12, 17–18, 105–6, 126–7,
     142–3, 216–22
   see also ecclesiastical reform, reform
     movement
reform collections 64–9, 78 n., 143
   'intermediate' collections 66 and n. 5,
     95, 104
reform ecclesiology 113–16
reform legislation 18–22, 37, 39, 64–5, 75,
   79, 83, 85, 95–6, 99, 104–6, 111, 143
reform movement 2–3, 11–15, 17–18,
   27–9, 31, 33, 64–5, 99, 143

Regino of Prüm, *Libri duo de ecclesiasticis
   disciplinis* 67
regnum 13, 23, 27, 32–4, 88–9, 171
res ecclesiae 126, 137–41, 190
Robinson, Ian S. 98 n., 111
Roman Church 12, 20–2, 28, 29, 32–3,
   38, 98, 99, 100–1, 107, 108, 115–16,
   117, 133, 148, 170–2, 221
Roman law 67, 71, 135, 192–3, 203–9
   see also civil law
Roman primacy 23–7, 37–9, 73, 75–6,
   79–80, 81–2, 85, 89–90, 91, 99–101,
   103–21, 142
   and episcopal authority 118–21,
     147–50, 153, 154, 157–60, 165–6, 170
   sources for 203, 210, 213, 216–22
   see also *plenitudo potestatis,* papal privi-
     leges
Rome 17, 22, 25, 29, 100–1

sacerdotium 13, 23, 27, 32–4, 88–9, 171
sacraments 94 and n. 117, 206–7, 211, 214
schism 27–9, 31–3, 95, 115–16, 122–3,
   137–8
   and ecclesiastical property 139–41, 175,
     185, 187, 188, 189, 190
schismatics 124–5, 127–8, 133, 139
Schmidt, Tilman 46–8
secular authority 123, 132–3, 135, 218
   kingship as *ministerium* 132–3
   see also secular power
secular power 129, 131, 187–9, 198–200
Seventy-four titles, see *Diversorum patrum
   sententie* (74T)
Siegfried, archbishop of Mainz 119
Sigebert of Gembloux, chronicler 2, 105
simony 19 n., 25, 39, 59, 62, 94 and
   n.117
social change 12–13, 44–5
sodomy 23
Somerville, Robert 12, 66 n.
Stephen IX, pope 27, 28 n.
Stickler, Alfons 5 n., 71, 102, 197, 198–9
Sutri (1046) 22 n., 45 n.
Swabian Appendix 70, 78 n., 126, 175–8,
   181, 182, 184, 185, 211, 215
   see also *Diversorum patrum sententie*
synods 49, 52, 53
   see also councils, Gregory VII

Urban II, pope ('Turbanus') 103, 104 n.
urban change 13–14, 44–5
utilitas 20, 37, 132

war 127 and n.17, 129–31, 133, 134, 135, 136–7, 193–4
  ius belli 129–30, 135
  ius gladii 129
  vis armata 129
Wazo, bishop of Liege 45 n.
Wenrich of Trier, polemicist 107 n., 123 n.

Wibert, archbishop of Ravenna (anti-pope Clement III) 123, 133–4, 135, 136–7, 138, 140
  see also Anselm of Lucca, *Liber contra Wibertum*
William I, king of England 5, 48 n., 132